Alternating Currents

ROBERT L. FROST

Alternating Currents

Currents

NATIONALIZED
POWER IN FRANCE,
1946–1970

Cornell University Press

ITHACA AND LONDON

First published 1991 by Cornell University Press.

International Standard Book Number 0-8014-2351-1
Library of Congress Catalog Card Number 90-55727
Printed in the United States of America
Librarians: Library of Congress cataloging information appears on the last page of the book.

♾ The paper in this book meets the minimum requirements of the American National Standard for Information Sciences— Permanence of Paper for Printed Library Materials, ANSI Z39.48-1984.

To my father, Bill Frost—
engineer, architect, humanist

Contents

Preface   ix

Abbreviations Used in the Text   xi

Introduction   1

1. Prelude to a Nationalization   9

2. The Politics of Nationalizing Electricity   39

3. The French State and EDF's Corporate Culture, 1946–1954   76

4. The Relations of Production: EDF Managers and French Political Economy   115

5. The Means of Production: Technological Choice at EDF   163

6. The Forces of Production: Work and Work Life at EDF, 1954–1970   206

Epilogue   247

Appendix   255

Selected Bibliography   264

Index   281

Preface

The idea for this book first germinated in 1978–79, at the height of the second oil price crisis and international opposition to nuclear-generated electricity. At that time, many activists presumed that public control of energy resources would mitigate the shocks caused by rising energy prices, guarantee against windfall profits by private energy suppliers, and give the public control over choice of technologies used to generate power. As a French historian, I was well aware that France had the largest publicly owned integrated utility in the capitalist world and that despite France's lack of access to cheap primary energy, power rates there were relatively low. Yet, France also has the world's most aggressive nuclear power program. In order to explain that apparent contradiction, I began research on Électricité de France, only to find, as many young historians do, that the issues were far more complex than I had envisioned. After a stint of rapid self-education in Wisconsin and Paris, I embarked on my study, concluding that at the very least public power is a highly worthwhile reform but it has little to do with socialism. In later research I began to discover a rich body of emerging scholarship in the history of technology, particularly that published after 1983. Historians of France, technology, political economy, labor, and business have therefore all contributed to the perspective that informs this work.

Funding for research performed in France in 1980–81 and the summers of 1984 and 1988 came from a variety of sources. The largest were fellowships from the French Ministry of Foreign Affairs (a bourse Chateaubriand) and the Wisconsin Alumni Research Foundation. Other assistance came from the Institute for Public Utilities at Michigan State University, the American Council of Learned Societies, the University

ix

of Wisconsin Department of History, the Association pour l'Histoire de l'Électricité en France, and the State University of New York at Albany. Various conferencing and seminar funds were provided by the National Endowment for the Humanities, Carthage College, Wabash College, the American University, and the State University of New York at Albany.

I did my research at several archives and other sites in Paris, with generous assistance from countless individuals. The most important sites were the Électricité de France archives, the Archives Nationales, the offices of the electrical workers' federations of the Confédération Générale du Travail (CGT-Pantin) and the Confédération Française Démocratique du Travail (CFDT), the press archives of the Fondation Nationale des Sciences Politiques, and those of the Bibliothèque de Documentation Internationale Contemporaine.

I received valuable criticism and assistance in Paris from Patrick Fridenson, Louis Puiseux, Bernard Court, René Gaudy, the collective at the CFDT national offices, Ernest Anzalone, Alain Beltran, Jean-François Picard, Antoine Prost, Karine Lowy, Sally and Huges Maquart-Moulin, Anne Saint-Guillain, François Caron, Frédérique de Gravelaine, and Sylvie O'Dy. In the United States Richard Kuisel, Donald Reid, John Weiss, Peter Kuznick, Darryl Holter, Herrick Chapman, Laura Hein, Cecil O. Smith, Kendall Birr, Raymond Ortali, and Robert Whitesell were similarly generous. Particularly valuable was the help Sidney Tarrow gave me during a stunning NEH Summer Seminar at Cornell in 1985. His colleague Peter Katzenstein clarified some political-economic issues. While working at the New York State Energy Office in 1985–86, I gained useful insights from Paul DeCotis. At Wisconsin, I received inspiration and worthy suggestions from Edward Gargan, Harvey Goldberg, Rodgers Hollingsworth, Domenico Sella, and Rodney Stevenson. John Ackerman of Cornell University Press provided invaluable assistance and insistence on problems of prose. Tyler Stovall gave me constant friendship and constructive criticism. Top honors, however, must go to Margaret Hedstrom, whose patience and criticisms have been nothing short of heroic.

ROBERT L. FROST

Albany, New York

Abbreviations Used

in the Text

CCOS   Conseil Central des Oeuvres Sociales, union-operated set of employee programs, from dining halls to vacation centers

CDF   Charbonnages de France, France's nationalized coal producer

CEA   Commissariat à l'Énergie Atomique, France's atomic energy commission

CFDT   Confédération Française Démocratique du Travail, leftist industrial union formed in 1964 by a break with the Confédération Française des Travailleurs Chrétiens

CFTC   Confédération Française des Travailleurs Chrétiens, Catholic trade union confederation

CGE   Compagnie Générale d'Électricité, France's largest electrical equipment manufacturer

CGT   Confédération Générale du Travail, largest industrial union in France

CMP   Comité Mixte à la Production, works committee, half workers and half managers, which advised local managers

CNR   Conseil National de la Résistance, National Resistance Committee, broad-based coalition of Resistance groups in France during World War II

CSC-CMP   Conseil Supérieur Consultatif des Comités Mixtes à la Production, the peak commission of CMPs, with representatives from lower CMPs

CSNP   Commission Supérieure Nationale du Personnel, labor-management body within Électricité de France that dealt with hiring, promotion, discipline, and work rules

EDF   Électricité de France, France's nationalized electrical uility

EEC   European Economic Community, organization founded by the 1957 Treaty of Rome for European economic integration

EEG   Études Économiques Générales, General Economic Studies, the mathematically oriented planning, performance evaluation, and rate-making section of Électricité de France

FNCCR   Fédération Nationale des Communes Concédantes et Régies, association of municipal utilities and localities having electrical facilities within their jurisdictions

FO   Force Ouvrière, anti-Communist industrial union that broke from the Confédération Générale de Travail in 1947

GDF   Gaz de France, France's nationalized gas utility

GNC   Groupement National des Cadres, professional-technical utility union associated with the Confédération Générale du Travail

LWR   Light water reactor, generic term for enriched uranium reactors developed in the United States

MRP   Mouvement Républicain Populaire, Christian Democratic party

PCF   Parti Communiste Français, French Communist party

Péon   Comité sur la Production d'Énergie d'Origine Nucléaire, a government commission charged with nuclear planning in the 1950s and 1960s

PROFOR   Professional formation, an internal program for training new managers at Électricité de France

PWR   Pressurized water reactor, a nuclear power-plant design utilizing enriched uranium, initially developed by Westinghouse

SFIO   Section Française de l'Internationale Ouvrière, French Socialist party

UNCM   Union Nationale des Cadres, Techniciens et Agents de Maîtrise, conservative professional-technical utility union affiliated with the General Confederation of Cadres

UNGG   Natural uranium, gas-cooled and graphite-moderated nuclear plant design, initially developed by France's Commissariat à l'Énergie Atomique

Alternating Currents

Introduction

In 1946 France's first elected postwar regime created Électricité de France by nationalizing virtually all the nation's electrical
utility facilities. The social goals for nationalization included efforts to
end the sharp class divisions that had hampered both political democracy and economic development. Political rationales flowed from
a perception that utility managers and owners had unduly influenced
the course of prewar French politics to their own advantage. Among
the economic reasons for the nationalization was the need to stimulate
France's utility sector, which had stagnated since the onset of the
Depression. Utility expansion had to precede major industrial growth
because electrical power was part of the infrastructure necessary for a
modern industrial economy, but France's private sector was woefully
short of the capital needed to modernize the capital-intensive industry.

Both France and Great Britain experienced a wave of nationalization
after World War II, but only the French took full control of the electric
power industry from power plants to meters. Far from being a case of
"lemon socialism," the nationalization of electricity in France targeted
an industry on the brink of massive expansion. Électricité de France
(EDF) emerged in 1946 as a potential pillar of a technically and economically modernized France, as a pilot firm in an industrial modernization process, and as a harbinger of a more egalitarian society.

A lopsided parliamentary majority in a strongly leftist political climate created EDF. Opponents remained quiet and resigned until mid-
1947 but then came into the open as the political majority moved to
the right with the onset of the Cold War. The opposition initially attacked the firm directly, but EDF and its supporters repelled the on-
slaught by pointing to EDF's productivity. An implicit "proof by

production" strategy preserved the nationalized industry and helped to table a more radical agenda, facilitating a fruitful (yet politically dubious) symbiosis between EDF and the private sector. By the mid-1960s, a consensus developed around a technocratic and productionist vision of EDF's place in the French economy and society.

The nationalization of electricity yielded not a socialist France but a far more efficient capitalist one. EDF became the largest and one of the most cost-effective, fully integrated power systems in the West, and ultimately helped to build a society of abundance, yet it failed to foster greater social equality. Productive triumphs, Promethean language, and mathematical modeling obscured the fact that by 1970 EDF managers were allied with the "trusts" that the nationalization of electricity was supposed to have undermined. The process that subordinated a publicly owned firm to the interests of the private sector is the central focus of this work.[1]

Many writers have presented the mixed results of French postwar reforms generally and the nationalizations in particular as reflecting the rise of a new class of technocratic managers who displaced traditional capitalists at the helm of France's political-economic order; a postindustrial society managed by experts replaced a class society based on wealth. Such an argument implies a fundamental change of elites. This work argues otherwise—that the elite was not replaced, but that it modernized, replacing heritage with meritocracy as a mode of sociopolitical legitimation. Technocratic circles within France's elite successfully convinced their more conservative peers that modernization, industrial rationalization, and planned economic growth were absolutely essential, and that economic renovation need not be accompanied by social upheaval. EDF technocrats played a crucial role in showing private sector managers that rational management and coherent planning could minimize the financial risks associated with productive expansion. In addition, EDF managers demonstrated that a generous and cooperative attitude toward labor yielded higher productivity and greater social stability than did the usual rigid opposition to organized labor's demands. EDF helped to set a clear trajectory toward modernization for the postwar French economy and it helped to lay the technical, economic, and ideological foundations on which a rejuvenated capitalism was erected.

EDF remains one of the purest examples of a modern technocracy. As with any hierarchical system, stability in a technocracy is predicated

[1] A recent sociological study of Électricité de France in the 1980s, *Le modèle EDF*, by Michel Wieviorka and Sylvaine Trinh (Paris: Éditions de la Découverte, 1989), begins its analysis with the assumption that EDF made a substantial political shift from the Resistance agenda to a moderate and technocratic one during the 1960s.

on the consent of those in the middle and lower ranks. In nontechno-
cratic social systems, that consent is usually attained by means of an
ideology that legitimates the status quo. Sociopolitical legitimation in
a technocracy, however, is based on confidence in the system's ability
to foster controlled change and growth—but that very approach inherently challenges the legitimacy of the status quo. As the history of
countless social upheavals indicates and as the conservative French
elite traditionally feared, a failure to legitimate the status quo could
lead to social cataclysm. The task of technocrats, therefore, was to foster
change while assuring that the changes would not stray beyond the
bounds of elite control. At EDF, a new legitimating ideology, technocorporatism, enabled the emerging technocrats to win the consent
of those not members of the elite to accept only limited change. One
of the keys to understanding the history of EDF can be discovered by
studying the reasons why potential opponents to technocratic power
surrendered to it.

The technocorporatist vision rests on notions of meritocracy and a
unilinear trajectory of all "progress." A meritocratic basis for hierarchy
serves to validate a new elite strategy by implying that expertise within
the productive system assures ascendency of the fittest individuals.
Mastery over the functional aspects of production is far easier to sell
to labor and consumers than simple status by birth, and it appears to
provide a measurable standard of success. The very notion of merit
remains largely undefined in popular discourse, though it is usually
derived from concepts of rationality and the capacity to abstract from
function to model. The intellectual tradition out of which technocorporatism emerged held that an analysis of component parts (or, in
modern parlance, subsystems) can lead the way to an understanding
of the whole. Analysis obviates synthesis, for synergy remains unde-
finable in an entirely quantitative framework. That which cannot be
quantified is irrelevant. Functionalism precludes aesthetics and most
qualities can be quantified; those that cannot are irrelevant. For the
technocorporatist, nothing succeeds like measurable success. The notion of unilinear progress within technocorporatism implies that each
problem has a single best and objectively knowable solution, and that
a succession of best solutions, implemented by qualified experts, will
inevitably lead to the best of all possible technological worlds.

Productive successes and the techniques used to attain them forestalled internal and eventually, external, opposition to the management
of EDF. Sophisticated models and specialized technical language effectively made it impossible for potential critics to frame a discourse
of opposition. Many of the managerial models passed off political and
social judgments as objective, science-based necessities. The new man-

agers presented as revealed truths capitalist economic models that implicitly subsidized large industry or limited EDF's presence on the capital market in order to avoid displacing private bond issues. The ostensible necessity for a market economy was as objective as Ohm's law; economic models emulated reality just as surely as $E = IR$ describes the relationships among voltage, current, and resistance. EDF managers ultimately used normative models of a purely competitive economy to make policy choices, just as engineers used hydrologic models to design dams.

The dynamics of consent explain why electrical workers and their unions, the key forces behind the nationalization, allowed EDF to cease challenging the capitalist order and to become allied with it. Ironically, whether an EDF union was Communist, Catholic, socialist, or purely "professional," its leaders fundamentally accepted the technocratic notion of progress and the meritocratic structures of legitimation on which the technocracy was based. Alternative visions of the possible remained elusive.

This work argues that progress is not unilinear, and analysis is not as objective as the experts claimed. While historical hypotheticals are always fraught with danger, it is clear that the characteristics of the nationalized power utility that oversaw all of France's electrical supply system in 1970 were not historically inevitable. It was possible to develop an institution more internally democratic and more open to public input. To gain a credible critical frame of reference, the opposition had to speak the language of the experts, yet it was incapable of doing so. The Marxist framework used by the majority of labor's leadership agreed with the technocrats on far too many issues—from a Promethean notion of progress to a respect for technically based hierarchy—and could not offer conceptual bases on which opposition could be built.

At EDF, the assumptions used to build models and the terms used to discuss them changed gradually and tacitly, but dramatically, between 1946 and 1970. Managers began with a highly politicized and fiercely independent stance toward the private sector. The private sector was viewed with disdain and EDF managers saw its methods as archaic and inappropriate for a firm that placed public service above private profit. However, the initial set of normative standards lacked concrete, systematic parameters, and EDF's early managers never succeeded in building an entirely new framework for decision making in a public enterprise. Unionists conceded provisional power to experts while EDF was under attack in the late 1940s, but that surrender became permanent. Cowed by the experts' technical successes, internal opponents systematically deferred to their superiors. The determination and skill with which early EDF managers defended the firm helped to quiet criticism permanently. Technocracy precluded democracy and made it easier to work with private sector managers who shared similar professional and cultural visions.

EDF managers who used private sector methods as normative standards shared several axioms with their erstwhile rivals: bigger is better (economies of scale), centralized is more efficient, and higher technology is intrinsically more productive. While these axioms may be true on small systems, they have a number of limitations when applied to large, leading-edge public systems. Reliability often weighs in favor of smaller and lower technologies. Intimacy with operational and social quirks as well as popular accessibility often weigh in favor of decentralized structures. Though largely a consequence of shared ideologies rather than overt conspiracies, the adoption of these axioms by its managers helped EDF operate to the benefit of large, centralized, and modern private firms. Modernist managers, whether in the public or private sector, shared a taste for hierarchy, scale, and novelty.

Marxist structuralists would argue that the process that integrated EDF with the private sector was inevitable because islands of socialism cannot exist in a capitalist sea. Parsonians would contend that the two sectors merged because a unified structure functioned most effectively. Instrumentalist approaches would stress the intelligence of the capitalist class, noting how the elite realized that by creating a nonprofit, publicly owned core in the industrial infrastructure, profits foregone at the core could augment revenues in the privately owned periphery. Evidence concerning EDF supports none of these analyses. The Marxist structuralist approach is overdeterministic because it neglects issues of human agency and will. The Parsonian stress on functionality begs the larger issues of initial intentions and political-social goals. While the instrumentalist theory may or may not be correct, its timing is wrong. Peaceful coexistence between the public and private sectors emerged only well after the nationalization, implying that private sector managers took several years to realize that nationalization could be turned to their advantage. The instrumentalist approach also implies a capitalist conspiracy on the part of actors inside and outside EDF to turn the firm to the service of the private sector. There is no evidence of any such conspiracy.

A more accurate analysis of the transition in management looks at of human volition and frailty. In the 1950s, EDF managers began to adopt private sector models for lack of alternatives. For example, cost and productivity analyses in business rely, in the largest sense, on profits as indicators of efficiency. In a nonprofit enterprise surrounded by the private sector, downstream from private suppliers and upstream from private bulk consumers, shadow profits became the most defensible measures and the normative standards of productive efficiency. In addition to the lack of nonprofit analytical models, one must also recognize the social background of EDF management itself. The most elite, technically oriented managers who occupied leading posts in government and industry were often graduates of the École Polytechnique, where they developed a collective sense of community and mission. Top EDF managers were also Polytechniciens and shared in the elite engineers' subculture. To swim against the social tide would have been unthinkable for EDF managers.

Any work dealing with a nationalized industry must address issues in historical political economy. The character of the French state changed critically from the Liberation era to the end of the Gaullist period. After World War II the Resistance coalition tried to build a new French state on a broad coalition cemented by a democratic, postliberal, and productivist political-economic consensus. That strategy failed with the onset of the Cold War, and the provincial, small-business coalition that had dominated the late years of the Third Republic retook power until it was eclipsed by Gaullism between 1958 and 1961. With the implantation of the Gaullist regime big business and centralized finance finally gained predominant political influence. EDF worked well with the initial postwar regime, but found little in common with the small-business conservatism and neoliberalism of the late Fourth Republic. The economic practices of the Fifth Republic—centralized and negotiated control over the economy by state-sector technocrats and the largest firms—offered the EDF managers a complementary set of partners. On that basis, EDF found a new and secure place within the structure of French monopoly capitalism.

Finally, this work addresses the issue of technological change and its social, economic, and political environment. The first wave of historians of technology, until the mid-1970s, tended to argue that technology determines society—man is *homo faber*, tools make the man, and the level of technology reflects the level of culture. More sophisticated supporters of this argument posit that the relations of production are also technologically determined. The notion of unilinear progress and the view that one technology or culture is higher than another are implicit in this technological determinism. This framework has recently been reversed. Many historians and technology analysts now argue that technology is socially and culturally constructed. Tools and techniques reflect not only the societies and cultures that produce them, they also reflect specific sets of political and social relations. Neither of these analyses transcends the notion of straight, causal vectors. At the extremes, they simply mirror each other, for causation remains unilinear and only the directions have been reversed.

This book argues strongly that the relationship between technology and its context is far more complex and that it is multifaceted, interactive, and almost chaotic. Technologies emerge from specific historical contexts, but once in place, they help to shape the dynamics of those contexts. Integrated power systems could only emerge from societies able to mobilize and centralize large sums of capital. Once in place, however, the technical attributes of power systems themselves and the language used to understand and discuss them reshaped social and economic geography. The inescapable technical characteristics of electrical transmission and distribution equipment make service more costly in sparsely populated areas, whether the social system is capitalist, socialist, or theocratic. Decisions on whether and where to install power systems, as well as on how much to charge for services, remain highly political because such choices can have considerable social and economic consequences.

This work is in two parts, one chronological and one thematic. The chronological part examines historical background to nationalized power (chapter 1), the nationalization of electricity (chapter 2), and the start up of Électricité de France (chapter 3). After 1954, with the major exception of the change of political regimes in 1958, there were few significant or cataclysmic events within or affecting EDF: process and evolution replaced events as the basic characteristics of change. By 1954, EDF management had already begun to shift its sense of purpose from the social reformism of the Liberation era to the efficient capitalism of the Gaullist Fifth Republic. Chapter 4 deals with political economy and managerial ideology and methods. It closes with a discussion of the emerging culture of high technology among EDF managers and thus acts as a transition to chapter 5, on the assumption that EDF management had near-total control over technological choice by the mid-1950s.

Chapter 5 raises a number of issues in technological choice, demonstrating the failure of unilinear explanations for technological change and the need for an interactive, nonlinear approach. The discussion focuses in particular on how pressures applied by private suppliers shaped EDF's methods for choosing and purchasing equipment, and how France developed its own nuclear power-plant design, only to abandon it under pressure from EDF's suppliers. Chapter 6 examines how labor and the unions dealt with a political and technological environment that was largely predetermined after the solidification of the new hierarchy. Labor's consent to technocratic power is discussed in this chapter. The work closes with an examination of the revolt of May 1968, dissecting the dynamics behind the one gash across the face of an increasingly complacent modernized France and the hopes that it raised for a postscarcity social order. The epilogue shows how the massive nuclear effort after 1970 solidified the current image of EDF— a public service firm run by expert managers in convivial concert with concentrated capitalist firms.

CHAPTER 1

Prelude to a Nationalization

Until World War I, France's electrical power industry rivaled any in Europe. Endowed with ample hydroelectric sites and an enviable pool of engineering talent, electrical power seemed to belle époque socialists and modernist businessmen to light the path toward a proud future. Nonetheless, by 1944, legal, institutional, ideological, and political factors had compromised the once-promising future of electrical power and more broadly, economic and technological modernization in France.

Administrative and managerial coherence eluded French utilities before nationalization, and the disarray slowed the maturation of power systems. As long as electrical facilities supplied only industrial consumers, there were few institutional or economic hurdles beyond obtaining the necessary site licenses and financing. Servicing large customer pools and interconnecting power lines among regions and firms demanded entirely new institutional arrangements, all of which faced political, economic, and technological complexities and barriers. Despite France's traditionally small firm size, utility managers argued that in order to assure sufficient financing and optimal use of facilities, corporate control over utilities had to be consolidated. This meant that after 1900, utilities constantly consolidated ownership and control, raising the specter in some minds of a sector dominated by faceless trusts operating for the benefit of their owners and to the detriment of consumers. In response, Parliament passed legislation in the 1920s that encouraged local cooperatives and municipal utilities, but this tactic failed to engender a coherent public power sector and further diffused control. Private and public utilities alike slowed system building during the Depression, and the stagnation and damage of World War II left French power facilities in a deplorable state.

Two superficially divergent ideological approaches to the industry emerged in the interwar period, one private and technocratic, the other public and cooperative. From their inception, the managers of French private utilities reflected the values and goals of the most modern section of French business opinion. In the 1920s, utility managers began to develop a coherent political and social philosophy that echoed their own predilection for expert rule. At the same time utility unions developed a sense of professional integrity and class consciousness and also began to advance their own ideas of how the sector should be owned and operated. Proud managers thus faced an equally proud labor force, and for similar reasons both sides agreed that the industry had to be centralized and controlled by experts. But utility managers failed to implement their visions, opening the path for a public and union effort after 1945.

The Status of French Electrical Services before 1945

In the 1890s, private hydroelectric production facilities mushroomed, serving primarily the papermaking and metallurgical industries. French electricity producers initially focused on industrial uses, leaving domestic and commercial consumers with scant power supplies, even in Paris and other major urban areas. Better interconnections within the utility system could have saved considerable capital costs by permitting more judicious use of existing equipment. Until 1918, however, utility managers showed little interest in grid building to connect multiple power-production sites with multiple points of consumption. Most links simply tied power plants to factories or cities.

Domestic and commercial electrical use expanded rapidly after 1918, and privately owned electrical utilities boomed in the 1920s. Utility entrepreneurs built several large coal-fired generating facilities near Paris and constructed a rudimentary power-transmission grid to link the hydro-rich South with the coal- and consumer-dense North. Grid building made good sense in France because coal-based power could be used to supplement cheaper, yet seasonally intermittent, hydroelectric energy. Coal-based power could also be derived as a by-product of the coal mining, steel, and coke industries. Grid building could thereby dramatically reduce costs by allowing an optimal mix of production facilities and by forestalling some costly construction.[1] In spite of these clear technical efficiencies, utility managers usually decided to install long-distance transmission links only to transport cheaply produced hydro power to user-dense, high-tariff areas such as Paris, and to supply the electrometallurgical and electrochemical industries with continuous power.[2] Utilities largely ignored smaller industries and rural consumers and tended to build simple transmission links rather than integrated interregional networks.

Having begun to pool supply and demand by developing transmission links, many utility managers saw financial and administrative consolidation as the natural complement to the technical centralization inherent in managing a power grid. Holding companies thus began to mobilize large amounts of capital, markets, facilities, and industry skills. Their consolidation strategies included absorbing or gaining control of other utilities. Utilities mobilized capital in part by urging small investors to purchase electrical securities as a method of saving, ironically creating a diffuse structure of ownership in a concentrating industry. In addition, many rural inhabitants purchased electrical securities in hope of luring new electrical facilities to their areas.

Utility managers constructed new electrical facilities only when they anticipated ample markets for additional output. This strategy to avoid smaller markets led to a relative overdevelopment of services in large urban areas (where user density and incomes were high) and reflected a dangerous tendency to seek rapid and low-risk returns. Paris, Lyons, and Marseilles thus developed rapidly as power markets while sparsely populated areas were often ignored. Utility managers followed a risk-averse strategy and often preferred less capital-intensive and more easily financed coal facilities over those of hydro. The electrical boom

---

[1] In cost characteristics, hydro and thermal can be viewed as opposites. Hydroelectric facilities are extremely capital-intensive, their costs often three to four times those of equivalent thermal generating capacity. Hydro has high fixed costs and low operating costs, whereas thermal has low fixed costs and high operating costs. Wise grid management entails using capital-intensive, cheap-fuel plants to meet the constant portion of demand (the base load) and running low-capital, expensive-fuel plants only to meet peak demand. For a fuller discussion of the possible savings from grid building, see Lionel Monnier, *La tarification de l'électricité en France* (1983), p. 18; for a specific case, see Christophe Bouneau, "La consummation dans le grand Sud-Ouest de 1914 à 1946: La formation d'un marché régional," in Fabienne Cardot, ed., *L'électricité et ses consommateurs* (1987), pp. 17–38.

[2] The structural-functionalist paradigm used in Thomas P. Hughes's study of gridding, *Networks of Power: Electrification in Western Society* (1983), tends to overstate the rationality of grid-building decisions on the part of utility managers. While demand-pull factors—an expanding popular demand for electricity—and supply-push factors—utility managers' recognition and encouragement of the growing power market—were undoubtedly present, there is substantial evidence that utility managers attempted to monopolize production and distribution concessions in order to extract high tariffs from consumers; see René Gaudy, *Les porteurs d'énergie* (1982), pp. 69–71.

decade of the 1920s thus meant an increased availability of electrical power in the major cities based on thermal production and only as much hydro production as utility managers considered necessary to serve large industry and dense urban markets.

Electrical supply and demand never successfully met in the power markets of interwar France. Regionally variable supplies faced highly price-sensitive demand. High-income domestic consumers showed little aversion to paying dearly for electricity, the rates for which included a luxury tax. Once the utilities satisfied the "luxury" market for electricity, they tried to sell to middle-income and working-class consumers. After the mid-1920s, utilities built new facilities, then set tariffs high enough to assure rapid capital recovery, only to discover that many consumers were reluctant to pay such high prices. Utility managers then became more cautious in their demand predictions and adopted less expansive investment programs in the late 1920s. Popular demand for electricity remained highly contingent on prices, and utilities rapidly discovered a common dilemma with new technologies. Suppliers could assure amortization by keeping rates high, but they risked forestalling adequate demand. Conversely, they could drop rates, expecting demand to expand, but risk not recovering their investments rapidly enough. By the late 1920s, utilities largely adopted the high-price strategy, leading to a construction slowdown in the 1930s.

Governmental regulation and control over utilities were as desultory as the construction and distribution practices of the utilities.[3] Electrical utilities' use of public and nonutility lands compelled the French state to assume a key role first in the regulation of utilities and later in the development of electrical facilities themselves. A law of 1906 set the regime for concessions on electrical distribution systems. These measures significantly affected many communities and helped shape France's power systems. French waterways had long before entered the public domain, and in 1909 the National Assembly passed the first laws regarding hydroelectric dams. In a rare move toward bureaucratic decentralization, Parliament granted communal governments the right to concede the use of rivers and their adjacent banks to private firms for installing small dams. Larger dam projects had to attain approval from Paris, yet local communities enjoyed benefits such as lease receipts

---

[3] For a complete analysis of the state's role in early electrical supply, see Pierre Lanthier, "The Relationship between State and Private Electric Industry, France, 1880–1920," in Jürgen Kocka and Norbert Horn, eds., *Law and the Formation of the Big Enterprises in the Nineteenth and Early Twentieth Centuries* (1979), pp. 590–601. Lanthier argues that the state and private utilities became deeply intermingled by the 1920s—largely at the behest of the utilities themselves.

and discounted power even from those. Utilities wanting to install transmission and distribution lines on nonutility properties faced similar requirements.

Usufruct legislation granted local authorities the power to regulate rates and exact a variety of payments from the utilities, yet the concession system further diffused public control over utilities. The legal rights associated with concession contracts opened new economic horizons to otherwise remote communities and gave them bargaining clout against the powers of the holding companies and the state. These prerogatives were jealously guarded and local discourse targeted outsiders, whether ministries, holding companies, or unions. Local political bosses often viewed electrical concessions as important parts of local patronage machines and adjusted concession contracts accordingly. Out of the array of concessionary agreements and political practices, France became a patchwork of varying rates, rules, and regulations.

Legislation also widened opportunities for electrification in areas where investors feared to tread and nourished decentralist sentiments in rural France. The municipal socialist movement of the mid-1920s expanded community control over local power supplies. In the era of the Cartel des Gauches, an electoral coalition of Radicals and Socialists, Parliament passed laws enabling communes and departments to develop their own facilities for producing and distributing electricity. Agricultural electrical cooperatives (organized under Sociétés d'Intérêt Collectif Agricole d'Électricité, SICAE) and *régies*, utilities owned by local governments, began to emerge in many areas, but they often lacked access to sufficient financing. Ironically, communities that operated local utilities became both concessionaires and conceding authorities, introducing a political and financial contradiction that would only increase with nationalization. Communes that owned generation and distribution facilities enjoyed considerable energy autonomy and could ignore Paris while they charted their electrical futures.

The concession system, the cooperative movement, and competition among private firms contradicted the centralization strategy of the holding companies and diffused authority over energy planning and operations. The maze of rival institutions made systematic interconnection ever more elusive, and supply efficiencies suffered accordingly. Local authorities were unable to develop gridding strategies among districts, and when private utilities developed interregional transmission links, régies and co-ops lacked protection against monopolist pricing practices. Thus, by the onset of the Depression, several problems in the utility industry were becoming clear: efficiency seemed to require centralized control, yet many citizens were reluctant to allow the controlling power to reside in private hands. At the same time, measures reinforcing local autonomy militated against the very centralization that efficiency criteria seemed to warrant.[4]

Measures taken during the Depression and the war did little to resolve crises of ownership and control in the industry. In the mid-1930s, the central state tried to gain the initiative in the utility sector and overcome the fragmentation of the industry, focusing on rural electrification and rate regulation. Legislators recognized that sufficient returns on capital invested in user-sparse rural areas would require inordinately high rates. High tariffs would cut potential demand and make profitability even more problematic. In a program more conservative than the New Deal's Rural Electrification Administration, Parliament created a system of tariff and revenue equalization among sparsely and densely populated areas. By 1939, over 90 percent of France's communes were electrified, yet new facilities were small and often inadequate for most uses beyond simple lighting. These systematic insufficiencies and a lack of consumer incomes retarded both agricultural electrification and broad domestic power consumption.

Rate-making practices were inconsistent and inequitable, and governmental intervention was largely ineffective before World War II. Rates had little basis in the actual costs of service. Wholesale and large industrial tariffs were usually set by negotiation and they reflected the corporate and financial relations among large utilities and industrial firms. Domestic users often paid premium prices to cover deficits engendered by preferential rates for industrial consumers and electricity resellers. Jules Moch later described this problem in the theoretical journal of the National Resistance Council. The utilities "go into debt because of the advantageous rates they grant to their subsidiaries, who are also their suppliers or their clients; they multiply these subsidiaries and by holding domestic ratepayers hostage, they can count on having their deficits covered. . . . The managers [of such firms] sit on the boards of directors of the major banks and the major industrial firms."[5] Rate reforms in 1935 created a crude tariff-indexing system. Basing power tariffs on production costs, the index used coal and labor costs as key variables, yet understated the impact of capital costs. The rate structure was inflexible in periods of economic and financial turmoil. Rigid rates emitted inaccurate "price signals" for consumers and managers and

---

[4] For a fascinating study and argument concerning the technical need for grid building and the problem of politically inspired roadblocks, see Hughes, *Networks*, chaps. 4 and 5.

[5] "J.M." (presumably Jules Moch), "Réflexions sur les socialisations," *Les Cahiers Politiques* (clandestine) 8 (March 1945), 26.

thus induced uneconomic choices. Acting under political pressure, the state reduced rates in July 1935, forcing tariffs to mirror falling production costs. This ad hoc approach failed to make rates more coherent.

Created in the 1920s and reformed in 1935, the state's Conseil Supérieur de l'Électricité was supposed to make utility regulation more systematic, but it largely failed. The council could only arbitrate conflicts over concession contracts, including rate cases. Its composition and judicial (rather than administrative) charge reflected the French approach to utility regulation before nationalization. In order to facilitate expert oversight and interest representation, the state allowed utility managers to hold the majority of seats on the council, where they could block actions of the Ministry of Public Works, which (like many local authorities) was in charge of utility oversight.[6] The council had little impact on the electrical power industry beyond providing career ladders for elite engineering graduates and offering a forum for cooperation between the state and the utilities.[7]

The French state also engaged in its own utility-development programs. In 1921, the French state created the Compagnie Nationale du Rhône to help develop the Rhône valley for irrigation, shipping, and electrical power production. Rhône valley communes, Paris-region private distribution firms, the City of Paris, and the French state owned the Rhône company. Through it, the state hoped to ease administrative barriers, to develop the entire Rhône basin as an integrated system, and to coax private developers to risk the requisite amount of capital. The Rhône company could not mobilize sufficient seed capital, particularly after the onset of the Depression. When World War II began, the company had not completed any projects, and the Génissiat dam, about sixty kilometers upstream from Lyons, was its only work in progress.

The state helped to charter the Groupement d'Électricité, a holding company with a 50 percent capital participation by the state, during the waning days of the Popular Front. Despite a bold portfolio of hydro projects estimated to cost three billion francs, the effort came to naught with the onset of war. The company did, however, foster cooperation among technocrats within the power industry and the state. That cooperation formed the embryo of a body of state and private utility technocrats, incubated during the war and born with the nationalization in 1946.

---

[6] [Pierre Le Brun], "La nationalisation nécessaire de la production et de la distribution de l'électricité," *Revue Syndicale Économique et Sociale* 3 (September 1937), 44.

[7] Monique Maillet-Chassagne, *L'influence de la nationalisation sur la gestion des entreprises publiques* (1956), p. 97.

Utility Management, Strategy, and Structure to 1939

French utility managers before World War II broke from French industrial traditions in their dedication to spur rapid technological change, yet their risk-averse investment strategies extended old French business habits. By 1939, an advanced technical and managerial elite oversaw technically backward utilities. The power companies had departed from the tradition of family firms and inherited managerial posts.[8] Top managers came from the elite École Polytechnique and middle managers and technicians from technical institutes such as the École Supérieure d'Électricité. Utility practices marked a key step toward managerial capitalism in France. Top managers acquired utility assets through generous employee stock options and though they often owned only minute proportions of corporate assets, they enjoyed considerable autonomous executive power. In addition, the utility trade association, the Syndicat Professionnel des Producteurs et des Distributeurs de l'Énergie Électrique, provided technocratic managers with a forum and helped to build their social networks.

Utility holding companies had begun to reinforce managerial autonomy in the 1920s. Ernest Mercier, like Samuel Insull in the United States, emerged as the top manager of utility holding companies sitting atop a pyramid of merged firms and joint-stock subsidiaries. While undoubtedly a wealthy man, Mercier owned only a small part of Compagnie Parisienne de la Distribution Électrique Union d'Électricité, and Lyonnaise des Eaux, all of which he managed. His corporate power arose from his control of shareholders' proxy votes. Mercier and other utility executives such as Louis Durand and Paul Huvelin liberally used that power to build and maintain strong personal positions in the industry.[9]

Controlling proxies was rather simple. Small shareholders often ceded their proxy votes to major banks, whose representatives generally voted with the managers at annual stockholders' meetings. Often only about thirty persons attended stockholders' meetings, even for firms with thousands of owners. Concentrated control and interlocking boards of directors assured strong ties across banks and utilities. Crédit Lyonnais tended to direct the policies of the Mercier group and the Compagnie Générale d'Électricité. By 1938, the five largest holding companies controlled 74 percent of the generating capacity and 66

[8] Pierre Lanthier, "Les dirigeants des grandes entreprises électriques en France, 1911–1973," in Maurice Lévy-Leboyer, ed., Le patronat de la seconde industrialisation, Cahiers du Mouvement Social, no. 4 (1979), pp. 106–10.
[9] Remarks of Paul Béchard, in France-Assemblée Nationale Constituante, Journal officiel, débats parlementaires (hereafter, JO, dp), 23 March 1946, p. 1076.

percent of all utility assets. The Giros-Huvelin group, the third largest, had links with the Société Générale d'Entreprise and the Compagnie Générale d'Électricité, leading civil engineering and electrical equipment firms, respectively. The fourth largest, the Énergie Électrique du Littoral Mediterranéen, had cross-ownership with Alsthom (as did the Mercier group), another major electrical equipment firm.[10] Further, the Empain group owned mechanical construction and metalworking firms and the Paris Métro. Its substantial power facilities supplied its factories and the Métro. Finally Ugine and Pechiney, the largest electrochemical and specialty-metals producers, owned considerable hydroelectric capacity, and both could sell surplus power at high rates and buy supplementary power at a discount. Electrometallurgical and electrochemical firms controlled 45 percent of the total hydroelectric reservoir capacity in 1946.[11] Holding companies bought many hydro concessions not for electrical production per se, but to preclude their use by competing firms. Like the diffusion of regulatory power, preclusive concession purchases hampered a coherent, planned use of energy resources.

Small utility investors saving for retirement were often well served by the domination of utilities by financial institutions, for both sought minimal risks, steady profits, and small capital gains. Utilities enjoyed both steady (or rising) dividends per share (Table 1) and saw no long-term share price deterioration between 1925 and 1940 (Appendix fig. A1). Utility strategies and structures were far less satisfying for those seeking rural electrification, particularly during the construction hiatus of the Depression.

Stagnant demand in the 1930s followed the expansion of the 1920s. Supply continued to expand well into the 1930s as works in progress were gradually completed, and utility executives became understandably uneasy. Electrical investments fell sharply in 1931, though by most accounts the Depression did not hit France until 1932. Executives anticipated reduced demand because of Depression conditions elsewhere and feared reductions of cash flow during construction. Utility managers based investment decisions on planning horizons of about five years and thus were hypersensitive to dim long-term financial prognoses. Production capacity grew after 1932 only as works in progress were completed. Reduced capital formation tended to enhance profits, for earnings once retained for reinvestment could be distributed as dividends. This helped maintain utility share prices as other share prices fell (Appendix fig. A1).

[10] Électricité de France, Conseil d'Administration, "Procès verbaux des séances" (confidential minutes of the EDF board of directors, mimeographed, nonpaginated, hereafter, CAPV) 3 (24 May 1946).
[11] Cited by André Girardot, JO, dp, 26 March 1946, p. 1074.

Table 1. Financial performance of French electrical utilities, 1920–1939 (price indexes based on 1927 = 100)

Years	A	B	C	D	E	F
1920–24	277	—	65	—	426	—
1925–29	364	+ 31.0	75	+ 15.0	485	0.943
1930–34	325	− 10.7	38	− 49.0	855	0.632
1935–39	284	− 12.6	55	+ 44.7	516	0.898

Sources: For average dividend per share and stock prices, Edmond Roux, Nationalisation sans spoliation (1945), p. 6; for industrial price indices, Jean-Marcel Jeanneney and Claude-Albert Colliard, Économie et droit de l'électricité (1950), Table 37.
Definition of columns:
A. Average dividend per share (in francs) D. Percent change in industrial price index
B. Percent change in average per share E. Dividend per share, constant francs
  dividends   (1927 = 100)
C. Industrial price index   F. Earnings-to-price ratios

While still exhibiting the visage and structure of managerial capitalism, French utilities reverted to the conservative strategies of traditional French businesses after 1932. Utility mangers moved from a low-price, high-volume marketing strategy to a high-price, low-volume plan. Debt-to-equity ratios were higher than those in other sectors because of the capital-intensive nature of the industry, but (like most French firms) utilities avoided debt financing and usually paid for new investments out of retained earnings. However, utility managers did not fear the loss of control associated with the sale of voting shares because proxies remained securely in thrall. A fall in issues of new stock in 1931 reflected reduced capital needs rather than a conscious move away from equity financing (Appendix fig. A2–a). Although Compagnie Parisienne de la Distribution Électrique increased its outstanding stock by 33.8 percent in 1934, its capital formation increased by only about 5 percent annually until 1939.[12]

High tariffs during the Depression also helped to maintain utility profits and to inflate utility stock prices relative to other stocks (see Table 1). Market values of utilities far exceeded book values. Rates seemed impervious to downward pressures, contributing to high profits in the period from 1930 to 1934. Between 1929 and 1935, while competitive sector profits fell 66 percent, utility profits rose 53 percent.[13] The rate reduction of July 1935 forced tariffs downward, but expanded consumption kept profits high. With the inflation of the Popular Front period, utilities were squeezed between rising low-tariff consumption

[12] Calculated from statistics presented in Charles Malégarie, L'électricité à Paris (1946), pp. 541–45. The author was a vice-president of Compagnie Parisienne de Distribution Électrique.
[13] Jean-Marcel Jeanneney and Claude-Albert Colliard, Économie et droit de l'électricité (1950), p. 107.

and higher production costs, causing a brief erosion of earnings. Nonetheless, overall utility financial performance in the 1930s was only slightly less impressive than that of the utilities' peak financial years in the 1920s.

Utility managers shifted their investment choices for generating equipment during the Depression, opting even more for coal over hydroelectric facilities (Appendix fig. A2–b).[14] Indeed, utilities built coal plants but used as much hydro power as possible in the 1930s. Hydro output as a percentage of total electrical production rose throughout the decade. This was caused not by investment decisions favoring hydro, but by plentiful rainfall and a policy of utilizing existing hydro capacity as much as possible.[15] The figures compiled by the Chambre Syndicale des Forces Hydrauliques are the best indicator of utility equipment plans. In 1932 utilities requested twelve hydro concessions for a total increase in power of 98.5 megawatts (mw); in 1933 there were only five such requests, for an installed capacity of only 30.14 mw.[16] At the World Energy Conference held in Washington in 1936, the French delegation, led by Mercier group managers, vowed "to struggle against an overcapacity that could be dangerous" and recommended "caution in building dams [for] fear of [an] overcapacity" that would "compromise our legitimate financial interests."[17] Mercier's biographer, Richard Kuisel, notes that the electric power industry eschewed hydro investments and concludes that "the power industry had made handsome profits, but it had done almost nothing to expand the facilities to meet the demand."[18] There was a certain logic to the antihydro view in the 1930s, however, with hydro being relatively more capital intensive as a method of production and with interest rates high compared to the anticipated growth in demand, managers needed to minimize fixed costs. Nonetheless, much of the coal needed for electrical production had to be imported, aggravating trade deficits and increasing dependence on foreign energy sources.

At the time of the Popular Front in 1936, leftists began seriously

---

[14] Figures presented in Appendix 2 tend to obscure this politically important fact. Actual annual investments in hydro tended to be less subject to major fluctuations owing to long construction times and a reluctance to close hydro construction sites once they had been started.

[15] État Français—Comité d'Organisation de l'Énergie Électrique, "Rapport de l'année 1944" (Vichy: n.p., n.d.), mimeographed; Électricité de France archives, series E8, "Statistiques 1," Centre de Documentation Murat-Messine, Paris. See also Edmond Lyon et ses Fils, Banquiers, ed., "Documents électriques," Étude A15 (Paris, February 1939), mimeographed, nonpaginated.

[16] Cited by Girardot, JO, dp, 26 March 1946, p. 1073.

[17] Cited in Annie Lacroix, "La nationalisation de l'électricité et du gaz," Cahiers d'Histoire de l'Institut Maurice Thorez 6 (n.s. 34, January 1974), 83.

[18] Richard F. Kuisel, Ernest Mercier: French Technocrat (1967), pp. 116–18.

raising the idea of nationalizing the power industry. They criticized utility managers for not upholding their proper capitalist role and not expanding the means of production. According to the Popular Frontists, utilities built thermal plants and maintained high rates in order to pocket higher profits, regardless of the effects on French living standards or the balance of trade. In addition, while many of the patents on hydro equipment used in France were French, thermal power required payments for patent licenses to German and American firms, particularly for boilers, heat exchangers, and alternators. Nationalization would thus revive the industry and foster technological independence. Nonetheless, pressing political crises prevented the Popular Front from submitting a nationalization bill to Parliament.

Political and Social Ideology in the French Electrical Industry, 1920–1939

Corporate concentration in the French electrical industry of the 1920s provided fertile ground for the seeds of technocratic ideology. In the rancorous and indecisive context of interwar politics, a political philosophy of technocorporatism emerged. In that philosophy, corporate paternalism merged with visions of efficient, technology-based growth, merit-based workplace hierarchies, and the rationalization of labor processes and investment decisions. Traditional corporatism envisioned a system of class cooperation based on "natural" status hierarchies. Technocorporatism encouraged class cooperation (as opposed to class conflict) within hierarchies of technical merit and mediated by the state.[19] Modernist corporatists wished to increase economic and technical efficiency and to foster economic growth; traditional (or conservative) corporatists could retard economic expansion by trying to preserve inefficient hierarchies at the expense of productive gains.

Technocorporatists strived to legitimate merit hierarchies by having engineers (or economists) manage a growth that ostensibly benefited producers of all stripes. This validated the ascendency of engineers and professional managers above owners and thus helped to map the

[19] This definition extends the one offered in Leo Panich, "The Development of Corporatism in Liberal Democracies," *Comparative Political Studies* 10 (April 1977), 61. Panich does not, however, discuss the concept of meritocracy as a legitimating structure. For an exhaustive study of a broadly defined corporatism in the interwar era, see Martin Fine, "Towards Corporatism: The Movement for Capital-Labor Cooperation in France, 1914–1936," Ph.D. diss. University of Wisconsin, 1971.

ideological terrain for the elite of managerial capitalism.[20] In techno-corporatist thinking, degrees of mastery over technical aspects of the productive apparatus determine status hierarchies. These technical characteristics are assumed to be value-free, arising from the irrefutable laws of mathematics, physics, and engineering. Social well-being is equated with technical efficiency, and the technocratic state is the ultimate guarantor of productive efficiency and hence of social progress.

Technocorporatists vaunt centralized high technology and an ever-increasing scale of the productive apparatus. Rejecting the Ricardian notion of diminishing returns to scale, *new* and *bigger* are synonymous with *better*. A corollary to this concept—that the minimum efficient scale of plant and machinery grows with the development of higher and more capital-intensive technology—supports industrial concentration, whether the firms be privately or publicly owned. Technocorporatist discourse thus relied on the language of scale, expertise, centralized power, efficiency, and empirically revealed truth. Technocorporatists of the right and left assailed what they perceived as French business practices that limited production in order to maintain high prices. Critics argued that this traditional Malthusianism enflamed class conflict over the distribution of limited output.

Several organizations promoted technocorporatist ideas in the interwar era, but none achieved appreciable political visibility. Redressement Français, a movement funded (and essentially founded) by Mercier and popular among power-industry managers and Polytechniciens in the 1920s, advocated a probusiness version of technocorporatism. At the same time, Polytechnique Socialists such as Jules Moch developed similar concepts with a more leftist tone. Parallel to a technocorporatist tendency within the Second International, Moch framed a socialist project that promised to supplant capitalist anarchy with socialist rationality, eliminating the material deprivation of the working class with a greater and better-distributed productive output.[21]

Because of its unusual technical and economic characteristics, the electrical power industry mirrored emerging technocorporatist busi-

---

[20] For earlier developments of this set of conceptions, see Charles S. Maier, "Between Taylorism and Technocracy: European Ideologies and the Vision of Industrial Productivity in the 1920s," *Journal of Contemporary History* 5 (1970), 27–61; Richard F. Kuisel, "Technocrats and Public Economic Policy: From the Third to the Fourth Republic," *Journal of European Economic History* 2 (1973), 53–99; and Kuisel, *Capitalism and the State in Modern France* (1982), chaps. 2, 3, and 4. While Maier locates the source of technocratic "macro" rationalization in the "micro" rationalization of Taylorism, Kuisel implies that it can be located more accurately in the engineers' conception of the power grid. In this respect, see Hughes, *Networks*, chaps. 4, 5, and 6.

[21] Jules Moch, *Socialisme et rationalisation*, pamphlet (1924), pp. 3–7; Ronald R. Kline, "Electricity and Socialism: The Career of Charles P. Steinmetz," paper presented at the University of Delaware Colloquium on the History of Technology, March 1985.

ness opinion perhaps more than did any other industrial sector. Mercier's ideas were typical within his milieu, and his association with Redressement exemplified the fate of business technocorporatism.[22] Mercier became politically active after the World War I when he joined the Messine utility group. His biographer Richard Kuisel states that with his boss, Albert Petsche, Mercier believed that "only an apolitical technical elite could provide the republic with sound and vigorous government."[23] From his association with the right-wing gadfly Maréchal Lyautey, Mercier developed respect for "team spirit" and for the technical elite's duty to protect and unify the fractious masses. Mercier eschewed unions, which, he felt, nurtured counterproductive egalitarian sentiments among workers. He sought instead to win workers' consent through corporate paternalism, evoking an *esprit maison* (company spirit) and treating personnel as a team. To reinforce the camaraderie of teamwork and fraternal competition, Mercier supported athletic teams, where workers could release workaday tensions, and offered home buyers' assistance plans, cafeterias, garden plots, and vacation resorts in the hope that these rewards would buttress personal commitments to the firm.[24]

Mercier felt that the politics of progress had to reach outside the firm. Echoing the hierarchical, neomilitarist predilections of many Polytechnique engineers, his Redressement tied a technocorporatist outlook to an elitist analysis of national politics. Redressement stated that the "political elite [had] submitted to the demagoguery of universal suffrage," so that "there remained only private business leaders who retained the capacity to act creatively and thus hold the levers of command" in French politics. Redressement wanted a new elite, naturally selected by the forces of competition and electrified by an "enterprising and audacious spirit."[25] Redressement produced a well-funded journal to disseminate these ideas, but it seems to have had few readers.[26] Redressement only preached to the converted.

Frustrated with Redressement's inefficacy, Mercier tried funding moderate politicians. He hoped that moderate politicians would at least encourage "rational" cartel building. Trying to build a right-center coalition government in 1928, Mercier contributed to the campaigns of

---

[22] For a fascinating study of another electrical sector manager who held rightist technocorporatist views similar to those of Mercier, see Richard F. Kuisel, "Auguste Detoeuf, Conscience of French Industry: 1926–1947," *International Review of Social History* 20 (1975), 149–74. Detoeuf headed Alsthom, France's largest electrical equipment manufacturer.

[23] Kuisel, *Mercier*, p. 46.

[24] Malégarie, *L'électricité*, pp. 413–25.

[25] Kuisel, *Mercier*, p. 48.

[26] Pierre Massé, *Aléas et progrès: Entre Candide et Cassandre* (1984), p. 37.

about one hundred deputies,[27] but the politicians were preoccupied with parliamentary wrangling and had little patience with technocratic ideology.

Once Redressement's academic technocorporatism waned in the face of popular indifference, fascist activism, and subsidized politicians' indifference, Mercier began to support fascists. Mercier and other business technocrats began to see ultrapatriotism and the "camaraderie of the trenches" as a powerful cement for class cooperation. Antiparliamentary fascists might, they hoped, create a state that could become technocratic. The Croix de Feu, France's largest fascist group, enjoyed considerable financial support from Mercier, but Colonel de la Rocque, the Croix's führer, cut the tie in March 1936 because Mercier's role as a prominent member of the "two hundred families" tainted the Croix's populism.[28] Rejected by the fascists and revealing the flexibility of technocratic thinking, Mercier toured the Soviet Union in 1935 and wrote a book lauding the expert Soviet planners who had overseen the first Five-Year Plan.

The twisted path of business technocorporatism underlined its lack of political efficacy. Fascist myths of male valor dwarfed fantasies of technological progress, and politicians were too opportunistic. Rightist technocorporatists lacked any effective institutional cachet until the Vichy period.

In the 1930s an apolitical, technocratic study group called X-Crise emerged, and it was a sieve through which technocorporatists of all stripes passed. As a circle of Polytechnique graduates, X-Crise members dreamed of solving the economic crisis by applying the expertise of apolitical technocrats. Many felt that the Depression had doomed the liberalism of the 1920s and that the alternative was the active intervention of the state in the economy. Aside from engineers, who made up nearly half of the membership of X-Crise, 23 percent of the members were high-level corporate managers in modern industries, 6 percent were bankers, and 3 percent were military officers.[29] On the left were reformers and socialists who argued for statist economic planning and technocratic control. On the right were corporate neoliberals, including

---

[27] Kuisel, *Mercier*, p. 84.

[28] Concerning the famous fascist revolt in Paris on 6 February 1934, the Communist daily *L'Humanité* of 23 July 1935 claimed, "The plans were well conceived; Mercier, Finaly, and Rothschild and their cohorts commanded, La Rocque executed." Kuisel accurately disputes Mercier's direct role in the fascist riots, but concedes that his financial support for the Croix was later quite large, and that it was the 6 February riots that attracted Mercier to the Croix; see Kuisel, *Mercier*, pp. 99–112.

[29] Philippe Bauchard, *Les technocrates au pouvoir* (1966), p. 21. On X-Crise generally, see also Kuisel, "Technocrats," pp. 74–75.

inspectors of finance, utility managers, and the head of the national employers' federation.

X-Crise's positions implied that rational economic management in many ways had to supercede popular democracy. Viewing democratic institutions as inefficient, rightists in X-Crise preferred to have a Bonapartist state implement their schemes. The left wanted the electorate to transfer power into the hands of unionist-expert committees. Nonetheless, the apolitical technocrat or bureaucrat so dear to Veblen could never exist in France. When faced with the political divisions that emerged with the elections of 1936, X-Crise faltered. Political realities in late interwar France simply became too divisive to be discussed at levels of comfortable abstraction. During the labor negotiations at the Matignon Palace in June 1936, X-Crise socialists sat on opposite sides of the bargaining table from one of their rightist colleagues. X-Crise and electrical power technocrats ultimately would have to choose sides between the Resistance coalition and the authoritarian collaborationists of Vichy.[30] X-Crise's failure echoed that of Redressement and underlined the fact that technocratic ideas elicited no broad support in the interwar era.

The French electrical power industry seems to have been far more productive conceptually than materially, particularly in the 1930s. While the industry languished, many persons within the sector developed increasingly coherent conceptions of how the industry and the economy could be reorganized. Neither leftist nor rightist technocrats gained predominant political power in the 1930s, but during World War II, the rightists gained power, only to lose it. That set the stage for the Left to implement its vision of industrial organization.

Electrical Workers and Unionism to 1944

Electrical workers were part of the upper strata of the working class before World War II. They had higher skills and enjoyed better pay and benefits than most other workers. Utility managers consented to generous remuneration in order to assure the stable pool of skills needed by their firms. Because labor costs were a small part of total utility operating expenses, monopolist utilities could pass most labor-cost increases on to consumers. Utilities could afford to be paternalist and to experiment with innovative approaches toward labor.

The history of French electrical workers' trade unionism broadly

[30] Robert O. Paxton, *Vichy France: Old Guard and New Order, 1940–1944* (1972), pp. 349–55, and Kuisel, "Technocrats," pp. 77–83. Kuisel asserts that the technocrats were essentially apolitical and served both Vichy and the Resistance well.

paralleled that of other pre–World War II unions.[31] Formed at the turn of the century as a union of gas and electrical workers, the Confédération Générale du Travail's Fédération de l'Éclairage (CGT-Éclairage) remained small and diffuse before World War I. CGT-Éclairage expanded somewhat as utility holding companies emerged in the 1920s, but the birth of Catholic trade unions under the Confédération Française des Travailleurs Chrétiens (CFTC) and the splintering off of the Communist CGT-Unitaire (CGT-U) divided organizing efforts. A lack of legally recognized institutional rights within firms also inhibited organizing. Unionized workers tended to be concentrated in Paris, Lyons, and Marseilles. At scattered power-production sites, thermal plant workers often belonged to miners' and steelworkers' unions, and hydroelectric workers frequently joined with chemical and specialty-metals workers.

Utility work itself often required that skills be enhanced as technology changed. Indeed, distinct from most industrial environments where higher technology meant a degradation of skill, electrical workers often gained higher skills, which bolstered their high status within the working class. Rapidly evolving technology and rising productivity represented a danger to electrical workers, not through layoffs, but by reducing the chances for promotion and impeding the entry of electrical workers' sons into the trade. Consumer demand had to expand apace with productivity increases if electrical workers' status was to be maintained. For this reason, workers at nearly all levels began to see growing electricity demand as the best guarantee of job stability and advancement. In addition, with their skills validated by the specific nature of electrical technology, many workers viewed technology itself as having an intrinsic, autonomous, and positive value. These factors lent workers a sense of allegiance to the industry and a solidarity with the technocrats' adulation of technology and growth, despite the strict status hierarchy within the industry. Many electrical workers allowed a subtle technocorporatism to alloy otherwise steely conceptions of class conflict.[32]

The power industry developed special technical schools to train a

[31] Excellent studies of electrical trade unionism are contained in René Le Guen, *Voyage avec des cadres* (1977), and René Gaudy, *Les porteurs*.

[32] The foregoing is based on conversations with militants of the Confédération Française Démocratique du Travail–Fédération Gaz-Électricité (CFDT-FGE), 5, rue Mayran, Paris, April-May 1981; similar conversations with militants of the CGT-FNE, Pantin, March-April 1981; and my interview with Ernest Anzalone, former secretary-general of the CFDT-FGE and a former board member of EDF, 21 April 1981. See also the series of articles in the CFDT-FGE's journal, *Gaz-Électricité*, in the spring of 1952. Theoretical framework for the foregoing is based on André Gorz, *Adieu au prolétariat* (1981), pp. 81–98, and Michael Burawoy, *Manufacturing Consent* (1979).

work force that needed ever-increasing levels of skill. Candidates for technical and skilled positions took competitive examinations to enter company schools and performed a stint of on-the-job training after completing their classroom training. Messine-group trainees usually attended the company school at Gurcy-la-Châtel, founded in the 1920s. This system undermined the potential collective strength of highly skilled electrical workers because the companies imparted such skills and because employers used technical schools to sell corporate ideological agendas. Curricula often became ideological training under the rubric of "moral instruction."[33] This type of training sometimes made utility personnel, especially in the middle and upper echelons, loyal company men. The division of loyalties between the community of workers and the hierarchy of the firm helped to preserve corporate power and weaken prounion sentiments. Finally, skilled electrical workers faced monopsonistic employers who did not hesitate to maintain blacklists.

Few electrical workers unionized before the Popular Front era. Daunted in organizing efforts, the CGT and CGT-U electrical workers' federations allied with leftist political parties and ran candidates for local government offices. Unionists on local councils helped shape utility-concession contracts so that workers gained *statuts*, provisions in concession contracts that guaranteed workers' rights to union recognition, advancement procedures, pension rights, and the like. Marcel Paul, a CGT-U militant and later head of the reunified CGT-Éclairage, was a councilor in Paris from 1936 to 1938.

In the new *statuts*, unionists wanted promotions to be based on seniority and job performance rather than on arbitrary selection. They also sought pension-rights guarantees, layoff protection, and safeguards against arbitrary disciplinary actions. While *statuts* formalized the implicit power that electrical workers' high skills would usually have conveyed, they did not directly attack strong hierarchies of command on the job. They demanded instead that hierarchies be based on merit and skill and that pay levels reflect them. The unions thus did not level a frontal attack on managerial prerogatives, but sought only to make management more merit-based and rational. Efforts for a nationwide *statut* bore fruit with an excessively vague law of July 1928 that required all new concession contracts to contain *statuts*. Employers routinely ignored the new law, which did not unify or specify the content of *statuts*. Competing unions could not force employers to observe the law, and further attempts at a national *statut* remained stillborn until the Popular Front era.

[33] Malégarie, *L'électricité*, chap. 5.

The reunification of the CGT in February 1936 sparked a rise in union membership among electrical workers' unions, whose numbers rapidly rose from 27,000 to 72,000, in a total labor force of about 105,000 workers.[34] The Matignon Labor Agreements, which were followed by a gas and electric labor contract dated 10 June 1936, granted official recognition to the CGT. In January 1937, the director of electricity (a subordinate of the minister of public works) established a model *statut* for electrical workers, but it fell short of guaranteeing the uniform salaries and pension systems sought by the unions. It also excluded technicians, engineers, and managers, who together made up 10 to 15 percent of the labor force. A decree of June 1938 created a *statut* that standardized pay and pensions, but the war began before it could be implemented. In addition, employers often used subcontracting to circumvent the new *statut*, a practice extended during the war and (under a new *statut*) after the nationalization.[35] Unions began to understand that subcontracting was a key managerial strategy to undercut workers' rights.

Having gained a pay hike of almost 100 percent and the promise of a *statut* in 1936, CGT-Éclairage ebulliently held its national congress in June 1937. Members recognized that the struggle for a statut was not complete. The CGT founded the Groupement National des Cadres (GNC) in response to the exclusion of white-collar workers from the Matignon agreement. The GNC's positions implied that middle management's interests were linked to those of blue-collar workers rather than with those of the employers. Reacting to the formation of the GNC, Énergie Industrielle (a part of the Durand group) helped to create the Union Nationale des Cadres, Techniciens et Agents de Maîtrise (UNCM), essentially a company union. UNCM became simply a rung on the career ladder for a number of engineers and managers.[36]

The GNC and UNCM both strongly supported the concept of merit-based workplace hierarchies despite divergent rhetoric toward management. UNCM's professional discourse offered white-collar workers proud roles, including leadership and guidance over subordinates, and mastery of sophisticated technological systems. Because the GNC insisted that technology was politically neutral and unaffected by the

---

[34] Émile Pasquier, "Une rétrospective," *Force-information* 190 (May 1971), 29.

[35] Roger Boutteville, "Circulaire No. D/78," 31 July 1942, from the head of the Vichy government's Comité d'Organisation de l'Énergie Électrique (COEE) to COEE members, carbon copy, CGT-FNE archives, Pantin, dossier: "Entreprises privées." See also infra, chap. 6.

[36] For a close examination of the UNCM's homologues in other sectors, see Ingo Kolboom, "Patronat et cadres: La contribution patronale à la formation du groupe des cadres (1936–1938)," *Le Mouvement Social* 121 (October-December 1981), 71–95. Kolboom shows how membership in cadre unions was almost a necessity for promotions after 1937.

class system, it could not coherently define the sociopolitical position of a labor elite with high-technology skills. Rooted in nineteenth-century positivism and influenced by the technological enthusiasm and productivism of 1930s Stalinism, GNC leaders saw technology as an engine of social progress. They were unable to critique technology choices in terms of how they affected job hierarchies and the character of work. GNC members led dual lives, as professionals and as union-ists, and the two seldom met. The GNC's perspective could not really counterweigh technocorporatism. It described work relations in class terms, yet, like the technocrats' view, did not recognize that class forces shaped technological systems and objects. Like many leftist techno-corporatists, the GNC sought only to replace hereditary hierarchies with meritocratic ones.[37] More practically, unionized managers had to enforce corporate dictates, sometimes in opposition to their unionized subordinates, and the GNC discouraged insubordination.

CFTC membership in the electrical services remained small in the interwar period. Founded in 1919, the CFTC's Fédération des Services Publics et Concédés was strongest in Catholic regions of France and in hydro production. Based on a humanist version of Catholic corpo-ratist paternalism, the CFTC vaunted the dignity of work and stressed the human rights of workers. The CFTC offered no effective path be-tween class struggle (in the CGT sense) and company unionism.

While electrical workers had considerable power through their skills, they were ultimately unable to develop a systematic vision of their political position within the industry, or of the industry's place within the economy. The CGT had called for the nationalization of utilities in 1918, but their demand had little resonance. Once unionists gained a powerful political voice during the Resistance, they placed nationali-zation at the top of the nation's political agenda.

War, Collaboration, Resistance, and Liberation

The political and social crisis from September 1938 until August 1944 allowed utility managers to recoup the social and economic affronts of the Popular Front era. Business technocorporatists found their first political opening in 1939 in the cabinet of the Minister of Armaments Raoul Dautry, a railway manager and frequent board member in the utility sector. The Vichy regime provided right technocorporatists a

[37] The foregoing analysis is drawn from the conceptual framework in Langdon Winner, "Do Artifacts Have Politics?" *Daedalus* 109: 1 (Winter 1980), 121–36; evidence from Le Guen, *Voyage*, passim; Gaudy, *Les porteurs*, part 2; and my conversations with René Gaudy and Bernard Court (CGT-FNE archivist), CGT-FNE offices, Pantin, March 1981.

framework to implement their industrial philosophy. Traditionalists and technocrats battled incessantly at Vichy, yet right technocorporatists enjoyed direct political influence for the first time at Vichy.[38] Wartime economic policies allowed electrical energy technocrats to pursue long-standing goals: taming the unions, implementing a transmission grid within a noncompetitive framework, allocating scarce resources to benefit the major firms, and centralizing sectoral control in a mixed corporate-state body.

Vichy's economic rhetoric feigned a campaign of trust-busting, yet used state-sponsored Organization Committees to nurture large corporations. In a speech in October 1940, General Philippe Pétain said: "By its coordinating role, the state must break the corrupting influences [of large corporations]. Far from constraining individual initiative, the economy must liberate that initiative from its present constraints while subordinating it to the national interest."[39] Antitrust rhetoric obfuscated economic policies that served the major firms well. Kuisel concludes: "Publicly Pétain supported the ideal of the National Revolution by denouncing the 'trusts' and by dissolving the strongholds of big business.... In practice, however, it was the technocratic managers from big business who actually ran the economy."[40] Arguably, the Vichy regime was not duplicitous but deeply divided between atavistic traditionalists and technocratic modernists.[41] Whatever the interpretation, it is clear that while Vichy claimed to serve the needs of the defeated French, it brought to power a dysfunctional combination of right-wing ideologues and technocratic economic managers.

The war-racked and shortage-ridden French economy needed some form of statist resource-allocation plan, and the issue of what was to be controlled and in whose interests echoed earlier political-economic debates. Socialist Albert Gazier later noted that the Vichy planners oversaw a "rational and systematic pillage of the economy, for the profit of the trusts working at the service of the Nazis."[42] Indeed, the Comité d'Organisation de l'Énergie Électrique (COEE) pushed for hydroelectric development in order to free up French coal for French and German industry.[43]

[38] Note, for example, the imbroglio over the "Synarchy": see Richard F. Kuisel, "The Legend of the Vichy Synarchy," *French Historical Studies* 6 (Spring 1970), 365–98, and Bauchard, *Les technocrates*, pp. 47–49. Business technocrats clearly perceived the differences between rightist technocorporatists of the Mercier type and overt fascists; see Kuisel, "Auguste Detoeuf," pp. 168–71.

[39] Philippe Pétain, "Le nouveau statut économique de la France," *Les Cahiers de la Jeune France* (Vichy: État Français, 1941), 9.

[40] Kuisel, *Mercier*, p. 146.

[41] Paxton takes this position; *Vichy France*, pp. 210–21.

[42] Albert Gazier, "Les comités d'organisation," *Le Peuple*, 25 November 1944, p. 2.

[43] Lacroix, "La nationalisation," p. 84.

Graduates of the École Polytechnique and veterans of the Corps des Ponts et Chaussées largely dominated the organization committees, particularly the COEE. Many had passed through Redressement and X-Crise to arrive at Vichy. Members of the Mercier network headed many of the committees: in addition to Roger Boutteville, Mercier's top manager at Union d'Électricité and later director of the COEE, Mercier's associates also headed the committees for aluminum and gas. Other Mercier confreres directed the petroleum and electrical equipment committees.

Though the Vichy regime dissolved the utility trade association, virtually the same body soon reemerged as the COEE and enjoyed far greater power. The Mercier and Durand groups had attempted in vain to rationalize service areas in the interwar era; the COEE gave three firms the concession for very high tension transmission on a national basis to divide as they saw fit.[44] A subsection of the COEE did the same for the lower-voltage grids. Centralized coordination and strong demand helped to maintain utility stock values and profits (Appendix fig. A3). Profits rose slightly with the onset of the war, and stock prices remained high well into 1943. COEE-directed rationing guaranteed large electricity markets by allocating power supplies to large firms engaged in war production for the Germans. Fear of demand shortfalls became a distant memory. The healthy financial performance of utilities stood in stark contrast to falling real wages for electrical workers and insufficient electricity for small consumers.

Utility managers seldom collaborated with Occupation authorities out of fascist sympathies. Most managers sought only to continue profitable operations under strained conditions. Managers cooperated when German and utility interests converged; when interests diverged, utilities resisted. Interests converged strongly in the case of the Belgian-based Empain group. Baron Empain owned a number of utilities and electrical construction firms in France. Under the auspices of Albert Bichelonne and Albert Speer, Empain divided the electrical equipment market in western Europe among major Belgian, French, and German firms. When Allied bombing disrupted production at the Siemens plants, Empain supplied the Germans and later installed machine tools from bombed Siemens plants.[45] Fernand Gambier, chief of Éclairage during the war, later noted how "a very tight clique of Ponts and

[44] Simone Deglaire and Edmond Bordier, *Électricité, service public; tome I: La nationalisation* (1963), p. 37.
[45] Fernand Gambier, "Le trust de l'électricité et son grand magnat Kollaborateur, le Baron Empain," *Le Peuple*, 25 November 1944, p. 4. Gambier called for the immediate sequestration of all of Empain's assets as retribution. Upon Liberation, Radio Belgium called for the assassination of Empain.

Chaussées engineers" had used the Occupation as an opportunity to give rate relief to their "friends" and to attack the unions.[46]

Ernest Mercier eschewed collaboration. Harassed by the Gestapo for his Jewish wife (a niece of the legendary Captain Dreyfus) and his less-than-enthusiastic response to the Occupation, Mercier joined the Resistance in 1942. He supplied information on the physical layout of the electrical system to the Resistance forces in London, thus helping the creative sabotage of the electrical system during Allied actions in France in 1944. Mercier even contributed funds to Communist representatives of the Resistance movement.[47] In terms of political symbolism, Mercier's Resistance activity undoubtedly helped to shield business technocrats from political attacks after the war.

Electrical workers often resisted the occupiers. The political climate for electrical workers after 1939 was deplorable. First, the Communist party, a powerful force among electrical workers, was banned after the Molotov-Ribbentrop Pact of 1939. Communists were expelled from the CGT later in 1939, and the central and confederate bodies of the unions were outlawed in the fall of 1940. The expulsion of the Communists from the CGT largely decapitated Éclairage and excluded many of its most militant members, leaving few militants to resist the ultimate suppression of Éclairage itself. In November 1940 several leaders of the CGT and CFTC published the famous Manifesto of the Twelve against the Vichy regime, even though some of the signatories continued to serve on government-sponsored committees. The Labor Charter, written by ex-CGT leader Belin in 1941, required all workers to join corporatist unions in tandem with the organization committees.[48] State attempts to enforce the charter propelled electrical workers toward resistance, and the CFTC fought at the side of the CGT. The power industry also resisted as a community, and joint actions helped to build a sense of internal solidarity. In a celebrated incident of quiet resistance, Pierre Massé, a Messine-group technocrat with prewar business ties to German officials in Paris, rescued Director of Electricity Roger Gaspard from a prison where he was held for trying to divert

[46] Gambier, "Plus que jamais, la nationalisation s'impose," *Le Peuple*, 11 November 1944, p. 4.

[47] Kuisel, *Mercier*, p. 150. Mercier gave 100,000 francs to Yves Farge and Pierre Villon; see Madeleine Braun et al., "Le Front National," *Cahiers d'Histoire de l'Institut Maurice Thorez* 8 (n.s. 39, November-December 1974), 91.

[48] For a full discussion of the promulgation and functions of the Charte de Travail (Labor Charter), see Georges Lefranc, *Les expériences syndicales en France, 1939–1950* (1950), chap. 3. The charter itself was more a paper organ than a reality. In the northern mining region where the Vichyite industrial and labor efforts were most effective, the bodies created by the charter emerged only in the spring of 1944, then dissolved in July of 1944. See Olivier Kourchid, "Un leadership industriel en zone interdite: La Société des Mines de Lens et la Charte de Travail," *Le Mouvement Social* 151 (April-June 1990), 55–78.

copper from the Germans. Gaspard then tried to keep Éclairage chief Marcel Paul from being sent off to certain death in a German internment camp. The three were later reunited atop EDF, with Gaspard named director-general, Massé titled as his assistant, and Paul celebrated as the founder of the firm.[49]

The CFTC did not initially oppose the Vichy regime directly. Traditionalists at Vichy publicly offered the kind of paternalist class cooperation and antitrust actions that the CFTC had long sought, but as the regime increasingly became an artifice for corporate power, the CFTC shied away. The technocratic style of the organization committees equally alienated the CFTC. The Labor Charter decisively ended any possible rapprochement between the CFTC and Vichy, for the charter violated the CFTC's insistence on trade-union pluralism. Vichy thus pushed a potential ally into resistance.[50] UNCM largely cooperated with Vichy, for as a technocrat's union operating in a technocratic regime, it was quietly allowed to continue after the Labor Charter ostensibly outlawed it. Many of UNCM's wartime leaders were purged after the war for their collaboration and were later excluded from EDF management.[51]

Electrical workers plied their skill and knowledge of the electrical system to cut power supplies to the enemy during the battles across France in 1944 and 1945. Lacking confidence in, and fearing the political impact of, the Resistance, the Allies bombed generating stations to achieve similar ends. By contrast, electrical workers understood that destroying power plants would ultimately make reestablishing service very expensive and time consuming. They therefore concentrated sabotage on key power pylons and transformers, making surgical strikes and minimizing lasting damage. Sabotage severed all of the major power-transmission lines in the summer of 1944. According to Roger Gaspard, 1,587 high-tension towers were downed, with an additional 1,160 damaged and 10 percent of all large transformers out of service.

[49] Massé, Aléas, p. 64, and interview by author with Gaspard, Paris, 3 June 1981. The CGT-sponsored biography of Paul, Pierre Durand, Marcel Paul: Vie d'un 'pitau' (1983), makes no mention of the incident. Later, when Massé joined the Resistance, his primary contact was Pierre Le Brun, head of the GNC and later a member of the EDF board of directors; Massé, Aléas, p. 59.

[50] For a discussion of the CFTC during the war, see Gérard Adam, La CFTC, 1940–1958, Histoire politique et idéologie (1964), pp. 15–32; see also Paxton, Vichy France, p. 348, and Robert Aron, Histoire de l'épuration, vol. 2 (Paris: Fayard, 1975), pp. 310–14.

[51] See "Réponse à M. G. Hérard," Tribune Économique, 1 November 1946. The author of this article, a defender of UNCM, claims that individuals within the UNCM, not the organization itself, collaborated. At the date of this article, the author claimed, to the disbelief of the CGT and CFTC, that there were no UNCM officers who had collaborated on the Labor Charter. In 1954 a CFTC author erroneously claimed that UNCM was born under the auspices of the charter, essentially as a collaborationist union; "L'histoire de la Fédération Gaz-Électricité de la CFTC," Gaz-Électricité 51 (January 1954), 4.

Upon the liberation of Paris, Parisian electrical workers "found" ten thousand tons of coal, which they had hidden from the Germans.[52] Electrical workers labored around the clock, often working over twenty-four hours on a shift, to reestablish services in the liberated zones. Underpaid and without union representation, they neither protested nor struck during the emergency reconstruction period. The Paris Métro was back into near-full service less than a month after the liberation of Paris, and the Paris-region grid was fully operational by late October 1944.

Despite Communist and CGT efforts to maintain order, electrical workers sometimes took matters into their own hands to achieve political ends. Workers often refused to work for their old bosses. They sequestered various enterprises and put them under the control of popularly elected *comités de gestion*, workers' self-management committees. Ignoring calls from de Gaulle and the Communists for discipline, workers dropped their tools to discuss ideas for reorganizing production and winning higher wages.[53] The gasworks of Gaz de Paris was seized, as were the tramways of Toulouse and the electrical distribution system of Marseilles. The departments of the Center and Southeast, particularly the Allier and Haute-Garonne, were centers of agitation.[54] Once services were commandeered, the *comités de gestion* and municipal councils allowed workers and communities to manage services without oversight by the usual authorities. The old managers were often retained, but they were monitored by the *comités* or the local governments. The *comités* clearly recognized that expertise was essential in operating electrical services.[55]

These actions gave electrical workers a taste of the role they envisioned for themselves in the nationalized electrical services of the future. Workers directly placed public ownership on the political agenda by seizing facilities and refusing to return them to the old owners. By their resistance activity and their reconstruction efforts during Liberation, the workers felt they had earned the nationalization of electricity. After twenty-five years of EDF's activity, Marcel Paul wrote, "It would

[52] Roger Gaspard (untitled), *Les documents C.T.E.P.* (mimeographed), 29 June 1946, p. 3.

[53] Annie Lacroix, "CGT et action ouvrière de la Libération à mai 1945," *Revue d'Histoire de la Deuxième Guerre Mondiale* 116 (October 1979), 55.

[54] For a general description and analysis of popular sequestrations, see Antoine Prost, "Un mouvement venu d'en bas," and Rolande Trempé, "Les charbonnages, un cas social," in Claire Andrieu, Lucette Le Van, and Antoine Prost, eds., *Les nationalisations de la Libération* (1987), pp. 66–88 and 294–300.

[55] "Exposé de M. Badiou, Haute-Garonne," "Exposé de M. Rougeron, Allier," and "Exposé de M. Foulon, Ille-et-Villaine," in Section Française de l'Internationale Ouvrière (SFIO), *Congrès national extraordinaire, Paris, 9–12 novembre 1944*, nonpaginated. BDIC microfilm 270/36 ext.

be perverse to mention the word *nationalization* without associating *resistance* with it; only unprincipled and gutless technocrats can attempt it, and they try to do so in order to deprive the nationalization of the character that the nation wanted to give it, and to contest the noble goals that were and continue to be assigned to this nationalization."[56]

Laying the Foundations for Nationalization

Many citizens saw broad anticollaborationist purges as a key to determining the political balance of the postwar regime. Before changing to a more accommodating political line in January 1945, the Communists ostensibly recognized that the wider the scope of the purges, the weaker the Right.[57] Leftists linked purges to a broader "democratization" of the economy. Purges would replace discredited collaborationists with reliable patriots. Some workers also wished to settle old scores and avenge suffering sustained at the hands of the occupiers and collaborators. Marcel Paul had spent much of the war at Buchenwald, and on his return to Paris he was welcomed by a sheepishly smiling Messine manager who had targeted him for arrest. Paul immediately asked why such a "collabo" had not been imprisoned. Many militants similarly felt that the purges had been incomplete.[58]

Established political parties helped limit the purges. Many officials argued that however necessary purges might have been, only calm and restraint could assure a rapid recovery. At the same time, the Communists were trying to win the confidence of the mainstream political parties and make a place for themselves in the postwar political order. They proffered an image of evenhanded justice throughout the Liberation period. Nonetheless, rank-and-file support for wide-ranging purges continued long after the Communists' change of line and the Socialists' move to the right in 1945.[59] After 1946, militants argued that a rightward turn in national politics arose from the influence of reac-

[56] Marcel Paul, *Le 25ième anniversaire de l'Electricité de France*, pamphlet (Paris: CGT-FNE, 1971), p. 3.

[57] Robert Aron, *Histoire de l'épuration*, vol. 1 (Paris: Fayard, 1974), p. 273, claims that Communist Resistance leaders in Paris intended to use the purges to discredit and destroy political adversaries of the party, whether they were actually collaborationist or not. Aron does not cite his source. If Aron's contention is true, it is certain that such a policy was not continued after January 1945.

[58] René Gaudy, *Et la lumière fut nationalisée* (1978), pp. 44 and 62, n. 46, and interview with Gaudy by author, 15 February 1981, CGT-FNE offices, Pantin. These sentiments were echoed in a number of reports from the provincial sections of the Socialist party in its November 1944 congress; see SFIO, *Congrès* (1944), nonpaginated.

[59] SFIO, *Résolutions du congrès national extraordinaire, Montrouge, 29–31 mars 1946* (1946), p. 32.

tionary personnel in the state and private sectors who had escaped the purges. Collaborators who survived the purges often did lose their professional standing.

Political conditions and the technical necessities of electrical services tended to make the purges less widespread in utilities than elsewhere.[60] Fernand Gambier, wartime head of Éclairage, assembled information and publicized acts of collaboration, yet his materials were routinely ignored.[61] Socialist Minister of Industry Robert Lacoste penned a decree in January 1945 instituting a purge commission within the power industry but allowing the pro–Labor Charter UNCM to judge putative collaborators.[62] Georges Maleville, a member of the Conseil d'État, sat on the commission in Paris which oversaw purges in the utilities and averred that it operated with the dignity of a high court.[63]

There were few tirades against Mercier in the leftist press after the war, in sharp contrast to press attacks on him during the Popular Front era. Orators rarely questioned the patriotism of the utility managers during the nationalization debates. The Communists occasionally painted the utility managers as collaborators in order to accelerate the process of nationalizing electricity, but the campaign had little effect. Indeed, many electrical workers recognized that some utility managers had protected them from the authorities.

Perceived technical necessities also helped to limit purges in the electrical power industry. Vital electrical services relied on the specialized skills, not the personal politics, of experts. The CGT moved toward this recognition after the Communists' change of policy and thus reinforced the image of politically neutral technology and technicians. On that consensus, the technocratic ideology that had guided COEE policy could survive unscathed into the Liberation era. Roger Boutteville escaped opprobrium, even though he had headed the COEE. In 1946 Marcel Paul, by then the minister of industry, named him chair of the Electricity Modernization Commission, a section of the Monnet Plan structure.

France faced reconstruction with grossly insufficient electrical systems. Though most of the transport grid had been pasted back together by the fall of 1945, 65 percent of all generating capacity was unavailable owing to coal shortages and aging or damaged plants.

[60] For example, concerning the coal industry, see Darryl O. Holter, "Miners against the State," Ph.D. diss. University of Wisconsin, 1980, chap. 2.

[61] E. Morel, "Les méfaits du trust gazier-électrique," *Le Peuple*, 3 March 1945, p. 3; see also F. Gambier, "Pour une véritable nationalisation du gaz et de l'électricité," *Le Peuple*, 13 January 1945, p. 5, and "Exposé de Foulon," SFIO, *Congrès* (1944).

[62] Only systematic pressure on Lacoste and the support of the CGT led to the seating of CFTC representatives on the purge commission; *Gaz-Électricité* 51 (January 1954).

[63] Georges Maleville, *Conseiller d'état: Témoignage* (1979), p. 51.

Only 168 of 250 thermal plants could be operated, and their average age was sixteen years. The utility trade association estimated total reconstruction costs of 7.8 billion francs. The 25 percent reserve margin that the power industry claimed to have had in 1939 was long gone.[64] Even if all extant thermal plants could have been repaired and supplied with sufficient coal, the available transmission and distribution networks could not have carried the load. Though the shoddy transmission grid had ironically made sabotage by the Resistance a bit easier, rural users faced a system that delivered power intermittently, and then only at widely varying voltages.[65] Severe rationing plagued all consumers. Well after Liberation, power was often available for only two to three hours daily.

A coal crisis lay at the heart of France's need to ration electrical energy from 1944 to 1948. In 1945, coal was the source of 75 percent of the primary energy used in France, and a switch from coal to electrical heating first by industry during the war and then by domestic users after the war made matters worse. Coal output had fallen considerably, and coal imports, which before the war had accounted for about half of France's foreign trade deficit, had to be bought with ever-shrinking foreign currency reserves. Facing financial losses in operating coal-fired power plants, at least one owner, Pierre-Marie Durand, at the height of the grave power shortages in the winter of 1944–45, instructed his managers not to operate coal plants unless forced to do so by public officials.[66]

Energy experts began to see hydroelectricity as the solution to energy shortages. A huge and heroic hydro program envisioned by Resistance study groups would end a dangerous dependence on coal, alleviate trade deficits, and contribute to national energy independence. On the Left, hymns of praise for hydroelectricity echoed expansively. Engineers also glorified hydro power, finding the massive curvilinear grace of dams far more exciting than the sheet metal of thermal plants. Gargantuan dams were to be icons of a new, modernized France, just as they had been in the United States with the Norris, Shasta, and Grand

[64] Edmond Roux, *Énergie électrique et civilisation* (1945), pp. 50–51. Syndicat Professionnel des Producteurs et Distributeurs de l'Énergie Électrique (SPPDEE), "Annexe à la lettre à M. le Ministre de la Production Industrielle," 30 December 1944, mimeographed; EDF archives, Series E8: "Équipement électrique." SPPDEE, *Réflexions sur l'équipement électrique en France*, pamphlet (Paris: SPPDEE, 1946), p. 3.

[65] *Nouvelles Économiques*, 15 March 1946, Union des Cadres Industriels de la France, "Programme d'action de la Résistance," *L'industrie française* (clandestine) (April-May 1944), p. 1, and "Un groupe d'abonnés," *Note sur la nationalisation de l'électricité*, pamphlet (Paris: n.p., 1945), p. 6.

[66] Letter to power-plant managers from Durand, 27 January 1945, reprinted in Le Guen, *Voyage*, p. 86; see also *Le Peuple*, 3 March 1945.

Coulee projects. Nature's freezes could be conquered, for titanic reservoirs could stock rains to meet winter peak power requirements in
the winter. Experts and politicians agreed that a utility (and preferably
hydro) boom was essential for France's economic revival.[67]

With emaciated share prices, depleted cash reserves, and dilapidated
facilities, electrical utilities were on the financial skids by 1945. Electrical
stock prices fell 67 percent between September 1944 and December
1945. The total market value of electrical stocks fell from 115 billion
francs in January 1943 to 45 billion francs in June 1945, when they
represented about 60 percent of total book values.[68] By March of 1946,
electrical stocks returned between 0.75 percent and 1.0 percent on
equity, while the average rate on other stocks was 1.8 percent.[69] Trepi-
dation at the costs of war damage and the threat of nationalization
induced a number of owners to sell off at a loss. Financial institutions
spread a great fear of expropriation among small investors, who rapidly
dumped their utility stocks. Prescient financiers—many of them the
same banks that had spread the rumors—in turn purchased the
spurned shares at bedrock prices.[70] As market values dropped, debt-
to-equity ratios rose, further eroding investor confidence.[71] With no
access to fresh capital and tariffs frozen under price controls, utility
managers virtually ceased to maintain financial reserves and even
drained many of them.[72] The power industry desperately needed
money, but rate increases or government subsidies were politically
unthinkable. The private sector could not afford to continue operating
for long, and a leviathan hydroelectric program was far beyond their
means. Electrical energy financing had to leave the private sector.

Industrial recovery and modernization seemed to demand state ownership, control, and financing of utilities. Even conservatives who tried
to limit nationalization efforts conceded that the industry needed a
massive infusion of capital from the state. Presumably, the state would
want control of the industry in return for the money it spent. Electricity
was a key part of the economic infrastructure, and growing electricity
use was considered the hallmark of a viable, expanding economy.

[67] This is the general tone of the Modernization Commission report; see France—
Commission de Modernisation de l'Électricité, *Rapport* (1946), entire. Similar sentiments
were expressed by Communists, Socialists, Catholics, and moderates alike; see infra,
chap. 2.
    [68] Frédéric-Dupont, *JO, dp*, 28 March 1946, p. 1158, and *Le Monde*, 20 July 1946.
    [69] Jean Curabet, *JO, dp*, 28 March 1946, p. 1162.
    [70] Gaudy, *Et la lumière*, p. 118; see also *L'entreprise* 634 (4 November 1967), 42–47.
    [71] Marcel Paul, *JO, dp*, 27 March 1946, p. 1110, and infra, chap. 4. Total utility debts
stood at 22 billion francs.
    [72] CAPV 13 (21 February 1946).

France ranked a pitiable ninth among all nations in per capita electrical use—national pride and a revival of French grandeur demanded more electricity. Only nationalization could provide the material and political precondition for that greatness.

CHAPTER 2

The Politics of
Nationalizing Electricity

Issues in the debate over the nationalization of electricity were as much symbolic as real, and the lengthy process offered a forum for expressing broad political disagreements. The vast majority of policymakers either strongly supported or reluctantly admitted the need for a public takeover because at the minimum they recognized that only the state could mobilize the capital needed for reconstruction, modernization, and expansion. Political groups also variously sought to punish unnamed capitalists who had ostensibly hindered industrial development, to reward patriots who had defended the nation in time of war, and to set the French economy on a path toward either socialism or a more efficient capitalism. These largely symbolic goals played a far more critical part in the nationalization process than did concrete discussions of exactly how a nationalized utility should be structured and financed. Given the political ambiguity of the electorate in 1945 and 1946, political posturing during the nationalization debate offered a way to create group identities. Each political formation seemed compelled to evoke lofty positions about either the intrinsic value of socialism or the need to take temporary measures to renovate an otherwise virtuous capitalist system.

Most policymakers agreed that the state had to take direct control of a key and expanding industrial sector and set it on a path of aggressive economic development. Opposition to nationalization thus took a largely symbolic form, for not only was it doomed to fail given the political context, but there was simply no other credible way to develop the industry in the immediate postwar political-economic context. Ironically, almost all political groups adopted an antistatist stance at the same time that they supported state ownership, and this contradiction prevented them from defining a coherent place for Électricité de France, as it stood on the periphery of the state yet abreast of the private sector. Similarly, though all recognized the vast capital needs of the power sector, few were willing to take the political risks involved in defining exactly how the infant enterprise would mobilize capital. Symbolic battles and position taking were politically easier than resolving issues, so that these two central issues of Électricité de France's life were never resolved by Parliament and thus became the source of contention for the next twenty-five years.

The French Political Landscape, 1944–1946

The law of 8 April 1946 creating Électricité de France nationalized the vast majority of electrical installations in France. The nationalization process had begun in May 1943, when the Conseil National de la Résistance (CNR) promulgated the concept in its Democratic Charter. In the charter, the CNR proposed the following reforms upon the liberation of France:

> ... The installation of a true economic and social democracy, compelling the eviction of the great economic and financial castes from the direction of the economy: a rational organization of the economy, assuring the subordination of particular interests to the general interest and exempt from the dictatorship of the professions installed in the image of the fascist states; the intensification of production along the lines of a plan set by the state after consulting the representatives of all the elements of that production; the return to the nation of the great monopolized means of production and the fruit of collective labor, of the sources of energy, of mineral wealth, of insurance companies and large banks; the development and support of consumers' and producers' cooperatives, both agricultural and artisanal; the right of access, in the framework of the enterprise, to the functions of management and administration for the workers possessing the necessary qualifications, and the participation of the workers in directing the economy.[1]

The ultimate goals of the reforms proposed in the Democratic Charter remained ambiguous; France was to be more economically and socially democratic, but was France to have a more efficient capitalism or democratic socialism? Whatever conflicting ends the authors may have had in mind, a "rational organization of the economy" and a "plan" implied that experts or technocrats inspired by the general will would

[1] Conseil National de la Résistance, *La charte démocratique*, May 1943, p. 8.

replace the "castes" as directors of the economy. An economic state-interventionist consensus based in humanistic egalitarianism and technocratic predilections inspired the CNR and the immediate postwar regimes. Such regimes, based on a coalition of Resistance parties—Socialists, Communists, and Christian Democrats—ruled France until the spring of 1947. One of their central concerns was to raise the popular standard of living, less by an explicit redistribution of wealth than by a massive effort toward economic expansion. Economic renovation was to concentrate first on production equipment, delaying greater popular consumption until a later date. The social position of the workers would immediately be improved by a vaguely defined participatory role in management.

The charter framed the methods for modernization and expansion more coherently than it did the goals. Aided by workers, technocratic managers were to oversee economic expansion, but popular economic improvement would be deferred until the productive infrastructure could provide more consumer goods at lower prices. Like the process of "socialist accumulation" in the Soviet Union in the 1930s, French modernization efforts would divert national income flows away from consumption and toward investment. A Plan Commission would administer the program.

Several contradictions were built into the modernization formula. Success hinged on an absence of class conflict and stiff wage demands during the period of rapid growth. Despite the notion of participation, workers had to consent to low salaries. Almost inevitably, the demands for rapid industrial expansion would stress efficient technocratic management over participatory democracy. Nonetheless, Resistance theorists believed that a technocracy could administer growth in a socially equitable fashion, and broad consensus supported that vision during the Liberation era.

Many citizens demanded and expected major political reforms when Paris was liberated in August 1944. Depression and military defeat had discredited the Third Republic, and collaboration with occupiers assured the demise of the Vichy regime. Popular enmity focused on France's elites, particularly the *haute bourgeoisie* and high civil servants. Marc Bloch's *Strange Defeat* and Léon Blum's *At the Human Level*, two famed wartime tracts, indicted the old economic and political élites for being conservative and reactionary in the most literal senses. The bourgeoisie had jealously guarded its wealth and position and viewed twentieth-century political economy with nineteenth-century prejudices. It responded to the need for modernization and social justice by rigidly defending its entrenched socioeconomic position.

In a nation rent by military defeat and economic depression, patriotism and productivism became key themes of reform. The General Studies Committee of the CNR accused the rich and powerful of suffocating democracy and economic growth in order to maintain hegemony, and it claimed that the dominant classes "could conceive of national renewal only in defeat." That "abdication" necessitated a revolution that would target high-level bureaucrats as well as the bourgeoisie.[2] The high state managers had been trained in an abstract fashion, caring little for genuine human problems and running the state as if it were an exclusive men's club. The *grandes écoles* and their alumni were culpable, and they, too, had to be replaced.[3] Despite scorching criticisms of the existing elite, however, the General Studies Committee could be no more specific than to call for, "a real democracy, freed from king-money, the equitable distribution of the nation's wealth, a dignified life for free workers, the sharing out of economic responsibilities and an end to the economic dictatorship. Briefly, more liberty, more equality, and more fraternity."[4]

Romantic rhetoric could not evade the need to lay concrete foundations for a new social order. Detached from the rank and file Resistance fighters, the General Studies Committee, an organization of experts, and the CNR, an organization of leaders, could not resolve programmatic differences among technocorporatists, neoliberals, and Communists. The ambiguous agenda of modernization, nationalization, and expansion glossed over a myriad of contradictions on political and programmatic levels, as the history of the nationalizations generally, and that of the electrical nationalization in particular, indicates.

France nationalized several industries between the liberation of Paris in the summer of 1944 and the legislative elections of June 1946. Under the authority of the Provisional Constituent Assembly presided over by de Gaulle, the state sequestered the coal industry (after its seizure by the coal miners) in late 1944 and nationalized Renault, whose owner was considered a traitor, early in 1945. These emergency measures were not inspired by a coherent political or economic agenda. Political-economic considerations did motivate later nationalizations.

In early March 1945, the Socialist and Communist parties further defined the CNR program by developing a list of industries to be nationalized and by outlining a nationalization process.[5] The two left parties won stunning victories in the municipal elections of mid-May

---

[2] Comité Général d'Études (CGE), "Pour une nouvelle révolution française," *Les Cahiers Politiques* 5 (January 1945), 11.

[3] "Un Catholique de la Résistance," "Pour la France de demain," *Les Cahiers Politiques* (clandestine) 2 (June 1942), 11.

[4] CNR, *Charte démocratique*, p. ii.

[5] For the text of the declaration, see *L'Humanité* and *Le Populaire* of 2 March 1945.

1945, and the CNR program seemed thus to receive a popular mandate.[6] Nonetheless, the Provisional Constituent Assembly only set up committees to study nationalizations before it recessed in August 1945. Elections to the National Constituent Assembly in October 1945 solidified support for the Liberation coalition. The Parti Communiste Français (PCF) emerged as the largest party, with 27 percent of the vote, trailed by the Christian Democrats with 26 percent, and the Socialists (Section Française de l'Internationale Ouvrière, SFIO) with 24 percent. De Gaulle remained chief of state. The PCF officially entered the government for the first time in November 1945. Even though "it [was] impossible for any postwar government to form itself against the Communists . . . and it [was] also impossible to govern without them," the PCF took a secondary role in the government.[7]

The National Constituant Assembly finally began to implement the CNR's nationalization program fourteen months after the liberation of Paris. Communists oversaw the ministries of labor, armaments, state, and most important, industrial production, which was administered by Éclairage's leader, Marcel Paul. By May 1946, the assembly had nationalized insurance, deposit banking, and electrical power, completed the nationalizations of coal and rail, and expanded the nationalized armaments sector.

The nationalization of electrical power was by far the most deeply considered of the nationalization processes.[8] In January 1945, the gov-

[6] In the municipal elections of the spring of 1945, relative to its prewar position, the PCF quadrupled the number of councils in which it held the majority of seats. In the first national elections since 1936, on 21 October 1945, the PCF nearly doubled its delegation in the National Assembly, with 26.1 percent of the vote.

[7] "Un Catholique de la Résistance," "France de demain," p. 11 (quotation). Philippe Robrieux, Histoire intérieure du parti communiste, vol. 2 (1981), p. 89, argues that de Gaulle imposed this limitation. In On chantait rouge (1977), p. 445, Charles Tillon, then a member of the PCF Political Bureau, argues that Stalin encouraged such a role. The PCF received only the ministries that oversaw the production apparatus (Industrial Production, Labor, Public Works, Armaments [manufacturing]) and were closed out of the posts that concerned state finances, defense, and foreign relations. Henry Rousso argues that the planning apparatus was in part framed as a counterweight to Communist influence in the industrial ministries; "Le ministère de l'industrie dans le processus de planification: Une adaptation difficile (1940–1969)," in H. Rousso, ed., De Monnet à Massé: Enjeux politiques et objectifs économiques dans le cadre des quatre premiers plans (1946–1965) (1986), p. 30.

[8] For an exhaustive study of the nationalization process itself, see Guy Bouthillier, "La nationalisation du gaz et de l'électricité en France," Ph.D. diss., Université de Paris, 1968. René Gaudy presents a more politicized analysis in his Et la lumière. A similar analysis is presented by Annie Lacroix in her "La nationalisation," pp. 81–110. For the view of the provincial mayors and the conceding communes, see Fédération Nationale des Collectivités Concédantes et Régies, Bulletin d'Information 100, special issue (February 1973), passim. See also A. Beltran, "EDF et la modernisation du service public électrique (1948–1952)," paper presented at the conference La France en Voie de Modernisation, Institut des Études Politiques, Paris, December 1981. Finally, Marcel Paul and his com-

ernment had named a commission composed of power-industry man-agers, state officials, legal experts, and trade unionists to develop the broad lines for the nationalization of electricity, but political divisions prevented it from authoring any coherent text. In the spring of 1945, a CNR subcommittee on nationalizations passed a sweeping nation-alization proposal written by the CGT's Pierre Le Brun, and in the process rejected a proposal that nationalized only electrical production and transmission. Though Socialist (SFIO) members of the CNR sub-committee had supported the Le Brun proposal, the SFIO parliamen-tary delegation later submitted a bill that nationalized only production and transmission and made the nationalized power enterprise a Cab-inet-style department. Similarly, a bill in April sponsored by the Mouvement Republicain Populaire (MRP) nationalized only transmis-sion and suggested that the nationalization of production and distri-bution could be entertained at a later date. The Catholic trade-union (CFTC) parliamentary delegation then entered a bill similar to that of the subcommittee, but only to point up its differences with the MRP.

Nationalization politics had indeed taken a strange turn, largely be-cause each party seemed more concerned with symbolic positioning than with real legislation. Though all Resistance parties formally backed the CNR program and the texts authored by the CNR, they proffered a raft of alternative bills. By June, this conflict spilled into the Provi-sional Constituent Assembly: the three Resistance parties and the Rad-icals entered the CNR bill in the name of the CNR, the assembly's Committee on Economic and Social Affairs (chaired by Le Brun) voted favorably on the CNR bill, but the SFIO reactivated its own bill. In early August, the CNR and SFIO bills went to the assembly floor for debate. The debate was divisive, but in its last session before permanent adjournment on 4 August, the assembly passed a resolution favoring the CNR bill.

After the Left's victory in the October 1945 elections to the National Constituent Assembly the Communists submitted the CNR (and Pro-visional Constituent Assembly) bill in the National Constituent Assem-bly in November, only to see the Socialists and Christian Democrats resubmit their own. Meanwhile, the association of municipal utilities, Fédération Nationale des Communes Concédantes et Régies, strongly influenced by Socialists, Christian Democrats, and Radicals, met jointly with the national conference of mayors and resolved in favor of the CNR bill. Marcel Paul, by then minister of industry, made minor ed-itorial changes to the CNR bill in December, but it still had to pass

rades recount their roles as nationalizers in an entire special issue of *Force-Information* 190 (May 1971).

through the Council of Ministers. After considerable criticism from René Pleven, the Radical minister of finance, and Georges Bidault, the MRP minister of foreign affairs, the ministerial council approved the bill on 18 January. Two days later (for other reasons) de Gaulle resigned. In the succeeding Félix Gouin cabinet, the SFIO and PCF held sixteen of twenty-four posts and the SFIO became the crucial swing party within the government. Similarly, in the Industrial Production Subcommittee of the National Constituent Assembly, the left parties held twenty-two of forty-two seats. To reach the floor of the assembly, the bill had to be reported out of the Industrial Production Subcommittee.

Jean-Marie Louvel, an MRP power-company executive, chaired the subcommittee. Paul Ramadier, a rightist Socialist with strong ties to the Socialist machinery of provincial politics, was named to oversee the path of the government bill in the committee and on the floor of the assembly. Beginning on 6 February, Ramadier and Louvel attacked the government's bill, seeking to delay reporting the bill until after the legislative elections in June. The committee voted the bill to the floor on 13 March, only after a massive public letter-writing campaign and a Communist threat to withdraw from the governing coalition. MRP representatives abstained, citing reservations on issues of scope and indemnities.

Debate on the government bill in the assembly began on 22 March, and a raft of counterproposals and over one hundred amendments assured that the process would be lengthy. Floor debate lasted nearly a week, but at 3:40 A.M. on 29 March, the government bill passed with few major changes. As a show of the strong support for the bill and despite political posturing, the vote was significant: 491 in favor, 59 opposed, 23 abstaining (including thirteen MRP members). However, a simple political and parliamentary chronology is misleading. The debate underscored a number of complex issues that had direct implications for the character of the postwar French economy. We shall examine those issues systematically, but first we shall place them in the context of party politics and ideology.

Conceptions and Politics of Nationalization

The Communists briefly enjoyed broad political support after the war due to their highly respected Resistance activity and their key position within the patriotic militias and local Liberation committees. The political line of the PCF remained ambiguous until early 1945, but a new program rejected any project for a radical transformation of

France.[9] The PCF cast its new platform in a way that would help it gain an institutionalized foothold in the postwar French state. In its efforts toward institutionalization, the PCF sought a quasi-corporatist system of interest-group representation, assuming that if a quarter of the electorate supported the PCF, the PCF should control a quarter of the state apparatus. By dint of the PCF's strong voice within the CGT, the PCF could legitimately claim to represent France's working class. To the Right and to the Socialists, the Communists seemed to be colonizing the state, but to the PCF, it was merely a question of getting its due.

Aware of its strategic political position, the PCF urged hard work in the present for deferred rewards. It urged a "battle of production" and delivered forceful tirades against strikes. Communists were willing to impose military-style discipline on the work force in order to speed economic recovery. Marcel Paul said: "The army has a unified command structure . . . and the high command of even the largest army in the world [the Red Army] is still at the human level. It is therefore possible to have unified management in our electrical system without going beyond the human level. Electricity is the army of the French economic recovery. Numerically, this army is insufficient; it can triumph only by discipline, an iron discipline."[10] As minister of industry after November 1945, Marcel Paul was simultaneously the advocate of management and of labor, so the demands of his two posts were often in conflict. Despite his impeccable union credentials, while trying to usher the electricity nationalization bill through the Industrial Production Committee of the National Constituent Assembly, he argued: "We are currently in the process of attempting to limit even further the already-limited supply of goods that the country can place at the disposition of the working class. We are primarily concerned with the economic revival of the country and thus the needs of industry must be met before others are considered."[11] Traditional notions of capitalist economic management and Stalinist "socialist accumulation" were oddly wedded in Communist strategy. The PCF could not simultaneously link participation in the government to satisfying popular demands, despite Paul's claims to the contrary.[12] Difficult choices had to be made between meeting immediate popular needs and building

[9] Stalin framed the program, hoping to allay Allied fears of a Communist France; Robrieux, *Histoire intérieure*, p. 81.

[10] Marcel Paul, *JO, dp*, 23 March 1946, p. 1107.

[11] Cited in Bouthillier, "La nationalisation," p. 327, n. 2.

[12] Cited in François Billoux "1944–1947: Des Communistes au gouvernement," *Cahiers d'Histoire de l'Institut Maurice Thorez* 34 (n.s. 6, January-April 1974), 142. Indeed, the PCF was ousted from the cabinet in May 1947 after it backed a strike at Renault, much to the displeasure of its governing partners.

the infrastructure necessary for a modernized economy. The PCF opted for the latter, and to this end, they sought a close alliance with leftist technocrats inside the SFIO.

In the Popular Front era, the PCF had argued that nationalization would only strengthen the private sector by having the state assume the burdens of operating the costly economic infrastructure.[13] In the Liberation era, the PCF did not concern itself with the relations between the nationalized sector, the state, and the private sector, or the modalities to prevent the nationalized sector from becoming a no-profit sectoral core that would divert profit to a privately owned periphery. It also remained virtually silent on the question of state planning. Retreating from theoretical considerations, the PCF conceded that nationalizations were useful structural reforms whose success would hinge upon "the intensity of the democratic forces," otherwise stated, the participation of the Communists in the government. For the PCF in 1945, nationalizing the industrial infrastructure would parallel the development strategy of the USSR. Nationalizations would also help to build an economically based political alliance with small business against the "trusts." The PCF therefore opposed nationalizations of entire sectors or of firms employing less than fifty workers.[14] Paul hoped to win small businesses' support for the electricity nationalization by turning over internal wiring verification and appliance sales (previously done by the utilities) to small businesses. This repartitioning would open new business opportunities and help build a multiclass bloc behind the nationalization.

The Communists also saw nationalizations as part of a democratization within the economy and as a starting point for the democratization of society as a whole. The nationalized sector would enhance national grandeur and independence, provide a shortcut to reconstruction, and provide shock troops in the battle of production.[15] Nationalizations "had nothing to do with socialism" as long as France

[13] Bouthillier, "La nationalisation," pp. 97–98. See also Georges Lefranc, *Le mouvement socialiste sous la Troisième République (1875–1940)* (1963), pp. 303–40, and Georges Lefranc, *Histoire du Front Populaire* (Paris: Payot, 1968), chap. 3. After the eviction of the Communists from the government in 1947, they readopted this analysis. See Kouziminov, "Le capitalisme monopole de l'état," *Études Soviétiques* 1 (15 May 1947), passim, and infra, chap. 3.

[14] PCF-Fédération Paris-Ville, "Ce que les parisiens doivent savoir: Pourquoi l'électricité est chère et rare," leaflet (Bibliothèque de Documentation Internationale et Contemporaine archives, interfiled with PCF materials), and "Interview with Maurice Thorez," London *Times*, 17 November 1946. See also "Rapport de Maurice Thorez," in PCF, *Rapports du Comité central pour le Xe Congrès national, Paris, 11–15 août, 1945* (Paris: PCF, 1945), p. 51.

[15] "Interview avec Marcel Paul," *Énergies* 799 (26 March 1971), 20, and Marcel Paul, "Les nationalisations et la lutte pour l'indépendance nationale," *Cahiers du Communisme* 35 (October 1959), 842.

remained capitalist.[16] At best, they offered a structural base for social-ism simply by being state enterprises and beginning to break the power of the two hundred families. Henri Martel made this point clearly in a speech to CGT coal miners: "We hear the slogan 'the mine to the miners.' The nationalization is not yet 'the mine to the miners,' but it is a first step to that dream of all workers. When that dream is realized, then we will have 'the mine to the miners.' But we should have no illusions; the nationalization still exists within the capitalist system . . . and we must remain vigilant."[17]

Communists found allies among Catholic unionists in efforts to de-velop comanagement strategies for EDF. Both groups supported na-tionalization bills that gave workers a strong presence on the board of directors. A new *statut* would also set forth a modest version of shop-floor democracy. Such measures would "extend democracy to the workplace."[18] The *statut* of 22 June 1946, coauthored by Marcel Paul, provided for consultative comanagement committees within EDF and created codeterminist boards and procedures to treat personnel mat-ters. The separation of personnel matters from other issues in the operations of the firm implied that shop-floor politics and managerial policy-making were to remain functionally separate. A meritocratic division of labor replaced the old class-based one, and the CGT was to defer to authority. In terms of designating the specific structures and methods of nationalizations, the PCF passed such tasks over to the CGT.

The Communists gained informal control of the CGT in the National Confederal Committee meetings of August 1945 and won control of the CGT executive committee at the CGT's national congress in April 1946.[19] Politically, the CGT was treated as non-Communist during the nationalization period, while at the same time the political positions of the CGT matched those of the PCF. Nominal nonpartisanship—a long CGT tradition—provided historical continuity for the new CGT and helped to legitimize the PCF-led CGT. A CGT majority in the industrial work force similarly raised its political stature. Éclairage's membership rose from 80,000 in 1937 to over 100,000 by April 1946 (in

[16] Speech of Jacques Duclos in the Assemblée Constituante Provisoire, 2 December 1945, cited in René Gendarme, *L'expérience française de la nationalisation industrielle* (1950), p. 103. See also Etienne Fajon, "Les Communistes et les nationalisations," *Cahiers du Communisme* 4 (n.s., February 1945), 31, 33–35.

[17] Cited in Darryl O. Holter, "Miners," p. 239.

[18] "Rapport de Maurice Thorez," p. 43.

[19] In that historic CCN meeting, the Communist "ex-unitaires," led by Frachon, re-ceived 89 percent of the votes; see Annie Lacroix-Riz, "Majorité et minorité de la CGT de la Libération au XXVIe Congrès confédéral, août 1944–avril 1946," *Revue Historique* 540 (October-December 1981), 472, and idem, *La CGT de la Libération à la scission (1944–1947)* (1983), chap. 2.

a pool of about 105,000 workers), and the GNC (CGT white-collar utility workers) had about 8,000 members in a pool of 10,000 workers.[20] In the nationalization, Éclairage and the GNC spoke for the majority of the electrical workers.

The movement of many prestigious non-Communists into the Communist camp also strengthened the PCF's influence in Éclairage, the GNC, and the CGT. For example, Pierre Le Brun, an influential member of the GNC and head of the CNR's study group on electricity nationalization, had become close to the PCF during the Resistance and thus sided with the PCF majority in the CGT. A massive influx of managers, engineers, and technicians into the GNC also strengthened the union. Many white-collar workers left the UNCM (the conservative white-collar union) to join the GNC out of opportunism and in response to the CGT's support for deferring to expertise in the battle of production. The purges also enhanced the position of the pro-Communist faction within the CGT by ridding the CGT of a number of prominent interwar corporatists.

The PCF compelled the CGT to support the battle of production and to discourage strikes. After September 1944, the CGT slogan became, "produce first, make demands later." As Annie Lacroix noted, "The usual demands of the CGT were relegated to the second rank of union tasks, in a position subordinate to the primary task of increasing production; [the CGT] condemned the proven weapon of the union movement, the strike, which, by definition, threatened production."[21] The CGT did protest the wage freeze and rationing practices, and often targeted Socialists in the government for alleged mismanagement. The CGT became more petulant after VE-day and the end of the public rationale for the wage freeze, also administered by the Socialists. Paul Ramadier, the Socialist minister of rationing (dubbed the "minister of penury"), was regularly lambasted.[22] The PCF and CGT seemed to play good cop–bad cop with with the government—if the PCF's coalition partners balked at the Communists' policies, mass action by the CGT remained a trump card.

Less cynically, in the politics of nationalization, PCF attitudes of ultra-

[20] "Rapport de Pierre Le Brun," in CGT, "XXVIe Congrès national, Paris, 28–30 avril 1946: Compte rendu sténographique" (typescript), pp. 262–63. Similar figures are recognized in CFTC—Fédération des Syndicats Chrétiens du Personnel des Services Publics et Concédés, La Voix des Services Concédés 6 (February 1946), 3.

[21] Annie Lacroix, "CGT et action," p. 47.

[22] Attacking Ramadier (a rival of the PCF in any event) helped to reinforce leftist calls for structural reforms by implying that shortages were caused by the systems of control over production and distribution, not by a real, net shortage of goods. In this respect, see John Hill, "Public Perceptions of the French Inflation of 1944–1952," conference paper, meetings of the Society for French Historical Studies, Québec, 21 March 1986.

"workerism" and statism merged with the CGT's stress on meeting the needs of consumers in a reaffirmation of the CGT's plan for equal representation of workers, consumers, and state officials on the boards of nationalized firms. For the CGT there was no contradiction, as some claimed, between meeting the needs of workers and performing public service.[23] The worker was also the consumer, and together they composed the Janus face of the productive citizen. The differing aspects of each could easily be mediated by state representatives on the tripartite boards. Finally, the CGT's long insistence upon workers' autonomy and the democratic character of the tripartite boards would prevent the state sector from becoming a sealed technocracy.

The CGT had supported nationalizations longer than any other political organization.[24] Its position on nationalizations joined older anarcho-syndicalist traditions with the interest-group approach of the PCF. The anarcho-syndicalist notion of shop-floor democracy as a precursor to workers' self-management fed into the PCF's notion of nationalization as a means to democratize society from the shop floor to the assembly. The corporatist tone of the CGT's 1934 plan blended with the PCF's multiclass alliance strategy. The CGT's long-standing vision of significant worker representation on planning boards softened the Communists' reticence toward both capitalist economic planning and the intervention of the capitalist state into the economy. Finally, the CGT's support for economic decentralization waned in favor of the PCF's penchant for centralization as a means to promote technical rationality and efficiency. Together, the CGT and PCF supported a wide scope for the electricity nationalization, a centralization of control over the firm's operations by the front office, a systematic autonomy from the state for utility managers, and a strong advisory role for workers in management.

The PCF and the CGT had essentially identical rationales for nationalizing electricity. Public ownership would help raise per capita use of intrinsically valuable kilowatt-hours, fortify and expand the electrical power supply, rationalize electrical production, transmission, and distribution by the massive introduction of the newest technology and

---

[23] The CGT's original 1919 nationalization program argued that nationalization had "no other goal than to procure the maximum of utility and economy for consumers"; quoted in Leon Jouhaux, "Ce que doit être le nouveau Conseil national économique," Le Peuple, 16 June 1945. On the apparent contradiction, see Pierre Uri, "La querelle des nationalisations," Les Temps Modernes 45 (July 1949), 165.

[24] For a history of the nationalization thinking within the CGT, see Valéry Paval, "Une vieille illusion réformiste: Les nationalisations, moyen de lutte anticapitaliste," Critiques de l'Économie Politique, 2 (n.s., January-March 1978), passim; Albert Gazier, "Brève histoire de l'idée de la nationalisation," Le Peuple, 9 December 1944; and Robert Goetz-Girey, La pensée syndicale française: Militants et théoriciens (1948), pp. 130–55.

thus lower production costs and make electricity cheaper and more popularly accessible.[25] Like the PCF, the CGT remained ambivalent on exactly how nationalized firms were to face the capitalist economy and state. Could a nationalized enterprise be autonomous from the state that funded it? Could islands of socialism exist in a capitalist economy? The worker-constituents of the PCF and CGT might have won an icon in nationalized electricity, but the PCF and CGT remained ambiguous on the new firm's political-economic position and future.

Socialist electoral support stagnated between the elections of 1936 and 1945. Because of its low public visibility during the Resistance, the SFIO did not share in the popularity of the Left upon Liberation. During the Occupation, Socialists practiced passive resistance, participated in anti-Vichy study groups, edited clandestine journals, or went into exile. They did not widely participate in partisan militias. A few collaborated with the Vichy regime, so the SFIO had to purge several of its once-prominent members.[26] The Socialists were divided between moderate anti-Communists led by Léon Blum, Paul Ramadier, and Robert Lacoste, and many rank-and-file party members amenable to unity with the PCF.[27] Though the overall economic position of the Socialist electorate had deteriorated with the privations of war, one could only assume that reconstruction, with its demand for technicians, teachers, and bureaucrats would rebuild the Socialists' clientele. The real question for the party, however, concerned reconstruction strategies and the place that the state would take in them.

Socialists strongly backed the CNR program, but they were divided over its concrete meaning. As they interpreted the charter, two poles of attraction emerged within the SFIO, parallel to those within the CNR as a whole. A dominant group around Lacoste and Ramadier supported neoliberal state intervention and piecemeal reforms, apparently to make capitalism more efficient and humane. A second group around

---

[25] Exposé de M. Marcel Paul, Conférence de presse du 18 janvier 1946, pamphlet (Paris: Ministère de l'Information, Direction de la Documentation, January 1946), p. 3.

[26] Daniel Villey, "Contre l'idéologie des réformes de structure," Les Cahiers Politiques 11 (June 1945), 31.

[27] This division came to a head in the SFIO's 1945 congress, in which, by a 3–2 margin, the unity motion was defeated. As a result, a number of youth sections left the party; Le Monde, 15 August 1945, and SFIO, XXXVIIe Congrès national, Paris, 11–15 août, 1945 (Paris: Editions du Parti, 1945). See also B. D. Graham, The French Socialists and Tripartisme (1965), pp. 87–114. Alexander Werth referred to Blum as being "almost pathologically anti-Communist," in France, 1940–1955, p. 266. In À l'échelle humaine (1971), p. 111, Blum referred to the Communist party as a "foreign party operating in France." There was little danger to the Socialists of being outflanked on the Left by the PCF. As the center party of the tripartite regime consisting of the SFIO, the PCF, and the MRP, the SFIO was virtually guaranteed a role in all governments in the then-foreseeable future.

André Philip and Jules Moch sought to replace capitalist market mechanisms with state economic management.[28] Many of the neoliberals eschewed comanagement out of a fear that union delegates would become cats' paws for Communist dominance. The neoliberal tendency reflected the provincial base of the SFIO and underscored the party's power in numerous local councils and mayors' offices. Through Lacoste, it also enjoyed connections with the reconstituted employers' federation.[29] For that and other reasons, Philip's *Cité-Soir* ultimately accused Ramadier of being an "agent of the trusts."[30]

The SFIO played a major part in the electricity nationalization by virtue of its long support of nationalizations, and because of its position in the governing coalition. In the politics of nationalization, the Ramadier-Lacoste bloc joined forces with centrist Christian Democrats to limit the scope, increase the purchase price, and decentralize the administration of EDF. As minister of industry Lacoste feared that rapid nationalizations would tangle authority and foster indiscipline and thus did little of substance before he left his post in November 1945.[31] The more technocratic Moch-Philip bloc sided with PCF efforts to give EDF a centralized administrative structure and a wide scope of operations.

Technocratic Socialists envisioned that the nationalized sector would prove its veracity by efficient production and thus help rationalize the economy.[32] Popular mobilization and class conflict would be unnecessary, for socialized production would make capitalism appear first anachronistic, then quaint. On the electricity question, technocratic Socialists wanted the nationalization to proceed in an orderly fashion, so they rejected the spontaneous requisitions of the Liberation era as counterproductive to rational planning and management. Moch wrote that "their spontaneity excludes any systematic plan . . . socialism demands order and coherent methods."[33] Siding with de Gaulle to delay reforms until the war was over, Moch broke with the CNR Charter's principle of implementing reforms immediately upon Liberation.[34]

[28] This division had opened up before World War II; see Jacques Amoyal, "Les origines socialistes et syndicalistes de la planification en France," *Le Mouvement Social* 87 (April-June 1974), 145ff.

[29] Henry Ehrmann, *Organized Business in France* (1957), pp. 229–30. While Lacoste can be placed in the neoliberal group, along with Moch he was in X-Crise in the 1930s; Philippe Bauchard, *Les technocrates*, p. 22.

[30] *Cité-Soir*, 2 March 1946; see also *Franc-Tireur* and *Front National*, both of 1 March 1946.

[31] Bouthillier, "La nationalisation," p. 127. The crisis of authority in the coal industry was often cited; see Holter, "Miners," chap. 3.

[32] Paul Ramadier, "Les entreprises nationalisées devant les problèmes de l'expansion économique," *Annales de l'Économie Collective* 514–21 combined (April-November 1955), 219.

[33] Jules Moch, *Le parti socialiste au peuple de la France* (1945), p. 45.

[34] Among the rationales given by Moch for the delay were (1) possible reduced le-

Technocratic Socialists' faith in the efficacy of experts left little opportunity for democratic management. Like the Communists, they supported strict workplace hierarchies and felt that power ultimately should reside at the top and flow downward, as in the army.

Socialist technocrats had a very coherent vision of how the electricity nationalization would fit within the economy as a whole. Nationalization was not an indictment of the owners (the SFIO nationalization bill applauded the competent management of the prewar utilities), but a concrete step in building an intermediary regime between "the liberalism of the nineteenth century and the socialism of tomorrow." White-collar experts would necessarily hold commanding positions. Planners would functionally integrate the policies of the nationalized firms with those of the state, using means-tested indemnities as a method of income redistribution and allowing operating losses in order to implement general economic policy. Future EDF directors were to stress demand forecasting and long-term equipment planning, but wider planning and budgetary power would reside in a technocratically dominated Central Electricity Council, over and above the more democratically structured board of directors.[35]

An alliance between the PCF, the CGT, and the Socialist brain trust assured that EDF would be cast in a left technocorporatist mold. Indeed, the CNR subcommittee developed a consensus around left technocorporatist theses. This political network formed a de facto common front on the question of management methods. Admiring the emerging functional division between owners and managers, this coalition supported workplace meritocracies and systematic industrial rationalization at the expense of more democratic procedures. Pierre Lefaucheux, later the head of Renault, wrote that such methods "absolutely conform to the principle of authority that must be maintained and even reinforced at any price."[36] In order for such methods to survive while workers had a consultative role in management, the unions had to consent to a secondary position. This position was accepted by the CGT, whose shop-floor philosophy Roger Gaspard later characterized

---

gitimacy of the nationalizations due to the nonelected nature of the government, (2) fear of radical action while seeking U.S. reconstruction aid, (3) the resistance of the still-implanted "Synarchie," and (4) with the shadow of collaborationists in mind, a fear of being accused of fascism; *Le Populaire*, 16 February 1945.

[35] Jules Moch, *Guerre aux trusts* (1945), p. 30 (quotation); idem, *Socialisme et rationalisation* (1924); idem, *Socialisme, crise, nationalisations* (1932); idem, *Le parti socialiste au peuple de la France* (1945). See also R. Tenaille, "La politique économique de demain," *Défense de la France* (clandestine) 40 (2–5 October 1943), nonpaginated; Georges Lefranc, *La nationalisation des industries clefs* (1936); and, reflecting Socialists in the CNR, "JM" (presumably Jules Moch), "Réflexions," pp. 21–36.

[36] Pierre Lefaucheux, "Passage au socialisme, pt. 2," *Les Cahiers Politiques* 9 (April 1945), 47.

as "take orders, do your job, and collect your paycheck."[37] Technocratic managers accepted a consultative role for workers in management as long as the hierarchy was not challenged.

The Christian Democratic party, formed in the spring of 1943, was the most moderate party in the postwar coalition. It enjoyed widespread popularity in the Liberation era due to an admirable Resistance record on the local level and to the fact that it was the only non-Marxist governing party. Nominally rooted in the social Catholic movement of the interwar period, the party included several diverse tendencies. The dominant groups were CFTC unionists and moderate businessmen; the latter sought a Resistance visage in an era of popular antipathy toward the Right. The fact that the MRP's first leader, Georges Bidault, was the first president of the CNR also reinforced its political credibility. However, Maxime Blocq-Mascart, a liberal of the CNR, said of Bidault: "He was a member of the CNR who ostensibly represented the Catholics, but in reality he represented nobody. But the Communists respected him. I could not accept a Communist chief of the CNR. They could not accept me. We agreed on a compromise candidate. That was Bidault."[38] The MRP thus functioned as an umbrella party arising from the peculiar political conjuncture between 1943 and 1947. Holter writes, "It was no easy task to square a Resistance program with one which could attract non-*résistants*, but the MRP managed to do just that."[39] The electoral base of the MRP included many peasants, a number of smaller industrialists and small businessmen, and Catholic workers.[40] It also included a small but influential circle of moderate technocrats led by Jean-Marie Louvel (a Polytechnique graduate, member of the National Assembly, and a top manager of the Huvelin electrical group) and René Perrin, of the Ugine chemical company.

The Catholic movement envisioned several different strategies for postwar modernization. Many MRP supporters rejected liberal capitalism, with its objectification of labor and its perpetuation of a class-divided society. That rejection of liberal capitalism cut two ways under the rubric of the humanization of labor. For traditionalists, it was profoundly conservative, striking its roots in the paternalist Catholic corporatism of La Tour du Pin at the turn of the century. This tendency reflected the traditional industrial paternalism of the small and medium-sized provincial family firms. Seeking a "humanization" of cap-

---

[37] Interview with author.
[38] Transcript of interview with Maxime Blocq-Mascart, in Sven Nordengren, *Economic and Social Targets in Postwar France* (1972), pp. 239–40.
[39] Holter, "Miners," p. 95.
[40] Transcript of interview with Robert Buron, in Nordengren, *Targets*, p. 244.

italism through an ambiguous concept of workers' participation, the CFTC bloc within the MRP rejected liberal capitalism in a more radical fashion.[41] The CFTC gas and electric federation led by Fernand Hennebicq of the progressive Reconstruction group saw an implicit contradiction between humanized work and capitalism. Though only gestating at the time, a concept of workers' self-management was beginning to emerge from the Reconstruction group.[42]

The MRP was deeply divided on the role of the state in postwar France. Moderate businessmen such as Louvel used Catholic antistatist doctrine to support neoliberal positions that sought to limit the state's intervention in the economy. The CFTC recognized the dangers of faceless bureaucratic control under an exaggerated statism, but it supported a strong state to aid reconstruction and promote social justice: "Economic evolution, the necessity for economic reconstruction, and above all, social justice demand that France adopt a directed economy in which the general interest takes precedence over that of the individual, where man is no longer ruled by money."[43] Among many Catholics, political unity could only be achieved under the vague program of patriotic productionism.

Divergent and contradictory positions on nationalizations deeply fractured Catholic unity.[44] The CFTC backed many of the CGT's positions on the creation of EDF, while Louvel and the moderates worked within the governmental coalition to limit the nationalization. Catholic doctrine accepted the necessity of nationalizations as long as they did not deny the sanctity of private property. As early as 1931, Pope Pius XI had written in *Quadragesimo Anno*, "There are certain categories of wealth that should be reserved for the collectivity, when they confer an economic power of such a scale that they represent a threat to the public welfare if left in private hands."[45] In Section 105 of the *Code Social* (1931), Maline added that any public takeover had to be accom-

---

[41] CFTC, *Programme revendicatif de la CFTC du XXIe Congrès de la CFTC* (1945), pp. 5–6.

[42] An excellent study of reconstruction and its role in guiding the CFTC's Catholic humanism into the CFDT's *autogestion* concepts is Paul Vignaux, *De la CFTC à la CFDT. Syndicalisme et socialisme: Reconstruction (1946–1972)* (1980). Of less importance is a Sciences Politiques thesis, Gérard Adam, *La CFTC*. A major arena for the development of reconstruction's ideas was the CFTC utility workers' monthly, *Gaz-Électricité*. For the early history of the CFTC, see Michel Launay, *La CFTC: Origines et développement (1919–1940)* (1987).

[43] CFTC, *Programme revendicatif*, p. 9.

[44] CFTC–Fédération des Syndicats Chrétiens du Personnel des Services Publics et Concédés, *Exprès* 15 (8 March 1946), 6. In his otherwise perceptive discussion of the Catholic origins of the modernist ideology, Luc Boltanski neglects this division; see *Les cadres, naissance d'un groupe social* (Paris, Éditions de Minuit, 1983), chap. 3.

[45] Cited in André Mater, "Réflexions d'un juriste sur une nationalisation," *Revue Juridique de l'Électricité et du Gaz* 15 (November-December 1948), 592.

panied by a "sufficient and immediate indemnity." Pius XII later eschewed direct state control of nationalized firms, yet he recognized
that they were sometimes needed to promote economic rationality,
avoid waste, remedy the abuses of individual ownership, and serve
the national community.[46] Statist nationalizations would only reproduce the problem of monopolies as the masters rather than the servants
of society, creating a state plutocracy in place of a private one.[47] Many
Catholics viewed non-bureaucratic management and workers' access
to managerial functions as preconditions for an increased dignity of
work. With its historic attention to the basic needs of workers and
consumers, postwar Catholic doctrine implicitly supported tripartite
boards of directors and a large autonomy from the state for nationalized
firms as a means for limiting state power.

Underlining the contradiction between class perspectives and party
labels, MRP moderates and CFTC progressives introduced separate
nationalization bills. The moderates' proposal was not a nationalization
bill per se, but a scheme for mixed public and private ownership. The
CFTC leadership said that it was "clearly inspired by the bosses."[48]
The CFTC bill closely paralleled that of Le Brun and Marcel Paul, except
for a provisions granting a larger representation of workers on the
board of directors, a smaller indemnity package, and a period of transition to full nationalization.

Reflecting moderate business opinion, Radicals and MRP moderates
coalesced to limit the scope, decentralize the management, and increase
the purchase price of EDF. These efforts only slightly weakened the
nationalization. On issues of economic *dirigisme* (state economic management) and nationalizations, MRP views often coincided with those
of Radical and SFIO moderates, all of whom adopted an essentially
neoliberal analysis, which accepted the general principles of *dirigisme*
and nationalizations, yet only insofar as they would not hinder individual initiative or free competition. Most neoliberals accepted nationalizations simply as a functional necessity for modernization and
reconstruction.

[46] Quotation in A. Dauphin-Meunier, "L'église et les nationalisations," *Questions Actuelles* (August-September 1946), nonpaginated. See also *Civita Catolica*, 7 September 1946;
G. Hérard, "La nationalisation de l'électricité et du gaz," *Tribune Économique*, 18 October
1946; and anon., "Vers les nationalisations?" *Fiches de l'Action Populaire* 47 (1945). See
speech by Pius XII, 11 March 1945, to the Italian Catholic Workers' Congress, cited in
Gendarme, *L'expérience*, p. 106.
[47] "Un Catholique de la Résistance," p. 6.
[48] CFTC–Fédération des Syndicats Chrétiens du Personnel des Services Publics et
Concédés, *La Voix des Services Concédés* 6 (February 1946), 3. The MRP bill was: "Annexe
au procès verbaux, n° 72," *JO, dp,* 11 December 1945; the CFTC bill was: "Annexe au
procès verbaux, n° 329," *JO, dp,* 31 January 1946. See also "Nationalisation de l'énergie"
(1946), mimeographed CFTC document, Hennebicq dossier, CFDT archives, Paris.

Neoliberalism was not a coherent ideology but a patchwork of vague Keynesianism, classic liberalism, and political expediency.[49] Neoliberals assumed that France had a class-divided society and that state intervention in the economy was a necessary evil. State interventionism was dangerous, according to the neoliberals, because if interventionism were institutionalized, one day the Left could permanently control the state and turn it against the capitalist economy. Neoliberals wished to circumscribe state interventions as narrowly as possible. René Courtin said from that perspective: "It is the bourgeoisie who have betrayed the country. We will therefore nationalize. It is a political necessity. In fifteen years, when a new bourgeoisie emerges that is worthy, we will denationalize."[50] Jacques Furaud of the MRP succinctly stated the main lines of the neoliberal philosophy during the electricity nationalization debates. "[We are] not opposed to the evolution of the liberal economy or of public control over this industry, but [we] desire that state intervention be only on the levels of overall management, financing, organization, and control. We are therefore totally opposed to the strategies of statist domination [étatisation] and of a bureaucratization that would impede the present system rather than ameliorate it.[51]

The Radical party emerged from the war in a relatively weak position. Many held it culpable for the political impasse of France in the 1930s, the voting of full powers to Pétain in 1940, and a mediocre role in the Resistance. In the Liberation era, many erstwhile supporters of the Radical party abandoned it for the Communists or Socialists. This left the Radical party considerably less "radical" than it had been in the 1930s, particularly on economic matters. Lacking a systematic ideology and torn between the economic dirigisme of Pierre Mendès-France and the liberalism of René Pleven, the Radicals offered little more than an ambivalent populism. They resurrected earlier rhetoric against the trusts and the large banks, defending "the middle classes in the community and their interests, and the middle classes, small businessmen, and tradesmen threatened with becoming workers."[52] Because of common socioeconomic constituencies and despite divergences on church and state issues, many Radicals shared neoliberal economic views with moderate Christian Democrats.

The MRP nationalization proposal reflected several neoliberal preoccupations also held by Radicals. The first, stated by Robert Buron, was that a depressed stock market and a virtually nonexistent bond market

---

[49] A systematic and sympathetic presentation of the neoliberal philosophy is Richard F. Kuisel, Capitalism, pp. 248–71.
[50] Courtin, cited in interview with André Philip, in Nordengren, Targets, p. 240.
[51] Furaud, JO, dp, 27 March 1946, p. 1104.
[52] Pierrot at the 1945 Radical Party Congress, cited in Nordengren, Targets, p. 89.

could not meet the capital needs of the electrical power sector.[53] In addition, the political base of MRP and Radical neoliberals consisted of small and medium-sized industrialists, and stockholders generally, some of whom owned electrical facilities or stock. Neoliberals proposed to grant generous indemnities and exclude cogeneration facilities from the nationalization. They also tried to set up a decentralized management that would be more subject to both political patronage and to provincial conservatism. Denationalization could then proceed by gradually chipping away at the periphery of EDF.

Alfred Krieger, a Radical, best stated the mixture of political, economic, and technical goals for the electricity nationalization as neoliberals perceived them: (1) to dissolve monopolies, (2) to extend and strengthen electrification, (3) to normalize and standardize electrical equipment, (4) to make electrical investments more systematic, (5) to suppress costly intermediaries, and (6) to extend electrical use by sales promotion.[54] Recapitalization goals could be achieved by a mixed ownership system, a state-owned power pool (as in Great Britain), or by subsidies to private firms, yet by December 1945 it was clear that the parliamentary majority would countenance nothing less than nationalization.[55] Neoliberals occupied crucial positions concerned with the electricity nationalization process. As tepid supporters of the concept, they were generally viewed as mediators between the enthusiasts for, and the direct opponents to, the creation of EDF. This rationale was behind the installation of Ramadier, a neoliberal Socialist, as the floor manager for the bill in the National Constituent Assembly's Industrial Production Committee.

There was no Gaullist political party or movement before 1947. Several authors claim that the MRP was a stand-in for de Gaulle in the assembly, but on the issue of nationalizations, the MRP and de Gaulle concurred only on the need to limit the scope of state ownership. Few other non-Marxists shared de Gaulle's vision of highly statist nationalizations. Some of the early contours of right technocorporatism were foreshadowed by de Gaulle's positions on the new role for the state and on nationalizations. The state was to "hold the levers of command" in the economy without "breaking the levers of private initiative and

---

[53] Cited by Deglaire and Bordier, *Électricité*, p. 185. This position was reiterated many times in the nationalization debates and later by Gaspard himself. See Roger Gaspard, "Dix ans de politique financière à l'Électricité de France," *Arts et Manufactures* 34 (December 1956), 32.

[54] Kreiger, *JO, dp*, 26 March 1946, p. 1069.

[55] Courtin, in *Le Monde*, 26 March 1946, and *Tribune Économique*, 21 December 1945.

private profit," always leaving a substantial "free" sector.[56] Agreeing with Marcel Paul that administrative centralization was necessary for managerial efficiency, de Gaulle disagreed with the PCF's pluralism and argued against a tripartite board of directors, supporting instead the position that the cabinet should have ultimate power.[57] De Gaulle despised politicized nationalizations, for they could have led to an overextension of the public sector. Contrary to the CNR charter, which called for reforms to be implemented directly upon Liberation, de Gaulle tried to delay action on the nationalizations until the popular élan of the Resistance faded. Furthermore, while de Gaulle conceded the positive virtue of a consultative role for workers on the shop floor, he balked at implementing such procedures.[58] He wished to limit workers' participation in management to consultations in the workplace with productive efficiency, not shop-floor democracy, as the central goal. Most crucially for de Gaulle, nationalizations could help rebuild greatness by providing the infrastructural base for economic renovation. In the end, however, lacking a political party and absent from government after January 1946, de Gaulle had little direct impact on the electricity nationalization process.

The traditional Right was not a strong political force in immediate postwar France because it was compromised by its past failures and a widespread belief that it had collaborated and profiteered during the Occupation. Joseph Laniel and André Mutter had been active in the CNR, but their participation did not remove the tarnish from the Right's image. Laniel and Mutter conceded to the Democratic Charter, though they disagreed with its radical tone. The Right nonetheless opposed nationalizations as well as most of the other postwar reforms. Still controlling a disproportionate share of the press, it proffered economic liberalism against the encroachments of a 'totalitarian' state. With its overtly fascist elements removed from political life as a result of the purges, only economic liberals enjoyed a public presence on the Right. Peak employers' federations, reconstituted after the war, tended to be far less overtly antiunion and antireform. They systematically attempted to limit the postwar reforms, but direct opposition to nationalizations could not succeed in the context of a general popular sentiment, echoed by prewar conservative General Giraud, that

[56] De Gaulle, *JO, dp,* 3 March 1945, p. 267; de Gaulle, cited in *Le Monde,* 22 December 1944; and de Gaulle on the BBC, 14 July 1943, cited in Moch, "Réflexions," p. 24. See also *Le Figaro,* 3 October 1944.
[57] "Interview avec Marcel Paul," *Énergies* 799 (26 March 1971), 5.
[58] Speech by de Gaulle to the Provisional Assembly in Algiers, 18 March 1944, cited in Georges Lescuyer, *Le contrôle de l'état sur les entreprises nationalisées* (1962), p. 17.

"France [had] been betrayed by her conservative classes."[59] Many conservatives accepted nationalizations with a sense of resignation. Mercier well expressed that sentiment at a Union d'Électricité stockholders' meeting, saying that he felt wronged by accusations that he lacked patriotism and had created a trust, but conceding to the nationalization as long as it was done as a legal expression of popular sovereignty.[60] Henri Davezac, the executive director of Vichy's organization committee on electrical equipment and head of the trade association, even saw potential benefits to his sector through the nationalization.[61]

Two schools of rightist opposition emerged. Edmond Giscard d'Estaing and a few others directly opposed the nationalization.[62] Others such as Edmond Roux and Joseph Laniel felt that by offering proposals for limited nationalization and mixed ownership they could preserve some of the industry from nationalization.[63] The major strategic lines of resistance were primarily to delay the nationalization process until the political atmosphere changed, to complain about small and foreign stockholders being wronged, and to claim that nationalizations would be too costly. In addition, some leveled ad hominem attacks against Marcel Paul, claimed that nationalization would mean large rate increases, vowed to protect local communities from the encroachments of the state, and warned against taking such action while seeking American aid.[64] Conservatives and moderates introduced a plethora of counterproposals and amendments to impede the government's bill.

The Right defended small and foreign stockholders because it rec-

[59] Cited in PCF, Xe Congrès, p. 27.

[60] Union d'Électricité, Assemblée générale, compte-rendu de séance du 18 mai 1945 (1945), p. 1. See also Ernest Mercier, "Préface," in Malégarie, L'électricité, p. iii.

[61] Ehrmann, Organized Business, pp. 115–16.

[62] Edmond Giscard d'Estaing, Les nationalisations (1945), nonpaginated. Giscard (Sr.) was a major owner of Thomson-Houston, a major electrical equipment manufacturer. His daughter-in-law (Valéry's wife) was heiress to a substantial portion of Schneider, another equipment firm.

[63] Joseph Laniel, La nationalisation de l'électricité: Un cri d'alarme (1946), p. 7; Edmond Roux, Nationalisation sans spoliation (1945); and Edmond Roux, L'industrie électrique au service exclusif de la nation (1946).

[64] L'Aurore, 13 June 1946, attacked Paul for his "totalitarian" penchant in managing the industrial power-rationing system. Paul calculated that the indemnities, when rolled into the electrical rates, would necessitate an increase of 20 centimes per kwh, a truly minimal sum; JO, dp, 27 March 1946, p. 1110. France-Soir of that afternoon proclaimed the rate increase with a banner headline. Claims of statist expansionism infringing on local autonomy were overstated, for the Congress of Mayors and the National Federation of Conceding Communes and Régies (FNCCR) met jointly in the fall of 1945 and passed a resolution supporting the nationalization of electrical services, with the caveat that the locals retain control of electrical distribution; see FNCCR, Bulletin, p. 17. That principle was contained in the government's nationalization bill. Fears vis-à-vis the United States were expressed by Bouvier O'Cottereau, JO, dp, 25 March 1946, p. 1065. Vie Française (23 February and 2 March 1946) openly called for delays, arguing that they were the best means for defeating the nationalization.

ognized that the holding companies themselves were politically indefensible. Utility managers had the utility stockholders' association send letters to its members with model protest letters to legislators enclosed, as the coal trade association had done in the face of coal nationalization.[65] They also sent a bulletin to legislators that stressed the diffuse ownership pattern in utilities.[66] Paul and Ramadier took note and made concessions on the indemnity issue. Foreign holdings in French power utilities were estimated by the Bank of France to be worth 5.68 billion francs (of a total of about 70 billion francs), 3.36 billion of which were Swiss held.[67] The Swiss financial press in particular led a campaign against the nationalization and for larger indemnities in the event of nationalization.

The Right also criticized the cost of the nationalization and modernization efforts. Faced with large indemnity charges and a projected 220 billion francs' worth of new investments in the electrical sector alone, the French state, itself anticipating a 1946 deficit of 487 billion francs, was considered incapable of carrying additional debt.[68] The new EDF would certainly have to seek fresh capital on the nonfunctioning bond market. In the event that the bond market revived, the Right feared that EDF bond issues would displace private issues and inhibit the recovery of private industry. This argument carried little weight, for regardless of who owned France's electrical system, such investments would have to be made.

Finally, like the neoliberals, the Right rhetorically claimed that public enterprise would undermine the free enterprise system. They averred that the state had a voracious appetite and that it would lap up everything in its path: first the nationalized sector, then (in concert with the unions) it would victimize the consumer, then it would turn on the unions, and it would finish by gobbling up the entire private sector.[69] Characterized as *étatisation* (roughly, statist domination), nationalization was decried as the first step toward totalitarianism.[70] This argu-

---

[65] Holter, "Miners," p. 125.

[66] Association des Porteurs d'Actions et d'Obligations de l'Industrie Électrique, "Les trusts ne tiennent pas les portefeuilles," *Bulletin* (19 January 1946), nonpaginated. This document asserted that there were 73,961 people who held less than 25 shares and only 161 who held more than 1,000 shares. Using *Le Monde's* statement of 20 July 1946, that there was a total of 21,000,000 shares outstanding, this author calculated that even if one allocates the maximum number of shares to the small holding categories given by the *Bulletin*, the top 161 owners held at least 82 percent of all electrical stocks.

[67] Laniel, *JO, dp*, 26 March 1946, p. 1065.

[68] Cost estimates by Bank of France, cited by Desjardins, *JO, dp*, 22 March 1946, p. 1006, and anon., "La nationalisation du déficit," *Questions Actuelles* 107 (January 1946), nonpaginated.

[69] Roux, *L'industrie électrique*, p. 32.

[70] Denais, *JO, dp*, 5 July 1945, p. 1296.

ment carried little weight, but it did compel a few changes in the government bill and elicited a promise for administrative decentralization. Rightist opposition to the nationalization thus largely failed, as the overwhelming parliamentary vote indicated.

Major Issues in the Electricity Nationalization

Many issues in the nationalization debate became significant only after the Paul–Le Brun bill had been approved in the Council of Ministers meeting of 18 January 1946. One would assume that because the SFIO and MRP had accepted the text, party discipline would assure rapid passage. However, many of the changes made to the initial bill were implemented at the insistence of the Socialists and Christian Democrats over the course of the legislative process.

Most policymakers agreed that *étatisation* was perilous, yet *étatisation* took on different meanings for different political tendencies. The widest condemnation of *étatisation* reflected the contemporary popular disdain for bureaucratic organizations. The Right and the neoliberals also saw *étatisation* as the process through which the state would utilize its powers to impose mandatory planning, state controls, and the like on the private sector. Many also feared that the nationalized sector would become a state within a state, a hermetically sealed technocracy, a new monopoly sector, or an independent bastion of Communist power.

The antibureaucratic analysis was elegant, yet simple, and it enjoyed broad public support. *L'Aube*, the leading Catholic daily, editorialized, "There is a bureaucratic smokescreen between the government and the country, an administrative mattress that dampens the decisions of political authority, dilutes the efficacy of all political authority, dilutes responsibility, and transforms the acts of government into an anonymous flurry of paperwork."[71] *Combat*, then edited by Albert Camus, went further: The bureaucracy "spreads through and infects the organs of the state administration. The disease is not new, but it has made progress. In the multitude of 'directorates,' 'subdivisions,' 'commissions,' and 'services,' the offices that intervene in the same areas and need to coordinate their activities instead of compete with each other, ignore and neutralize each other. Finally, with each passing day, there is a reaffirmation of the horror of anything 'that lives.' "[72] If the imagery of the postal service with its petty bureaucrats and lethargic window occupants elicited universal disdain, that of an impersonal technocracy

[71] *L'Aube*, 27–28 May 1945.
[72] *Combat*, 26 July 1945.

seemed to worry only leftist Catholics and a few other non-Communist leftists. A Catholic journalist wrote of his fear of a system in which "individuals are treated either as pawns on a chessboard or as ciphers in economic calculations."[73] *Combat* feared the "replacement of the republic of the 'good old boys' by the republic of the technicians."[74] A commonly cited solution to bureaucratic infestation was to counterbalance the power of the state by placing worker and consumer representatives in the boards of directors. Since 1919, that model had been the darling of the CGT, and by 1945 it was adopted by Communists, Socialists, and many Christian Democrats. The CFTC went further by arguing for an even greater worker representation (more than one-third of the board) and by seeking to have constituency groups rather than the minister of industry appoint worker and consumer representatives.[75] The Right opposed the tripartite boards, claiming that two-thirds of the board would be dedicated to parochial rather than general interests, thereby necessitating a stronger state role.[76] The Ministry of Finance also opposed such a structure, insisting that state-appointed technical and financial experts predominate in order to assure technical expertise and financial responsibility.[77]

All three of the major parties supported EDF's autonomy from state controls, but for different reasons. For MRP neoliberals, an autonomous EDF was the the best guarantee that the government could not use EDF as another agency through which to implement economic *dirigisme*.[78] The PCF recognized the fragility of the political moment and saw an autonomous EDF as the best guarantee that the influence of the firm and of the CGT would not be undermined by a change in cabinets. Like the left technocrats, the PCF saw EDF as potentially threatened by the conservative Finance Ministry, and it attempted to grant EDF managers "a taste of initiative and a sense of responsibility," free from that ministry.[79] Moderate Christian Democrats unsuccessfully sought to give state-appointed managers the power to veto the board's decisions. The final law gave the cabinet only the power to appoint the director-general, on the recommendation of the board. EDF was to have an "industrial and commercial" rather than an administrative

[73] Dauphin-Meunier,"L'église," nonpaginated.
[74] *Combat*, 3 March 1945.
[75] CFTC, *Voix*, pp. 3–4.
[76] Courtin in *Le Monde*, 22 March 1946, and Daniel Villey, "Les étapes du capitalisme d'État," in André Armengaud, ed., *Vingt ans de capitalisme d'état* (1951), p. 29.
[77] Bouthiller,"La nationalisation," p. 189. A decree by Louvel in May 1953 replaced several of the consumer representatives with "experts"; see infra, chap. 3.
[78] Furaud, *JO, dp*, 27 March 1946, p. 1104.
[79] Paul, *JO, dp*, 27 March 1946, p. 1120 (quotation). See also Moch, "Réflexions," p. 32, and Lefaucheux, "Passage," p. 47.

character, using private rather than public sector accounting and budgetary procedures. Parts of the financial press welcomed a power company that could be dealt with as a private business.[80]

However, that structure risked replacing a clique of private trusts with one mammoth public monopoly. The Socialists' solution and the one written into the law (though it was insufficient to the neoliberals and the Right) provided that EDF accounts would be open to public scrutiny and verified by a special state accounting board.[81] The Center-Right feared that EDF could use its simultaneous monopolist and monopsonist positions (as the major vendor of electrical power and the major purchaser of electrical equipment) to victimize the private sector. For this reason, Louvel (MRP) was willing to risk a break in the governmental coalition in order to have separate gas and electric firms, and to break EDF into a set of relatively autonomous regional firms. Left technocrats and the PCF-CGT saw such decentralization as technically inefficient, for economies of scale would become elusive.[82] On the Right, Edmond Roux saw decentralization as a sham, noting that technical necessities–the same ones cited by the Left–would demand recentralization.[83] The PCF's Political Bureau conceded to the moderates on these issues and thus prevented a break in the governing coalition by promising to decentralize EDF.[84] Decentralized distribution services were also a means to avoid a strong, imperial EDF. Preexisting localized *régies* and cooperatives were retained, while all other distribution services were integrated into EDF, with the promise that the latter would someday become locally operated *régies*.

Out of the debates on *étatisation*, EDF emerged as a centralized and relatively autonomous industrial and commercial firm, with the inherent risks of becoming either a technocratic citadel or a simple extension of the cabinet in power. Legislators made concessions to decentralist arguments, but the state retained the power to determine how decentralized EDF would ultimately be. The political autonomy of a state enterprise can, in the end, only be relative—there are no neutral technocracies, just as there are no neutral technologies. Indeed, political factors will always impinge on (if not control) the decisions in any technocracy, yet a technocracy can often carve a slice of autonomy based on its internal expertise. Though provincials and neoliberals were

[80] *Tribune Économique*, 5 April 1946.

[81] Béchard, *JO, dp*, 26 March 1946, p. 1076. The accounting board was the Cour des Comptes until 1949, and the Commission de Vérification des Comptes des Entreprises Publiques thereafter.

[82] "Compte rendu de la Commission de conciliation," *Force-Information* 190 (May 1971), 32–37.

[83] Roux, *L'industrie électrique*, p. 28.

[84] Gaudy, *Et la lumière*, p. 127, n. 95.

later able to pare small zones of patronage out of EDF, the lack of any systematic definition of EDF-state relations potentially made EDF a centralized extension of the cabinet in power.[85] Such centralization was possible partly because the state was the sole "shareholder" of EDF, but mostly because political forces were constantly battling for political power. Indeed, in the final analysis, with the exception of the PCF, all groups eschewed *étatisation* when they envisioned political rivals controlling the state, but accepted it when they believed that they themselves might have political predominance.[86] The debate on *étatisation* conveniently obscured this fact, much to the future detriment of EDF.

The indemnity issue constituted the most discussed—but ultimately the least significant—question of the nationalization process for EDF.[87] While the neoliberals and the Right sought to make the indemnities as large as possible, the CFTC, CGT, PCF, and left Socialists attempted to minimize them. However, when the neoliberals (led by Louvel) became recalcitrant, other groups conceded on several major points, thereby creating one of the most lucrative sets of financial bonds ever issued in France. For publicly traded firms, the plan entailed simply exchanging utility stocks for a new set of EDF bonds. For nontraded firms, it meant issuing EDF bonds based on an appraisal of existing assets. Two steps were involved in structuring indemnities, first, evaluation of existing assets and equity, then determination of the character of the bonds.

From the outset, legislators assumed that the stock prices of March 1946 were far too low to serve as an indemnity reference base, for if they were indexed with 1938 values equal to 100, then-current quotations would be at 222 for the utility stocks, in the face of far higher stock indicies elsewhere and a vastly higher cost-of-living index.[88] The question thus concerned a suitable reference period for setting an index base that would not penalize current stockholders for the massive stock sell-offs between 1943 and 1946. The CFTC wisely proposed using wealth tax declarations as a base (thus justifiably rewarding or penalizing people for the veracity of their tax declarations), but they were

[85] Legislation defining relations between the nationalized sector and the state was slated for all of the nationalized industrial sector. Several bills were debated until 1949, but the divergent purposes and appetites of the political parties precluded passage.

[86] Bernard Chenot, "Direction et contrôle des entreprises nationalisées," *Le fonctionnement des Entreprises nationalisées en France: IIIe Colloque des Facultés de Droit, Grenoble, 9–11 Juin, 1955,* p. 30.

[87] For a complete discussion of the indemnity question, see EDF, *Comptes d'activité et rapport de gestion, 1946–1949* (Paris: EDF, 1950), pp. 85–87. See also Georges Maleville, "Les modifications apportées à la loi du 8 avril 1946 sur la nationalisation de l'électricité et du gaz," *Cahiers de Documentation Juridique de l'Électricité et du Gaz de France* (1949), 2–14, and Pierre Loiseau, *L'indemnisation des entreprises nationalisées* (1950), passim.

[88] "Compte rendu de la Commission de conciliation," p. 37.

ignored. The government's text set the base at 333 (again, 1938 = 100), and it had the support of the PCF and the SFIO. Louvel insisted on a base of 398, yet 333 became the base in the nationalization law, a figure that was nonetheless 50 percent higher than current quotes on the stock exchange.[89]

The yield on the bonds was variously proposed at 2 percent per annum (PCF), 3 percent (SFIO and most of the MRP), and 3.5 percent (Louvel, many Radicals, and the Right). Bonds for the nationalized banks had been set at 2.5 percent with little debate in December 1945. The current rate on savings was 3 percent, and the average yield on utility stocks was less than 1 percent. When Parliament set bank bond rates at 2.5 percent, bank stock prices rose slightly, indicating investors' acceptance of the rate. Much of the financial press considered the 3 percent rate sufficient,[90] and Minister of Finance André Philip argued that bonds at 3.5 percent would inflate overall interest rates, but Louvel insisted on 3.5 percent. Paul and Ramadier wanted to pass the nationalization by a large majority, so Ramadier took a PCF proposal that placed a 1 percent levy on the firm's total annual revenue as a supplement to the return on EDF equipment funding bonds and offered a similar scheme for the indemnity bonds if they were kept at 3 percent. It passed in that fashion. The package in the law therefore had the reference base at 333, with fifty-year bonds paying 3 percent per year. In addition, 1 percent of EDF's total revenue in a given year was to be distributed over all of the remaining indemnity bonds. The indemnity bonds were to be divided into fifty equally sized series, with one series retired annually based on a random drawing. An independent state agency was created to service the bonds.

The financial community warmly received the indemnity bond formula. *Bulletin Économique* said that the system would "aid the healthy functioning of the bond market," and a number of other journals responded likewise.[91] Nonetheless, some still felt that the formula was insufficient. In 1948, Louvel sponsored a bill to hike the reference base to 380, to rearrange the formula used to distribute the 1 percent share over the bonds, and to grant an additional indemnity to those whose bonds were drawn early.[92] Together, these measures raised EDF's in-

---

[89] At the urging of many large banks and brokers, many of the small blocks of stock had been sold off well before the nationalization debates. This stampede of sales depressed the market so that many small holders sustained losses long before the nationalization, while prescient speculators were able to buy the stocks at low prices (often at 205). Consequently, the major beneficiaries of generous indemnities were not necessarily the oft-mentioned small holders, but a small group of speculators.

[90] *Bulletin Économique*, 14 March 1946, and *Le Pays*, 20 January 1946.

[91] *Bulletin Économique*, 1 April 1946.

[92] "Loi du 12 août 1948, n° 1260," *JO, lois et décrets*, 14 August 1948. At the same time,

demnity bill by 3.3 billion francs.[93] Furthermore, indemnity-valuation commissions excluded EDF managers while representatives of the old utilities were welcomed. Finally, valuation commissions later used a reference base of 600 to calculate the liquifiable values of nonpublicly traded firms.[94]

EDF received equipment with a replacement value of about 200 billion francs (in mid-1947 francs) for which it issued about 82 billion francs in bonds, the difference due in large part to the low market-to-book ratios for Bourse-quoted firms, to depreciation, and to inflation.[95] The losers were, first, those who dumped their stocks in the fever before December 1945, and second, those who unwisely sold their stocks between April 1946 and January 1951, when the indemnity bonds were issued. Nonetheless, even conservative Daniel Villey said that EDF indemnities "led to exhorbitant advantages for the bondholders."[96] Moch's fears that indemnities would create new "trusts" were realized. France's largest electrical equipment firm, Compagnie Générale d'Électricité, once included several private utilities; it expanded in the 1950s by using EDF indemnity bonds as a major part of its finance capital.[97] A similar pattern held true for France's other major electrical equipment constellation, the Empain-Jeumont-Schneider group.

Legislators debated two major issues concerning which facilities would be nationalized, the capacity floor below which power facilities would remain private and the fate of electrical coproduction and self-generation facilities of manufacturing firms. A broad scope supported by Paul, Moch, and Philip prevailed, with a few concessions to Louvel. An amended MRP nationalization bill, authored by Louvel and René Perrin, had targeted only those facilities that produced more than 200 million kwh in 1942. This was unacceptable to the overwhelming majority of the legislators, for it would have left 45 percent of the French generating capacity in private hands. While it was generally conceded

---

insurance companies began to offer policies to bondholders to insure against the danger of having their respective bond series drawn.

[93] EDF, Conseil d'Administration, "Procès-verbaux des séances," CAPV 32 (4 February 1949).

[94] "Décret du 14 août 1947," JO, lois et décrets, 20 August 1947.

[95] On the value of the equipment, see CAPV 18 (13 June 1947); on the total value of the bonds, see Gaspard, "Dix ans," p. 32.

[96] Villey, "Les étapes," p. 28. To this day, the performance of the EDF indemnity bonds on the Bourse could not be less spectacular, particularly because the 1 percent bonus is distributed over a continually diminishing number of bonds, as 1/50 of the bonds are rolled over annually. For a given value of bonds issued in 1951, Bourse quotations indicated a twofold increase in value by 1956, 3.5 fold by 1963, 7.5 fold by 1971, and 29 fold by 1981; drawn from ibid., p. 31; Deglaire and Bordier, Électricité, p. 233; Gaudy, Et la lumière, p. 115; and Gaspard interview.

[97] Moch, Réflexions, p. 30; on CGE, Gaspard interview and L'Entreprise 634 (4 November 1967), 42–47.

that "small" producers would not be nationalized, *small* ultimately came to mean a production of less than 12 million kwh in 1942, even though a figure half that size had been proposed by Paul and Moch. On the issue of who had rights to build new plants, Paul accepted a proposal by Ramadier to allow *régies* and private firms to build new plants if their annual production capacities were less than 12 million kwh, subject to the approval of EDF.

Electrical coproduction and self-generation facilities (called auto-producers), primarily those in electrometals, electrochemicals, coal mining, and railroads, made up about one-third of French generating capacity in 1946.[98] The Paul-Moch-Philip bloc wanted to nationalize these facilities and the Ramadier-Lacoste-Louvel bloc (along with the Finance Ministry) opposed it. Extricating coproduction plants from their parent facilities was no easy task, but Paul argued that it was technically necessary in order to pool all power in France and derive greater overall efficiency. A wide scope would also assure systematic utilization of river basins, long a problem in hydro production. Louvel and others countered that efficient pooling could be done without nationalization through a system of designating interruptible users. Ultimately, on a compromise offered by Ramadier, coal and rail power plants remained with their nationalized parent firms (though EDF was to control those facilities), while private sector facilities were nation-alized.[99] Joint committees between EDF and private firms were to op-erate the latter installations, with a rate guarantee promising that "the power supplied will be at economic conditions corresponding to those which such firms would have been able to obtain had they continued to own and operate the facilities themselves."[100] These provisions were written into the law as Article 8 and the price-guaranteed power, often sold at one-tenth the going rate, came to be known as "Article 8 power."[101] The financial press attacked Article 8 as governmental med-

---

[98] Coal and rail installations were 18 percent of all French generating capacity at the time, and those industries were also state-owned, yet Alais Froges et Camargue (the predecessor to Pechiney) had owned 15 percent of France's hydro capacity in 1939; Bernard Legrand and Georges Yelnik, "Un consommateur bien particulier: Aluminium Pechiney," in Fabienne Cardot, ed., *L'électricité et ses consommateurs*, p. 140.

[99] SNCF (rail) and CDF-HBD (coal) were later allowed to build their own new plants; letter of 19 March 1949, from Lacoste to Varlet, director of electricity, cited in Simone Deglaire, ed., *Recueil des lois, décrets, arrêtés, circulaires et cahiers des charges intéressant la production, le transport et la distribution de l'énergie électrique*, vol. 11 (1952), p. 719.

[100] Paul, *JO, dp*, 27 March 1946, p. 1106. The joint committees' powers were later ignored; the price for power supplied to the aluminum industry was set by the minister of the national economy, entirely circumventing the joint committees; see CAPV 21 (1 August 1947).

[101] *Vie Française*, 27 April 1946, bemoaned the fate of the aluminum industry under Article 8, claiming that if power tariffs were too high (electricity constitutes about 30

dling in the affairs of private businesses, particularly in its provision prohibiting the further construction of private generating plants.[102]

Legislators agreed that EDF's purview should stop at the power meters, leaving internal wiring, appliance sales, and maintenance to the private sector. These activities had previously been performed by the utilities.[103] Secondly, the nationalization law prescribed that firms primarily engaged in electrical power were initially to be nationalized in full. Evaluation commissions would then decide which facilities were necessary to EDF and would return the remainder to the original owners, pursuant to Article 15 of the nationalization law.[104] Finally, the political influence of the Herriot circle prevented the nationalization of the Rhône Company. The nationalization law thus gave ownership of 75 percent of France's electrical facilities and near-total control over all installations to EDF. EDF was in a position to be the designer and manager of France's entire electrical system, with the potential for becoming the master of all energy policy in France.

Legislators ignored the issue of capital financing in the nationalization process and thus forced EDF to start up without capital reserves, working capital, or even operating funds. The private utilities had systematically depleted such funds before the nationalization.[105] EDF also inherited over 20 billion francs' worth of debts (exclusive of pension commitments) incurred by its predecessors. The law thus created a conundrum: if EDF was to act as an autonomous industrial and commercial enterprise, without stockholders, where was it to find the financing it needed? If EDF was to borrow to meet its needs under tariff controls, it risked snowballing debts, borrowing ever more to cover old debts. There was also a danger of replacing an old stockholding class with a new bondholding class. Given the time gap between ground breaking and the first economic returns on new facilities, there were no means to pay the bills in the interim. Robert Buron raised this issue during the parliamentary debates, with little effect. Internal fi-

---

percent of the total production costs in aluminum production) manufacturers would leave France in search of cheaper electricity.

[102] *Tribune Économique*, 5 April 1946.

[103] A vacuum was created by the nonnationalization of internal wiring verification. As a result, for several years, verifications were not performed, resulting in a large number of accidents among consumers; CAPV 66 (28 September 1951). The marketing of appliances was very slow in getting off the ground, much to the dismay of the CGT and the FNCCR.

[104] The evaluation commissions under Article 15 took a very narrow definition of EDF's needs. As a result, the land on which EDF central offices now stand, originally owned by the Messine group, was first nationalized under Article 6, returned to the Messine group under Article 15, and ultimately repurchased by EDF at a much higher price; CAPV 63 (29 April 1951).

[105] "Interview avec M. Pierre Simon," *Force-Information* 190 (May 1971), 13. Pierre Simon was EDF's first chairman.

nancing could never meet EDF's capital needs without large and immediate rate increases. The CGT presented a coherent logic: if EDF was publicly owned, the state was essentially the sole shareholder and, like any shareholder, the state periodically had to infuse EDF with fresh capital. EDF ultimately floated on Marshall funds, but at the outset, it was desperate.

EDF's managerial autonomy, addressed only in a bureaucratic sense by legislators, was predicated on its financial autonomy. If EDF had to seek financial assistance from the government, the government would surely insist on controls over EDF.[106] The financing issue thus silently doomed EDF's vaunted autonomy from the start. The financial health of France's largest industrial firm became subject to the political and budgetary whims of each passing cabinet. Furthermore, the government would soon begin to affect the capital flows between the private and public sectors by deciding to subsidize, allowing EDF to issue bonds, or permitting rate increases.

The Labor *Statut*

The nationalization was a clear victory for the electrical workers. The head of their largest union oversaw the writing of a progressive nationalization bill and ushered it through the obstacle course of Parliament. At every moment of the process, electrical workers were prepared to conduct work actions to increase the pressure to nationalize. The keystone of their victory was the new *statut*, promulgated on 22 June 1946. Marcel Paul and his staff, drawn largely from Éclairage, wrote the text in the late nights after the nationalization, rushing it to completion out of a fear that the perfect political moment could pass in a few weeks' time. Paul preferred a decreed *statut* to a labor contract, for a contract could expire during a period when labor was far less powerful.[107] The nationalization law empowered Paul to write the *statut*, and only the countersignatures of the minister of labor (Croizat, PCF) and the prime minister (Gouin, SFIO) were required.

The provisions of the *statut* were quite advanced compared to the work rules in nearly all other industries in the West. Paid leave was offered for everything from marriage to a child's first communion or a death in the family. Promotions, hiring, and pay levels were to be public, guaranteeing an end to managerial discretion. Disciplinary actions were to go before comanagement bodies meeting openly, with

[106] See infra, chap. 3.
[107] Paul, in *Force-Information*, p. 14; René Gaudy, *Les porteurs*, pp. 140–42; and Pierre Durand, *Marcel Paul*, p. 223.

subordinates in the hierarchy able to sit in judgment of their superiors. All workers were guaranteed one month's pay as an annual bonus, with one-half payable for summer vacation. Sex discrimination in salaries and hiring was prohibited. The unions gained full control over all benefit programs through the Conseil Central des Oeuvres Sociales. Pensions were based on the pay levels of the last year worked and were to be raised along with the pay of active workers, a provision that encouraged the retirement of the old antinationalization managers.[108] The most advanced aspect of the *statut* was its implementation of codeterminist principles. The CFTC had designed codeterminist procedures of its own, and Paul's text satisfied them.[109] The *statut* created a codeterminist (50 percent workers, 50 percent managers) National Superior Commission for Personnel (Conseil Supérieur National du Personnel, CSNP) to deal with hiring, promotion, discipline, job descriptions, and all other nonwage issues concerning electrical workers, even those not employed by EDF. Secondary commissions fulfilled these same functions on a local level with appeals rights to the CSNP.

Workers saw codetermination as a way to break the traditional paternalism of the employers and to achieve a new respect and self-confidence. According to Roger Pauwels and Yves Morel, former CGT and CFTC representatives on the EDF board, such measures signified a radical democratization of the electrical power industry and represented the workers' greatest victory in the entire nationalization.[110] Charles Tillon, state overseer of the nationalized armaments industry in 1946, thus spoke of industrial democracy in the armaments sector: "The spirit of a search for a new life, learned in the Resistance, compels us to ask ... that the highest technicians consider the opinion of the worker who sits on the codetermination committee and to receive his proposals for economies of work time and raw materials with confidence. [The technician] thus renders homage to those who have acquired direct knowledge, a knowledge that only grows and is humanized by human activity. It is in this school that people learn to be more than mere breadwinners."[111]

[108] Gaspard interview; Paul, Gaspard, and Simon met in the summer of 1946 and decided which managers to pension off. According to Gaspard, part of EDF's early success was due to the silencing of that potentially very hostile opposition through the use of such pension-bribes.

[109] The CFTC sought (1) open disciplinary procedures, (2) experiments in workers' control in the management of workers' social programs, and (3) autonomous work groups in production. See CFTC, *Programme revendicatif*, p. 3.

[110] Interview by author with Roger Pauwels, at the CGT-FNE offices, Pantin, 23 June 1981; and interview with Yves Morel, Embrun, 17 July 1981.

[111] Charles Tillon, *On chantait rouge*, p. 447. A similar analysis of *cogestion* was offered by Pierre Simon, in 1946–47 the president and director-general of EDF, to a congress of the EDF shop committees in Paris, 26 February 1947; FNCCR, *Bulletin*, p. 75.

The right of workers to have a say in matters treated by the CSNP and the secondary boards marked a major break in the history of French labor relations. Even though they were attacked for undermining the principles of job hierarchies and the "rights" of managers, codeterminist bodies reinforced workplace hierarchies. When positions within the hierarchy were subjected to a merit-oriented scrutiny and when workers helped to elect and confirm their own superiors, they legitimized the chain of command. In this way, pay differentials were easily justified and deference was reinforced by workers' acquiescence. When management later became less benign toward the workers, codetermination became "a means for investing antilabor policies with the mantle of workers' consent."[112]

The mixed production committees (Comités Mixtes à la Production, CMP) and subcommittees (Sous-CMP, S-CMP), and a Superior Council of CMPs (Conseil Supérieur Central des CMP, CSC-CMP) represented the reform with the greatest potential for workers. These codeterminist bodies, half workers and half managers, had only a consultative role in overseeing the production process, yet for the first time, managers and workers could meet face-to-face and discuss the methods and organization of work. Managerial paternalism was to be forever banished in these meetings among equals. Viewed by the CGT as necessary in aiding the battle of production, the mixed committees were seen by the CFTC as precursers to democratic and collective management and as arenas in which workers could demystify managers and managerial functions.[113] The CMPs could become either shadow managerial bodies or mere echo chambers for premade decisions. Paul wrote that the CSC-CMP could be the place where "the elected representatives have . . . the possibility to debate the problems of the operations in the nationalized firms, covering the questions of tariffs, equipment, investments, and other things."[114] Pierre Simon, the first president and director-general of EDF, agreed with this conception of the CMPs, and with Paul, he set up the CSC-CMP accordingly.[115] Many Socialists had less confidence in the technical competence of manual workers and thus argued for more traditional managerial methods.[116] A lack of competence among lower-level workers may have inhibited *cogestion*, yet

---

[112] Interview by author with Ernest Anzalone, former head of the CFDT-FGE (ex-CFTC), Paris, 9 July 1981.

[113] The differing expectations for the mixed committees were profound. Once the PCF was felt to be out of the government permanently and the battle of production was ended, the CGT allowed the committees to fall into abeyance. The CFTC made the committees an object of major attention and continuously attempted to revive them.

[114] Paul, in *Force-Information*, p. 17.

[115] Marcel Paul, *Le statut national*, n.d., nonpaginated.

[116] Ramadier, "Les entreprises nationalisées," p. 207.

as EDF's subsequent history indicates, successful *cogestion* hinged equally upon the unions' commitment to comanagement.

Immediately upon its publication, the *statut* elicited a strong negative reaction from the press, with headlines reading: "The *Statut* of Gas and Electricity: Anarchy in High Places," "The Degradation of the Public's Welfare," and "The Finance Minister Must Change the Scandalous *Statut*."[117] Not only did the conservative press such as *Figaro* (7 July) and *L'Époque* (30 June) question the *statut*'s legality, even the Socialists' *Breton Socialiste* argued that the *statut* overpaid the workers.[118] The codetermination provisions were a major target of criticism. *Tribune Économique* wrote that they did not "provide the indispensible conditions to encourage the personnel and maintain the proper spirit of emulation" of workplace superiors, substituting the authority of managers with "the arbitrary will of a small number of men chosen by a political party."[119] UNCM made similar allegations. *Le Monde* criticized the pay levels, arguing that high gas and electric salaries would engender wage increases in the entire public sector.[120] Raymond Aron not only saw the pay as too high, he also sensed a double game in allocating a 900 percent spread between the lowest and highest salary categories: "Without a doubt, the ministers have been careful in their attempt to extend their influence among engineers and technicians, in order to show that they are the defenders of the managers and elites as well as the masses, but their attitude has some more profound causes. Everywhere that the interests of production are paramount, the inequality of salaries is strong."[121] The Communists' battle of production had its costs, yet employee benefits, which cost an additional 40 percent above the total wage bill, tended to be far less hierarchically applied. In response to the spate of criticism, several MRP leaders began legislative action against the *statut*, but Éclairage vowed to cut off power if any changes were made.[122] The MRP quickly backed down.

Why did Paul write such a profoundly progressive *statut*, the most advanced that France had ever seen? Was it merely to serve partisan political purposes, as Aron and the Right claimed? Undoubtedly, a *statut* that ostensibly required union membership in order to participate in the life of the firm aided the CGT, but the vast majority of electrical workers were already in the CGT, and Paul gave plenty of room for the CFTC to operate. Large-scale social and economic gains no doubt

[117] These headlines are reviewed in *Tribune Économique*, 18 October 1946.
[118] Cited in Gaudy, *Et la lumière*, p. 159.
[119] *Tribune Économique*, 11 October 1946.
[120] Robert Jacomet, *Le Monde*, 6 July 1946.
[121] *Combat*, 5 July 1946.
[122] Paul, *Le statut national*.

won the workers' support, but that support was already guaranteed. Perhaps the *statut* represented an attempt to create a CGT-PCF bastion within EDF, an institutionalized position in postwar France, but the CGT had gained that status through a half-century of agitation and a key role in the creation of EDF. In the final analysis, the major purpose of the *statut* was to guarantee the success of the nationalization. Marcel Paul later wrote: "It was a question of making the personnel the body and soul of the nationalization, of attaching it to the two [gas and electric] industries that are equal to the tasks incumbent upon the personnel, but at the same time, of demonstrating [the personnel's] real participation in setting up and managing a branch of the national economy. It was no longer a question of manual workers, office employees, and managers being considered as mere adjuncts to the production process under the orders of nationless financial groups, but of a human grouping attached to a noble cause, tied to it by their participation."[123] The *statut* did create a team spirit within EDF. The *statut*, the personnel, and EDF were thus inextricably linked: an attack on one has since been seen as an attack on the other. In the subsequent history of EDF, the workers have been its most ardent defenders, though sometimes merely in defense of acquired rights. At the birth of EDF in 1946, many saw its creation as the work of the workers themselves. The *statut* put that recognition into writing.

Richard Kuisel writes, "The Left's reforms made the French economy more managed and more dynamic but not more socialist."[124] From the opposite perspective Annie Lacroix wrote, "The repulsion of the enemies of nationalization showed perfectly that the nationalization, even attenuated by measures favorable to grand capital, touched capital to the core in a sector of strong accumulation."[125] After conceding that the statut was a major victory for labor, André Marty wrote: "The nationalization assured some monstrous giveaways to the electricity trust in the form of indemnities. Moreover, it forced the rate payers to pay for the enormous investments (great dams, new thermal and hydro power plants) that the electricity trust had avoided making before the war."[126] Did the creation of EDF represent the nationalization of an otherwise doomed industry, or did the nation take control of a potentially dynamic sector? Was the new EDF going to be a workers' paradise or a citadel of consenting robots? Would it combatively conquer its own independent territory in the capitalist French economy or would it sell

[123] Ibid.
[124] Kuisel, *Capitalism*, p. 202.
[125] Lacroix, "La nationalisation," p. 101.
[126] André Marty, *L'affaire Marty* (1955), p. 247.

itself and its services as the opportunities arose? Could it be an island of participatory socialism in a capitalist economy, or would capitalistically inclined managers and government officials make it capitalist? In essence, would EDF provide a basis for a transition to socialism or for a more scientific and rational capitalism?

After a long, mostly rhetorical parliamentary process, EDF emerged in April 1946 with many options open to it, though its freedom of action was already limited by price and wage controls and by the immediate financing problem. In its sphere, EDF could become a powerhouse of its own, with a power equal to that of nearly any minister. Whether or not it would do so depended upon the esprit of its workers and managers. Its relationship with the state would, however, be determined by the state itself during the Cold War era. Regardless of the internal philosophy of EDF, it would be only relatively autonomous from the state and the private sector. The textures of changing political conjunctures and the internal life of the firm would define the character of that relative autonomy. EDF was cast in a leftist mold and it was immediately to face formidable enemies.

CHAPTER 3

The French State and
EDF's Corporate Culture,
1946–1954

Électricité de France emerged in the spring of 1946 amidst a wave of enthusiasm within the electrical power sector. Workers were excited to see that they could shape the daily life and help determine the long-term direction of the firm. Indeed, the head of their largest trade union, Marcel Paul, essentially laid the political groundwork for the enterprise, and the workers expected immense sociopolitical gains for themselves and for the working class as a whole. As workers in a pilot firm dedicated to building a renovated France, EDF personnel felt both a deep sense of joy and a strong sense of responsibility to make the nationalization succeed. Managers, engineers, and technicians felt a similar sense of enthusiasm and responsibility, to which was added a sense of liberation within their own careers. As technocrats, they would no longer be constrained by the demands of profitability as they framed and executed their ambitious technical and productivist tasks. Managers and workers also saw the emergence of an EDF family, a community that was to be reinforced daily by collective participation in building a new France. The EDF family not only shared work time as a productive community, but by dint of the massive social programs sponsored by the personnel-operated Conseil Central des Oeuvres Sociales (CCOS), EDF personnel were to be trained in EDF schools, dine in EDF cafeterias, spend their leisure time in EDF vacation resorts, and live in EDF-subsidized communities. EDF was to become a new form of convivial "total institution."

The euphoria was very brief. In the midst of a nation rent by deep financial problems and raging inflation, EDF was soon plagued by a systematic campaign against it by more moderate external forces. EDF was created at the height of a period of legalistic leftism in France and it was only a matter of time before a renascent Right would have the power to attack almost all of EDF's important aspects, from the strong workers' presence within the firm, to the generous salary and benefit programs, to the expansionist visions of the EDF community, and finally to its very autonomy as a modern enterprise. The EDF family nonetheless stood firm, buttressing its internal unity and defending itself from attack by a strategy of proof by production, showing the nation that the nationalization was an incontestable success. The logic of proof by production helped to rebuild the workplace hierarchy within the firm and to reduce workers' shop-floor power. Yet even as the era of besiegement waned in 1953, the internal solidarity of the EDF family survived.

"La belle france que nous allons faire . . . "

"The beautiful France that we are going to make"—so said Marcel Paul to Pierre Simon, the cabinet's choice as president and director-general of the new EDF, in April of 1946, as he described his vision of the new firm. Workers, managers, and private sector capitalists were to cooperate in creating a France that was to be more socially egalitarian, more democratic, more productive, and more modern. The centerpiece of a new France was to be the new, high-technology electrical utility, leaving its permanent mark on the landscape of France with its mammoth dams taming powerful rivers and its massive power transmission lines tying all of French society together in a common path to the future.

In the opinion of many, Pierre Simon was just the man to guide the enormous task that lay ahead. For the neoliberals, his experience as a top manager of the Durand utility guaranteed that EDF would be run responsibly and with due attention to the balance sheet. Simon also enjoyed strong union support and could expect acquiescence in a period that demanded hard work and low pay. For the Communist leadership of the CGT (Fédération de l'Éclairage), Simon first had proven himself by advocating hydroelectricity in the 1930s, when the rest of the industry eschewed it. Then, in 1939, when the Communists within Éclairage were excluded from union positions, Simon met with them and vowed to remain in close contact.[1] Finally, as a badge of political legitimacy, Simon, who had been appointed director of electricity by the Popular Front, was fired from that post by the Vichy government. Simon assumed his post voluntarily without pay and promised Marcel

[1] René Gaudy, *Et la lumière*, p. 140.

Paul that if the workers struck against EDF, he would promptly resign. Without reservations, Paul consented to a no-strike pledge.[2]

Pierre Simon set up the basic administrative structure for EDF, with directorates for operations (including production, transmission, and distribution), equipment, personnel, research and development and administration (the general directorate). Simon chose many top Durand managers as his direct associates because of their common working experiences and because the ex-Messine managers were distrusted by the rank-and-file electrical workers. There were a few exceptions: Pierre Massé and Pierre Ailleret, both of the Messine group, took the directorships of the equipment section and the research and development section. Roger Lescuyer, Paul's top administrative aide, took the post of secretary-general, essentially the head of internal administration. Simon and Lescuyer symbolized the esprit of the firm itself: Simon, the progressive manager, and Lescuyer, the militant unionist and leader of the Fédération Nationale des Communes Concédants et Régies (FNCCR), who could guarantee a connection between Paris and the provinces. With few exceptions, the initial top managers were almost entirely from the Corps des Ponts et Chaussées, excluding their higher-ranked classmates from the École Polytechnique, the Corps des Mines. In those halcyon days of "la belle France," Paul even invited Roger Boutteville, Vichy's top electrical power technocrat, into EDF management, but Boutteville declined, preferring to join a major electrical equipment firm. The only overt exclusion from EDF was that of Jean Dupin, a top Messine manager and a head of the Pechiney aluminum group, who had openly disavowed the legitimacy of the nationalization.[3]

The first EDF board of directors echoed the specific political conjuncture of April 1946 (Appendix fig. A4). Among the state representatives were F.-L. Closon, the director of the census (and later the director of France's national economic and statistics agency), who reflected the new attention to mathematical rigor among the modernizers; Léon Delfosse, the Communist head of the CGT miners' federation; and Paul Abeloos, a high functionary of the Ministry of Public Works, who had considerable experience in negotiating public works projects. Among the consumer representatives were the two leaders of the FNCCR, Georges Gilberton and Alexis Jaubert, three Communist mayors (also FNCCR members), and Eugène Roy, a former Resistance activist and owner of the Longwy steelworks. Paul chose three militants of the GNC, two from Éclairage and one from the CFTC, to represent

---

[2] Interview with Pierre Simon, cited in *Énergies* 799 (26 March 1971), 19.
[3] *Le Monde*, 9–10 June 1946.

the personnel, thus entirely excluding any representative of the UNCM, which was generally viewed as collaborationist and opposed to the nationalization. As self-conscious progressives, the first board members soon tried to break from the conservative traditions of French industrial management.

The new directors and board broadly defined EDF's new territory and powers. Pierre Grezel, an ex-Durand manager who became director of operations, combined the 86 electrical transport firms, 1,150 distribution firms, and 154 production firms and literally thousands of separate concessions into one system in less than a year. Jacques Rigolot, a Durand man, performed the immense task of combining the accounts of the old companies. The board of directors boldly used Article 19 of the nationalization law to annul twenty-three of sixty-three existing equipment contracts, which constituted 60 percent of outstanding contract values. The new EDF managers saw these contracts as sweetheart deals, which often included exhorbitant cost-plus provisions, between utilities and subsidiaries of equipment manufacturers.[4] Similarly, the board of directors tried to break a number of below-cost rate contracts between old utilities and many bulk industrial users, only to be blocked by the Price Controls Bureau and the courts. The board expansively interpreted Article 8 of the nationalization law and thus decided that only EDF could build new power plants, even those under the capacity floor of 12 million kwh and those in direct association with rail and coal-mining activities.[5] Robert Lacoste, the new minister of industry, soon reversed the action. Article 15 of the nationalization law forced EDF to return its nonutility assets to the successor firms, yet on recognizing the extent to which the former utilities had emptied their cash and depreciation reserves, the board decided that EDF should deduct such funds from returnable assets under Article 15. Finally, wary of the dangers of *étatisation* inherent in accepting government subsidies, a number of board members refused direct capital subsidies from the state.

EDF never decentralized distribution services as Article 23 of the nationalization law required. Neoliberals and provincials supported decentralization as a way to avoid economic and managerial gigantism. Instead, in cooperation with Gaz de France, EDF created an internal administrative decentralization that allowed the joint distribution services to share the twenty-five regional and local offices of their predecessors, yet real control stayed with EDF and GDF offices in Paris. Decentralization schemes that would have reduced EDF-GDF control

---

[4] CAPV 8 (18 October 1946), and EDF, *Rapport d'activité et comptes de gestion, 1946–1949* (Paris: EDF, 1950), p. 23.
[5] CAPV 2 (16 May 1946).

were opposed by technocratic managers and the CGT for technical and political reasons. Along with the CFTC, the CGT feared that a plethora of distribution *régies* would fragment the utility work force, 60 percent of whom worked in distribution services. Roger Lescuyer clearly set forth Éclairage's deepest reservations in a letter to Marcel Paul.

> The creation of these [local *régies*] would create a number of bases for [the Socialists], which they would not hesitate to use for their own base political ends.
>
> In effect, the so-called public distribution establishments would hire and supervise a large labor force; moreover, [they could implement] a rate-making system that would serve their own political propaganda without having to worry about the resulting deficits, for EDF would pick up the tab.
>
> In the Political Bureau [of the Communist Party] we concluded that to accept the public distribution establishments would amount to offering our enemies a method for isolating us politically via their economic policy [and to giving them] major financial resources; these funds would undoubtedly be used against us by all of the bourgeois political parties, including the Socialists.[6]

Representatives of the FNCCR (and later from the anti-CGT union Force Ouvrière) had elicited a promise from the front office that the EDF-GDF control would be only temporary.[7] However, EDF's temporary control over distribution gradually became permanent. All of the ministers of industry up through the mid-1950s allied with EDF managers and the two major unions at EDF to keep control over distribution centralized, though few agreed with the CGT's motives. The CGT did agree with the ministers' assumption that technical and economic efficiency required centralization. Despite their formal authority, Socialist and centrist deputies and FNCCR representatives on the EDF board could not force EDF to surrender its power.[8] Finally, in 1957, the cabinet created consultative committees parallel to the twenty-five "provisional" regional distribution centers. EDF largely ignored the new bodies.

[6] Lescuyer to Paul, 30 January 1958, CGT-FNE archives, dossier 18/4: "Sabotage nationalisation."

[7] CAPV 12 (7 February 1947).

[8] FNCCR, "Allocution du Président Jaubert, Compte rendu du XIIIe Congrès," *Bulletin d'Information* (August 1948), 16. Jaubert said that the Direction Générale "show[ed] deep hatred for the distribution services even before they existed." G. Gilberton and Jaubert both hotly protested the modes of consultation used when circulating the *régie* proposals in the provinces, and Gilberton went so far as to term the procedures "undemocratic," particularly since an absence of response from a collectivity was counted as a vote approving the plan; CAPV 50 (25 May 1950).

Centralized control over distribution detached managerial responsibility from local services. EDF operated a dual system of services, one owned by the pre-1946 *régies* (which delivered only 5 percent of all power) and one owned by EDF. Without coherent representation on the board of directors, domestic users often felt that their interests were slighted. Early EDF and Plan Commission technocrats' penchant to concentrate on production facilities and industrial supply compounded the problem. Distribution was simply too tedious and lacking in grandeur to be of interest, and EDF's modernization strategy called for building production and transmission facilities before reinforcing distribution. When capital funds were short, distribution investment programs usually saw the deepest cuts.[9]

Electrical workers and cadres were rapidly integrated into the new, unified system of job rankings. On the national level, Paul, Simon, and Roger Gaspard, the director of electricity in 1946 and Simon's choice for assistant director-general, sat behind closed doors and decided which cadres from the old firms to retain and which to retire, resulting in 3,522 retirements.[10] Simon appointed the provincial distribution center managers with the aid of the FNCCR. Local Éclairage stewards met with the new managers and integrated blue-collar workers into the new job structure. Much to their dismay, representatives from the CFTC were usually excluded from the process.[11] The CFTC was also initially closed out of some of the codeterminist personnel bodies, but Paul and Simon rapidly respected their demands, and the CFTC received its share of seats soon thereafter.[12]

The keystone of the new system of labor relations at EDF was a direct association between workers and managers and close cooperation between EDF and the private sector. On both counts, the CGT willingly cooperated. Not only did Paul give a no-strike pledge to Simon in the earliest months of EDF's existence, but Le Brun accepted the principle

[9] In the 1950s, the distribution grid was so insufficient that line losses on it grew at twice the rate of the growth in actual consumption. See EDF, *Rapport d'activité et comptes de gestion, 1951* (Paris: EDF, 1952), p. 49; in the Mayenne district in 1951, of twenty-five thousand farms, only seven thousand had electrical services; see Georgette Elgey, *La république des contradictions, 1951–1954* (1968), p. 11. EDF admitted in its publicity brochure, "Dix ans d'efforts" (Paris: EDF, 1957), p. 17, that it had slighted distribution. Even into the 1960s, though power was available in all communes, the system capacity was low.

[10] Many of those pensioned off had been opponents of the nationalization, and the generous retirement provisions of the *statut* helped to quiet the opposition of the retirees; interview by author with Roger Gaspard, Paris, 3 June 1981. See also CAPV 23 (31 October 1947).

[11] Interview by author with Yves Morel, CFTC representative on the EDF board of directors, 1948–1968, at his home in Embrun, 17 July 1981.

[12] Fédération CFTC des Services Publics et Concédés, *Exprès* 18 (26 April 1946).

of pegging pay increases to productivity,[13] and even went so far as to accept the notion that "industrial rates must not go beyond a certain level that would hinder the national recovery."[14] The CGT/GNC also supported an equipment strategy that had EDF cover the costs of reconstructing and modernizing the electrical equipment sector through the high prices it paid for equipment—provided that deliveries were made as soon as possible.[15]

The CGT led efforts to keep wages from increasing EDF's operating expenses. When state employees' salaries were increased in January 1946, Éclairage kept its demands far lower than the increases granted to the state workers and below the rate of inflation. The above-average pay levels of May 1946 at EDF were outstripped by higher wages in other industries by July of the same year while prices rose over 30 percent.[16] The CGT also helped to trim the EDF work force by 8.6 percent between the time of the nationalization and March 1948. Productivity and real salaries at EDF fell steadily between 1946 and 1948.[17] By 1949, letters from local managers flooded the EDF front office, complaining that the low pay had caused a widespread malaise among the workers.[18] By February 1949, EDF found it difficult to recruit and retain cadres because the pay was considerably better in private industry. In return for the CGT's rigorous cooperation with the front office, the board of directors often backed the workers' wage demands, even when domestic tensions over the Cold War peaked. Finally, attentive to the Communists' "battle of production," the CGT/GNC accepted frequent fifty- to sixty-hour workweeks and the use of temporary workers. The CGT and GNC led the battles to cut absenteeism and operating costs, even when the cuts entailed a systematic degradation of living standards.

Cost cutting, even in the face of eroding real salaries, was a key part of the cooperative relationship that unions sought to create between workers and managers. The codeterminist bodies set up by the labor *statut* were the centerpiece of this strategy. For management and the CGT, comanagement offered the means to cut costs and to cement

[13] Agreement between Éclairage and Direction Générale, 11 June 1947, formalized in Personnel Memo 82, of 17 June 1947.

[14] Éclairage circular of 26 July 1946.

[15] *Deuxième rapport de la Commission de Vérification des Comptes des Entreprises Publiques*, p. 24, cited in Monique Maillet-Chassagne, *L'influence*, pp. 194–95. See also EDF/GDF, "Rapport sur l'activité d'EDF et de GDF depuis la nationalisation" (31 March 1948), p. 39.

[16] CFTC Circulaire 27, August 1946, Hennebicq papers, CFDT archives, Paris.

[17] The fall in productivity was largely the arithmetic result of booking considerable new interest charges (associated with the buy out and the new investments) into operating expenses as output grew only slowly.

[18] Morel in *Gaz-Électricité* 21 (July-August 1949).

unity within the firm. The CFTC hoped that the committees would help blue-collar workers rise within the firm by educating them in the modalities of management. Simon, a social technocrat and a leftist Catholic, saw the role of the committees in a much more radical light. In a speech to the first (and only) congress of works committee (CMP) delegates, Simon said: "In contrast to the spirit of routine, we must have a revolutionary spirit. Without a doubt, the workers can be very intelligent and can even escape their roles to become governmental ministers. Until now, there was a widespread tendency toward a separation between the roles of workers, who were to perform mechanical tasks, and managers, whose role was to define the methods of work. Today, that distinction is being suppressed. Under the old system, those who performed direct work were excluded from its conceptualization; today, we seek to associate the workers in that conceptualization." Lest one overestimate the revolutionary thrust of his views, he added: "One can sufficiently understand and judge only what is within his purview. Commit yourselves to address only those questions that you know fully. The top managers alone have the responsibility for the overall functioning of the service and they must exercise it fully."[19]

Comanagement reinforced productivist cooperation between workers and managers during the heroic period. Early in 1947, Éclairage even circulated a leaflet in EDF workplaces that urged workers to respect job hierarchies and to cease viewing EDF as their own, rather than the nation's, property.[20] As minister of industry, Paul could rely on labor's support as he strictly rationed power to domestic electrical users while allowing metallurgical and other industries to run at full tilt. In addition, if dam construction demanded the destruction of centuries-old villages, productivist logic allowed the trampling of peasants under the march of progress.[21]

Ironically, the height of class-blind productivism was attained after the onset of Cold War tensions. In the fall of 1948, Paul toured the Monnet Plan dam projects with J.-M. Louvel and a number of other influential private sector industrialists. In the publicity brochure produced after the tour, the collective authors vaunted the camaraderie

[19] "Extraits de l'allocution de M. Pierre Simon, Réunion des Comités d'Entreprises d'EDF du 26 février 1947," appendix 6 of FNCCR, Bulletin d'Information 100 (special, February 1973), 75–77.
[20] Cited in Robert Lacoste, "Liberté et production," France-Documents 9 (July 1947), 3.
[21] For a detailed case study of the flooding of an Alpine village by an EDF–Monnet Plan dam at Tignes, see Robert L. Frost, "The Flood of 'Progress': Technocrats and Peasants at Tignes (Savoie), 1946–1952," French Historical Studies 14:1 (Spring 1985), 117–40.

of the construction workers, who labored up to ninety-four hours per week as the pioneers of the emerging new France. At the Bort dam site, "in less than five years, men correct[ed] the work of millennia." Peasant resistance to the dams was written off simply as a result of "medieval fear and superstition." Heroic language underlined a vision of a classless social order: "Social barriers are abolished, unknown. The hierarchy exists, [it is] normal and natural, but as a function of value, competence, and love for the task ahead."[22] This brochure did more than buttress the significance of dams as icons of a new France; it was also devoted to the voluntaristic cooperation between workers and managers within EDF and between EDF and the private sector.

The informal reward for hard work, declining real salaries, long hours, and dutiful subservience was the system of personnel-operated cafeterias, vacation centers, and living communities that EDF had inherited from its predecessors and continued to build. These aspects of the EDF community became almost inescapable for the personnel. Inside and outside the workplace, EDF became a total institution, even to the point of encouraging the sons of EDF workers to work there. A heroic notion of the new relationship between workers and technology began to emerge. Protected against technologically induced layoffs by the *statut*, new technology did not represent a threat to employment security as it had in the past. Instead, it became an essential element in liberating the working class, for it positively revalorized workers' skills. Social technocrats were to break new paths to the high-tech future. A culture of high technology soon became a central ideational structure within EDF, and widespread adherence to it, reinforced by a prolabor front office, became the basis for a cohesive rapport within the firm. The culture of high technology was so powerful that in later years, when management abandoned its side of the social productivist partnership, the unions were loath to recognize its passing.

Financial Crises at EDF's Birth

When Pierre Simon assumed the directorship of EDF in April 1946, he found EDF's treasury entirely bereft of funds. Simon met with the director of the treasury and said, "I'm the head of the new power company, I guess you're my banker."[23] The Finance Ministry granted EDF enough funds to solve its cash flow crisis, but the money did not last long. Faced with the massive costs of the Monnet Plan projects

[22] Comité pour l'Équipement Électrique Français, *Cinq jours au pays du kilowatt* (1949), pp. 9, 40.
[23] Simon, cited in *Énergies* 799 (26 March 1971), 19.

and with rates that were too low to ensure solvency, EDF was deeply in debt.

Up to November 1947, the government tried to keep utility rates low in order to combat inflation and aid industrial recovery. As part of efforts to reduce inflationary pressures on the economy, the government had forced EDF to reduce its tariffs in late 1946. The government granted a rate increase in March 1947, only to rescind it in May. Simon immediately resigned in protest and Roger Gaspard replaced him as director-general. Rates were so low that by June 1947, average tariffs were 3.75 times 1938 levels, while salaries were at eight times 1938 levels, and construction costs were fifteen times higher.[24] A 53 percent rate hike in November 1947 sparked considerable social protest, but it was not enough to balance EDF's accounts, and a retroactivity clause in it gave the Conseil d'État cause to annul it. Lacoste continued Paul's policy of keeping power rates low, especially for industrial sectors critical to industrial recovery. By September 1948, EDF bought power from the Rhône Company's Génissiat hydroelectric plant at 1.8 francs per kwh, yet sold it at 0.6 francs per kwh to the electrochemical industry.[25] Rates were endemically so low that Raymond Villadier, EDF's financial director, was able to say in 1951 that EDF had helped to stabilize prices and "gave veritable subsidies to both industry and individuals."[26] The government refused to allow any tariff increase between October 1948 and April 1951, despite considerable inflation in that period.

As successive cabinets moved to the right after mid-1947, the government's rationale for the low-rate policy lost its basis. The emerging "free market" policy implied that EDF would be allowed to increase its rates enough to permit EDF to finance its equipment program, yet the government still forbade rate hikes. Ramadier cut the subsidies allotted to EDF's equipment budget by 10 percent in 1948. Ten thousand workers who had been employed at EDF's building sites were furloughed. The government had to make difficult policy decisions, but Ramadier echoed the financial press in asserting that France had to "guard against a costly overequipping of the electrical power sector."[27] Power rationing continued.

[24] *Vie Française*, 20 June 1947.
[25] *Perspectives*, 23 September 1948.
[26] *Le Figaro*, 28 September 1951.
[27] Marcel Paul, "Les nationalisations," p. 845. In his position, Ramadier was actually further to the right than Louvel, who defended the Monnet Plan equipment program. Louvel himself ran into resistance when faced with Minister of Finance Petsche's call for further cuts in Monnet Plan spending. In response to Louvel's position, Petsche echoed Ramadier in saying, "would you prefer to allow France to die from overbuilding than to permit six billion francs in savings?" *JO, dp*, 24 September 1948.

The state would not permit EDF any measures to solve the firm's financial problems. In addition, EDF had to cover the endemic operating losses of Gaz de France. EDF's only recourse was to high-interest, short- and medium-term bank loans. The Bank of France and other banks refused overdraft protection for EDF greater than 5 billion francs until 1949, even though EDF had an annual cash flow of 120 billion francs and 30 billion francs' worth of accounts receivable.[28] The inevitable result was snowballing debt, the carryover of debts from year to year, and a dubious ability to pay outstanding debts. Many top EDF managers understood that the bankers' opposition was ideologically motivated, fueled by spite against a state firm that had, according to conservatives, despoiled legitimate investors.[29]

France began to receive Marshall Plan aid from the United States in 1948. EDF's share of that year's funding (67.1 billion francs) and the next year's (97.3 billion francs) went largely toward refinancing old debts incurred by EDF and its predecessors.[30] Indeed, debt service costs throughout the 1950s commanded an ever-increasing share of EDF's operating income.[31] In addition, as EDF needed to install more equipment each year, its volume of new debt continued to rise. By the 1950 operating year, EDF paid combined finance and indemnity charges of 20.6 billion francs, while its total labor costs were only 56 percent higher than that, at 32.1 billion francs.[32]

The financing problem raised several important issues. EDF faced three possible avenues for funding new projects: rate increases, state subsidies, and bonded debt, yet all of these had potentially negative repercussions. Rate hikes were politically unpopular because domestic increases alienated the public, and industrial increases might have hindered modernization efforts. State subsidies potentially fueled inflation by implicitly expanding the money supply, and they reproduced the vertical inequality of France's regressive tax structure. EDF often had to sell new bonds to repay older bonds. State subsidies would have been the best financial solution, but the political and economic preconditions for them—a restructuring of the tax burden and a halt in inflation—remained elusive.

The debt crisis made EDF vulnerable to attacks from the conservative

---

[28] EDF, *Comptes et rapport, 1946–49*, p. 74.

[29] Martine Bungener, "L'électricité et les trois premiers plans: Une symbiose réussie," in Henry Rousso, ed., *De Monnet à Massé*, pp. 110–12 and 114.

[30] *Comptes et rapport, 1946–49*, p. 74.

[31] There was one exception to this rule: in 1957, the government forgave one-third of EDF's debt to the French state. This subsidy helped to drop EDF's indebtedness temporarily, but by 1960, such debts returned to their 1957 levels.

[32] Philippe Empis, "Les aspects financiers d'Électricité de France," *Nouvelle revue de l'économie contemporaine* (March 1950), 10.

press. It was easy to document the financial problems of EDF, yet it took a large measure of dishonesty to attribute those problems to incompetent management or to the entire nationalization experiment. Once EDF's financial problems became obvious, the conservative press had endless ammunition with which to attack EDF. Paul Reynaud, a moderate who became minister of finance in August 1948, termed the entire nationalized sector a "machine for losing money."[33] Though denationalization remained impossible, many conservatives believed that a successful press campaign could at least chip away some of EDF's profitable activities and make EDF managerial practices more conventional and probusiness. Such attempts began in 1947, as did attacks on Communists within EDF.

Labor Power under Siege

Historians typically mark the beginning of actions against Communists in the nationalized sector with the elections of November 1946, and the ousting of Communists from the government in May 1947.[34] Measures at EDF had features in common with anti-Communist campaigns elsewhere, but those at EDF were counterbalanced by the persistence of the Communist–social technocratic alliance, actions of mutual defense between the CGT and the front office, and the unflagging loyalty of the CGT to the firm. Though the purges caused a number of profound changes at EDF, particularly with respect to Communist power at the top of the firm, CGT and GNC influence in the daily life of EDF survived.[35] The failure of the campaigns to root out the Communists allowed the social technocratic and productivist alliance within the firm to continue. Most of the social gains of the nationalization were preserved, but the purges fostered an isolation of EDF from the neoliberal private sector and state. At the same time, the productivist

[33]Cited in L'Observateur, 14 June 1951.

[34] This chronology is presented for the Charbonnages by Darryl Holter in "Miners," and by the CGT/GNC in René Le Guen, Voyage.

[35] Gaspard, general director of EDF at the time, contended that the purges were "relatively insignificant" (interview by author with Gaspard, Paris, 3 June 1981); Yves Morel, CFTC militant and board of directors member at the time, affirmed Gaspard's position (interview by author with Morel at Embrun, 17 July 1981); Louis Puiseau, a GNC militant at the time, concurred with that position (interview by author with Puiseau, Paris, 18 February 1981). Only the past and current militants of the GNC and of Éclairage claim that the purges were a major break in the history of EDF. Roger Pauwels, lifelong CGT militant and board of directors member, supported that position (interview by Michel Beltran with Pauwels, 13 January 1981, and interview by author with Pauwels, Pantin, 23 June 1981); LeGuen, Voyage, pp. 134–43, makes a similar argument.

strategy helped build the bases on which a more conservative managerial milieu would later take power.

On the original board of directors named by Marcel Paul, nine of eighteen members were either in the Communist party or closely allied to it; similarly, on the Conseil Supérieure de l'Électricité et du Gaz, the majority of members were Communists or sympathetic to them. Marcel Paul was accused of having "packed" those bodies, though he had appointed a CFTC member and a number of technocratic experts to the EDF board and had designated Simon, decidedly a non-Communist, as chief executive officer.[36] Minister of Industry Robert Lacoste began to reshape the board by ousting Léon Delfosse in March 1947, yet the GNC and Éclairage remained publicly silent.

Throughout 1947 the Communists avoided conflicts with the government, even as salaries plummeted. When blue-collar electrical workers struck in May 1947, Paul encouraged GNC cadres not to strike and Éclairage tried to get the workers back on the job.[37] The CGT only halfheartedly participated in a nationwide strike wave in the fall, and CFTC and UNCM members continued to work. Contrary to accusations by the Socialists, the Communists were not preparing a coup and using the nationalized sector as a flash point. Indeed, Moch, by then the minister of interior, easily broke a December strike by bringing in a few naval engineers to Paris-region facilities, whence the strikers peaceably retreated.[38] Despite a public show of opposition, behind the closed doors of EDF board meetings, CGT representatives sought joint meetings between chiefs of local distribution centers and stewards in order to organize layoffs, and Le Brun urged collaborative efforts between EDF and the electrical equipment trade association. Finally, to ease the firm's financial crisis, Marcel Paul donated 700 million francs from the workers' social fund (CCOS) to the EDF treasury.[39]

The Communist line changed radically in September 1947 with the founding conference of the new international Communist organization, the Cominform. At that meeting, Soviet leaders lambasted their French comrades for cooperating too closely with the bourgeoisie and the

[36] Paul did not suggest Gaspard as EDF's first chief executive officer because the latter was "suspected by many [in the business community] of being a socialist" (Gaspard interview).

[37] In the EDF board meeting, Gaspard lauded the strikers' "moderation," and the board unanimously encouraged the government to accept the strikers' demands -- the atmosphere was such that Emile Pasquier, an Éclairage leader, asked the front office of EDF to set up a strike vote; CAPV 16 (27 May 1947).

[38] The strike was called for 1 December, but was broken by Moch the same night, much to the embarrassment of the Communists, who, expecting the strike to succeed, headlined L'Humanité on 2 December with the false news that the power and Métro in Paris were down owing to the victorious strike effort.

[39] CAPV 22 (26 September 1947), 25 (28 November 1947), and 45 (27 January 1949).

Socialists, and they ordered the PCF to oppose the government directly. The theoretical foundation of the new strategy was a conception of two irrevocably irreconcilable worlds, the popular-democratic Eastern bloc and the imperialist western bloc.[40] Cooperation between the PCF and any other political party in France became henceforth impossible. Ironically, this position mirrored the worldview emerging among non-Communists in the West: both sides eschewed any compromise.

The party's new line put Communists in the nationalized sector in an awkward position. The very existence of that sector had been a stunning victory for a political strategy that was suddenly branded as class collaborationist. Those within the nationalized sector could not credibly shun it as a part of the bourgeois state because nationalized firms were not classically bourgeois employers. Communists at EDF found their solution in targeting the state rather than the firm as the class enemy. While under attack, Communists sought stronger links with the EDF social technocrats, and when the Right and the Socialists attacked the CGT and EDF, the Communists posed as the productivist defenders of the beseiged citadel. For his reluctance to adapt fully to the harsh party line, Paul was compelled to pronounce a mea culpa in front of the PCF's twelfth party congress in April 1950, where he admitted that he had not seen the emerging community of interests between the state and the large corporations.[41]

The fall of 1947 marked the beginning of massive, unrelenting social agitation in France and a decisive break between Socialists and Communists. During the May strike, Prime Minister Ramadier had appealed to the Liberation esprit of the workers; in the fall, the Socialists replied with force.[42] The U.S. State Department and the American Federation of Labor (AFL) supported Socialist efforts against the Communists. In 1945, the AFL had sent Irving Brown to Paris to undermine Communist influence within the CGT. Brown distributed funds to anti-Communist trade unionists, including Éclairage's Clement Delsol, but Brown failed

[40] Philippe Robrieux, *Histoire intérieure*, pp. 224–40.

[41] Cited in *Énergie Électrique et Gaz* (FO electrical workers' journal for the Paris region), November 1949–March 1950; see also *Gaz-Électricité* 26 (April 1950) and *L'Humanité*, 5 April 1950.

[42] The government issued a back-to-work order against the May strikes, but Ramadier pleaded on the radio: "Do not go on strike. . . . I cannot believe that you would act in 1947, after the nationalization, as you did when the industry was still owned by the companies. You are no longer working for a boss, your labor no longer goes to fatten capitalist profits. You are at the direct service of the nation. . . . Your attitude would no longer be a threat to a boss, but it would be a blow directed against the nation and against the republic"; cited in Georges Lescuyer, *Le contrôle*, p. 105. Following the fall strikes, Force Ouvrière, the anti-Communist faction within the CGT (and a splinter union as of December 1947), even accused Gaspard of being a lackey of the Communists because of his support of the strike; leaflet of Force Ouvrière, June 1947, FNE archives, dossier: "Scission FO, 1947–1948."

to prevent the Communists from gaining control of the CGT. He felt that Éclairage was Communist-dominated.[43] AFL and State Department funds continued to support the anti-Communist faction, Force-Ouvrière (FO), and probably subsidized FO activists within EDF and their newsletter, *Bulletin Syndicale de Liaison*.

The State Department also encouraged the French government to act against the Communists. Though much of the documentation of American involvement in French internal affairs remains classified, there were probably pressures to oust Communists from the nationalized sector, a major recipient of American aid, after the Blum-Byrnes Accords of May 1946.[44] However, Washington did not simply pull anti-Communist puppet strings, as the Communists have often claimed. French anti-Communists had their own reasons for encouraging the purges. Anti-Communism was a means to outflank a rival political party, to diminish popular pressure for progressive income redistribution, which, many assumed, would hinder economic modernization, and to ensure that the modernized French economy would not stray too far from the realm of neoliberal capitalism.

In 1946 and 1947 FO tried to change the methods for delegate and steward selection and to rally opposition to the Communists' productivism by accusing Paul of protecting cadres and doing little on the wage issue.[45] With its political base among foremen and lower management, the FO faction accused Paul of circumventing intermediate authority by building an alliance between blue-collar workers and upper management.[46] FO activists worked with Socialists outside of EDF

[43] Irving Brown, "Report to Woll," 10 December 1945, secret memo to the AFL-CILR, April 1946, papers of Florence Thorne, AFL Director of Research, State Historical Society of Wisconsin, US MSS 117a/8a, box 16, file CILR, 1945, and Brown, "The CGT Convention," memo to the AFL-CILR, April 1946, Florence Thorne papers. For a discussion of Brown's activities in France more generally, see Ronald Radosh, *American Labor and U.S. Foreign Policy* (New York: Random House, 1969), pp. 308–26.

[44] See infra, discussion of the ouster of Le Brun and Pasquier from the EDF board in May 1950. Elgey, *La république*, p. 292, asserts that in May 1946, Blum had agreed with Secretary of State Byrnes that American relief would be linked to a major anti-Communist effort. Darryl Holter, "Politique charbonnière et guerre froide, 1945–1950," *Le Mouvement Social* 130 (January-March 1985), 33–53, points out a subtle double game played by the French government: recognizing that the Americans' political logic behind reconstruction aid was to counter Communist agitation with promises of prosperity, the French maintained the Communists within government positions in order to gain more aid and a better reparations package from Germany. See also Edward Rice-Maximin, "The United States and the French Left, 1945–1949: The View from the State Department," *Journal of Contemporary History* 19 (October 1984), 729–47.

[45] Letter, Delsol to Paul, 30 August 1947, and leaflet of FO faction, June 1947, Éclairage archives, dossier: "Scission FO, 1947–1948"; *Bulletin Syndical de Liaison*, 1 and 1bis (August-September 1947).

[46] FO leaflet, summer of 1947, Éclairage archives, dossier: "Scission FO, 1947–1948."

to lay the groundwork for the Socialists to disavow any alliance with the Communists and thus to open the way for systematic purges at EDF.

The Socialists had concrete reasons to break with the Communists. They feared that Communists were displacing them, particularly in the nationalized sector.[47] An anti-Communist campaign would isolate the Communists and allow the Socialists to ally with the Center and stay in power. The SFIO did not abandon its commitment to national economic management, but it did undermine the political basis for it by placing the alliance between social technocrats and Communists in jeopardy. Many Socialists followed Jules Moch as he evolved from a social technocrat to a neoliberal anti-Communist.

While PCF officials may well have initiated the strikes of autumn 1947 in order to create a political crisis, Communists within EDF opposed such a strategy because they feared that it would only strain the delicate unity within the firm. Nonetheless, fearing that Communists had initiated strikes within the nationalized sector in preparation for a coup, President of the Republic Vincent Auriol ordered Lacoste to oust Communists from the nationalized firms' boards.[48] As a first step, the Socialist labor minister recognized the tiny (5 percent support) UNCM as a legitimate union at EDF. In December 1947, Lacoste ousted three Communist or pro-Communist consumer representatives and replaced a GNC member (Claude Deluche) with a UNCM member (Ambroise Cornat). The CGT remained publicly silent.[49] In addition, representatives of the Finance Ministry on the board began to attack the codeterminist personnel board, the CSNP, a bastion of CGT power. Gaspard defended the CSNP as the CGT quietly offered to limit its powers.

Formalizing the split in the CGT, Force Ouvrière held its founding congress in December 1947. Lacoste responded immediately, appointing Émile Peyras (FO) to replace John Ottaway (GNC) on the board in April 1948, before the degree of support for FO at EDF had been determined. The CGT protested verbally, but it did not organize any work actions. Lacoste then lent his support to a UNCM lawsuit against Paul's decree that had created the first EDF board. The Conseil d'État responded favorably and suspended the board in June 1948. Lacoste

---

[47] *Lumière CPDE socialiste* (March 1947), newsletter of Paris-region Socialist gas and electrical workers.

[48] Vincent Auriol, *Mon septennat* (1974), p. 585.

[49] The CFTC joined the CGT's protest within the board against the appointment of Cornat, for the UNCM had recently not only attacked EDF in the press, it had red-baited both the CGT and the CFTC; CAPV 26 (18 December 1947).

then ousted the three remaining CGT representatives and André Cold-ers (CFTC) as well.[50] With the EDF board in indefinite recess, Lacoste began to reshape the EDF front office. The point of hottest contention was Lacoste's firing of Lescuyer.[51] Lescuyer was generally viewed as the "eye of Moscow" within EDF, and UNCM supported Lacoste's action, claiming that Lescuyer had "exhibited a partisan [i.e., pro-Communist] spirit in his functions as Secretary-General."[52] Gaspard tried to replace Lescuyer with an anti-CGT cadre, but the CGT pro-tested, so Gaspard withdrew the appointment and abolished the post.

Lacoste seriously underestimated EDF's internal unity when he au-thored a pair of decrees in September 1948, one ordering the state to take control of the workers' social fund (then controlled by the CGT majority in the EDF work force) and the other immediately cutting the EDF work force by 10 percent. Backed by Gaspard and the front office, the CGT and CFTC responded with sporadic work stoppages, power cuts, and demonstrations, forcing Lacoste to rescind the decrees.[53] Later in 1948, Lacoste had to reconstitute the board to include three Communists and André Colders (CFTC), who then retired and gave his seat to Yves Morel, one of the CFTC's most progressive leaders. Lacoste could not purge EDF as he had the coal industry, and further actions had to wait until the Cold War deepened. Nonetheless, in reappointing the board, Lacoste replaced progressives Etienne Audi-bert and F.-L. Closon with financially conservative Louis Escallier and Didier Gregh as state representatives on the board.

The CGT still tried to reinforce solidarity within EDF by urging the board to pass resolutions supporting EDF's autonomy and the labor *statut*, and it won Gaspard's support in resolving that the nationali-zation law and the *statut* were inextricably tied.[54] To anti-Communists, this proved that EDF was dominated by a party-controlled union, and that Gaspard and the front office were patsies of the Communists. The

[50] Letter, Lacoste to Paul, 14 June 1948, Éclairage archives, dossier: "Discrimination anti-syndicale."

[51] Transcript of interview by Alain Beltran with Roger Pauwels, supplied by Pauwels, used with permission.

[52] *UNCM Bulletin*, 15 March 1948. Lescuyer was probably a fairly hard-nosed Com-munist within EDF—Pierre Massé referred to him as "the eye of Moscow" (*Aléas*, p. 90); Alice Saunier-Sëité, a future minister of universities who worked directly under Lescuyer at that time, made similar allegations; see Jean Choffel, *Seule, une femme: Alice Saunier-Sëité* (1979), pp. 15–16.

[53] The work-force reduction excluded any consultation between the government, the front office, the EDF board, and the CSNP; *Le Monde*, 16, 19, 21, and 30 September 1948. According to Ernest Anzalone, a CFTC activist at the time, the October 1950 decrees were merely a pretense for further purges; interview by author with M. Anzalone, EDF offices, Paris, 23 March 1981. See *Gaz-Électricité* 16–18 (September-November 1948), for an exhaustive discussion of the movement resisting the decrees.

[54] CAPV 31 (14 January 1949).

Socialists therefore sought to strengthen state controls over EDF because "when the disasterous political strikes have broken out as a result of the calls of the Cominform, they have faced . . . powerless directors who sacrifice everything out of a fear of losing popularity."[55] FO made similar accusations.[56] During this period, real wage levels were declining rapidly, and mandatory overtime was still more the rule than the exception.[57] Consequently, EDF was having trouble attracting new workers and retaining old ones. Gaspard and the front office thus had incentives to back union demands, often in opposition to the state representatives on the board. The CGT allied with the front office against the board, thereby undercutting the power of the board itself.

The GNC tried to implement innovative managerial strategies while it was on the EDF board. Early in 1949, Le Brun proposed issuing bonds upon which interest would be paid in free electricity. The board rejected the idea, only to have the finance minister approve it later, at which time the board conveniently forgot the source of the plan.[58] When the government announced cuts in the EDF equipment program in April 1949, the majority of the board went along while the CGT led the resistance against the cuts. The CGT's resistance attracted the support of other unions and successfully restored the program.[59] Finally, Le Brun circumvented EDF's top managers and consulted directly with EDF's equipment contracting section in order to find ways to cut capital spending without reducing equipment programs, primarily through a closer cooperation between EDF and its ts suppliers. The board and front office sharply criticized Le Brun for circumventing their prerogatives.[60]

Sensing its own isolation during 1949, the CGT tried to draw EDF into its political ghetto. In 1948–49, the CGT defended EDF's autonomy, but shifted toward noncooperation and rivalry with the private sector. The CGT thus noisily protested when Henri Lafond, a major big business figure, was appointed to the board in October 1949, though Paul's own nationalization law required the appointment. Relations between the CGT and the board continued to degrade throughout 1949 and 1950, often deteriorating into shouting matches between GNC and state representatives. The friction encouraged the state representatives to

[55] *Le Populaire*, 21 July 1949.
[56] *Lumière et Force* 7 (April 1949).
[57] By April 1949, real wages were 14 percent below 1914 levels (*Gaz-Électricité* 22 [April 1949]), and by April 1950, they were only 58 percent of 1938 levels (transcript of Éclairage and GNC press conference of 3 April 1950, Éclairage archives, dossier 2/4: "Tarifs EDF-GDF").
[58] CAPV 32 and 40 (4 February and 22 July 1949).
[59] CAPV 35 and 36 (6 April and 25 April 1949).
[60] CAPV 45 (27 January 1950).

demand the removal of the CGT once and for all. Thus, by the spring of 1950, with the exception of tepid support from the CFTC and the front office, the CGT was isolated, making it an easy target for the next round of purges.

A disastrous strike in March 1950 and the end of a Socialist presence in the cabinet fueled a second wave of purges. By that time, EDF salary levels had become untenable. All the unions struck initially, but UNCM, FO, and CFTC leaders ordered their members back to work after only a few days when faced with a back-to-work order and a clearly regressive settlement offer. The proposed agreement cut the maximum seniority bonus from 60 percent to 40 percent of current pay, deprived many retirees of inflation protection, and vaguely promised that wages would be tied to productivity increases. The CGT argued that the wage-productivity link was an empty promise on which the government would renege (which it did). The CGT stayed out for several weeks and became entirely isolated, fighting a lonely and losing battle and heightening political tensions.

In May 1950, the French government was deeply in debt, in part because of its rearmament program and its war in Vietnam. Ratings on state bonds were so low that the government enviously eyed EDF's better credit as a channel for raising more money. The Finance Ministry therefore allowed EDF to sell 15 billion francs in bonds, yet the government actually received half of the proceeds. EDF thus issued 15 billion francs' worth of EDF bonds, when in truth, it was acting as guarantor of 7.5 billion francs for itself and 7.5 billion francs for the government. It was a case of securities fraud and Gaspard later admitted it as such.[61] The CGT publicized the fraud, for which they were soundly chastized by the board and threatened with sanctions.[62] Five days later, Minister of Industry Louvel removed Le Brun and Pasquier, leaving Jules Plicault as the only CGT representative on the board.[63]

[61] Gaspard interview.

[62] CAPV 49 (12 May 1950). The CGT's position, that the Vietnam War was a costly diversion from the reconstruction and modernization, formed the ideological basis for its opposition to the modalities of the bond issue. This point of view was even shared by the highly technocratic *Revue Française de l'Énergie* (hereafter, *RFE*) in an editorial, "Réarmement et Plan Monnet," 15 (December 1950), ii, which argued that the diversion of state funds into the war helped to forestall France's program of constructing a modern economic infrastructure.

[63] Plicault stayed on the board for another three years. It remains a mystery why Plicault had not been removed as well, for he had taken the same position as Le Brun and Pasquier. He wrote a letter to Escallier on the twentieth, daring Escallier to oust him; Escallier did not take up the challenge; Éclairage archives, dossier: "Révocation de Le Brun et Pasquier." The CGT initiated judicial action against the revocations and even elicited testimony from Louvel, but the procedures did not bear fruit until 1958, with a decision in favor of the CGT; report from Éclairage attorney Le Seuer, 15 February 1958,

Whether the bond sale imbroglio was intended as a provocation to the CGT is unclear; for the Right, it was certainly a happy coincidence. The fact that the the 8 May 1950 issue of *Newsweek* reported the removal of Le Brun and Pasquier before it happened indicates that Bidault had told Americans of his plan even before informing the EDF board. *L'Observateur* placed the affair within the context of similar purges at the Charbonnages and France's Atomic Energy Commission. In regard to the bond issue itself, *L'Observateur* wrote: "The maneuver was a little grotesque. Being unable to borrow the money itself (what French citizen would be willing to furnish money to the government to fight the war in Indochina?), the government reserved half of EDF's bond money for itself. . . . It would be a matter of decency to inform the bond subscribers that half of their money will go for something far different from electrical equipment."[64] The conservative press fully backed the government. *Le Figaro* noted the CGT's opposition to the bond issue, but not its circumstances, and invited the government to oust the CGT: "what will the government be forced to do to end this inadmissible duplicity?"[65] The financial press generally did not mention the incident except under the usual rubrics of bond issue announcements.

The GNC was henceforth without any representation on the board, even though it represented about 55 percent of the cadres, engineers, and technicians at EDF. Éclairage (which then represented about 75 percent of the blue-collar and office workers) had Plicault on the board, but Éclairage had him abstain in all votes on the board. This represented the zenith of the "two worlds" conception—to the Communists, the bourgeoisie itself had proven that the worlds were irreconcilable, and it was certainly not the duty of Communists to help make capitalism operate better.

The state also attacked codeterminist institutions in which the CGT enjoyed considerable power. In May 1950, Louvel decreed rule changes that gave managers the final say on the CSNP and secondary personnel commissions, made many of the commission's decisions advisory, and prohibited inferiors from judging superiors. The CGT nonetheless continued to enjoy some power where sympathetic managers sat on the commissions. However, comanagement was seriously undermined, because once the CSNP had become largely advisory, management ceased to take it seriously.[66] In a similar vein, the press attacked the CCOS as a Communist-run war chest. Paul Reynaud wrote in 1949:

---

idem. Regardless of the legal decision, de Gaulle soon afterward decided to allow CGT representatives back onto the board.

[64] *L'Observateur* 7 (25 May 1950).
[65] *Le Figaro*, 18 May 1950.
[66] *Le Monde*, 20 February 1951.

"Électricité and Gaz de France, this company [sic] which costs us so much and enlightens us so little, has a deficit of 26 billion [francs]. But Marcel Paul can receive 600,100,000 [francs] for his workers' social welfare program and use it to set up hunting trips for the personnel and to buy an island in the Marne near Champigny, where priviliged couples can take nature hikes."[67] EDF's most renowned Communist, Marcel Paul, was president of the CCOS, and the CCOS board could hire, fire, and discipline the 290 CCOS workers independently from EDF.[68] Decrees in October 1950 ordered Paul to turn over lists of CCOS workers to EDF and to integrate those workers into the EDF personnel regime. Paul refused, claiming that the decree undermined the workers' control of the CCOS. The CGT called strikes in the Paris region, but interunion divisions caused them to fail.[69] The other unions urged Paul to turn over the lists, but he continued to refuse. During the early morning hours of 22 February 1951, a fully equipped riot squad descended upon the CCOS offices and forcibly took them over. It did not return to workers' control until 1964.

By mid-1951, the CGT was virtually absent from the formal positions of power it had once held. Informal CGT power prevailed at the local level and forestalled wide purging, despite the relatively autonomous power of local distribution-center chiefs. CGT records indicate only three or four cases of overt political discrimination on the local level.[70] Local anti-CGT discrimination was far more subtle. It usually involved the hiring of temporary nonunion workers and the use of non-EDF subcontractors. Subcontractors were often operated by old utility managers who had been excluded from EDF for political reasons. This created a politically docile parallel work force, just as the use of temporaries created an economically vulnerable group.

In the final analysis, anti-Communist actions destroyed the CGT's formal power, but it retained substantial influence in the daily life of

[67] Cited in Pierre Durand, *Marcel Paul*, p. 252.

[68] The Communist party did, however, consider the CCOS to be a party fief: during the 1950 party congress, Thorez mentioned to Auguste Lacoeur that the party needed better access to the CCOS and suggested that Léon Mauvais, an Éclairage member who sat on the Political Bureau of the party, replace Paul as CCOS chief. Lacoeur replied that Éclairage was one of the strongest pro-Communist unions and that it was somewhat of a fief in Paul's personal domain, and Paul was, he said, extremely popular at EDF. He therefore advised against the change, and his advice was heeded. See Robrieux, *Histoire intérieure*, vol. 2, p. 278.

[69] *Gaz-Électricité* 43 (October-November 1952).

[70] Éclairage archives, dossier: "Discrimination anti-syndicale." Most of the discrimination cases involved barriers to promotion, usually characterized by CGT members being passed over in favor of FO men. The lack of purging for simple membership did not exclude firings for supporting CGT work actions; in the 1950 strike, cadres were ordered to replace striking blue-collar workers; two cadres in the Valence district were fired for refusing to do so; see Le Guen, *Voyage*, p. 179.

the firm. Enjoying the support of the vast majority of blue-collar workers and a weak majority of cadres, Éclairage and the GNC were simply not going to disappear. CGT members continued to enjoy the normal rights of other EDF workers and were by no means excluded from promotions to top jobs at EDF. Nonetheless, as the board of Directors had been purged, so had the Conseil Supérieur de l'Électricité et du Gaz (CSEG) and the CSNP. The CGT held seven of nine seats on the CSNP in 1946, but after May 1950, it had only seven of thirteen seats. The survival of a CGT majority on the CSNP underscored the reluctance of EDF management to move against the CGT, particularly in light of the latter's continuing productivism and loyalty to the firm. However, the changes that did occur as a result of the Cold War meant the inclusion of UNCM and FO members in the CSNP and the CSEG, and those unions scarcely represented the interests of the blue-collar majority of EDF workers because both organizations were largely composed of foremen and cadres.[71]

Though the relations between the CGT and the front office were sometimes very acerbic, a basic community of interests survived. While the Center-Right attacked EDF during the Cold War era, the CGT staunchly defended a strong, productivist, and autonomous EDF. On the basis of mutual defense and proof by production, the internal alliance continued. The CGT later took its alliance with the front office for granted. Once united with management in a common culture and community of productivism and technology in the firm, the CGT failed to detect management's abandonment of the alliance after 1960. In the process, the CGT became essentially a tame company union and its centrality to the EDF community waned.

EDF under Attack

The leftist alliance within EDF correctly surmised that attacks against Communists were only part of a larger campaign against EDF itself. The onslaughts coincided with the return to power of the Center and Right during the Cold War era. Ironically, the anti-EDF campaign reached its zenith just as EDF was becoming broadly accepted by French society.[72] These attacks included attempts to increase indem-

[71] Emile Pasquier, "Note sur les discriminations dans les industries électriques et gazières," undated Éclairage memo, carbon copy, Éclairage archives, dossier: "Discrimination anti-syndicale."

[72] In the period up to 1950, the financial press was divided in its opinion of EDF; most journals reluctantly agreed that EDF management was competent but feared the influence of the Communists. With the exception of journalists in Switzerland, the financial press reluctantly began to accept the nationalization after the purges and the successful pro-

nities and the value of assets returnable to the private sector under Article 15, efforts to denationalize the peripheral activities of EDF, and measures to reduce EDF's massive hydroelectric construction campaign.

In 1948, EDF estimated its total indemnity bill at 70 billion francs.[73] Later campaigns to increase indemnities easily gained stockholders' support, though most had accepted the original indemnity plan.[74] Changes in the indemnification process thus hiked the indemnity costs to 96 billion francs.[75] A law in 1946 had forced EDF to cover war damage costs on nationalized utilities, and a law in 1948 raised the valuation coefficient for publicly-traded firms to 3.98 times 1938 stock values and provided for interim indemnities based on imputed asset values before

---

ductivity campaigns at EDF. *Bulletin Économique, L'Économie,* and *Tribune Économique* followed this pattern, as did *L'Information* and *Semaine Économique et Financière;* for synopses of business opinion in this respect, see in particular *L'Information,* 11 May 1951; *Les Documents CTEP,* 5 March 1948; and *Semaine Économique et Financière,* 16 July 1948. *Bulletin Économique,* 2 June 1947, and *Cahiers Français d'Information,* 15 June 1947, were almost alone among financial journals in fully backing EDF's position as the antinationalization campaign got underway in early 1947; *Bulletin Économique's* position had changed from its initial antinationalization stance of little more than a year earlier; see the issue of 14 March 1946. After the Cold War shake-up, the best presentation of sympathetic business opinion toward EDF is Philippe Empis, "Les aspects," pp. 6–12. Only once did a Swiss paper support the nationalizations, in a pair of articles by Raymond Aron in *Journal de Lausanne,* 8 and 11 June 1949. For more typical examples of the extremely negative response of the foreign financial press, see *Journal de Lausanne,* 28 February 1950; *Financial Times* (London), 20 September 1949; *Journal de Genève,* 8 October 1948; and *Gazette de Lausanne,* 29 October 1948. In the nonfinancial press, EDF's major defenders were, of course, the press of the CGT and Communists, but EDF also found support (albeit strongly anti-CGT and anti-Communist) in the left Christian Democratic *L'Aube* (2 November 1948) and *La Croix* (series of articles in May-June 1951), and in the Socialist *Le Populaire* (series of articles in mid-July 1949). The nonparty progressive press also lent support to EDF; see *Combat,* 24 September 1949, and *La Réforme,* 15 May 1948, in particular. The popular press opposing EDF was led by *Le Figaro,* with support from *Le Pays,* 20 March 1947; *Vie Française,* 20 June 1946; and *L'Aurore,* 22 March 1947. These journals often asserted that EDF was to be the flashpoint for a Communist revolt. Senator Chaladon repeated most of the assertions of the right-wing popular press in *Revue Politique et Parlementaire* (June 1949), but deleted allegations of an impending Communist coup. Marcel Ventenat's *L'expérience des nationalisations* (Paris, 1947) was the first book-length antinationalization tract, replete with coup rumors. Finally, Louis Baudin, André Armengaud, and Marcel Pellenc edited *Vingt ans de capitalisme d'état* (Paris: SPID, 1951), the most systematic rightist critique of the nationalizations. Henry Ehrmann, *Organized Business,* p. 252, found many of Pellenc's assertions to be doubtful.

[73] Électricité et Gaz de France, *Rapport sur l'activité d'EDF et de GDF depuis la nationalisation,* pamphlet (Paris: EDF/GDF Direction Financière, 31 March 1948), nonpaginated.

[74] For example, at the last shareholders' meeting at CPDE, there was no criticism of the system; *L'Information,* 8 December 1951. Upon the issuance of the first series of indemnity bonds, *Le Monde,* 21 January 1951, heralded them as a very good deal.

[75] Article 6 of a decree of 26 May 1952 (No. 52–601, *JO,* 27 May) set the total indemnity bill at 93 billion francs; *Recueil,* vol. 14, pp. 57–63. Simone Deglaire, an official in the Electricity Directorate, later tallied up the indemnity bill at 96.37 billion francs; see Deglaire and Bordier, *Électricité,* p. 231.

the appraisal of nationalized assets was completed.[76] Though EDF was not responsible for a slow evaluation process, it was forced to make an advance payment of 4 percent on estimated assets in June 1947. EDF managers barely protested the changes, for such amendments merely compensated for inflation after April 1946. In the end, EDF issued equity purchase bonds that reflected an initial undervaluation of the assets it obtained, but interim adjustments and the provision granting bondholders 1 percent of EDF's revenues until 1996 more than compensated for any undervaluations.

EDF was excluded from the valuation process of both the assets it directly needed and the nationalized nonutility assets, which it had to return to the private sector (Article 15 assets). A decree of 1948 and the Rousselier Report of 1949 prohibited EDF from setting Article 15 assets against the estimated working capital deemed appropriate for the nationalized assets.[77] Article 15 assets included large cash and securities reserves accumulated by private utilities during the nonexpansion years of depression and war, and land once bought for future expansion. Assets returnable under Article 15 were worth about 15 billion francs, and Article 15 decisions cost EDF from 3 to 5 billion francs.[78] EDF returned at least 3 billion francs in securities alone. Returns of properties under Article 15 were evaluated based on book values while indemnities were calculated on market values; this meant that some firms recieved more under the restitution provisions than they had lost through the nationalization.[79] On the EDF board, only the CGT and CFTC representatives resisted the report. In addition, an early interpretation of Article 8 gave EDF a number of small hydroelectric plants, but later interpretations forced EDF to return 1,086 of the 1,604 hydro plants it had originally received. In the end, conservative interpretations Articles 8 and 15 undermined EDF's pretensions to be the master of all electrical power activities in France.

EDF's greatest disappointment in the legislative arena was the Ar-

[76] Georges Maleville, "Les modifications apportées à la loi du 8 avril 1946 sur la nationalisation de l'électricité et du gaz," *Cahiers de Documentation Juridique de l'Électricité et du Gaz de France, Année 1949*, pp. 2–4, and Deglaire and Bordier, *Électricité*, p. 221. For an exhaustive discussion of the texts affecting indemnities and the modalities of their calculation, see Pierre Loiseu, *L'indemnisation*, passim.

[77] A. Alleaume, "La bataille de l'énergie," carbon copy of rough draft of Éclairage position paper, Éclairage archives, dossier: "Problèmes énergétiques: L'électricité," and "Réponse de la CGT au rapport Roussilier," 30 September 1949; CGT report to the EDF board's Finance Committee, carbon copy, same dossier. For details on the Roussilier Report, see the "Faits et travaux" section of *RFE* 4 (November 1949), 232. The stocks of the old utilities continued to be traded on the Bourse until the actual issuing of the EDF indemnity bonds; with the Roussilier Report, those stock values rose on the Bourse; see "P.J.," "Le marché des valeurs de l'énergie" *RFE* 10 (June 1950), 319.

[78] CGT, "Réponse."

[79] Aubry in *Le Monde*, 15–16 August 1948.

mengaud law of 2 August 1949. Senator Armengaud had opposed the nationalization and presented himself as the key defender of free enterprise. He argued that EDF had forestalled the construction of cogeneration facilities, that it ignored smaller facilities, and that energy could be conserved by allowing private firms to build their own electrical production facilities.[80] Armengaud himself wanted full denationalization, but he found sufficient support only for denationalizing cogeneration (generation from waste heat) and autoproduction (generation for on-site use). The EDF board resolutely opposed the Armengaud bill. The CFTC pointed out that the bill would increase production costs for EDF, that it would induce private firms to compete with EDF for the limited output of the electrical equipment firms, and that workers in the "Armengaud plants" would not be covered by the labor *statut*.[81] Anticipating a measure of the Armengaud variety, EDF had already softened its position on cogeneration and autoproduction. EDF never addressed a potential salutary effect of the Armengaud bill— an expansion of the nation's power facilities at no cost to EDF or the state. An important question of principal was never raised: should EDF have provided equipment for the exclusive use of private firms? Because EDF could gain access to cheaper financing and had the greatest expertise in electrical power in France, would not EDF's engagement in cogeneration have been an implicit and costly subsidy to the private sector? Without attacking the nationalization itself, it can be argued that if private firms wanted power facilities for their own exclusive use, they should, as provided by the Armengaud law, have financed and built such plants, freeing EDF to supply less well-heeled consumers.

The Armengaud bill represented a largely symbolic attack on EDF's pretensions because its concrete effects were minimal. Sponsors of the Armengaud law vastly overstated the number of new cogeneration plants that would be built. They claimed that the law would affect three hundred factories in the leather, food processing, paper, distilling, textiles, and rubber industries, but between 1949 and 1954, no new cogeneration facilities were built.[82] When Pechiney built a power plant in 1954, it hired EDF to design and oversee construction and operation.[83] Private cogenerating capacity grew only slowly, to 700 mw in 1963 (equal to 10 percent of EDF's thermal capacity); in 1971, only 1,039 mw of capacity existed. A decree of April 1955 forced EDF to transport

---

[80] "Exposé des motifs, Prop. de loi n° 4223 du 14 Mars 1948" (Paris: Imprimerie Nationale, 1948), offprint.

[81] *Gaz-Électricité* 21 (July-August 1949).

[82] "Rapport de la Commission de la Production Industrielle sur la proposition de loi no 4223," *JO, annexe au procès verbaux du 29 mars, 1949*.

[83] Letter from Pechiney director to Gaspard, cited in CAPV 98 (23 December 1954), and EDF archives series E8, dossier: "Économie Générale."

the power produced by Armengaud plants and to purchase any of their excess power. This decree forced EDF to subsidize the operation of private cogeneration. EDF lost in a number of ways: first, it had to build transmission facilities for power over which it had little control; second, it had to buy excess power at low rates whether or not the grid needed it; and finally, it had to supply reserve power. In essence, the transport decree created a power-pooling system disadvantageous to EDF and advantageous to the owners of non-EDF plants. Private plants received the benefits of pooling while EDF and consumers as a whole supported the costs.

An additional set of measures focused on the hydroelectric construction campaign, an artifactual totem of the productivist coalition. These attacks had a deep psychological impact on EDF, and they reflected not only the financial community's distaste for EDF's choice of capital-intensive hydro over cheaper (in the short run) thermal facilities, but also economic traditionalists' resentment toward the new technocrats. In contrast to other attacks on EDF, the antihydro campaign was in part conducted within the EDF board by a Ministry of Industry representative, Gabriel Taïx.

Taïx had gained his fame by reorganizing the power-rationing system in 1947 and 1948. On the EDF board, in public speeches, and within the government, he sharply criticized the Monnet Plan's concentration on hydroelectricity.[84] Taïx claimed that the hydro program was too expensive and involved too long of a lead time between decisions to build and on-line dates, and he even asserted that the hydro program was a Communist plot to drain the state's finances. He had confidence in no one: the unions were puppets of Moscow, energy technocrats were "phony experts" who defended Monnet with a "technician's vanity," and the planners themselves were a cabal of subversive technocrats.[85] In a report of July 1952 to the Economic and Social Council, he misrepresented EDF's prohydro position and presented his own prothermal position as that of EDF. For his efforts, he was publicly attacked by both Gaspard and Massé, who defended EDF's position.[86] He also infuriated minister of Industry Louvel, a strong supporter of the hydro strategy, so Louvel ousted him from the EDF board in November 1952. The Taïx imbroglio was ironic in that his prothermal and antihydro position was later adopted by EDF itself. The interim thermal program that Taïx pushed sounded to many like the position taken by

[84] Gabriel Taïx, L'énergie et son utilisation (1949), pp. 7–10.
[85] Gabriel Taïx, Le Plan Monnet est-il une réussite? (1953), pp. 85–86 and 150.
[86] Editorial, "Le Rapport Taïx," RFE 34 (September 1952), 347. Gaspard and Massé responded by letters in RFE 35 (October 1952), 423, and Taïx's response is in RFE 36 (November 1952), 45–46.

the Messine managers of the interwar era. It is no coincidence that when EDF itself began to opt for thermal power in the mid-1950s, it was largely the work of Massé, a former Messine manager.

EDF thus sustained several blows to its solvency, its territory within French industry, and its internal social cement. None of these assaults particularly damaged EDF, for they constituted minimal reductions of EDF's real industrial and political power. They did, however, contribute to a sense of beseigement within EDF, and they were concurrent with massive press campaigns against EDF management and the CGT. The social productivist alliance withstood the attacks and buttressed internal solidarity in resistance to them. Efforts to place bureaucratic controls over EDF management similarly reinforced EDF internally.

The Controls Campaign

Moves to implement administrative and bureaucratic controls over EDF decisions began in late 1947, concurrent with the pervasive economic crisis and EDF's own financial problems. In 1947 and 1948, EDF was inundated by state officials overseeing accounts on a day-to-day basis, surveying equipment purchasing, enforcing concession contracts, and helping to implement overall state industrial policy, such as it was. EDF saw these actions as mere irritants, for the first wave of bureaucrats could act only in a consultative fashion. The controls campaign in part reflected a need for scrupulous accounting of the use of public funds, but some of its other causes were far less honorable. The Right reversed its position of 1946 against controls once the Communists were ousted from the government and controls could be used to break the internal alliance at EDF. The Right despised the nationalization as a symbol of creeping socialism, and conceding that denationalization was impossible and using economic liberal rhetoric, it set out to encumber EDF with armies of bureaucrats. The Center supported the controls campaign not out of ideological motivations but out of political opportunism because it needed rightist support in its coalition governments. Campaigns against the nationalized sector were an easy way to gain those votes. Finally, many suspected that the Monnet Plan had stressed the development of productive facilities without due regard to the financial returns (*rentabilité*) of public investments. Controls were thus proffered as a way to implement an emerging set of *rentabilité* criteria against the continuing productivist ethic within EDF.

The Socialists delivered the opening salvos in the controls campaign while they continued to pose as defenders of EDF's autonomy. All decrees implementing controls in the period up to 1950 were authored or countersigned by Socialists. The most outstanding acts of direct state intervention by Socialists into the internal affairs of EDF were a November 1947 decree that cut EDF capital funds and the September 1948 attempt to reduce EDF's labor force. In the 1947 action, Ramadier posited that France was overequipping itself with electrical facilities, and he thus lent credence to the argument that EDF's capital demands were bleeding capital markets.[87] The personnel reduction decree set the precedent that a minister could circumvent the normal channels of the EDF board and front office to compel changes in managerial policy. Finally, the Socialists also set the dangerous precedent of arbitrarily revoking and replacing EDF board members without consulting the respective constituencies.

Controls measures multiplied after Paul Reynaud became minister of finance in mid-1948. As a precondition for accepting the post, Reynaud demanded a law allowing the cabinet to reorganize the management of the nationalized sector by decree. Thus, by late 1948, a broad political front sought controls over the nationalized sector, but the purposes and content of them differed widely: "The supporters of *dirigisme* or of planning [mostly Socialists] saw the nationalizations as levers in their economic policy; controls were to be a set of long-term directives in the areas of public investments and production; for the supporters of liberalism, keeping the state out of the affairs of the nationalized sector had been viewed as a lesser evil, but, by their very hostility to the principle of nationalization, they rallied to a policy of systematic controls."[88] Socialists used controls largely as devices against their Communist rivals, so they did not develop a coherent controls program until 1953. On the Center and Right, the impetus for controls was divided between those who wished to set EDF at the service of the private sector and those who sought to undermine EDF itself. Industrialists saw wage controls as a way to keep workers in the nationalized sector from setting wage and benefit patterns for labor in the private sector. A lack of consensus on the motives for, and modalities of, controls forestalled any law systematizing relations between the state and the nationalized sector. Hence, controls were imposed in a haphazard fashion.

The first report of the Commission de Vérification des Comptes des Entreprises Publiques (CVCEP) in August 1949 called for inspectors of

---

[87] Despite complaints that EDF was exhausting available investment capital, the private sector received 36 percent of its investment capital during the Monnet Plan in the form of state subsidies and loans; Ehrmann, *Organized Business*, p. 290, n. 24. In terms of bonded debt for the private sector, it has been generally conceded that the private bond market did not revive until 1951; see Philippe Brachet, *L'état-entrepreneur* (1976), p. 82.

[88] Georges Lescuyer, *Le contrôle*, p. 101. The author was the son of Roger Lescuyer.

finance to have additional power over EDF managers. The report conceded that the government's policy of low tariffs was at the root of EDF's deficits, but it chided EDF's financial section for inadequate attention to depreciation accounts and for irregular accounting practices in general. It thus supported assertions that EDF was badly managed financially. The CVCEP claimed that an incompetent EDF board was the source of managerial problems and recommended that experts from the private sector or the state bureaucracy replace labor and consumer representatives on the board.[89] The CVCEP also sharply attacked the unions' influence in general management and personnel decisions. Finally, the report applauded the fact that pay decisions were controlled by the cabinet rather than directly set by EDF managers.[90] The report carried considerable political weight as a document authored by prestigious inspectors of finance, and nearly all its recommendations were ultimately implemented. Clearly, the earlier popular distrust for the Inspectorate of Finance had waned and been replaced by a traditional trust of financial experts as value-free oracles of the nation's financial well-being. Many Socialists agreed that workers were incompetent as managers, but the critique was often couched in anti-Communist rhetoric: "Unions cannot be the commanders and the commanded at the same time. . . . One can only hope that someday French unions will become conscious of the national interest and no longer associate themselves with acts of treason. . . . Worker representatives should not sit on the boards in order to implement the demands of their colleagues against those of other board members."[91] From 1949 to 1953, politicians added controls in a piecemeal fashion, often depending on the need to create or preserve parliamentary coalitions. Nonetheless, the second wave of controls gave bureaucrats a priori control over EDF's activites, reduced unions' formal power within the firm, and intervened in EDF contracting procedures.

Despite the Right's accession to power following the elections of June 1951, the government rarely attacked EDF until May 1953. From mid-1951 to early 1953, divergences within the Right between traditionalists such as Antoine Pinay and modernists such as René Mayer and Louvel made the formation of cohesive cabinets difficult. Indeed,

[89] The complete text of the report can be found in *Journal Officiel, Annexe Administrative*, 21 August 1949, p. 386ff. The latter recommendation was directly contrary to the nationalization law.

[90] An admirable analysis of the report from a business perspective is in *Tribune Économique et Financier*, 9 September 1949; from a labor perspective, see Delsol in *Force Ouvrière*, 29 September 1949, and by the CFTC staff in *Gaz-Électricité* 43 (October-November 1949).

[91] Christian Pineau, "Sur la gestion des entreprises nationales," *Revue Banque et Bourse*, 14 (June 1950), 251–54.

modernists needed traditionalist votes to stay in power. As early as 1949, most modernist neoliberals accepted the nationalizations, if for no other reason than that the expansion of assets during the Monnet Plan made resale to private firms financially impossible.[92] In 1952, Louvel wrote, "By now, we must admit without reservations that after proof by performance, the nationalizations are essentially a success."[93] Furthermore, despite endemic financial problems, EDF's productive successes reflected a management that was competent beyond question. Finally, by 1953, the Communists held few formal positions of power within EDF and controls could do little to weaken the informal power of the CGT.

In the second week of May 1953, the Mayer cabinet needed to enact measures that would augment its support on the Right. To that end, during the night of 10 May, Louvel issued ten decrees that set a priori bureaucratic controls over virtually all aspects of management in the nationalized sector. All equipment purchases above a certain monetary floor henceforth required prior approval by controllers from the ministries of finance and industry. All long-term equipment plans, annual budgets, bulk power and concession contracts, wage and benefit settlements, and even most purely technical managerial decisions were likewise subjected to direct ministerial controls. A tight bureacratic straitjacket replaced the relative autonomy once enjoyed by EDF and other nationalized sector firms. Other decrees reduced the EDF board from eighteen to twelve members and replaced consumers with "experts" (bankers, for the most part) on the board.

As acts of political opportunism, the decrees were unrivaled; after the CFTC attacked him for the decrees, Mayer responded, "What do you expect? You have a bad press and I needed to strengthen my majority; it was essential that I satisfy them [the Right]."[94] The wave of protest following the decrees was almost universal, with the exception of the most conservative financial press.[95] The ouster of all but one of the FNCCR representatives from the board enraged provincials and disturbed a fragile internal equilibrium. The decrees were a major political blunder, for any attack on the FNCCR was a challenge to the still-powerful provincial patronage system of the Fourth Republic. In

---

[92] Raymond Aron in *Journal de Lausanne*, 11 June 1949.

[93] Cited in *Forces Nouvelles* (CFTC journal), 12 July 1952.

[94] *Gaz-Électricité* 50 (December 1953).

[95] André Thiers expressed the prevailing opinion in the financial press in criticizing the controls as entangling bureaucratically and obfuscating legally, asserting that the controlled were more competent than the controllers; see *La Cote Financière et Économique*, 20 August 1954. In *Aux Écoutes de la Finance* (28 May 1953), Severus (a pen name) expressed the more conservative business opinion, applauding the decrees as viable measures for preventing social agitation and assuring that the state's money was well spent.

response to the opposition, Louvel later restored one of the three FNCCR seats and raised the number of board seats from twelve to fifteen.

The protechnocratic press was large and influential by 1953 and it directly criticized the decrees. Louis Armand, the model *homo technocratus* of the 1950s, had already characterized the controls movement in 1951 as "demagogic and ill-conceived;"[96] in 1953, he became entirely frustrated: "How many state's attorneys, how many inspectors of finance, how many Polytechnique alumni spend their time looking over our shoulders? . . . Could not their time be better spent?"[97] In an editorial, *Revue Français de l'Énergie* called the decrees "absurd and incoherent."[98] The director of legal relations at EDF wrote that "the autonomy of GDF and EDF, guaranteed by the law of 8 April 1946, has become an illusion, a mirage."[99] The unions and leftist parties responded with similar defiance. On 20 May, 90 percent of the utility work force struck to protest the decrees and effectively blocked a decree that would have empowered the cabinet to modify the *statut* by decree.[100] Sensing that the decrees were a disguised means to install former utility executives on the boards, the parliamentary Left entered a bill (which did not pass) prohibiting such people from sitting on the boards. Most directly, however, Albert Gazier, a Socialist and FO activist, authored legislation to overturn the decrees. The Gazier bill passed in 1955 and made most of the a priori controllers consultative again. The power of the bureaucratic spiderweb was reduced, but the structure remained. Gaspard was asked in an interview what Louvel's motivation was and what were the effects of the May decrees—did Louvel intend to hamstring EDF out of a basic resentment toward its existence? "Absolutely not," replied Gaspard, "we were classmates at Polytechnique, and Louvel had nothing against us. He had several political enemies he wanted to get rid of—he hated the Communists, so he purged them. As for the controls, they were not an impediment."[101]

The May decrees reflected some of the broader predilections of the emerging right technocorporatists. As state planners shifted from defining productivity in physical terms toward defining it by financial

[96] Louis Armand, "Entreprises nationalisées et entreprises privées," *Bulletin ACADI* 53 (December 1951), 418.

[97] Cited in Georges Lescuyer, *Le contrôle*, p. 155.

[98] Editorial, "La mission de contrôle, forme dissimulée de la tutelle," *RFE* 42 (May 1953), 275–76.

[99] Georges Maleville, "L'autorité de l'état sur les services nationaux," *Cahiers Juridiques de l'Électricité et du Gaz* 5 (October–December 1953), 141.

[100] *Gaz-Électricité* (special issue, May 1953).

[101] Gaspard interview.

criteria, *Revue Française de l'Énergie* wrote that the decrees gave priority to the Ministry of Finance over the Ministry of Industry, particularly because Finance received two seats and Industry received only one on the new board.[102] The battle between engineers and economists thus began, though many did not yet recognize it. Observing that the government had arrogated the power to decree changes in the board, Georges Lescuyer argued that the new controls helped the more purely technocratic front office eclipse the more democratic board, opening an avenue to the highest levels of government for EDF managers.[103] Nonetheless, the emergence of powerful links between the front office and the government could not occur until the front office evolved sufficiently to gain dominance over the board. Once set in the 1960s, those links became the centerpiece of right technocratic state policy toward the nationalized sector.

The Right did not learn from its errors of May 1953. Decrees in August 1953, promulgated with the hope of avoiding opposition while most of France was on vacation, took direct aim at the rights of nationalized sector workers. The decrees integrated public enterprise workers into the *statut* of state employees, raised the retirement age, and gave the Finance Ministry ultimate power over all public sector wage and benefits agreements. The Right had assumed that assailing public workers' rights would reduce labor pressures in the private sector. FO, UNCM, and the CFTC staged a two-hour warning strike against the decrees on 24 July. Postal workers began a strike wave even before the decrees' 10 August publication. On 8 August, Paris-region gas and electric workers staged "rolling strikes," keeping power down to 70 percent of normal levels and shutting power in various parts of the city, district by district. Later the same day *Le Monde* recommended that the government concede defeat. Faced for the first time since 1947 with a united labor movement and one of France's largest strike waves, the government backed down. The attack on the *statut* was parried, but the Finance Ministry retained control over wage settlements.

The defeat of the August decrees marked the end of the controls movement for the balance of the Fourth Republic. Up to 1958, occasional measures increased controls, but the framework for the relationship between the state and EDF had been set. Subsequent moves to impose controls carefully avoided direct attacks on the unions; instead, they approached the unions with a more subtle strategy of cooptation and circumlocution. The imposition of a myriad of controls (see Appendix fig. A5) did not fundamentally change managerial practices

---

[102] Editorial, "La mission de contrôle," p. 276.
[103] Georges Lescuyer, *Le contrôle*, p. 164.

at EDF. In terms of labor settlements, equipment programs, and tariffs, EDF had been promised autonomy by the nationalization law, yet had never enjoyed it. Controls only formalized preexisting governmental power over EDF.

The army of accounts overseers, contracting surveillance officers, and technical controllers within EDF did little beyond delaying paperwork. The controls clouded the legal status of EDF, obscuring whether it was subject to corporate or administrative law procedures; the legal section of EDF burgeoned as a result.[104] Bureaucrats who oversaw equipment orders for the Ministry of Industry reviewed an average of about 150 contract proposals per year, but from 1948 to 1970, they refused to certify only two contracts. In both cases EDF circumvented them, and in one the controllers were criticized and quieted by the Minister of Industry's own governmental commissioner.[105] Philippe Brachet interviewed members of the Cour des Comptes on the role of the overseers, and he was told that the controllers did nothing concrete, that they were outside the flow of information, lacked office space, specialized in parlor chatter, and that such jobs were a convenient means to put aging, nonproductive bureaucrats out to pasture. Brachet found that the controllers who represented the government against the nationalized sector often did precisely the opposite and defended the nationalized firms in the councils of the government.[106]

Attempts to impose controls on EDF sought to integrate EDF into the state and to coordinate EDF and governmental policies more directly. These tasks proved impossible, for the state itself was in transition from economic traditionalism to modernism.[107] Controls usually

[104] Roger Combet, the director-general of GDF, wrote that in 1956 there were twenty-two legal texts pertaining to economic and financial controls, ten texts concerning parliamentary controls, eight applying to real estate operations, seven referring to the CVCEP, seven applicable to administrative and technical controls, seven concerning the investments commission, and seven pertaining to the contracting commission, for a total of sixty-two different texts; "L'administration et les affaires nationalisées," *Revue des Arts et Manufactures* 59 (November 1956), p. 53. EDF was subjected to almost exactly the same regime.

[105] The first contract the Contracting Commission blocked was for a Stein-Roubaix 125-mw thermal boiler in July 1954; their pressure on the manufacturer led to a a 0.7 percent lowering of the original bid; CAPV 105 (23 July 1954). This cut was far less than those usually garnered by the EDF contracting services. The second contract blocked by the Contracting Commission was for a civil engineering contract on a hydro project in January 1961; the commission was chided for delaying progress by the EDF board, by Gaspard, and by the Governmental Commissioner; CAPV 179 (27 January 1961).

[106] Interview by Philippe Brachet with an unnamed member of the Cour des Comptes, 21 September 1968, in Pierre Naville, ed., *L'état-entrepreneur: Le cas de la régie Renault* (1971), p. 139.

[107] See infra, chap. 4. See also Sidney Tarrow, "The Crisis of the Late 1960s in Italy and France and the Transition to Mature Capitalism," in Giovanni Arrighi, ed., *The*

only reinforced the internal solidarity between workers and managers, Communists and anti-Communists, and technocrats and unionists in opposition to the beseigers of the citadel. The impasse of the controls movement after 1953 reflected the political reality of EDF: EDF in the 1950s was a social technocratic island with its own delicate set of internal relations, ideology, and politics. Neoliberals and conservatives in the 1950s could not break the firm's internal unity from the outside. Effective integration between EDF and the state apparatus had to wait for changes to occur within EDF itself.

EDF as Pariah: Politics and Ideology within EDF in 1954

EDF entered 1954 at a definite turning point. EDF's successes were indisputable, as output steadily grew and labor's share of total costs fell (Fig. 1), but success had its costs. The heroic era of the great dams and the liberation esprit had long been surpassed by the period of Cold War politics and attacks on EDF itself. The abyss was early in 1953, and in the summer of that year both the purges and the controls movement reached impasses. The death of Stalin, the end of the Korean War, and the astounding working-class unity in the August strikes all contributed to making the Communists more amenable to "frontist" activity and, in turn, to reducing anti-Communist sentiments. This shift made the long-term survival of the internal coalition at EDF possible. Events up to 1954 did, however, levy a serious toll on internal morale. The social productivists had placed their material hopes for EDF in the Monnet Plan dams; consistent cuts in state funds for EDF and the promulgation of the interim thermal equipment plan in 1948 belied such aspirations. By 1952, thermal capacity was 20 percent above the Monnet Plan projections and hydro capacity was 17.5 percent short.[108] To many within EDF, the shortfall in hydro meant a dream deferred, if not destroyed. The dams were monuments to the social productivist alliance, and the inability to expand hydro further was an outward sign of failure.

Relations with the private sector improved as the government routinized EDF's tariff and equipment-purchasing policies. The EDF board

---

Political Economy of Southern Europe (Beverly Hills: Sage Publications, 1985), and André Granou, *La bourgeoisie financière au pouvoir* (1977), chap. 3.

[108] Henri Varlet, for the Comité Consultatif de l'Utilisation de l'Énergie, "Où en est-on de la réalisation en 1952 des objectifs du Plan Monnet?" mimeographed report, 18 January 1952, EDF archives. Technically, hydro capacity figures reflect "average annual productability."

Figure 1. EDF output and labor force, 1946–1970

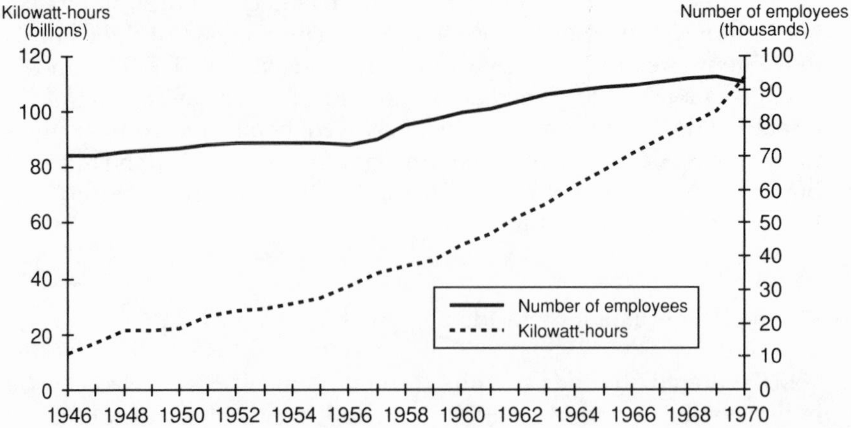
Kilowatt-hours
(billions)
Number of employees
(thousands)
120
100
80
60
40
20
0
100
90
80
70
60
50
40
30
20
10
0
1946 1948 1950 1952 1954 1956 1958 1960 1962 1964 1966 1968 1970
Number of employees
Kilowatt-hours

Source: "Électricité de France, entreprise nationale, industrielle et commerciale," *Notes et Études Documentaires* 4,329–4,331 (2 November 1976), 87.

had tried to revise the below-cost bulk-power contracts while simultaneously subsidizing domestic hookup fees and meter rentals in order to improve popular access to electrical services. The first reform was to help pay for the second. The government granted EDF only the second half of the deal, and this mildly exacerbated operating deficits and perpetuated cross-subsidies within the rate structure. Inequalities remained startling: while Pechiney paid 0.72 francs per kwh and Bozel-Maletra, a steel company, paid 0.47 francs for its power, the City of Paris paid an average of 4.12 francs per kwh.[109] Different costs of service justified some of this differential, yet many large industrial consumers were subsidized while smaller nonresidential users and municipalities were not.

EDF initially denounced many prenationalization equipment contracts, yet nonetheless assumed that it would pay to modernize and reconstruct the electrical equipment industry. EDF was periodically too pliant in contract negotiations up to 1950, but it was rewarded with prompt delivery dates and state-of-the-art technology. EDF negotiators began to bid very aggressively after 1950. The board's equipment committee frequently sent back all of the bids it had received and reopened

[109] *Bulletin Officiel de l'Office des Prix* 87 (15 April 1953). In all of the following discussions of power tariffs, it must be noted that systematic information on the actual rates charged is very hard to come by, particularly after 1954, because it became increasingly secret.

the bidding process. This tactic often yielded cost reductions of up to 10 to 20 percent. By 1951, equipment manufacturers regularly complained to Louvel about EDF's practices. Louvel first prohibited foreign bidding (thus reverting to prewar protectionism), then he ousted Paul Abeloos, EDF's toughest negotiator, from the board. Ambroise Roux, later the head of the mammoth Compagnie Générale d'Électricité, replaced Abeloos.

The EDF board itself changed considerably between 1947 and 1954. By 1954, the board on the surface looked like that of any large French firm, except for the presence of three union representatives and a deep set of internal divisions. Jacques de Fouchier was a banker, Henri Lafond was in the inner circle of the national employers' federation and sat on numerous boards of major industrial firms (many of the major suppliers to, or buyers from, EDF), and Roux was an industrialist. Gilbert Devaux and Bernard Clappier, the Finance Ministry representatives, came from the traditionalist Inspectorate of Finance. Albert Caquot, one of the most loquacious board members, personally symbolized the ambiguous position of EDF: after a long and distinguished career in public service, he simultaneuosly sat on the boards of EDF and one of its suppliers. Unlike some of its predecessor's, the board seldom passed resolutions backing the unions' wage demands.

The front office subtly became more autonomous from the board. Increasingly tight control of information by the front office and a lack of profound discussion reflected this trend. Major decisions tended to be relegated to top-level conferences between Gaspard, Marcel Flouret (the chairman of the board), Caquot (occasionally), and representatives of the relevant ministries. The board was then faced with faits accomplis. The unions did not resist the gradual eclipse of the board because some militants undoubtedly considered the change salutary. The relatively progressive front office was a definite ally as labor faced a board dominated by bankers and industrialists. Conversely, though many board members wished that the front office would oppose the unions more directly, the permanent consensus of the firm made that impossible.

Relations among the unions were often vicious between 1948 and 1953. Though unified in defense of the nationalization experiment, FO, UNCM, and the CGT undermined one another's work actions, spread ugly rumors on union bulletin boards, and consistently attacked one another. UNCM and FO frequently refused to participate in joint demonstrations and campaigns simply because the CGT called them.[110]

[110] Indicative of this position was an article in the Socialist *Le Populaire*, 13 October 1950, at the opening of the CCOS crisis. The author chided the government for attacking the worker-controlled character of the CCOS, but at the same time, it deeply criticized

Cohabitation within the same firm demanded a measure of civility among the unions, but FO and UNCM refused to recognize the CGT's legitimacy. The CGT won little sympathy by using its grip on personnel administration procedures as a way to lure the membership of other unions. The CFTC became an essential intermediary among the unions, but by 1952, its patience had worn thin.[111] These tensions echoed those of the Cold War and only a thaw could reduce them.

The social productivist alliance survived within an isolated and divided EDF. The persistent personal relationship between Paul and Gaspard exemplified a maturing internal coalition. The relationship hinged on mutual respect, with Paul respecting Gaspard's managerial skill and political acumen and Gaspard recognizing Paul's de facto parentage of EDF. When Paul occasionally became caustic toward Gaspard, the latter sought a tête-à-tête between the two to resolve the problems.[112] Other unionists sometimes felt ignored and they implied that management prostituted itself to the CGT, but the front office and the other unions maintained cordial relations.[113]

Productivity bonuses were included among the costs necessary to assure the survival of the alliance. They were a way to allow hidden wage increases and thus to circumvent the government's wage freezes. Bonuses also implied enormous rises in worker productivity, particularly in hydro. They thereby helped to defend EDF from political attacks. Unfortunately, the bonuses shortchanged retirees (because pensions were calculated on base pay exclusive of bonuses) and promoted an inequitable distribution of pay increases, particularly between hydro and thermal workers.[114] Another compromise was the use of subcontractors and temporary workers. EDF accounted subcontracting costs under nonlabor rubrics and because many labor-intensive tasks such as maintenance on distribution networks were subcontracted, the nominal productivity of EDF workers was falsely enhanced. Temporary workers also performed the least-efficient tasks and hiring them also kept down the size of the work force. EDF thus sidestepped another possible source of rightist attacks.

By 1954, the fruits of productive efficiency provided the EDF community with a solid strategy of defense. By secreting the social gains of the nationalization in order to deter political pressure and by choosing productivism as the basis for political security, the progressive

---

and red-baited the CGT, recommending to Socialist electrical workers that they not participate in joint actions with the CGT in defense of the CCOS.

[111] *Gaz-Électricité* 43 (October-November 1952).
[112] Gaspard interview. Gaspard described Paul's political posturing as "superficial."
[113] *Gaz-Électricité* 68 (March-April 1956).
[114] Morel interview.

internal alliance unwittingly laid the groundwork for a transition to apolitical and antilabor management policies. Economic models increasingly displaced coherent social policies. Dreams of *cogestion*, a major promise of the nationalization for the workers, began to fade with the demise of the Communists' battle of production in the 1947–48 crisis, and by 1954, they were largely replaced by "objective" charts and graphs. This dehumanization did not sit well with the CFTC, which continued to seek a more humanistic style within the firm. Morel wrote:

> Must we deal with all of the questions concerning the life of the firm by the use of graphs, curves, flow charts, and diagrams, which are all the result of more or less complicated formulas? In our opinion, the title of upper-level manager gives responsibilities that go beyond the simple acrobatics of turning the firm into a massive data base and operationalizing it all with equations. There is the human factor, which any manager befitting that title must not forget. In most of the discussions that the unions have been having with managers, we constantly confront the response, "the program, the cost savings, the organization chart." . . .
>
> [Addressing the cadres:] If you continue to refuse a dialogue, we can also change our attitude. Our unionism is sufficiently strong to counterpose your vaunted theories with other data and other conclusions based on our own research. This confrontation of ideas can be the basis of dialogue; if you refuse that dialogue, we will publicly create it in our journals and circulars, and you would not be pleased to see, posted on the union bulletin boards, technical information that belies your vaunted competence.[115]

The CFTC's voice opposing the technocratic style of EDF management echoed into a shadowy future. Workers' confidence in their own capacities to create a participationist and humane alternative did not emerge until the late 1960s.

The strategy of proof by production dangerously implied that success could be measured in quantitative terms alone. The social productivist alliance had contented itself with measuring success by increases in physical output, arguing that some essential public services had to be provided regardless of the costs. Henri Varlet, Louvel's top overseer of EDF, said in 1951 that "the question of production costs, however crucial, must be balanced against the notion of public service."[116] Led by Massé, the emerging economist-managers began to present financial rates of return, *rentabilité*, as the only true measure of productivity. The language of productivity survived, but the meaning had subtly shifted. Using claims of economic neutrality and assuming that bigger

---

[115] *Gaz-Électricité* 37 (November 1951).
[116] CAPV 62 (27 April 1951).

was better, the emerging right technocorporatists ultimately helped to strengthen the position of the modernist corporate milieu. The new position not only blurred the social vision of the nationalization, it also obscured the larger political and social goals once envisioned for EDF.

The emerging strategy promoted peaceful coexistence and fruitful collaboration with the same corporate entities that the Liberation-era coalition had once intended to destroy. Equipment-purchasing practices began to evolve from rivalry and competitive bidding toward grouped and allocated orders based on generously indexed price series. The emerging managers linked the health of EDF to that of its suppliers. Similarly, some EDF managers not only began to accept a regressive tariff structure, which EDF had sought to demolish, they cloaked a more regressive rate structure in the raiment of mathematical certainty. Finally, in 1950 they developed the Blue Note, a financially driven equipment-choice model, which delegitimated once-vaunted hydro projects.

Bernard Chenot recognized as early as 1955 that nationalizations had failed to undermine the concentrated private sector: "Private profits have reappeared laterally, grafted to the very flanks of the public enterprises, which, created in order to abolish them, have helped to increase them. . . . It was impossible that it be otherwise."[117] In 1946, many had thought it possible to do otherwise, that the social and technical superiority of the nationalized sector would provide the bases for a peaceful transition to humane socialism. Cold War politics closed off that option, preventing even the possibility of experimentation to discover whether it was a real option or a mere fantasy. Popular opinion broadly recognized by 1954 that the nationalization was a technical success but a social failure.[118]

---

[117] Bernard Chenot, "Les paradoxes de l'entreprise publique," *Revue Française de Sciences Politiques* 4 (October-December 1955), 728.

[118] Note in particular in this context the series of interviews that *Le Croix* ran in the first week of June 1951; with the exception of Marcel Pellenc (whose disdain for the nationalizations was well recognized; *La Croix*, 2 June 1951), all of the respondents, ranging from Le Brun to Maurice Guérin, the MRP deputy who authored that party's bill for a *statut* for the public sector, conceded that the nationalizations were a technical and managerial success but a social failure.

CHAPTER 4

The Relations of Production:
EDF Managers and
French Political Economy

Governing power in the mid-1950s alternated between traditional conservatives such as Joseph Laniel and Antoine Pinay, who
represented the interests of provincial, family-oriented industrialists,
and neoliberal modernists such as René Mayer. Deep divisions among
non-Marxist parties rendered majorities elusive, and acrimony within
the Center-Right precluded it from addressing and resolving the in-
cessant crises of the Fourth Republic's closing years (1954–58). The
generals' revolt in Algeria directly indicted the Fourth Republic for its
inability to solve foreign policy crises, and parallel incertitudes plagued
state industrial and financial policy. The installation of the Fifth Republic in 1958 resolved a previously uncertain colonial policy and likewise offered a rightist technocratic solution to conflicts surrounding
the nationalized sector.

The period from 1954 to 1965 embraced France's final transition from
traditional to modern capitalism.[1] A Parisian-based corporate and managerial elite replaced a geographically diffuse and small business milieu
as the central clientele of the state. The political-economic instability
of the Fourth Republic was rooted in the disequilibrium between a state
structure that had most of the attributes of a fully modern capitalist
state and a configuration of political-economic forces that reflected an

---

[1] This is the central point in André Granou's *La bourgeoisie*. See also Colin Crouch and
Alessandro Pizzorno, eds., *The Resurgence of Class Conflict in Western Europe*, vol. 1 (New
York: Holmes and Meier, 1978); C. Bergquist, ed., *Labor Systems and Labor Movements in
the World Capitalist Economy* (Beverly Hills: Sage Publications, 1984), and Sidney Tarrow,
"The Crisis of the Late 1960s in Italy and France and the Transition to Mature Capitalism,"
in Giovanni Arrighi, ed., *The Political Economy of Southern Europe* (Beverly Hills: Sage
Publications, 1985). Such is also the tone of other recent works, among them, Henry
Rousso, ed., *De Monnet à Massé*.

earlier phase of capitalism. Before the transition, statist and parastatist institutions such as EDF were poorly integrated into the practices of state economic policy; after, they gradually became fully integrated with state policies that reflected a commitment to make the state, the nationalized sector, and the dominant firms of the private sector work in concert.[2] The transition to a fully integrated, mixed capitalist economy required that the political and private sector elites modernize and that managerial thinking in the nationalized sector converge with the larger political-economic synthesis. This process can be viewed as a convergence—a successful search for a middle ground—between a relatively traditionalist political and business elite and a new corps of rigorously modernist state managers.

Changes in the Nature of the French State

The Second Plan (1954–57) echoed the conservative nature of the regime, yet it nonetheless reflected the conservatives' reluctant admission that a planning process was necessary, even if it was only to allocate public investments. Whereas the Monnet Plan had concentrated on simple *rendement*, an increase in physical output, by 1950 at the urging of EDF's Pierre Massé and Marcel Boiteux, state planners began to adopt *rentabilité*, the rate of financial returns on specific investments, as its central decision-making criterion.[3] While financial calculations were essential tools in defining the economic value of potential state sector projects, the normative reference for financial returns soon became that of the concentrated private sector. *Rentabilité* criteria easily collapsed into a conservative goal of short-term, calculable returns on investment and therefore disadvantaged capital-intensive and slowly returning investments such as hydroelectricity. Only after 1958 did *rentabilité* calculations, replete with mathematical finance, planning, and productivity models, yield a strategy to guide the economy toward concerted policies between public and private sectors.

Although state economic policy in the period from 1954 to 1962 reflected the vacillations of the regime itself, it remained vaguely Keynes-

---

[2] Lionel Monnier, "La complémentarité des capitaux publics et privés," in *Le rôle des capitaux publics dans le financement de l'industrie en Europe occidentale aux XIXᵉ et XXᵉ siècles,* colloquium (1981), pp. 177–205. For key works on the transition, see Richard F. Kuisel, *Capitalism,* and Henry W. Ehrmann, *Organized Business.* Some recent edited volumes address the nationalized sector; see *Le rôle des capitaux publics,* colloquium; Rousso, ed., *De Monnet à Massé;* and Patrick Fridenson and André Straus, eds., *Le capitalisme français XIXᵉ–XXᵉ siècle: Blocages et dynamismes d'une croissance* (1987).

[3] Martine Bungener, "L'électricité et les trois premiers plans: Une symbiose réussie," in Rousso, ed., *De Monnet Massé,* p. 116.

ian. The state occasionally tried to stabilize the economy by variously turning on or off the valve of public investment in order to regulate overall demand in the economy. The nationalized sector, which represented about 25 percent of all capital formation in France, was the obvious target for such a strategy. When the state pursued anti-inflationary policies by cutting public spending, it contradicted another goal, that of providing necessary economic infrastructure. The need for demand contraction seldom coincided with less need for state-provided infrastructure. This contradiction was at the heart of the conflicts between EDF and the state in the period from 1954 to 1962. The state also cut EDF's equipment budget according to budgetary exigencies, even though such cuts threatened EDF's ability to meet the demand for electricity.[4] Furthermore, because state budgetary crises often coincided with economic recessions, budget cuts for the nationalized sector, implemented to balance the state's finances, only exacerbated downturns.

Efforts to contain inflation in 1956 and 1957 highlighted another conundrum in state economic strategy. The government cut public sector capital spending and froze tariffs, thus allowing more capital to flow to the private sector, hoping that fresh capital would be invested or passed through in price cuts. New investment was to yield higher productivity and help lower prices, thereby striking directly at inflation. Neither of these results materialized.[5] The state did not require that the additional capital be invested productively, nor did policymakers allow a sufficient lead time for more private capital to be translated into cheaper goods. The mediocre result of flaccid macroeconomic management underscored the need for the private sector to respond positively, as it had with the Pinay stabilization of 1952, rather than to close ranks and reinforce its ententes.[6]

The crucible for the emerging alliance between technocratic managers in the nationalized sector and the modernist managers of the government and private sector was ACADI, the Association des Cadres Dirigeants d'Industrie, a group not unlike X-Crise a generation earlier. ACADI membership included a number of high-level EDF managers (among them Gabriel Dessus and Pierre Grezel), Henri Lafond (an EDF board member and an associate of the metals entente), Henri Davezac (head of the electrical equipment entente), and René Perrin (head of

[4] CAPV 86 (27 March 1953).
[5] Philippe Brachet, L'état, chap. 4, and Jean Lecerf, La percée de l'économie française (1963), chap. 8 and passim.
[6] The "Pinay stabilization" well reflects the character of premodernist state economic policy. By public appearances across the country and speeches at business luncheons, Pinay succeeded in reducing inflation. His structural solution for inflation, trust-busting, failed miserably in the face of a wave of increased industrial concentration.

Ugine). Louis Armand, one of France's most famous technocrats, also participated. Pierre Mendès-France, though only on the periphery of ACADI, shared many of its positions.[7] In sharp contrast to the small business and antitrust orientation of cabinets between 1949 and 1954, ACADI favored private sector ententes as a way to assure a rational allocation of resources and markets among capital-intensive firms within the same sector.[8] Rationalization would, they argued, mitigate risk, minimize research and development costs (henceforth shared by a number of firms), and use standing capital more efficiently by meeting growing and well-allocated demand. ACADI opposed competition among French firms yet saw competition as most effective among sectors and nations. For this reason, they welcomed France's entry into the Common Market.

The Fifth Republic did not bring the modern corporate elite immediately to power. From 1958 to 1962, neoliberalism transmuted to rightist technocorporatism as Gaullist modernists slowly managed to convince economic traditionalists that political and economic modernization could proceed without creating an opening for the Left. In 1958 de Gaulle appointed Jacques Rueff, a doctrinaire liberal, as his economic czar in order to woo traditionalists and coordinate state interventionist institutions and practices. Rueff and Pinay, another traditionalist-cum-Gaullist, were used skillfully to gain provincial business support for the new regime. Shortly thereafter, genuine modernists such as Valéry Giscard d'Estaing replaced Rueff and Pinay. Combined with de Gaulle's nationalism, early traditionalist policies effectively tied traditionalist businessmen to the Gaullist regime.

The transition to modern capitalism occurred more rapidly within the infrastructure of the ministries than it did at the top levels of the state. A number of the directorates within the Ministry of Industry had become resolutely modernist as early as 1952. This was particularly marked in the directorate for the heavy metalworking and electrical equipment industries (called the Direction des Industries Méchaniques et Électriques). That bureau consistently countered the balanced-budget fervor of the Finance Ministry, and in close association with the proconcentrationist views of Industry Minister Louvel, it insisted that EDF frame its equipment-purchasing policy to promote industrial concentration and "rationalization" among its suppliers.[9] Along with ACADI, many ministry experts argued that the new model for industrial concentration would reject antigrowth Malthusianism and instead use ententes to reduce the risks associated with growth-oriented and

[7] Jean Baby, "La formation des trusts," *Économie et politique* 5/6 (1954), 55.
[8] Ehrmann, *Organized Business*, p. 197.
[9] Baby, "La formation," p. 55, and CAPV, 1954–1962, passim.

capital-intensive investments. By the mid-1960s, the erstwhile conservative Finance Ministry, reshaped by a new wave of young graduates from the École Nationale d'Administration, ceased to reflect the views of traditionalists in the Inspectorate of Finance and began to seek a coordination between private and public sectors.[10] As corporate and public officials jointly managed an integrated economic system, cooperation began to replace rivalry.

As Jean Bouvier noted, the "economic triumphalism" of the Fifth Republic meant inducing economic growth rather than directing it.[11] To this end, state officials pursued several broad goals, including sustained growth without inflation (something unattainable during the Fourth Republic), French technological leadership, high rates of investment, and higher incomes, but only to the extent that they would not engender demand-pull inflation. These goals implied specific strategies. Attentive to a pervasive capital shortage, experts focused capital accumulation on the sunrise private firms—those with technological growth potential, high capital intensiveness, and competitive potential in international markets. Under the banner of a return to economic liberalism and a rejection of *dirigisme*, Gaullist policies offered healthy, oligopolistic firms few governmental encumbrances and granted state-subsidized loans to firms vulnerable to market pressures. In theory, the Common Market would apply competitive pressure on oligopolies, thereby reducing the danger that they might abuse their power. According to Gaullist experts, subsidies for nonprofit enterprises had to be restricted because such funds would not recirculate to augment the total capital supply. Similarly, income gains had to be focused on those economic groups with the lowest marginal propensities to consume, thus allowing relatively greater savings rates and a further augmentation of the capital stock, while reducing the tendency toward demand-pull inflation. Finally, average salary increases had to be restricted to a level slightly below the rate of economic growth, again permitting an expansion of the capital stock. In short, Gaullist economic strategies were highly growth-oriented, yet they gave pride of place to the stronger segments of society and to the firms that were already on top.[12]

---

[10] Gilbert Devaux, a Finance Ministry representative on the EDF board, characterized the generational shift even within the Inspectorate of Finance as a change from 'literary types' to 'quantifiers'; interview with Devaux on 12 June 1984 by Jean-François Picard and Alain Beltran, coauthors with Martine Bungener, *Histoire(s) de l'EDF* (1985).

[11] Jean Bouvier, "Financement public et re-démarrage industriel en France, 1944–1950: Une prise de relais ambigüe pour l'investissement," in *Le rôle des capitaux publics*, colloquium, p. 90.

[12] For detailed discussions of Gaullist economic policies from a variety of perspectives, see Granou, *La bourgeoisie*, passim; Alain Prate, *Les batailles économiques du Général de Gaulle*, passim; and Jean Lecerf, *La percée*, part 3.

EDF and the Modernist State

EDF resented the Finance Ministry's imposition of highly restrictive controls on capital budgets more than it had the army of petty controllers imposed during the Cold War period. However, in the mid-1950s, a politically embarrassing conjuncture in its production situation undermined EDF's protests. Electricity demand weakened during the post–Korean War recession, which began in mid-1953. Much of the Monnet Plan equipment finally came fully on line between 1951 and 1953, along with considerable thermal capacity started during the fear of capacity shortfalls in 1950 and 1951. This gave EDF a relative overcapacity of productive equipment well into 1954.[13] Though quite transitory, this overcapacity starkly contradicted EDF's perennial claims of insufficient capital funds. EDF had followed Plan Commission advice and concentrated its efforts on building productive capacity, much to the detriment of transmission and distribution networks.[14] In 1954 a transmission failure in the Alpine region caused a domino effect and blacked out half of Paris for a short period of time, pointing up the insufficiency of the transmission grid. Given the lag time between a decision to invest and actual production from new equipment, Massé foresaw power shortages looming for 1955.[15] By 1956, the production reserve margin during peak demand hours was near zero. EDF had to operate woefully inefficient thermal capacity on peak, and operating costs skyrocketed accordingly. France avoided power failures in 1957 only because considerable rainfall had filled EDF's hydro reservoirs to the brim.[16]

EDF thus became an easy target for accusations of mismangement and subsequent budget cuts: billions of francs had been poured into EDF's capital equipment, yet EDF could still not deliver abundant and consistent power to all French citizens. In spite of the fact that funding cuts had caused the capacity shortfalls, EDF's credibility concerning its financial situation was in doubt. The government therefore found ostensible cause to be as parsimonious as possible toward EDF. Virtually every year between 1954 and 1959, Parliament cut EDF's budget requests, passed the reduced budgets, and cut them again after passage and after EDF had already begun to contract on the basis of the legislated budget. "Periodic massacres" of the equipment budget aggravated the misallocation of equipment spending.[17] Cuts were first made

[13] EDF, *Comptes d'activité et rapport de gestion, 1953* (Paris: EDF, 1953), p. 13.
[14] *Gaz-Électricité* 52 (February 1954); see also supra, chap. 3.
[15] CAPV 119 (7 October 1955).
[16] CAPV 136 (22 July 1957).
[17] Term used by Raymond Villadier, EDF finance committee chief, in *Vie Française*, 10 January 1958.

on the distribution budget, then on reservoir hydro, then on the transmission grid and thermal plants (see Appendix fig. A6 for sources of EDF capital and Appendix fig. A7 for capital-expenditure allocations).

When conjoined with electrical rates that only occasionally covered operations and maintenance, budget cuts made EDF perennially capital-short. By the late 1950s, EDF needed a massive catch-up equipment program, which required large orders for equipment. Massive orders fueled price hikes more than regularly paced orders would have, and EDF had to pay the higher equipment prices. Indeed, delays in the execution of the Serre-Ponçon and Roselend hydro projects added an extra 30 percent to the original projected costs.[18] Furthermore, delays arising from the cuts forced EDF to opt for investments with the shortest lead times. This compelled a choice for thermal power. Imported coal and oil further aggravated France's foreign exchange and inflation problems. The Plan Commission began to recognize this problem in 1957, when in preparation for the Third Plan it wrote: "Already, between 1951 and 1953 [the years of the deepest cuts], in the interim between the First and Second Plans [and] because of financial difficulties, it was considered impossible to envision large investments in the energy sector, and that resulted in a number of our foreign exchange problems. It is not possible to imagine repeating that mistake in the 1957–58 period."[19] Nonetheless, EDF had to defer much of its 1957 equipment program and could not begin any new hydro projects in 1958, including its innovative tidal power plant at Rance.[20]

EDF's capital shortage increasingly forced it to issue larger bond series in order to procure sufficient capital. To make the bond issues attractive, EDF offered various forms of inflation protection on the bonds, ranging from indexed principal and interest to redemption bonuses. These measures diverted risks from investors and forced EDF to pay the costs of the inflation. EDF's bonds continued to be some of the most valuable on the Bourse. In addition, to minimize the periodic costs for the bond repayments, EDF offered special incentives to bondholders to exchange old bonds for new issues. This raised the long-term finance charges paid by EDF and aggravated the snowballing debt. Of the 111.5 billion francs in the 1958 bond issue, for example, 58 billion francs went toward bond redemptions.[21] Faced with high debt retirement charges, EDF occasionally sought short- and medium-term bank loans to cover its debts to the state.[22] The government forgave 4.7 billion

[18] CAPV 158 (14 January 1958), and CGT-Fédération de l'Éclairage, *Gaillard-Pflimlin et le gouvernement actuel conduisent le pays à la récession* (1959), p. 12.

[19] Cited ibid, p. 14.

[20] EDF, *Rapport d'activité et comptes de gestion, 1956* (Paris: EDF, 1956), p. 27, and CGT–Fédération de l'Éclairage, *Gaillard-Pflimlin*, pp. 10–11.

[21] CAPV 147 (28 February 1958).

[22] CAPV 109 (17 December 1954) and CAPV 136 (22 July 1957).

francs in finance charges owed it by EDF in 1957 and a similar moratorium in 1962 only slightly ameliorated the debt situation.[23] Ideally, EDF wanted to cover its investments as follows: one-third from bond sales, one-third from state subsidies, and one-third from retained earnings.[24]

As a result of the constant cuts in the EDF equipment budget, EDF's share of total electrical power production fell steadily in the mid and late 1950s. While this symbolically undercut EDF's pretentions to be the master of all electrical power in the country, it also devastated operating accounts. Forced to buy power from the public coal and rail firms, the Rhône Company, and private producers, EDF paid more for replacement power than it would have if it had had sufficient equipment to produce the power itself. EDF also had to pay to build transmission facilities for such power, regardless of whether its location conformed to an optimal geographical configuration of power plants and transmission facilities.

High coal prices, high capital charges, and insufficient electrical rates forced EDF to run up large operating accounts deficits in the mid-1950s. EDF also paid the extra costs engendered by running inefficient thermal plants and by paying high prices for subcontracted work because the government did not permit EDF to hire enough of its own workers. Excessive production costs in the nationalized coal industry were directly passed on to EDF. The public coal firm, Charbonnages de France (CDF), had systematically modernized during the Monnet Plan, only to find that many coal consumers had switched to petroleum products. The state directed EDF to buy CDF's surplus coal and had CDF build its own coal-fired power plants. With France's entry into the Franco-German Coal-Steel pool in 1952, EDF paid a 1 percent surcharge on each ton of CDF coal it consumed, yet the state forbade EDF from including the coal-price increases in its electrical tariffs.[25] Conversely, when France and Great Britain stumbled into the Suez crisis in the fall of 1956, thereby closing off the canal and the Middle Eastern oil supply, many oil consumers switched back to coal. The state then forced EDF to purchase less CDF coal in order to make it available to private industry. At the time, CDF coal cost 5,450 francs per ton while the American coal EDF purchased as replacement fuel cost 8,700 francs per ton.[26] Again, EDF was not allowed to pass through the cost increases. Instead of implementing internal controls as before when EDF

[23] CAPV 132 (23 November 1956).
[24] EDF, Services Financiers, "Considérations sur l'Électricité de France," mimeographed document, 15 February 1954.
[25] CAPV 91 (24 July 1953).
[26] CAPV 136 (22 July 1957).

faced financial crises, the government informally initiated a new pattern of state influence over EDF, measures that were implemented entirely from outside the firm.

In the closing years of the Fourth Republic, the government increasingly tried to make EDF adopt policies that would aid its suppliers and largest customers. Such efforts were crude and unsystematic, and they ran into constant resistance from EDF managers and unionists. The reason for EDF managers' reluctance to submit to the state's intrusions in the mid-1950s was quite simple: the state systematically placed the financial and productive solvency of EDF in jeopardy. A concession to the state's pretensions to control in that context would have been a dereliction of managerial duty, so EDF managers resisted.

The Fifth Republic placed far greater power into the hands of the executive branch of the French state and ultimately permitted the government to develop a consistent and coherent state industrial policy. The changed nature of the state deeply affected EDF. Henceforth, the interventions of the state in EDF management changed from the plethora of petty interventions in EDF's daily affairs to allowing EDF greater autonomy over its quotidian conduct. At the same time, the government rationalized larger-scale controls over EDF policies that had macroeconomic or intersectoral effects, such as salary and tariff levels, bond issues, capital budgets, and contracting procedures.

Though the ACADI perspectives favoring concentration in the private sector and stressing the technical expertise of the new managerial milieu were undoubtedly attractive to a number of EDF managers as a way to use expertise to circumvent statism, they only slowly became a matter of policy at EDF. Several factors account for this delay. First, the politics of the nationalization were still fresh within EDF, and a proentente policy contradicted EDF's original inspiration. Second, there was no guarantee that the firms allowed to enjoy entente status in order to reduce costs would not turn around and victimize EDF with fixed prices, as the aluminum cable manufacturers did every year when EDF bought power-transmission cable.[27] Finally, the government directly prohibited EDF from openly imposing rationalization on its suppliers by insisting on bidded contracts and by setting EDF budgets on an annual basis, thus forestalling a coherent pacing of orders, which might have reduced equipment costs.

The transitional policy entailed increasingly closer ties among the prime minister, the ministers of finance and industry, and top EDF managers. By the mid-1960s, the salary and tariff controls, which had

[27] The minutes of the EDF board reveal this to have been a pervasive problem from 1948 to 1970, as revealed by a systematic reading of the CAPV series for the entire period.

been exercised in a haphazard fashion under the Fourth Republic, became far more conscious, systematic, and planned. As a result, not only did the EDF board of directors become increasingly meaningless, but so too did the previous set of governmental controllers.[28] The government and EDF top managers sought direct ties between the EDF front office and the ministries, but EDF itself—unions, middle managers, and even some board members—still retained a sense of autonomy and tried to preserve a distinct set of internal social relations. State technocrats and EDF managers could not consummate their marriage until EDF management evolved out of its alliance with the trade unions, shedding its nostalgia toward the nationalization élan. Finally, rightist technocrats within EDF could only rise after the first generation of EDF managers retired and were replaced by a much more self-consciously expert and probusiness group.

The decade-long transition from a state entanglement in EDF's day-to-day affairs that rarely addressed long-term policy to interventions that oversaw major policy and left EDF free to conduct routine business ultimately bore fruit in 1970 when the state and EDF management signed a Program Contract. The contract gave EDF considerable autonomy in its daily affairs in return for EDF's efforts to meet goals for growth, costs, budgets, and salaries. The contract essentially allowed EDF to behave like a large private sector firm. A major step in this direction had already been taken in the mid-1960s when the state cut EDF's access to state-subsidized loans and allowed EDF greater access to the bond market. EDF also faced less state opposition to raising its tariffs. In all, EDF was to be cut from the state's financial umbilical and become increasingly self-reliant.[29]

The Finance Ministry's actions reflected both petty and policy-oriented motives. As the Fifth Republic solidified, the latter eclipsed the former. After 1958–59, state intervention into EDF's affairs tended to make EDF activities more beneficial to leading-edge private sector firms, often at EDF's expense. The first moves focused on equipment-

[28] In the December 1954 meeting, participants spent an hour and a half discussing motorbike garages, yet only five minutes on substantive policy issues; CAPV 98 (23 December 1954).

[29] The state's new logic on capital funding was clear: the nationalized sector was no longer considered the motor of growth in the economy, EDF's high-rated bonds could be sold to more people, and more state-subsidized loans could go to the private sector. This was a reversal of the policies of the Fourth Republic, which tried to cut EDF's expenses (and its crowding-out effect on capital markets) by issuing it subsidized loans. In order to reduce EDF's presence on capital markets after the policy change, EDF was allowed more revenues by tariff increases. This general policy of greater financial autonomy for EDF was abruptly abandoned in the 1970s, following the 1973–74 oil crisis and the adoption of an aggressive and costly nuclear power program (the Messmer Plan) in 1975.

purchasing policy. In the fall of 1958, the government changed EDF's contracting methods to allow an upward adjustment of contract prices between bid and actual contracting dates, forcing EDF to bear the risks of inflation in the interim.[30] In addition, the arbitration procedures in force for civil engineering contracts, which opened another avenue for hiking equipment prices once they had already been contracted, were extended to all equipment contracts. The percentages allowed for cost overruns on equipment contracts were likewise increased.[31] Finally, the Green Tariff, a boon to large industrial customers, was phased in between 1958 and 1961. After Wilfrid Baumgartner replaced Pinay in 1961 and Giscard d'Estaing assumed the post in 1962, the finance ministry more coherently pushed EDF toward a functional integration with leading-edge private firms.

The EDF community made only tepid efforts to resist increasing *étatiste* pressures after 1958. In January 1959, amidst the period of de Gaulle's personal rule, Finance Minister Pinay appeared on television and claimed that EDF was his personal fief, angering the EDF board and reviving old fears of *étatisation*.[32] Pinay had already irritated EDF two months before by refusing to accept EDF's 1959 operating budget because it fully included the costs of a government-approved salary agreement. Pinay also issued a decree that cut the frequency of domestic meter readings in half in many areas, threatening meter readers with layoffs and infuriating domestic users who had to pay out more when the meter reader–bill collector arrived.[33] In a similar vein, conforming to EEC rules, Pinay imposed a value-added tax on EDF in the summer of 1959, but allowed EDF only partial cost recovery. Finally, the Finance Ministry forced EDF to borrow five billion francs from the European Investment Bank. Terms of the loan gave EDF no protections against fluctuations in the international exchange rate of the franc.

The *étatisation* question became a major issue at the January 1959 EDF board meeting, called to approve the usual annual bond issue. Recognizing that the government was unilaterally imposing policies on EDF, union representatives Émile Jouhanny (CGT) and Yves Morel (CFTC) asked that the board address the assault on its powers. They also protested the government's insistence that EDF bear the cost of inflation on its bonds while it rejected similar cost-of-living protections for EDF salaries.[34] The board discussed the problem, but did nothing,

---

[30] Circular from the minister of public works, 15 October 1958, cited in CAPV 156 (19 December 1958).
[31] CAPV 156 (19 December 1958).
[32] CAPV 158 (14 January 1959).
[33] CAPV 154 (24 October 1958).
[34] CAPV 158 (14 January 1959).

thus acquiescing in its own implicit demise. Jouhanny and Morel voted against the 1959 bond issue, but only as a symbolic gesture.

Gaspard and the unions again united to resist what the CGT termed an "authoritarian" industrial rate cut in October 1959. Pinay single-handedly reduced power tariffs for industrial consumers, with the espoused policy goal that the cost reductions would be passed on to final consumers. He presented the board with a fait accompli by announcing the discounts to the press before the board could act. At the time, EDF salaries were at the center of EDF's concerns, and Gaspard argued that the workers would be quite legitimately infuriated to see big industry receiving yet another subsidy while salaries remained frozen.[35] Gaspard, the unions, the board, and the even minister of industry sharply protested, but to no avail.

EDF was both ill equipped and halfhearted in its attempts to resist a forced collaboration with the modernist private sector. Throughout the 1950s, the EDF community had prided itself in its leadership position in French industry because of its high rate of capital formation, its technological and managerial innovation, its progressive social programs, and its convivial internal ambiance. Managers and workers alike at EDF had viewed their private sector counterparts with a strong dash of condescension. To many at EDF, simple comparison—not to mention systematic partnership—with the private sector represented a denial of EDF's sociopolitical raison d'être. Such coordination would undoubtedly mean a loss of status for the EDF community. The unions publicly protested but performed no work actions—salary issues remained conveniently concrete as broad policy issues became more elusive. Gaspard wished to make strong protests but deferred to the board, and the board wanted to avoid angering the government that had appointed it. EDF became more irresolute internally as it faced a more resolute state.

Within EDF, a new generation of manager-economists, who fundamentally agreed with Gaullist policies of industrial integration, began to emerge. These "neutral" technocrats saw their role not as leaders of a progressive enterprise, but as technically expert organization men working within a larger system and trying to make it more "rational." The social productivists could resist integration with the private sector either by union-led work actions or by direct confrontations between the front office and the government. The unions still feared that work actions would only open up EDF to renewed attacks. Led by Gaspard, the front office offered a center of possible resistance, but only as long as the social technocrats predominated over the economist-managers.

[35] CAPV 166 (23 October 1959).

Gaspard himself had often been chastized for resisting the government. Even had they wanted to, the new managers were ill-prepared to confront the combined power of the new Gaullist state and the integrated oligopoly sector.

After the early 1960s, EDF management followed the path of least resistance. The state became far more coherent in directing EDF, and rising young managers who had not experienced the nationalization found enormous advantages in obeying. Compliance offered the promise of positions in the upper reaches of the state itself. The half-baked alternatives of the unionists counted for little in the face of the coherent political-economic program promulgated by the Gaullists. During the Fourth Republic, led by Gaspard, the EDF community could often manipulate vacillating ministers and politicians; under the Fifth, the vacillation ceased. Moreover, the perspectives and ideologies of the new EDF managers and high-level state officials began to converge. With the political élan of the nationalization gone as a force repelling managers away from their elitist training, the magnetism of solidarity among elitist technocrats prevailed.

Changes at the Top of EDF, 1954–1970

A board of directors divided among business moderates, state technocrats, and labor militants, symbolic of the Fourth Republic regimes that appointed it, stood in constant contrast with the solidly modernist managerial infrastructure of EDF. The board maintained close ties with the political levels of the state and often acted as a rubber stamp to preformulated government decisions. In contrast, EDF managers tended to ally with the permanent technocratic infrastructure of the technical and industrial ministries. However, little conflict emerged between the board and the managers, primarily because Gaspard pursued a strategy of maintaining a strong front office in the face of a weak board, and because Gaspard adroitly used the respect that the political elite held for him.[36] The front office maintained tight control over all information flowing from the firm to the board and the government, and the only major conflicts were over questions of the volume of EDF's capital spending.

[36] The practice of political arm-twisting eventually proved to be Gaspard's undoing. In a confrontation with Prime Minister Pompidou in 1962, Gaspard overplayed his hand and was soon forced out by Pompidou. Later, de Gaulle, looking after a strong-willed individual like himself, arranged for Gaspard to take over the helm of the Schneider metals combine. At the time, de Gaulle was concerned that controlling interest in Schneider, held by Finance Minister Giscard d'Estaing's wife, would be sold to the Belgian Empain group.

Secrecy became the rule for conducting EDF's business, and the minutes of the board were made secret in 1954, thus making board members less responsible to the public. The official rationale for secrecy was to keep "professional secrets" from firms that were major clients of, or suppliers to, EDF. This was absurd, for at the time of the decision, Roux (from the Compagnie Générale de l'Électricité, one of EDF's largest suppliers) and Lafond (from the metals trade association) sat on the board.[37] Any information available to the board was certainly available to EDF's suppliers and clients. A clearer rationale for secrecy was to insulate EDF from informed criticism from the general public or the CGT, which still represented the majority of the workers at EDF yet was absent from the board. Bernard Chenot wrote: "The rule of professional secrets is aberrant when it is applied to the board of a public enterprise. In the first instance, it makes the representation of specific interests entirely illusory. [More broadly,] it inhibits the control public opinion should have over public affairs."[38] As a result of the secrecy, board members were increasingly responsible only to the state that appointed them, and the interests of domestic power consumers and EDF workers could be slighted. Unions were forced to go public in order to resolve problems within the firm, and elitist managers were able to rise far more easily.[39] Unionist board members or top managers who dared to disseminate privileged information even within the EDF community risked censure and professional suicide.

Technocratic managerial practices put down deep roots in the transitional period, 1954 to 1962. In the remaining years of the 1960s, the apolitical technocrats became solidly entrenched at the top of EDF. Economist-managers slowly gained the upper hand over social technocrats, and acquiescence by the CGT added the finishing touches to the technocratic citadel (see Appendix fig. A8 for the composition of EDF's top management). An internal ideology and culture of high technology facilitated labor's consent to elite technocratic management and reinforced the hermetic character of EDF. Safely cloistered in secrecy, the EDF board moved closer to the private corporate sector through the inclusion of, and domination by, people who held similar views on the needs of a modern capitalist economy. The mainstay of

---

[37] The annual budget bill passed in December 1952 prohibited the state representatives sitting on the boards of nationalized firms from having ties with private firms doing business with those nationalized firms; cited in "Sommaire des lois," *Cahiers Juridiques de l'Électricité et du Gaz* 5 (January 1953), 17. This provision was later passed independently as Law No. 53–75 on 6 February 1953 (*JO*, 7 February 1953), cited in Simone Deglaire, *Recueil*, vol. 13, p. 85. Despite these legal provisions, Ambroise Roux stayed on the EDF board until July 1955.

[38] Bernard Chenot, *Organisation économique de l'état* (1965), p. 450.

[39] Frédérique de Gravelaine and Sylvie O'Dy, *L'état-EDF* (1978), p. 136.

their consensus was a notion of a symbiosis between EDF, its suppliers, and its largest industrial customers.

The final victory of the economists over the engineers and social managers did not occur until after Prime Minister Georges Pompidou removed Gaspard from the EDF directorship in December 1962. Until then, the new generation of economist-managers had slowly moved up in the EDF ranks, often enjoying the sponsorship of Massé and the older generation of rightist technocrats. They used the growing technical complexity and the need for management science to deal with EDF's immense scale as their entrée to the upper echelons of management. Their incontestable expertise placed them largely beyond criticism, particularly since EDF had already based its public reputation on its managerial acumen. The social productivist alliance could not resist the new generation of managers frontally, for the latter utilized and extended many of the same productivist views that had been the basis for the earlier alliance. With sophisticated programs for advertising electricity, the new managers adopted a more marketing-oriented version of the progressive public service concept.[40] The new managers mobilized the resources of expert techniques and language as well as connections to powerful social networks. Against that bulwark, the participatory and progressive nostalgia of the social productivists counted for little.

The membership of the EDF board shifted considerably between 1962 and 1965. The chairmanship passed from Marcel Flouret, former director of the nationalized railroad and chairman of EDF since 1952, to Gaspard in April 1963. André Decelle replaced Gaspard as director-general. Gaspard left the chairmanship late in 1963 and later became chief executive officer of the Schneider metals combine. André Decelle was a mild-mannered, likable fellow who symbolized the transition to unshakable technocratic management at EDF. After a long initial stint as a regional hydro-equipment director where he experienced the pride of the social productivist hydro engineers, he briefly oversaw the high-powered economics and econometric sections of the firm, then became director of distribution. Through his career path, he had seen the managerial extremes within the firm and remained torn among them. Under his leadership, the alliance between unionists and top managers was maintained on an illusory basis. He lent a receptive ear to the demands

---

[40] Several longtime veterans of EDF noted informally to the author a shift symbolic of the change in managerial outlooks: in 1955, many EDF managers thumbed through the Communist *L'Humanité* over morning coffee; by 1965, they were reading *Le Figaro*. EDF advertising sustained a similar shift. In the same period, it changed from a Spartan (and tacky) socialist realism reminiscent of *L'Humanité* to the slick commercial style of *L'Express*.

of the social productivists but responded far more consistently to the manager-economists. Decelle formally controlled the firm, yet allowed actual management to devolve toward the Pierre Massé–Marcel Boiteux dyad, with President Gaspard briefly as a shadow director-general. Decelle was "retired" out in 1967, citing personal reasons and health problems, but there remains considerable controversy concerning the real reasons for his departure.[41] Marcel Boiteux, the leader and darling of the economist managers, replaced him. Boiteux was not a Polytechnique graduate, not even an engineer—a radical departure from past practice—but a renowned mathematical economist trained at the École Normale and Sciences Politiques.

The change in the EDF board that was most resented within EDF was the replacement of Henri Lafond, who died in 1963, with Raoul Vitry d'Avaucourt. Vitry had been a major figure in the technocratic industrial circles at Vichy during the war, and when he acceded to the EDF board, he was the chief executive officer of Pechiney, EDF's largest client and the major beneficiary of EDF's preferential industrial power rates. The conflicts of interest were obvious, though never attacked legally. By sitting on the EDF board, he had privileged access to critical EDF operating costs and financial information, thus enabling him to demand rate discounts with a full recognition of EDF's ability to adjust rates in Pechiney's favor. Pechiney was also EDF's sole supplier of reactor-quality graphite. Vitry's presence on the EDF board represented a typical form of interfirm ties among large corporations, that of interlocking directorships.

Pierre Guillaumat, one of France's leading energy technocrats, was another major figure on the EDF board. Like Massé, Guillaumat had come through the old Mercier network after graduation from the École Polytechnique. An archetypical Gaullist civil servant, Guillaumat had been a minister of armies, then oversaw the nationalized oil industry through its period of reorganization in the 1960s.[42] He had sat on the EDF board from 1955 to 1959 as the representative of the Ministry of Industry and the Atomic Energy Commission (Commissariat à l'Énergie Atomique, CEA) but was a minor figure at that time, focusing his energies on the CEA and the oil industry. As a veteran of the Corps

---

[41] Sustained by an article in *Combat* (18 September 1967) and by numerous interviews, Picard et al., *Histoire(s)*, p. 201, imply that the nuclear imbroglio caused Decelle's downfall. On the contrary, Pierre Massé argues that the reasons for Decelle's exit were much more mundane; *Aléas*, pp. 131–33.

[42] Guillaumat was initially the chief executive officer of the Société Nationale des Pétroles Aquitaines, the nationalized petroleum exploration firm. Under his leadership, it began to act as an oil-importing agency and became the Bureau de Recherche des Pétroles (a member of the mixed-ownership consortium, Union Génerale des Pétroles). Today, it is the Société Elf-Aquitaine.

des Mines, Guillaumat's rise to the top of EDF represented the first invasion of the strongly Ponts et Chaussées EDF by engineers from the Corps des Mines. EDF was then still concentrating on coal and hydro as primary energy sources; the major push for oil-burning thermal power at EDF began just as Guillaumat first left in 1959. Guillaumat returned to the EDF board as chairman when Gaspard left early in 1964, and stayed only two years, but long enough to facilitate long-term contracts between EDF and the oil industry and to seal the shift from Ponts et Chaussées energy, particularly hydro, to the new Mines energy, oil.

The most telling change of all in the EDF board and front office was the rise of Massé and Boiteux in the mid-1960s. Throughout the 1950s, Massé had been second at EDF behind Gaspard, who had kept him out of crucial positions of power, particularly those dealing with the unions, which Massé deeply distrusted. Massé left EDF in 1959 to become plan commissioner, France's leading planning official. While heading the Plan Commission, Massé helped draw up a plan to reduce sharply France's nationalized coal industry, and he presided over a three-member commission of experts in 1963 that developed the neoliberal Toutée pay procedures (see below) for nationalized sector workers. Massé came back to EDF as chairman of the board, replacing Guillaumat in 1965 and helping to elevate the independent status of the charman's position. Thus, in the late 1960s, Boiteux and his old sponsor, Massé, headed EDF. The ascension of the Massé-Boiteux pair symbolized the final victory of the rightist technocrats at EDF.

Conceptual Revolutions in EDF Management

By 1954, EDF's institutional position within the French economic and political terrain was largely unchallenged. The great battle of production had largely been won, though the distribution and secondary transmission networks were still inadequate. Reliable and low-cost power supplies to key industries (though not to the public at large) were assured. EDF was a stunning technical success. Despite the Finance Ministry's parsimony toward EDF's equipment budget, EDF had built a solid productive system, and upgrading of the distribution system was in sight. Real costs per delivered kilowatt-hour were dropping steadily, owing to rising thermal efficiency, vastly greater labor productivity, falling capital-output ratios, and—much to the disdain of the financial community—the effectively negative interest rates EDF paid to finance system expansion.

EDF had ended power rationing in 1949 and then turned to meet expanding demand and to cut production costs. To guide the new orientation, the EDF managers and the state chose to stress the financial aspects inherent in the concept of *rentabilité* rather than the more elusive notions of productivism and public service. EDF was proud to state that it was France's largest investor, representing 5 percent of all capital formation in France, and that for every franc of value added, EDF used one-third of the average amount of labor and three times the average amount of capital.[43] The task for management was thus to derive the highest economic returns from the massive quantities of capital it used.

Rentabilité analysis promised an optimal allocation of resources within EDF and across the economy. The shift in stress from *rendement*, the specialty of engineers concerned with technical efficiency, to *rentabilité*, the province of economists concerned with capital efficiency, fore-shadowed the ultimate predominance of economists over engineers within EDF management. The mavens of *rentabilité* used quantitative methods of analysis almost exclusively. Something that could not be quantified was considered irrelevant. The social character of work and consumption and the quality of service became analytically elusive because quantitative designations could not be placed on such things.[44] This approach implicitly defined workers and consumers as mere factors of production and units of demand. Workers and consumers thus became objects for analysis and management rather than the subjects of the production process.

Expressing the government's consensus in the mid-1950s, Ramadier had noted that the key word for the nationalizations in 1945 was *reconstruction*, but that in 1955, it was *expansion*. He argued that if the nationalized sector should not serve the private sector directly, it should at least assure that it not drain capital from the private sector.[45] Indeed, the notion of cooperation between the public and private sectors was shot through with the concept of *rentabilité*: criticisms that EDF constituted in the words of conservative critics, "disloyal competition," centered on EDF's activity in financial markets, and they implied that EDF was not using its capital as effectively as the private sector. In 1961, to end the "disloyal competition," Giscard d'Estaing called for

---

[43] EDF document, "Exposé de M. Boiteux devant le Conseil d'Administration d'EDF, 5 Février, 1969," EDF archives, Centre Murat-Messine (Paris), dossier E8: "Économie Générale."

[44] In an implicit response to Massé's assertion that quality could be quantified (see infra), Decelle later argued, "The quality of service is a central preoccupation, and it is not [merely] mathematical"; Picard et al., *Histoire(s)*, p. 144.

[45] Paul Ramadier, "Les entreprises nationalisées," p. 201.

an economic coordination, based on high *rentabilité*, yet limited capital resources in the nationalized sector.[46]

As a comparative framework, *rentabilité* analysis could refer either to the firm's past performance or to the current performance of other firms. Between 1949 and 1963, *rentabilité* analysis used EDF itself for reference; later, large private firms became the normative standard. *Rentabilité* thus became equivalent to shadow profitability rather than technical or economic efficiency, with efficiency gains and net operating surpluses essentially reflecting shadow profits. The shift in reference standards was fraught with more subtle meaning. Though the private sector reference standard reflected a necessary turn outward, it implied that as a leading firm in the economy, EDF would no longer set its own standards but reflect upon less-efficient, profit-oriented firms as the standard. It was a managerial surrender of EDF's leading position. The new mathematical models defined efficiency with respect to a hypothetical competitive firm operating in a fictive free market. This shift represented the abandonment of attempts to forge a new definition of internal management approaches or of noncapitalist relations within the firm or the society as a whole. In simple terms, an emulation of modern business methods replaced the last vestiges of experimentation with humane and democratic socialist approaches.

Rivalry between the public and private sectors had been healthy for the economy and would have been even more fruitful had the Finance Ministry not restricted EDF's access to capital and skilled labor markets. EDF competed with private firms in many factor markets, but few firms could claim decreases in unit production costs of 2 percent annually in constant francs, as EDF could, or a similar fall in their product prices. Certainly no other firm could claim an almost 9 percent annual growth in worker output.[47] By virtually any measure, EDF was France's most efficient firm, and its rate of productivity growth was among the fastest. Particularly because roughly 75 percent of EDF's output was sold to other firms and thus represented a production-cost component in rapid decline, it would probably have made macroeconomic sense to allow EDF to displace other firms in factor markets. Competition in factor markets would have demanded that private sector firms strive to meet EDF's factor productivity levels. As EDF managers shifted from rivalry to cooperation with private sector firms, many of which were relatively inefficient oligopolies, the normative standards for economic efficiency for all firms fell.

[46] Pierre Massé, "Les conceptions et les objectifs du VIe plan," *Bulletin d'Information des Cadres* (in-house journal for EDF managers, hereafter *IDC*), article 62 (May 1961), 6.
[47] All figures are for the period 1950–65.

Massé denigrated the early productivist approach as "irrational" and linked the battle of production to a "war economy" mentality.[48] He had argued for the private sector reference since the early 1950s. It took years to become generalized throughout EDF management, for it represented a sharp break from the original inspiration of nationalization. The emerging standard was first popularized within the EDF equipment office by Massé, and it subsequently spread into the Études Économiques Générales (EEG) section, the group responsible for economic modeling, founded in the early 1960s. The chief executive section, Direction Générale, and the personnel division were the last to accept it because the daily resistance of workers to it and the old nationalization esprit was most sharply felt in those sections. Nonetheless, by the mid-1960s, the private sector reference became unassailable. Uncritical cooperation with the private sector among economist-managers replaced the fruitful rivalry of the social productivists.

Gaspard characterized his management style at EDF in the 1950s as "artisanal," and though his methods were sometimes paternalist, he seemed to view EDF workers as people dedicated to their work and to the successes of the nationalization experiment and the productivist alliance.[49] Gaspard often circumvented the hierarchy and dealt personally with crises within the firm, thus minimizing tendencies toward authoritarianism and indifference toward labor. Though committed to a formal hierarchy of power within the firm, he often used informal face-to-face meetings as a way to reinforce the internal sense of community. In contrast to Gaspard, Pierre Massé pursued an approach toward management that was centered exclusively on economics. He was convinced of the need for a strictly vertical hierarchy and for labor costs to be carefully calculated so that EDF workers would not inordinately benefit compared to private sector workers.

Massé approached economic analysis as a neoclassicist. He set EDF's equipment programs according to private sector financial indicators rather than to real productive returns in the private sector or the most efficient strategy for EDF. He wanted EDF to minimize its recourse to financial markets in order to make more capital available for private investment. Similarly, labor costs had to be kept to a minimum so that EDF's pay levels would not set wage patterns across the economy and erode private profitability. Massé's approach was rightist technocorporatism writ large and his past in the Messine group was no coincidence. Like his mentor, Mercier, Massé believed that both liberal capitalism and class struggle were outdated and that cooperation had

---

[48] Picard et al., *Histoire(s)*, p. 335.
[49] Interview with Roger Gaspard, Paris, 3 June 1981.

to replace class conflict in order to increase the size of the economic pie.[50] His conceptions of economic cooperation implicitly denied the value of the competition he simulated in his models. The rate of financial returns in the economy and within EDF, not the efficiency of production itself, was the measure of success. Quantity was a viable substitute for quality because "the notion of the quality of service, approximate and intuitive until the present, has been rendered quantitative and calculable."[51] Along with the technique of quantification came a taste for scale. To Massé, EDF's success came not from the qualitative or political fact of the nationalization per se, but from the opening the nationalization gave for creating economies of scale and for calculating the future in terms of long- rather than short-term costs.[52]

The CFTC alone seems to have understood what the change in managerial perspectives implied for the workers and for the larger economic role of EDF. After reviewing the text of the Second Plan, largely authored by Massé, Morel stated the CFTC's opposition to its stress on the "renovation of financial methods, entirely capitalist in spirit, from which our nation suffers." He then criticized the plan's call for EDF to cooperate with its suppliers, proposing trust-busting instead.[53] Later, in discussions of the Third Plan (to cover 1958–61), Morel sought to tie the industrial plan to a social plan, without which the private sector alone would benefit.[54] Though the CFTC did not fully comprehend what the shift toward private sector–public sector cooperation meant, the CGT virtually ignored the entire set of issues. It discovered them twenty years too late, when Le Guen observed: "Henceforth [after 1950], what counted was not the social and economic *rentabilité* of a public service that was created to develop the social life and well-being of the nation; what counted above all was financial *rentabilité*, a notion that led to the abandonment of the notion of public service, while [EDF was to] furnish energy to the private industrial sector at below-cost rates."[55] As a result of the their inability to comprehend the changes in managerial philosophy, the major unions at EDF were unable to resist them until the events and recognitions of 1968. By that time, the rightist technocrats had fully installed their own definition of *rentabilité*, at great expense to EDF workers and society as a whole. Similarly, the FNCCR, represented on the board by its powerhouse president,

[50] Brachet, *L'état*, p. 97.

[51] EDF, *Dix ans de progrès* (1956), p. 19.

[52] Pierre Massé, "Intervention de M. Pierre Massé," *Annales de l'Économie Collective* 514–21 (April–November 1956), *Compte rendu du deuxième congrès international de l'économie collective, Liège, 17–21 septembre 1955*, p. 232.

[53] CAPV 90 (10 July 1953).

[54] CAPV 127 (25 May 1956).

[55] René Le Guen, *Voyage*, p. 157.

Georges Gilberton, resisted Massé throughout the 1950s, but, cowed by expertise, he succumbed to Boiteux in the mid-1960s.

In opposition to neoclassic calculations of *rentabilité*, Bernard Chenot wrote, "the state did not nationalize in order to act as a marketing agent, but to modify the course of economic phenomena in the name of the public's interests."[56] As they built their models, the economist-managers quietly assumed that EDF's activities did not systematically affect the distribution of income and resources in the society. The famous caveat of the microeconomists, ceteris paribus—all other things being equal—lost its meaning with a firm of EDF's scale, especially through its tariff and equipment-purchasing policies. Ironically, the economist-managers recognized EDF's macroeconomic effects on financial and labor markets. In addition, the normative assumptions that the marketplace was the best allocator of resources and that all important variables could be quantified were political assumptions and not neutral principles.[57] Such axioms denied the purpose of the nationalization, for the qualitative facts of workers' participation in management and of public service had crucially inspired the nationalization law, while the notion of intersectoral economic cooperation had not.

The assumptions embedded in *rentabilité* analysis led to specific political outcomes. At Massé's urging, Boiteux used these criteria in his work with the Second Plan's energy work group and directly undercut the prohydro position favored by EDF.[58] The CGT argued that *rentabilité* was a squarely political notion: "The [analytic] pretext of *rentabilité* at the level of production, so often put forward when it is a question of raw materials or French workers, makes no economic sense when the basic needs of the country are in question. . . . The problem of *rentabilité* rests on other elements: it is a function of the methods of management . . . [and] it is emminently a question of national policies."[59] Following the logic of shadow profitability, Massé attempted to introduce the notion of a negotiable "labor costs item" into EDF's labor relations and analytic accounting procedures. Gaspard quietly opposed him on this for a number of years. When Massé was plan commissioner, he imposed the "labor costs item" conception on EDF from the outside.[60]

---

[56] Bernard Chenot, *Organisation*, p. 444.

[57] Brachet, *L'état*, p. 207.

[58] Massé later apologized for undercutting the EDF board; see CAPV 96 (18 December 1953).

[59] CGT-Fédération Nationale des Industries de l'Énergie Électrique, Nucléaire, et Gazière [ex-Éclairage], *Pétition pour une politique française de moyens énérgetiques dont l'urgence est criante* (1956), p. 12.

[60] Subcontracting of work properly the purview of statutory EDF workers continued, as did the use of nonstatutory temporary workers as ways to adjust employment and productivity figures. Éclairage estimated in 1963 that on any given day there were about

While the economist-managers attempted to compress the "labor costs," they viewed financial charges as an inflexible cost of doing business. For this reason, even though the unions remained powerful at EDF throughout the period, in 1955, the "labor costs" item was 23.9 percent of total operating costs, but only 21.6 percent of 1962 operating costs, while capital charges (principal, interest, and amortization) rose from 30.8 percent to 33.1 percent.[61] Shadow profitability was a fitting criterion when applied to labor, but it could be disregarded when dealing with high finance. Massé also argued that despite private firms' recognition that inflation lowered long-term capital costs, a nationalized firm should not follow investment practices that disadvantaged savers.[62]

Ironically, Massé's notion of shadow profitability was precisely that which Taïx had supported in 1952, much to the chagrin of the worker-manager alliance within EDF. Taïx's problem was one of tactlessness. When Massé presented the same position in a scientific form, the CGT and Gaspard remained virtually silent, unwilling to question the mystical power of expertise.

Economists as Managers

The Equipment-Choice Model

In a midstream reorientation of Monnet Plan goals in 1949, the government compelled EDF to build a set of coal-fired plants. At the height of this thermal equipment push, EDF's equipment office made a science out of necessity. Forced to install thermal plants to cover the time lag involved in waiting for the completion of the Monnet Plan hydro projects, Massé and Equipment Director Raymond Giguet developed the Blue Note, a mathematical model used to calculate the economic value of different projects and thus to choose between thermal and hydro plants. First developed in 1950 and finalized in 1953, the Blue Note

ten thousand subcontracted workers working parallel to the roughly eighty-five thousand statutory EDF workers; *Force-Information* 103 (May 1963), 24.

[61] Calculated from EDF, Études Économiques Générales, "Les progrès de productivité à l'Électricité de France et leur répartition: Résultats passés et perspectives actuelles," report submitted to EDF board's Operations Committee, April 1969, appendix 2, nonpaginated. Following Massé's lead, as director-general in 1968, Boiteux tried to impose total factor productivity analysis on EDF, but rigorous contestation over the allocation of productivity increases to various factors (especially labor) led to its abandonment by 1973. On Boiteux's advice, Pierre Lhermitte (EEG director) attempted to use the analysis to eliminate ten thousand workers. He failed. See Picard et al., *Histoire(s)*, p. 145, and Massé, *Aléas*, pp. 248–49.

[62] Pierre Massé, "L'électricité devant un nouveau plan," *RFE* 30 (April 1952), 221.

represented EDF's first move toward shadow-profit criteria, as well as the first foray into applying mathematical models to managerial decisions.[63]

Running the Blue Note model, which included many simultaneous equations, was no easy task before the computer. After deriving historical correlations between the expansion of electrical consumption and the growth in gross national product, economists forecast electrical demand for the medium term. Projections for future fuel costs, estimated plant lives, the costs of supplying reserve capacity sufficient to protect against system failures, and the extra benefits derived from valuable hydroelectric peak power capacity were then calculated and entered into the model. Crucially, modelers assigned a discount rate to respective project costs to account for the very different capital and variable cost ratios between projects. A potential hydro project was then stacked up against a standardized thermal plant as reference (coal-fired at 125 mw), based on a comparison of cumulative present-worth calculations. Even if all of the previous variables were correctly calculated, the key variable, and the one most open to question, was that of the discount rate: a relatively high rate disadvantaged more capital-intensive hydro.[64]

Economists could credibly set several different discount rates. These included: (1) the real (net of inflation) rate of interest EDF paid for its capital (about −6 percent), (2) the nominal rate EDF paid (about +3.5 percent), the average real financial market rate of return (about −5 percent), and the average nominal financial market rate (about +4.0 to +4.5 percent). The two most practical and credible options were the two nominal rates, both of which ignored inflation. The most accurate discount rate for EDF itself would have been the real rate EDF paid for capital (−6 percent); lacking that, EDF's nominal rate would have been a workable compromise. Nonetheless, political forces and neo-classic economic wisdom demanded the use of the nominal financial market rate. The use even of the nominal rate paid by EDF would have demanded a relatively greater use of hydro. Thus, arguing that EDF had to gauge its investment not according to the least-cost criterion for

---

[63] The use of linear programing models for managing hydroelectric reservoirs remains an exception, but that procedure was confined to the engineers.

[64] The use of discount rates is a method for determining the present value of future investments. The method accounts for the fact that present-day investments are essentially loans from the present to the future at an interest rate given by the discount rate. The standard formula is $K/(1+r)^n$, in which K is the capital invested, r is the discount rate, and n is the projected useful life of the project. This quantity, calculated for each year of a plant's expected life, then summed, represents the present worth value of a project. In this case, a higher value for r makes the present worth of a capital-intensive investment appear lower.

itself but according to the needs of the economy as a whole, Massé adopted the financial market rate, ignoring the fact that it was set not by real productivity but by investors' assumptions about movements in security prices and earnings.[65] Massé's decision reflected concerns that EDF have a quantitative weapon to defend its investment program, but not to crowd private firms in capital markets.

The problems with the Blue Note ran deeper because using the nominal financial market rate put the returns of EDF investments on par with those of the private sector. The clear financial advantage of the nationalization inherent in special access to low-interest capital was thus annihilated. The high rate forced EDF to choose investments with short-term rates of *rentabilité* comparable to those of large private firms. The economists claimed that the choice of discount rates had to be oriented toward "the collective rate of preference for the present over the future,"[66] but in reality, the financial market rate reflected in part the inefficient allocation of resources in the private sector. If investors sought rapid returns on capital, EDF was compelled to do the same through the use of the Blue Note formula. When the Blue Note was submitted to the EDF board for approval in 1951, the reception was tepid: Plicaud of the CGT opposed the formula's favoring of thermal, and others opposed the notion of *rentabilité* in the model.[67] With the exception of Plicaud, the board unanimously approved the Blue Note, owing to a lack of alternatives and despite reservations. In later years, Caquot and Gilberton, both strong advocates of hydro, argued forcefully within the board for a lower discount rate—Caquot even performed a massive study to support his position—but they were ignored.

Despite the vaunted accuracy of the Blue Note, it compelled EDF managers to choose less economical thermal facilities. The Blue Note enabled economists to calculate how much hydroelectric capacity could be profitably built, and when *rentable* hydro capacity or capital were short, they installed thermal plants to meet projected demand. At the discount rate of 4 percent, which EDF used in the 1950s, France had 100 twh (100×10^9 kwh) of hydro capacity. When the discount rate was hiked to 7 percent in 1960, France's equipable hydro capacity fell to 81 twh, and when the rate shot up to 10 percent in 1969, only 63 twh were available. Ironically, though the use of the Blue Note over a protracted period and the gradual exhaustion of hydro sites should have closed the gap between the average production costs of thermal

[65] Henri Rousseau, "25 ans de progrès économique et financier," in EDF, ed., *Le service et les hommes* (1971), p. 36.
[66] "Le taux d'actualisation," *IDC*, article 262 (March 1969), 5.
[67] CAPV 62 (27 April 1951).

and hydro power, thermal production costs consistently ran about 40 percent over those of hydro (capital costs and depreciation included), and the gap was only beginning to close by 1969.[68] In addition, the thermal reference assumed a rate of available thermal capacity of 76 percent for all thermal plants at any given time. Any availability rate for thermal lower than 76 percent in practice would thus further overvalue thermal plants. The availability rate for the 125 mw thermal series averaged 63 percent between 1959 and 1969, and 59 percent for the 250 mw thermal series between 1961 and 1969.[69] In both instances, thermal facilities enjoyed the benefit of the doubt.

The objective character of the Blue Note was disputable, as some EDF managers reluctantly admitted. Wishful thinking often replaced scientific calculation, particularly with respect to projected fuel costs, consumer demand, and thermal plant reliability. Francis Bessière of EEG later admitted the modelers' guesswork: "There is no decision criterion that can be purely mathematical or logical. . . . In the face of the major uncertainties involved in nuclear power production or in projecting future fuel costs, the decision maker can use mathematics as a tool for critical analysis, permitting him to have the best knowledge of the conditions in which he must decide. But it must not serve him as an 'alibi': the mathematical tool does not relieve him of his freedom of choice, and it should not protect him from the weight of his responsibilities. Each must employ this tool for the best ends, but in the end, he must [openly state] his opinions."[70] Raymond Giguet and Massé both implied that the Blue Note yielded mathematical certainty. In 1961, when Equipment Director Didier Olivier-Martin presented a revised version of the Blue Note to the board, he falsely implied that the discount rate under the revision would be that paid by EDF on its capital, not that of the financial market.[71] In that year, the gap between the two figures represented a 27 percent difference in EDF capital expenses.[72]

Proponents of thermal power also used the Blue Note to justify other agendas. Giguet explicitly stated his economic rationale by stressing the mathematical predictability of thermal output, its operational flexibility, and its lower initial cost. The Finance Ministry supported him on the latter point.[73] More significantly, however, between 1949 and 1954, political centrists saw imports of American coal as a way of sealing

---

[68] CAPV 275 (May 1969).
[69] Calculated from EDF, *Statistiques de production et de consommation*, 1969 (1970), p. 30.
[70] Cited in Claude Berthomieu, *La gestion des entreprises nationalisées* (1971), p. 217.
[71] CAPV 179 (20 January 1961).
[72] EDF-EEG, "Les progrès de productivité," appendix 2, table 1.
[73] Cited in Michel Herblay, *Les hommes du fleuve et de l'atome* (1977), p. 99.

the NATO alliance.[74] Finally, the social productivists' penchant for hydro had allowed considerable autonomy to a large number of hydroelectric engineers and technicians who enjoyed a convenient detachment from the authoritarian atmosphere of the Parisian equipment directorate. The Blue Note reduced their autonomy by centralizing decisions on planning and siting. This was the first step in reducing the power of the early heroes of the EDF experiment, the hydro engineers and technicians.

The 4 percent discount rate that EDF used throughout the 1950s was not far from the nominal rate EDF paid for capital. The real rate was far lower, but equipment programs derived on that basis demanded more capital than the government would allow. For that reason, the state consistently cut EDF's equipment programs and concentrated the cuts on hydro equipment. In order to make the Blue Note a formula for the derivation of equipment programs safe from after-the-fact cuts by the government, the plan commissioner (Massé) imposed a 7 percent discount rate on EDF in 1960. The use of less efficient thermal power demanded by the high discount rate made EDF as a whole less efficient. In the end, the Blue Note oriented EDF not toward choices that promised the highest efficiency at the lowest costs, but toward choices that tended to reduce EDF's overall efficiency down to levels prevailing in the private sector.

Reforms of the Electrical Rate Structure

Parliamentarians, utility trade unionists, and utility managers agreed that the rate structure in 1946 needed substantial reform. The prenationalization rate structure reflected patterns of Malthusian profitability in domestic sales and cross-ownership between industrial firms and utilities in industrial sales rather than any economically rational or socially responsible plan. In addition, because one of the largest components of production costs was that associated with constructing generation, transmission, and distribution capacity, many utility experts hoped that if the rate structure were properly designed, consumers would schedule their demand in such a way as to increase the utilization of existing facilities. For all of these reasons, the nationalization law ordered EDF to develop a new rate structure as soon as possible.[75]

Before and after rate reform, consumers essentially bought two prod-

---

[74] Picard et al., *Histoire(s)*, pp. 106–7.

[75] For a complete and detailed discussion of rate reforms designed and implemented by EDF, see Robert L. Frost, "Economists as Nationalised Sector Managers: Reforms of the Electrical Rate Structure in France, 1946–1969," *Cambridge Journal of Economics* 14 (1985), 285–300.

ucts, capacity (measured in kw) and quantity (measured in kwh). Ideally, capacity charges reflected the capital costs of the power facilities needed to provide service, and quantity, or commodity, charges reflected the variable costs, including fuel, labor, administration, maintenance, and the like associated with the quantities of power consumed. Typically, consumers rented the portion of the facilities needed to meet their demand via monthly kw subscription fees and then paid for power actually consumed via conventional kwh charges. To simplify metering for domestic consumers, some capacity and commodity charges were rolled together into a declining block rate structure, which charged according to quantities consumed, with discounts for greater use.[76] In the two-part high-voltage rate structure before 1958, kw fees, fixed at 165 francs per kwh and not adjusted for inflation thereafter, no longer covered capacity costs. Lost capacity revenues were recovered through the more flexible commodity rates. EDF therefore received little revenue to cover the capital charges on its own equipment from large users during economic recessions as industrial plants stood idle. The costs that industrial power consumers should have paid during recessions were borne by EDF; it thus unintentionally subsidized them at such times.[77] EDF lost badly in slow economic periods and only covered its costs in upswings.

EDF created its own problems with low-voltage rates. Attentive to the fact that popular electrical use was low and assuming that more electrical use meant a more satisfied populace, EDF intentionally kept its domestic capacity charges, meter rentals, and hookup fees low. Originally, EDF had received a 15 percent premium above the cost of new hookups to pay for new capacity. In April 1954, EDF ceased collecting that fee. In like fashion, it tried to keep capacity charges for the larger domestic rate blocks low in order to encourage more domestic power use. EDF recognized that consumers resented having to pay high fixed costs regardless of how much they consumed. EDF willingly paid handsomely for this strategy to improve its public image.[78]

---

[76] To illustrate the capacity and commodity distinctions, assume that a consumer uses 50 kwh of power. At the extremes, he can utilize 50 kw over one hour or one kw over 50 hours. In the former case, more capacity is necessary and he should therefore pay a higher kw fee. Similarly, the latter consumer utilizes only one kw of capacity and his his kw charges should therefore be lower. The capacity/commodity distinction becomes slippery when one considers problems of varying efficiencies of power plants—an inefficient plant may be cheap to build and expensive to operate, as with older thermal plants, or it may be expensive to build and cheap to operate, as with hydro facilities. Because almost any utility has a mix of facilities, the commodity/capacity distinction is easily blurred; therefore, most rate structures carry some capacity fees within commodity charges, and vice versa.

[77] CAPV 95 (27 November 1953).

[78] CAPV 109 (17 December 1954).

The government often unilaterally limited or restructured rates. Because the higher domestic rate blocks were part of the 214-article consumer price index on which social security and other income-support programs were based, in the fall of 1953 the government forced EDF to cut them for the winter of 1953–54. The costs were paid by EDF. EDF resisted a similar demand in the winter of 1954–55, fearing that it would become permanent. Instead, discounted summer rates started two months early; again, EDF paid the difference.[79] In June 1954, Louvel forced EDF to cut its industrial rates 10 percent, claiming that cheaper power would encourage economic expansion. EDF again resisted, arguing that electrical power rarely constituted more than 1 percent of all industrial production costs, so that such a cut would barely benefit industrial users, while it would wreak havoc on EDF's accounts. Nonetheless, the government insisted.[80] To soften the blow, the government lowered coal prices for EDF and slightly increased its loans to EDF. EDF managers hoped that a new rate structure would prevent the state from meddling with power tariffs and other EDF affairs.

Designing a new rate structure, later known as the Green Tariff, was no easy task. First of all, few agreed on the axioms for the new tariff design. The principle of marginal cost pricing, that each user should pay the costs of meeting the marginal demand induced, was popular among experts, but problems of incalculability, conceptual complexity, and interest-group conflicts meant that few could envision implementing marginalist rates. The principles of means-tested rates, with each user paying according to his ability to pay, of targeted rates, wherein tariffs were set in order to subsidize industrial or domestic development, or of inverse elasticity pricing, wherein higher prices were charged those users who had the least propensity to shift their demand as a result of tariff changes, competed with marginalism as possible theoretical frames. After briefly toying with other approaches, the EDF board accepted marginalist principles in 1948 and delegated authority to EDF economists to develop a design. Led by Gabriel Dessus and Marcel Boiteux, the economists came up with the framework for the new structure in 1955. While the intricacy of the power system perhaps justified the complexity of the marginalist model, the same complexity insulated the economists from popular criticism. Facing resentment from Gilberton, the unions, and others who perceived cross-subsidies among consumer classes in the Green Tariff, the economists took the higher ground of expertise.

The Green Tariff was applied to high- and middle-tension consumers;

[79] Ibid.
[80] CAPV 104 (25 June 1954) and 106 (24 September 1954).

low-tension consumers remained a rate-protected class, though significantly, the Green Tariff set rates for EDF's billing to its own distribution services. When the EDF board discussed the Green Tariff between 1954 and 1958, the complicated mathematical model eluded the comprehension of many board members. On this point, Roger Pauwels of Éclairage later noted, "The proper role of rate making in a nationalized enterprise such as Électricité de France must be to permit any citizen, however small his level or interest or expertise may be, to judge [the structure], and, if it is difficult to respond to this need, owing to some of the very abstract notions that are bandied about (for example, the distinction between power and energy), democratic management in that context becomes impossible."[81] The political acceptability of the Green Tariff was never subjected to a rigorous political trial. Indeed, de Gaulle decreed its implementation in December 1959, his last month of emergency powers. The mode of implementing the Green Tariff meant that political authorities delegated the immense power of rate making, the cash nexus between EDF and the public, to a select group of technocrats.

Few contested the general principles behind marginalist rate making, that prices should reflect production costs and that rates should direct customers to use utility capacity efficiently. When the economists converted marginalist principles to a concrete rate structure, the new structure gave larger-than-ever discounts to the biggest industrial users. According to the economists, marginalism justified a structure of discounts for bulk power purchases, high subscription levels, high load factors (i.e., high utilization rates of subscribed capacity), modulability of demand over time and space, and high delivery voltages.[82] By neoclassic economic prejudice—that bigger is more efficient—most of the discounted factors were enjoyed by financially concentrated and capital-intensive firms, particularly those in chemicals and metallurgy.

The Green Tariff contained many questionable aspects of neoclassical economics. Ceteris paribus was a convenient theoretical starting point, but a false assumption in practice. Arguing for neutral tariffs—neutral with respect to the nation's distribution of income—all criteria concerning the ability to pay or the actual ability to adapt electrical use to minimize user costs were ignored. The new tariff model was supply-

[81] Roger Pauwels, letter to Massé, 19 September 1966, CGT-Éclairage archives, dossier: "Problèmes énergétiques."

[82] The mathematical derivations behind the Green Tariff are presented in Gabriel Dessus, "Perspectives commerciales sur les fournitures d'énergie électrique à l'industrie," *RFE* 1 (November 1949); Marcel Boiteux, "Sur la détermination des prix de revient et de développement dans un système interconnecté de production-distribution," *Revue Générale de l'Électricité* 68 (August 1949); and EDF–Études Économiques Générales, *Le calcul économique et le système électrique* (1979), chaps. 3, 4, and 7.

side economics before the fact. Boiteux wrote, "The policy of tariff neutrality ... explicitly seek[s] to restitute to the market its arbitrating role and to leave to parliament the task of redistributing revenues." Yet economists, not the market, set electricity prices. Even if the allocation of goods and services to individuals and groups was inequitable, according to Boiteux, EDF should not try to redistribute economic resources: "In the name of a restrictive conception of equality of all in the face of the public service, the state often forces its enterprises to sell its services at the same price for all.... Equality has nothing to gain [from this], and collective output has a lot to lose in these generalized equalizations, which result, for example, in penalizing non-peak consumers in order to subsidize over-consumption ... in other activities."[83] Gabriel Dessus went further, arguing that if the state wanted to redistribute income, it should do so through taxes and welfare payments, leaving the nationalized firms alone.[84]

EDF economists suggested that electricity rates could act as "price signals." By guaranteeing that rates reflected the costs that individual consumers imposed on the nation's system, the Green Tariff would induce users to adapt their electricity demands and bring society to a least-cost Pareto optimal solution. Accurate price signals would shift part of the peak load to nonpeak periods, thereby reducing necessary investment. This ignored the fact that not all consumers could equally vary their demand according to time, place, intensity, and the like. Demand elasticities were assumed to be uniform and near zero. However, Pechiney could (and did) relocate its plants and adjust its demand according to EDF's criteria, but small industrial users serving local or regional markets often could not. The price elasticity of demand was clearly not uniform for different consumer classes. This was why J. M. Buchanan rejected the Green Tariff: "If we could assume that the service in question is characterized by zero elasticity of demand, the...Boiteux model could be rescued in all essential respects."[85]

Because elasticities of demand varied widely within consumer classes, the benefits of the Green Tariff went to those who could adapt their demand, most often, large integrated industrial firms, especially those with coproduction facilities. The Green Tariff thus probably shifted payment ratios within and across consumer classes, thus cre-

[83] Marcel Boiteux and Louis Puiseux, "Neutralité tarifaire et entreprises publiques," *Bulletin de l'Institut International d'Administration Publique* 12 (1969), 111.
[84] Gabriel Dessus, "A propos de réformes tarifaires," *RFE* 57 (October 1954), 14.
[85] J. M. Buchanan, "Peak Loads and Efficient Pricing: Comment," *Quarterly Journal of Economics* 80 (1966), 470. Later economists have argued even more strongly, fully rejecting the assertion that marginal cost pricing yields Pareto optimality; see Donald J. Brown and Geoffrey Heal, "Equity, Efficiency, and Increasing Returns," *Review of Economic Studies* 46 (October 1979).

ating cross-subsidies within the overall rate structure.[86] The Industrial Production Committee of the Conseil de la République (Senate) recognized this in a report on the proposed tariff:

> The proposal in question [which ostensibly] establishes equality of treatment seems to assert that there is an analogy between an industrial firm and a [local] distribution service consuming the same quantities of energy under the same conditions. That is absolutely false. The industrialist always retains his freedom of action; he is completely free to install his own energy source, he can move his operations to a location more favored by the rate structure, [and] he can shift the hours in which he consumes electricity in order to attain the maximum benefits from the rates. . . . The case is totally different for a distribution service [,which] must, in effect, supply current to whomever demands it, at whatever hour or situation of demand. It is rooted in the area set for it. . . . As a result, it is impossible for it to address any of its legitimate demands to its supplier, the nationalized firm. . . . The concept of specific times, places, and uses as bases for sales at cost is also seductive in the abstract, but we shall see that it leads to a total negation of the principle of public service.[87]

Ramadier and Gilberton initially opposed the Green Tariff for similar reasons.

The Green Tariff retained the language of public service, that of equal treatment of equals, but EDF manager-economists stressed the specificity of each user, arguing that most users were indeed not equals. This position was justified, for production costs varied for almost every industrial user according to location, power consumed, supply voltage, and duration and time of use. Using these variables and the axiom that electricity is nonstorable (a fact that requires productive capacity slightly above peak demand), the economists defined different sets of costs and rates for different users.

The gap between marginalist theory and the rates charged under the Green Tariff arose from a set of arbitrary decisions, and the plethora of variables requiring specification spawned major calculation problems. Cost allocations required mathematical, statistical, and computing techniques at or beyond the frontiers of current knowledge. Boiteux's mentor, Professor Maurice Allais, saw this as the greatest problem of the Green Tariff.[88] On the positive side, Lionel Monnier

---

[86] Lionel Monnier recognizes this cross-subsidization, yet claims without much evidence that such a structure was framed as a way to pursue industrial policy; "La tarification de l'électricité depuis la crise du pétrole," *Revue de l'Énergie* (June 1978), 305.

[87] France, Conseil de la République, Commission de la Production Industrielle, "Rapport No. 418," pamphlet, addendum to the 21 July 1954 meeting (Paris: Imprimerie Nationale, 1954), p. 3.

[88] M. Boiteux and L. Puiseux, "Neutralité," p. 89.

has noted: "There are certain economic incalculables and it is unthinkable that they could ever be entirely resolved. But the obvious limitations should not deter us from coherently formulating models. In constantly forcing the analyst to explain all hypotheses, economic calculations alone allow him to define what he knows and leave the rest aside."[89] Michel Gabet, an EDF economist, admitted that calculability problems broke the link between the Green Tariff and marginal costs directly, so the cost analyses rested on "the mathematical *hope* [*espoir*] of marginal costs" [emphasis added], and even Boiteux and Stasi admitted that there were considerable "imputations" between theory and practice.[90] Hans Nissel, a critic of the Green Tariff, concluded that, "after all of [the] assumptions and adjustments, it is difficult to say to what extent the Green Tariff reflected marginal costs."[91]

When faced with problems of calculability, the EDF economists tended to impute in favor of the largest users. In these adjustments, they broke from the usual distinction between subscription fees to meet fixed capacity costs and commodity charges to meet operating costs. In a mathematical demonstration, Boiteux showed that Pareto optimality for the power system as a whole was assured by adding the capacity costs for inframarginal plants into the commodity charges during peak periods, thereby further pushing up on-peak energy charges. He assumed that the operating costs of the last generating plant on line (the marginal plant) were so high (owing to operating inefficiencies) that the revenue surplus gained by charging kwh rates based on such costs would cover the capacity costs for all but the marginal plant.[92] Boiteux claimed that the revenue surplus would cover not only short-term operating costs but long-term developmental mar-

[89] Lionel Monnier, *La tarification*, p. 46.
[90] M. Gabet and M. Francony, "Aspects économiques et tarifaires de la modulation des charges à l'Électricité de France," paper presented to the EEC's Committee on Electrical Energy, conference on the coverage of load curves in future electrical production systems, Rome, 10–14 October 1977, p. 2, and Marcel Boiteux and Paul Stasi, "Sur la détermination des prix de revient et de développement dans un système interconnecté de production-distribution," Report 6, UNIPEDE Rome conference, September 1952, p. 33. Jean Lorgeou of EDF's Service d'Étude et de Promotion de l'Action Commerciale noted in an internal EDF document, "La tarification de l'électricité" (document AC/T 700, May 1978 p. 6/1), that the gap between the marginalist theory and the actual rate schedule was filled with many compromises and arbitrary decisions, so that filling the gap was essentially a game of probability.
[91] Hans Nissel, *The Electrical Rate Question: Europe Revisited* (1976), p. 17.
[92] For example, if at a given time the operating costs on a new base-load plant were 1 franc per kwh, and those on an old and inefficient peak-power unit (in 1958, most likely a 55-mw unit built in the 1920s) were 9 francs per kwh, EDF could easily cover all of its costs by charging 9 francs per kwh on peak. If, however, EDF replaced that inefficient peaking unit with one whose operating costs were 5 francs per kwh, it would charge 5 francs per kwh on peak, thereby cutting its revenue surplus at a time when it needed more revenue to cover the capital expenses of the new peak unit.

ginal costs as well. He asserted that the model would work correctly if the equipment-planning discount rate was identical to prevailing rates of return on the financial markets, all producers in the economy priced their outputs at marginal cost, and interest rates were identical to the rate of growth in the economy.[93] Since the latter two conditions were not met, the theory could not work effectively in the real world. In addition, as the efficiency gap among plants narrowed owing to the diminishing rates of growth in technical improvements, the revenue surplus would shrink over time. This misconception reduced the allocation of costs to nonpeak, high load-factor industrial consumers.

Once EDF had developed a tentative rate schedule, projected EDF revenues fell 7 percent short of what EDF needed.[94] Strategies of marginal cost pricing could not yield sufficient revenue to meet EDF's needs. Boiteux attributed this to the decreasing cost character of the industry, in which, at virtually all levels of output, marginal costs were less than average costs. EDF filled the gap by selectively increasing certain rates above the derived marginal costs.[95] Boiteux claimed to follow the second-best theory of Lipsey and Lancaster, making a distinction between the private sector (assumed to be competitive) and the public sector and calling for the latter to cover the difference. This meant that if below-cost sales to large industrial consumers on the Green Tariff induced losses for EDF, the state should cover them.[96] Roger Pauwels of Éclairage replied that marginal cost pricing would work only in an economy in which all goods were priced at marginal cost, otherwise, without subsidies, "the result can only be an erosion of the substance of the nationalized firm."[97]

Indeed, the introduction of the Green Tariff necessitated state subsidies, for without them, EDF would have not had sufficient investment capital. Its introduction in 1958 was immediately followed by a drop in overall EDF investments, and in particular, a 36 percent fall in EDF's

[93] Boiteux, "Sur la détermination," p. 31.
[94] Marcel Boiteux, "L'énergie électrique: Données, problèmes et perspectives," RFE 123 (August 1962), 196.
[95] Ibid, p. 87.
[96] On the contrary, Paul Stasi ("L'utilisation rationelle de l'énergie électrique: L'apport de la tarification," paper presented to the UNIPEDE Warsaw conference, May 1962, p. 9) claimed that the 7 percent revenue gap was filled by selectively raising the rates of consumers whose rates under the Green Tariff were substantially less than they had been before the changeover; on the contrary again, Nissel (The Electrical Rate Question, p. 14) claimed that the gap was compensated by simply hiking the rates in the North to cover the difference. The issue remains rather mysterious, for it was never presented to the EDF board for resolution. Nonetheless, when EDF made a set of revisions to the Green Tariff in the late 1960s, Boiteux noted the complaints of industrial consumers in the North and sought rate reductions for those consumers; CAPV 278 (24 October 1969).
[97] R. Pauwels's draft of paper on rate making, 1967, p. 21, Éclairage archives, dossier: "Tarification."

ability to finance its investments from retained earnings between 1959 and 1960.[98] That drop ended only when systematic state subsidies to EDF began in 1963, accompanied by a rate hike for low-voltage (non-industrial) consumers. By giving EDF more revenue, the later rate hikes also reduced EDF's presence on the bond market.[99]

The phase-in of the Green Tariff also benefited large high-voltage industrial users and hurt low-voltage users. The government and EDF had already agreed that rate reform would not increase rates for any Green Tariff clients.[100] The government also recognized that EDF was operating at a loss, so it allowed EDF to raise capacity charges from 165 to 1,500 francs per kw for the industrial users who did not opt for the Green Tariff.[101] The government then decreased EDF's revenue by imposing a kwh rate cut for the same users in November 1959.[102] To compensate for EDF's losses incurred between 1957 and 1959, low-tension users collectively saw an increase of 17 billion (old) francs in meter charges and 10 billion (old) francs in general rate hikes.[103] EDF also reinstated the 15 percent surcharge it had earlier removed from new low-voltage hookups.

The introduction of the Green Tariff meant substantial rate cuts for several industries. Aluminum producers that did not already benefit from specially discounted rates saw reductions of about 20 percent, large metallurgical firms enjoyed cuts of about 12 percent, and a number of cement producers received reductions of 12 to 13 percent.[104] Specific figures are unavailable, but regionally based, medium-sized firms seem to have sustained large rate increases, particularly those in such industries as textiles, metal fabricating, and other energy-intensive, yet small-scale, activities. Indeed, at the insistence of these firms inter-regional rate differences for medium-tension users were

---

[98] EDF-Direction Générale, "L'évolution du financement des investissements," single-page document, June 1981.

[99] Thatcherite conservative Henri Lepage (*EDF et la tarification au coût marginal* [1988]) argues in favor of privatization for EDF and attacks the marginal cost model for its incalculability and its tendency to generate overpriced rates, yet deeply confuses the issues of operating subsidies and cross-subsidies.

[100] Administrative order of 27 November 1958, *JO*, 2 December 1958, cited in Deglaire, *Recueil*, vol. 13, p. 547.

[101] CAPV 133 (21 December 1956); the kw charges for non–Green Tariff industrial users were hiked to 2,000 old francs per kw in December 1958, to 2,500 old francs in December 1959, and to 3,000 old francs in December 1960; *Journal Officiel, Textes d'intérêt général, électricité: Concession du réseau d'alimentation générale en énergie électrique (cahier des charges)*, pamphlet No. 58–211-S (December 1958), p. 4. Perhaps low-volume industrial users were reluctant to opt for the Green Tariff because they themselves had to pay the $900 it cost to install the special meters used for the Green Tariff.

[102] CAPV 167 (4 December 1959).

[103] CAPV 164 (24 July 1959).

[104] Jean Vilain, *La politique de l'énergie en France* (1969), p. 201.

reduced just before the Green Tariff was implemented. In addition, the EDF front office back dated rate reductions to 1 January 1956, and EDF paid 40 million francs to General Motors, 32 million francs to Duralumin, 23 million francs to Ciment Français, and 10 million francs to Ciments Lafarge.[105] Boiteux justified the rebates by asserting that they were given to reflect the time between a request to go onto the Green Tariff and the time when the new rates were implemented. Contending that EDF should pay for delays in implementing rate reductions, Boiteux insisted that the payments be based on imputations rather than direct meterings.[106] Though many industries that had enjoyed preferential tariffs before the reform saw rate increases, within a short time, their real rates dropped to preform levels or below.[107]

The Green Tariff explicitly did not apply to low-voltage power supplied to homes, artisanal enterprises, or commercial consumers, though it did apply to EDF's sales to its own distribution networks. Over 90 percent of all power consumers fell into the low-tension category and they accounted for well over half of all EDF revenues, but their total electrical consumption was about one quarter of that among higher-tension consumers. Reform of low-tension rates began in the early 1960s, and because of technical, legal, and fiscal problems, the phase-in period for the low-voltage Universal Tariff ran from 1964 to 1974. The EDF front office refused the GNC's request that the Green Tariff be reviewed while developing the Universal Tariff in order to eliminate cross-subsidies.[108]

The Universal Tariff was introduced like the Green Tariff, by subjecting higher-volume users to lower percentage rate increases than low-volume users. This placed a greater responsibility for paying overall system costs onto the shoulders of smaller consumers. For example, in the rate hike of July 1965, nominally at 1.85 percent, the average low-voltage users saw increases of 7 to 10 percent.[109] Increases in 1963 and 1964 meant a 2.3 percent hike for very high voltage users, 2.8 percent for high-voltage users, 3 percent for middle-tension users, and 4.2 percent for low-voltage users. As a result of the rate reforms, by 1970 the rate gap between low- and high-voltage rates was higher in France than elsewhere: in Great Britain, the ratio was 1.16 : 1, in West

[105] "M.G.," "Réponse de [name blacked out] aux questions posées," undated carbon copy of document marked "très secrète," Éclairage archives, dossier: "Problèmes énergétiques: tarification."

[106] S. Deglaire and E. Bordier, Électricité, p. 91.

[107] Picard et al., Histoire(s), p. 161.

[108] Draft of untitled paper by Claude Tougeron on tariffs, 1962, GNC archives, dossier 2/4: "Tarifs EDF-GDF," p. 18.

[109] Pauwels draft, p. 20.

Germany it was 1.65 : 1, in the United States, it was 1.83 : 1, while in France it was 2.3 : 1.[110]

Rather than seeking implicit or explicit subsidies to help cover capacity costs for low-volume domestic power consumers, EDF economists decided to use advertising to promote sales, recognizing that after raising the voltage (and the revenues) of the low-tension systems, there would be substantial excess capacity.[111] In addition, because most domestic consumption occurred off-peak, increased use by that group improved overall system-load factors. Almost any increase in low-tension consumption would require no additional capacity.[112] Hence, EDF began its famous "Blue Meter" sales campaign in 1962, starting out by painting many of the low-voltage domestic meters in the country blue, and following with advertising brochures and consumer centers. The advertising efforts reflected an implicit admission that the demand elasticity assumptions in the marginalist model were faulty: had the elasticities been as high as EDF claimed, consumers would have adapted demand to prices, making advertising unnecessary.

EDF economists promised substantial reductions in peak loads and commensurate savings on capital investments and operating costs. Massé optimistically claimed that the peak shaving induced by the Green Tariff would amount to 540 mw, constituting five thousand dollars a day in coal purchases and 42.5 billion old francs in capital investments by 1965.[113] Paul Stasi claimed that the new rates had shaved the morning peak by up to 700 mw and the evening peak by 200 mw.[114] Massé repeated Boiteux's figures to a skeptical EDF board.[115] EDF economists attributed any and all load-factor improvements to the salutary effects of the Green Tariff. They ignored the fact that over

[110] Nissel, *The Electrical Rate Question*, p. 67. EDF itself admitted that the rate gap between high- and low-voltage rates had widened considerably as a result of the rate reform; see "Niveau de prix de l'électricité," *IDC*, article 227 (September 1967), 2–6.

[111] In the mid-1950s, realizing that physically expanding the capacity of the distribution network was far too expensive and time consuming, EDF decided to raise the voltage on the distribution network, thereby doubling the wattage it could carry and giving EDF time to rewire the entire nation.

[112] J. Rouchon, "Une expérience de mise en place d'une réforme tarifaire en basse tension: Les problèmes posés par l'introduction en France du tarif universel," conference paper no. 4.2, UNIPEDE conference on electricity tariffs, Madrid, 21–23 April 1975, p. 13.

[113] Pierre Massé, "Quelques incidences économiques du tarif vert," *RFE* 97 (May 1958), pp. 392–93. This promise helped to gain the government's approval of the new rate structure. In the wake of the energy shortages after the Suez Crisis, any cuts in energy use were welcome. In addition, the Finance Ministry was expectedly happy to see any cuts in EDF spending.

[114] Stasi, "L'utilisation rationnelle," p. 18.

[115] CAPV 149 (25 April 1958).

time electrical use rose fastest among high-utilization consumers. As an arithmetic consequence, total system load factors rose regardless of the Green Tariff. Undoubtedly, industries for which electrical power was a major component of total production costs did reduce their peak demands.[116] Nonetheless, between 1952 and 1956 (before the Green Tariff), the utilization rate of the system rose from 61 percent to 64 percent, but between 1956 and 1964, when load characteristics were supposed to have been ameliorated, the total system utilization rate remained constant.[117]

Large industry probably applied considerable pressure on EDF, via the government, to grant rate relief. In a secret internal memo in 1964, Boiteux noted that among "subscribers for whom electrical power costs play a major part in total production costs, the existence of [special low rates] is indispensable for resolving problems between ourselves and them; were we not to resolve these problems in this fashion, the industrialists would go to the government and seek its support [for cutting our rates]."[118] EDF thus set high volume and high load utilization rate tariffs that were probably lower than production costs. When the General Economic Studies section proposed revisions to the Green Tariff in 1969, it refused to increase any of the largest industrial users' rates regardless of whether or not marginal cost analyses justified them, which they did. They justifiably claimed that if such rates were too high, large consumers would simply move their operations overseas.[119]

Under the Green Tariff the aluminum industry had all of the most desirable consumption characteristics, so it received the cheapest power. However, when it considered expanding its facilities in 1964, Pechiney sought even greater discounts on its power. Undoubtedly, Pechiney could use information on EDF's ability to discount its rates via the seat held on the EDF board by Pechiney's chief executive officer, Raoul Vitry d'Avaucourt. After receiving offers for discounted rates for

[116] André Requin and Jean Lorgeou, "Experiences with French Tariff Structures: Technical Means for the Implementation of Tariff Structures," in Charles J. Cicchetti and Wesley K. Foell, eds., *Energy Systems Forecasting, Planning and Pricing: Proceedings of a French-American Conference, University of Wisconsin–Madison, 23 September–3 October 1974,* pp. 301–2.

[117] Nissel, *The Electrical Rate Question,* p. 49, verified against EDF, *Statistiques de production.*

[118] "MB/JB," "Le tarif d'appoint," EDF internal document (confidential) 19 September 1964. Boiteux later noted that for large power consumers, pressuring the government to force EDF to lower certain rates yielded easier production-cost reductions than real improvements in productive efficiency; cited in Picard et al., *Histoire(s),* p. 366.

[119] EDF-EEG, "Étude relative à la révision du 'tarif vert,' " Report to EDF Board of Directors' Operations Committee (confidential), 23 October 1969, p. 2. Pechiney had built new plants overseas for years, installing an aluminum-production facility in Greece directly after the war and one in West Africa in the late 1950s.

a mine-mouth plant in the German Rhur and a gas-fired plant in the Netherlands, Pechiney presented them to EDF and demanded lower rates, lacking which Pechiney would move away. Boiteux initially stood firm, telling Pechiney that the Green Tariff made economic sense and that if Pechiney wanted cheaper rates, it could indeed go elsewhere. The government sharply disagreed and told Boiteux that EDF had to meet Pechiney's demands. Boiteux then sent his modelers back to the computer, and they soon came up with mathematical justifications for further reducing Pechiney's rates.[120] The revised model factored lower oil prices into the rate structure in such a way as to give all the benefits of falling oil prices to the largest consumers, thus violating the assumption (used in framing the Green Tariff) that aluminum smelters were supplied by cheap hydro power at the base of the load curve.[121] EDF economists thus showed that their science could bend according to political pressure. In doing so, they undercut any claim that the marginal cost rate structure was scientifically based.

No covert capitalist conspiracy framed rate reforms that ultimately benefited large industries. With honorable intentions of public service, EDF economists attempted to apply rational models in order to benefit society as a whole. The problem was not of intention, but of a naïve, neopositivist faith in building value-free models. The very impossibility of value neutrality in the models yielded socially inequitable and sometimes economically inefficient results. Neoclassic assumptions, particularly a normative notion of the free market, reflected the social and cultural instincts of the moderate technocrats. By delegating rate making authority to a group of elite economists, EDF shifted responsibility and power from the politically representative environment of the board to an undemocratic one. Despite the scientific veneer, rate making was a political process in which the ascendant political forces at a given time—domestic consumers and infrastructure industries in the 1950s, and large, integrated firms in the 1960s—got the rates they wanted.[122]

---

[120] CAPV 276 (27 June 1969); in this meeting, Boiteux recounted the Pechiney blackmail and mentioned that the synthetic textiles firm Progil had played a similar game. For Pechiney's side of the story, see Bernard Legrand and Georges Yelnik, "Un consommateur bien particulier: Aluminium Pechiney," in Fabienne Cardot, ed., L'électricité, pp. 142–43.

[121] "MB/JB," "Le tarif d'appoint."

[122] This follows a broad pattern of pricing public power in the United States; see Sam Peltzman, "Pricing in Public and Private Enterprises: Electrical Utilities in the United States," Journal of Law and Economics (1971), and John P. Blair, "The Politics of Government Pricing: Political Influences on the Rate Structure of Publicly Owned Utilities," American Journal of Economics and Sociology (1976). Both works are cited in Lawrence J. Hill and Richard C. Tepel, "Regulation, Pricing, and Comparative Performance in the U.S. Electric Utility Industry by Ownership Type," technical report no. ORNL/TM-9509 (Oak Ridge, Tenn.: Oak Ridge National Laboratory, 1985), p. 3/28.

In the final analysis, technocrats and the economic modernists had quietly taught an important lesson: nationalized enterprises could ultimately be turned into subsidy mechanisms that redirected tax and rate payers' money toward the private sector.

The Culture and Ideology of High Technology

Real salary levels at EDF declined steadily after 1947. As early as 1949, graduates from elite engineering schools (Polytechnique, École Centrale des Arts et Manufactures, and École Supérieure d'Électricité) virtually ceased entering EDF.[123] France severely lacked enough engineers in the 1950s, and the gap was made worse because many Polytechnique graduates worked not as engineers but as corporate managers, not unlike Gaspard and Massé.[124] By 1954 and 1955, the problem of recruitment was so grave that EDF managers, the EDF board, and conservative cadre unions publicly complained, breaking from engineers' usual professional silence on such issues.[125] By the late 1950s, such higher-status workers virtually fled EDF. In 1962, though EDF was France's largest and most technologically oriented firm, less than 4 percent of all Polytechnique graduates worked there.[126] The obvious solution to the cadre recruitment and retention problems was to raise salaries. The government granted cadres a few salary increases between 1957 and 1961, but they were insufficient. Just as the government had limited EDF's access to the capital markets for fear that EDF would crowd out other borrowers, it restricted EDF's access to the elite labor market. A wave of retirements beginning in the late 1950s further aggravated the cadre crisis.

The crisis strongly influenced the esprit of the EDF community, and the burgeoning bureaucracy at EDF created a rift between middle and upper management. In 1959, Distribution Director Touz noted in a speech to local distribution center managers, "There is a certain malaise among the cadres, a certain state of doubt, a certain disenchantment . . . a sense of being cut off from the directing conceptions of the firm,

---

[123] Editorial, "La grève à EDF-GDF," *RFE* 7 (March 1950), 4.

[124] A-J. Capocci, "Les cadres d'EDF-GDF," *Vie Française*, 15 September 1961, and "AIII", "L'électricité de France en 1955," *Les Documents Politiques, Diplomatiques et Financiers* (August 1956), 33–35.

[125] The Fédération des Cadres Supérieurs de l'Électricité et du Gaz went public with these complaints in *Figaro*, 12 May 1954. The same group reiterated its complaints in their journal, *Les Écoutes du Monde*, 24 December 1954; even *Le Parisien Libéré*, 9 January 1957, noted that pay levels at EDF made the hiring of engineers and cadres impossible. See also CAPV 118 (22 July 1955).

[126] Jacques Billy, "Les 'X' dans les affaires," *Entreprise* 376 (24 November 1962), 49–52.

and the rather discouraging impression that there is no longer a permanent exchange between those who think and those who do."[127] In its 1957 congress, the GNC noted that a deep apoliticism and careerism among the new cadre entrants into EDF exacerbated these problems.[128] Finally, though high job security somewhat compensated for low salaries, EDF did not treat young cadres well. A young cadre reported: "The situation we faced at the beginning of our careers at EDF was truly insulting. We were forced to relocate time and time again and we were never paid back for our moving expenses."[129] After considerable agitation by the workers and numerous complaints from the front office, in January 1960, the Ministry of Industry allowed EDF to restructure salaries, giving disproportionate pay increases to cadres as part of a generalized salary hike. The 1960 settlement also set a trajectory toward pay equity between then-underpaid EDF workers and private sector workers. However, the government blocked the scheduled increases, just as it had after similar promises in 1951 and 1957.

Barring pay increases sufficient to attract technical and managerial personnel, the next option, affirmed variously by unions and managers alike, was to stress nonsalary issues as incentives for joining EDF and staying there. Continuing an early EDF tradition, many within the EDF community sought personal and collective validation through association with leading-edge technological systems. Conceptions of technological futures were very different between the unions (particularly the CFTC) and the EDF front office, but both positions stressed the progressive role of high technology. The general approach, implicit in the earlier social productivist vision, characterized technical progress as the foundation for social progress and the promoters of electrical use as missionaries for the gospel of growth.[130] While this new ideology among managers continued the older notion of public service, it contradicted the class conscious and inward-looking views of the social productivists, replacing them with a stress on the intrinsic value of

---

[127] Speech of Distribution Director Touz to distribution center managers, cited in *Bulletin d'Information des Cadres*, article 6 (April 1959), 4–5.

[128] Cited in René Le Guen, *Voyage*, p. 242.

[129] Interview with an unnamed EDF cadre, in Capocci, "Les cadres."

[130] Marxist writings have traditionally reflected a strong implicit notion of unilinear technological development. For example, see Langdon Winner, *Autonomous Technology: Technics-out-of-Control as a Theme in Political Thought* (1977), pp. 77–89, and David MacKenzie, "Marx and the Machine," *Technology and Culture* 25 (1984), 473–502. Louis Puiseux, a one-time high official of EDF who is now in the academy, has referred to this view as "the Promethean aspect of marxism"; noted in his seminar on French Energy Policy, École des Hautes Études en Sciences Sociales, February 1981. For a vibrant discussion of the broad identity between electrical system expansion and social progress in the United States, see Richard F. Hirsch, "Culture and the Paradigm of Growth in the Electric Utility Industry," paper presented at the annual meetings of the Society for the History of Technology, Cambridge, Massachusetts, November 1984.

expertise itself and a paternalist rather than participationist notion of service. The darker side of the culture of high technology was a brave new world vision of the future—it was no coincidence that Jean-Luc Godard chose to film *Alphaville*, a movie about postmodern social and cultural vacuity, in the new Murat-Messine office complex of EDF's Central Services.

EDF's top managers expanded technical assistance to developing countries as a way to stress the high social status among cadres associated with technical progress. In addition, they promoted domestic electrical use, metaphorically implying that it would help build warm, happy nuclear families. Though both programs had other, equally important goals, one to support a French Alliance for Progress, the other to encourage a better utilization of EDF's facilities, they both had crucial cultural components. The emerging culture of high technology was tied in part to the slowing of hydro development. Hydro totemism had fostered internal cohesion in the early years, but the economist managers' slowing of hydro development and the exhaustion of *rentable* hydro sites demanded the construction of a new operative myth. Exported hydro expertise, domestic consumerism, and nuclear power provided the new icons. Between 1958 and 1962, the photographs adorning the walls of EDF offices slowly changed from domestic hydro to nuclear, foreign hydro, and domestic consumerist imagery. Those of the massive transmission facilities, wired as they were to the image of a rational framework over the nation, stayed. Nuclear high technology offered an opportunity to buttress collective self-conceptions as experts safe within security perimeters. Finally, in the new managerial mentality, closed nuclear technology and the inward-looking nuclear family were part of the same historical impetus.

EDF increasingly engaged in consulting for foreign electrical utilities after 1958. Top EDF managers hoped that foreign consulting would help build internal solidarity among EDF managers and engineers by giving them a stronger sense of world leadership in electrical power technology. Less importantly, by opening overseas markets for French electrical equipment manufacturers, EDF might not have to cover all of its suppliers' research and development costs. Finally, consulting would valorize engineers' work on a world scale and offer self-esteem beyond the paycheck and outside the politics of the EDF community.

EDF's foreign consulting activities were initially directed by an internal office, the Inspection Générale pour la Coopération hors Métropole (IGÉCO), under hydro expert Marcel Mary. IGÉCO concentrated specifically on the finer points of utility management: rate making, accounting methods, electrical law, and the like. Broad technical, managerial, and engineering assistance was quite limited. In 1958, EDF started a joint subsidiary, called Sofrelec, with private electrical think tanks and French banks. EDF owned 33 percent of Sofrelec. When the proposal for Sofrelec was first submitted to the EDF board for approval in 1958, it was met with mixed reactions. Bernard Clappier, the representative of the Finance Ministry, applauded the proposal as a measure to increase exports from French manufacturers, but Morel feared that EDF would become a shill for the French equipment firms and that Sofrelec would undercut EDF's independence.[131]

Morel's fears were not unfounded. In 1957, EDF had consulted on the preparatory work for the Konkouré hydroelectric project in Guinea, but the project eroded EDF's market in France and encouraged industrial power consumers to expand outside France. With an average annual productive potential of 3 billion kwh, the Konkouré project provided cheap power for a multinational aluminum production complex of which Pechiney and Ugine owned one-half.[132] The power from Konkouré was to cost a mere 1 franc per kwh, compared to French rates of about 0.85 franc for limited quantities of Article Eight power and 5.0 francs per kwh for all power thereafter.[133] The Konkouré project allowed Pechiney and Ugine to threaten overseas production as a way to pressure EDF to cut its bulk power rates. EDF's overseas consulting activities were to "strengthen ties between the technical elites of foreign countries and the French industrial milieu" in more than just a social sense.[134] Sofrelec wrote: "These studies will tend to open the door to precise industrial activities, and one can easily understand that [consulting work] will interest the mechanical and electrical construction firms in a number of countries, particularly in France. There is a clear role for Sofrelec to play in that respect, and [consulting activities] can lead to requests for direct work following requests submitted to Sofrelec managers."[135] Similarly, EDF participated in the National Center for Foreign Trade, helping to increase French exports through the center's activities, which were, in the words of a representative of the center, "to play an important role in helping . . . French exports."[136]

EDF genuinely sought to spread the good life associated with electricity. Implicitly rejecting the prevailing simplistic notion of a single,

[131] CAPV 156 (19 December 1958).

[132] Les Échos des Finances, 17 October 1957.

[133] "Lettre du conseil municipal de Saint-Denis sur la question des tarifs cadeaux," Force-Information 12 (June 1955), 44, and Revue des Applications de l'Électricité 200 (January 1963).

[134] "Considérations sur l'engineering à l'étranger et sur le 'sofre' en général," Bulletin d'Information des Cadres, article 159 (November 1964), 7.

[135] EDF, Manuel de l'expert d'Électricité de France en mission de coopération technique (1967), p. 142.

[136] Aristide Antoine, Les relations d'Électricité de France avec l'étranger (n.d. [1956?]), p. 12.

unilinear development model for the Third World, EDF was laudably careful to orient developing countries toward appropriate technologies rather than simply the highest technology available from French manufacturers. Part of that recognition of the need for appropriate technology in the Third World came from a paternalism of the technically advanced toward "backward" countries, but it would be unfair to view EDF's activities in that light. In its manual for EDF engineers doing overseas consulting, the stress on appropriate technology and respect for indigenous culture was far too systematic to indicate simple paternalism.[137]

Crucially, EDF's overseas consulting helped to buttress the intrafirm mentality of technical expertise. With a missionary zeal comparable to the power-sales campaign at home, overseas consulting offered EDF engineers higher self-esteem at a time when their intrafirm status was waning. Consulting also reinforced the view that technical development was a mission accomplished in France, one naturally leading to similar missions elsewhere. Public service at home was transformed into humanitarian service overseas, further reinforcing an emerging element of internal solidarity within EDF, that of technical superiority on a world scale. Foreign consulting also helped to stress technical and economic expertise over more classically political notions of public service. However, EDF's missionary work grew at the same time as the Gaullist state sought national grandeur both as a supporter of Third World nationalism and as a supplier of modern technologies. As with the Alliance for Progress, consulting elegantly dovetailed national interest, economic expansion, humanitarian service, and collective self-satisfaction.

Just as overseas consulting represented a turn outward, a stress on domestic sales reflected a turn toward rapprochement with emerging French consumerism. A naïve notion that technical progress was both politically neutral and socially beneficial inspired the promotional fervor of EDF managers and the CGT toward domestic sales. In this analysis, technological development was autonomous and unilinear: it had a dynamic all its own, and progress itself unfolded embedded possibilities. These conceptions of technology fired a zealous promotion of electricity in and of itself—more electrical use did not, it was assumed, reflect higher living standards, it caused them. Ironically, EDF embarked on these campaigns at a time when the available funds within EDF for the expansion of domestically available power were very scarce.[138] By 1963, however, domestic rate reforms had generated

[137] See, for example, EDF, *Manuel*, p. 62ff.
[138] Not only were there few funds for the reinforcement of the low-voltage network, EDF managers were not particularly enthusiastic to expand that sort of equipment, for

sufficient funds for extensive domestic promotion and network reinforcement. The finance ministry's largesse also helped sales campaigns. The major promotional campaigns after 1959 also reflected a
sense of subtle embarrassment in the EDF community due to relatively
low electrical use per citizen. Indeed, as late as 1957, over one-half of
French households had few electrical appliances other than lamps. At
the same time, internal wiring in homes was so insufficient that before
a voltage change on low-tension networks, most French households
could operate few resistance devices (lights, irons, toasters, etc.) at the
same time. The sales campaigns thus genuinely sought to raise levels
of domestic comfort. Nevertheless, if the benefits of increased domestic
electrical use were as obvious as one would be led to believe, it can be
surmised that promoting electricity and appliances did not only serve
consumers.[139]

The change in the approach toward sales campaigns can be best
understood by contrasting the views of Gabriel Dessus, a top EDF
manager, in 1952 to those expressed by EDF managers in the early
1960s. Dessus argued: "To sell as many kilowatt-hours as possible no
longer [i.e., since the nationalization] makes any sense: perhaps it
satisfies the engineers; it certainly satisfies the statisticians . . . but vanity of vanities . . . why use labor power, coal, and public credit in order
to to supply the French people with a given type of energy when
perhaps they would prefer to consume more sausage? . . . After all, is
a public service there to satisfy the public, or to impose its tastes on
the public?"[140] More technically oriented managers at EDF also argued,
"Our métier is to satisfy [existing] needs as well as possible—it is not
up to us to provoke [more demand]."[141] Nonetheless, by the 1960s,
EDF management was determined "to impose its tastes on the public"
because they were, as an anonymous manager said, conscious of the
"change in moral climate" as EDF moved from parsimony to plenty
and as the economy as a whole did the same.[142] In its Four-Year Plan

they claimed that economies of scale did not operate in electrical distribution services;
see EDF-Direction Générale, "Les investissements de la distribution dans les agglom-
érations" (Plan V Distribution Plan) mimeographed (1965), EDF archives, series E8:
"Économie générale."

[139] Though she does not discuss the ontology or intentionality of appliance giving, in
*More Work for Mother: The Ironies of Household Technology from the Open Hearth to the
Microwave* (New York: Basic, 1983), Ruth Schwartz Cowan provides a very useful point
of departure for addressing the ritual giving of appliance-gifts by husbands to their
spouses.

[140] Speech by Gabriel Dessus to EDF commercial agents, in Gabriel Dessus, "Le service
national et le client," *RFE* 32 (June 1952), 301.

[141] Jean Dubois, "Le réveil commercial d'EDF: Compteur bleu et chauffage électrique
intégré," in Cardot, ed., *L'électricité et ses consommateurs*, p. 288.

[142] "Le développement des ventes d'énergie électrique en basse tension," *IDC*, article
165 (January 1965), 3.

for Commercial Action of 1963, among other goals, EDF wanted to provoke and promote electrical use, rather than wait for the demand to appear, and to cultivate a confident image.[143] EDF worked symbiotically with Moulinex, France's largest home-appliance manufacturer, in its promotional efforts.[144] The EDF community justified sales promotion in the 1950s as a way to raise the utilization rate of the low-voltage network; in the 1960s, EDF ostensibly sold an intrinsically valuable commodity, electricity. Undoubtedly, the latter justification helped to validate EDF workers' self-image. Reflecting these image-building efforts, between 1958 and 1965, EDF's promotional budget rose from 1 to 3 percent of its total annual operating revenues.[145] The CGT urged these campaigns forward, reinforcing the culture of electricity and recognizing that a positive public image for EDF meant greater political security for the workers and the firm.

Sales campaigns after 1959 promulgated a gently sexist and middle-class vision of the nuclear family living in a single-family home. Appliances enhanced the warm, happy, inward-looking family, for they were "so appreciated by the little queen of the household [maîtresse de maison] because of the help they give her."[146] In order to attract the housewife to appliances, EDF built many neighborhood-based consumer-action centers, all clean, brightly lit, and filled with all the newest appliances. A recurring image in the EDF brochures of the era (not unlike those of the All Electric Home campaign in the United States at the same time) was that of the new mom standing beside her shining range as an appreciative family sat around the television set. Missionary zeal aside, EDF well understood who could best afford the new image of the family: when increasing the capacity of the Parisian distribution network to allow more use of appliances, EDF worked first in the wealthiest districts.[147]

Several major EDF figures agreed that sales campaigns were consciously framed to influence the internal mentality at EDF and to reshape the collective self-image of electrical workers.[148] They also

---

[143] "Le plan quadriennel d'action commerciale," *Bulletin d'Information des Cadres*, article 127 (June 1963), 4.

[144] Moulinex's performance was a true success story. In 1962, it was tiny, and most of the French appliance market was dominated by Philips (Holland), but by 1970, Moulinex had the largest French market share and also had a significant presence throughout the EEC.

[145] "Le développement des ventes," p. 1.

[146] Speech by Jacques Gallot to EDF commercial agents, cited in *IDC*, article 151 (August 1964), 9.

[147] Evidently, the sales campaigns succeeded. During the famous "blue meter" campaign, which began in 1963, the number of French homes with washing machines rose from 24 percent to 65 percent in five years; Dubois, "Le réveil," p. 290.

[148] Interviews by author with Roger Gaspard, Paris, 3 June 1981, and Ernest Anzalone, Paris, 14 April 1981.

recognized that special in-house journals played a similar role. The first of these, *Vie Électrique,* a journal for blue-collar workers, started in 1955; it was followed by *Bulletin d'Information des Cadres* in 1959, for white-collar workers. Both publications were self-consciously apolitical and entirely ignored the place of unions in the life of the firm. Instead, they lauded EDF's technical and managerial expertise, carefully presenting photographs of smiling workers, scenic power lines, tamed nature, or warm and well-lit families. These publications most succinctly presented the image of high technical progress in a nuclearized future. A missionary vision and a stress on depoliticized technical expertise became the cement for the EDF community as its managers shifted from social productivism to symbiosis with the private sector.

The evolution of the relationship between the state and EDF and the changes in managerial thinking within EDF could be encapsulated as a change from traditionalism to modernism within the state and a replacement of social technocrats with economist-managers in EDF management. Such terms are loose, yet useful. Though there is little consensus on the exact political-economic dimensions of the political changes in France between 1954 and 1965, the term *modernization* encompasses almost all views, from those who see the rising walls of the technostate or technoprison, to those who see the victory of rationality over instinct and prejudice. With respect to a long-standing debate over the issue of *dirigisme,* François Caron and others argue that the Fifth Republic rejected the *dirigisme* of the Fourth in favor of a more liberal, free market approach.[149] While elements of this view seem valid, the persistence of macroeconomic controls over EDF and the explicit policy of the state to use the nationalized sector (and state subsidies) to aid private industry bespeak a public liberalism and a tacit *dirigisme.* Conversely, while EDF itself openly represented a facet of a directivist state, the increasing use of normative free market assumptions in shaping corporate policy reflected a growing adherence to liberalism. From opposite ends, therefore, state and EDF policies began to converge and tensions were lessened.

Jean-François Picard and others also argue that EDF went through a major shift similar to that described here, yet they ascribe it to the era from 1965 to 1975.[150] The character of that shift was fairly clear: the participationist, nationalist, and self-reflective EDF community gave way to a technocracy operated from the top by an insulated group of highly competent experts. Their credentials were beyond reproach, and they led EDF to the height of its glory in 1970. The trajectory of the

---

[149] François Caron, *An Economic History of Modern France* (New York: Columbia University Press, 1979), p. 327.

[150] *Histoire(s),* pp. 213–26.

changes documented by Picard and others was set in the years 1954–
65. At that time, EDF managers chose to reject their original alliance
with the trade unionists and left technocrats and fully affirmed their
allegiance to the modernist capitalist system.

CHAPTER 5

The Means of Production:
Technological Choice at EDF

The nationalization of electrical power in France gave EDF the power to determine the techniques and technologies it would use to fulfill its mission. As in much of the history of technology, a key issue for EDF was that of technological choice, and it was in that realm that nationalization liberated French electricity. EDF made the most of its liberation in its early years, freeing engineers to envision bold choices, but by the mid-1960s, economists and finance men made economic decisions that sometimes negatively reshaped technological choices. For example, by selecting oil as a primary energy source, EDF chose to erode France's already-limited energy independence, and by moving toward cost-plus methods of equipment purchasing, EDF became less capable of controlling the costs and characteristics of its equipment. In opting for American nuclear technology in 1969, EDF largely surrendered control over a key component of its technological future. Ironically, just as EDF managers were losing control over technological choice, EDF workers were learning to gain political control of the technology with which they worked.

Many writers on technology—those whom David Noble refers to as technological Darwinists—and much of the general public believe that the internal characteristics of artifacts impose technological choices.[1] Technological Darwinists believe in a technological jungle where only the most economically fit technologies survive, and where there is only one best way to do a job. *Best* in this context is measured by capitalist standards on the free market. The dustbin of technological history is filled with the refuse of technologies that the market in its impersonal

---

[1] David F. Noble, *Forces of Production* (1984), pp. 145–47.

wisdom proved unfit. For such analysts, technologies are not chosen but uncovered, and the role of the engineer, economist, or marketing expert is merely to uncover the best technology, which always either lies hidden just beneath the surface of current material culture or can be discovered by rational investigation by means of larger data bases, more sophisticated models, or more powerful computers. Such investigation is based on the natural laws of physics, engineering, neoclassical economics, and revealed consumer preference, and those who succeed are today's discoverers. In this context, technological change is little more than the discovery and development of a unilinear trajectory of embedded potentialities. What is more, to borrow Langdon Winner's term, this school views technology as "autonomous," a force that constructs society and culture rather than being constructed by them.[2] More accurately, one can argue that there is a dialectic between technology and its context, that as an iterative dynamic, technology and its environment simultaneously construct each other.[3]

The Darwinist approach begs the very issue of what is the best or fittest technology. The normative assumption of a free market gives little guidance, for it exists only in the minds of certain experts. *Best* can be defined, as it was by the second generation of EDF managers, in entirely neoclassical terms; it can be defined in Keynesian terms, systems analysis terms, and certainly Marxist-Leninist terms. Though systems analysis has shed light on the contours of interrelatedness and thereby eroded unilinear conceptions, systems analysts have always had to draw the fateful line around the system they wish to examine. As with the economist-managers at EDF, what is excluded conceptually by the systems approach is analytically irrelevant. Until the late 1960s, EDF managers drew lines around fossil fuel plants, judging their efficiency only on a heat-loss basis. Soon, popular attention forced the line to be expanded to include polluted air and overheated rivers, and in 1973, OPEC stretched the line further to include not only the security of supply but the politics of the suppliers. The efficient 600 mw oil-fired plants started in the mid-1960s, which were the best technologies of their day, became embarrassing behemoths by 1975. Similarly, the abandoned nuclear plants at Shoreham, New York, Zimmer, Ohio, and Midland, Michigan, represent monuments to systems analyses that underrated the probability and consequences of plant failures.

Were we to concede that systems analysis, along with cost-benefit analysis and least-cost modeling, are the most appropriate starting points for technological analysis, we would have to recognize their

[2] Langdon Winner, *Autonomous Technology.*
[3] For an ecosystem application of this framework, see Richard Levin and Richard Lewontin, *The Dialectical Biologist* (1985), intro. and chap. 1.

limitations—an inability to deal with all factors, particularly the non-quantifiable ones—as well as our own. It is impossible to foresee all possibilities or to construct algorithms to simulate them. Criteria for making choices must be made explicit, and the means for making choices (not to mention the recognition that choices even exist) must be rational. Were taste, instinct, and class predilection allowed to allocate massive quantites of capital, we would oversee a monumental waste of social resources. At EDF, the early efforts of the economists and engineers to define criteria for technological choice were laudable and necessary tasks. As time passed, however, EDF managers were wont to articulate their criteria and tended (often unintentionally) to choose technologies that reinforced the positions of powerful economic, social, and political groups, using the franchise of expertise to legitimate their choices. The axioms for rational choice were presented as neutral, not unlike Boiteux's assertions about the Green Tariff, and when the process of making choices had to go beyond the quantitatively explicable frontiers of the models, the new managers passed off instinct, taste, and class predilection as rationality. When they were democratically and openly derived, models could set frameworks for choice, but they could not make choices. Then as always, that task remained within the realm of human frailty and politics.

Choices of Primary Energy Sources

EDF at the outset systematically chose to use domestic coal and hydropower for the bulk of the power it produced. These two forms of energy met a number of pressing demands. With sufficient French coal production, both were absolutely domestically based and fostered energy independence and a minimal drain on France's limited foreign exchange reserves. In addition, both industries were in public hands, assuring (in the Liberation-era climate of distrust for private ownership) that their development would benefit the nation rather than a small circle of corporate profiteers. For these and other reasons, the Monnet Plan focused on hydro and domestic coal development. Nuclear power technology will be discussed later in this chapter.

Within the domestic coal and hydro logic, however, different groups competed over which should be stressed. By political tradition, thermal power was viewed as reactionary and hydro was seen as progressive,[4]

[4] Picard et al., *Histoire(s)*, pp. 68–72. See also Pierre Lanthier, "Les dirigeants," pp. 101–36. Specifically, thermal power was identified with the Mercier utility group and hydro was identified with the CGT's 1937 nationalization plan and the Popular Front's "Plan for Three Billion" of 1938 (see supra, chap. 1).

so the self-conscious progressive politics of EDF's early years demanded hydro. EDF drew much of its early management from the
Corps des Ponts et Chaussées, who, as specialists in bridges, roads,
and public works, were inclined toward the earth-moving and concrete
of dam projects. This stood in stark contrast to their rivals from the
Corps des Mines, whom they had well-nigh defenestrated in constructing the EDF front office and who favored the development of
fossil fuels. Engineers found particular satisfaction in hydro. Liberated
by the nationalization, utility engineers could let their technical imag-
inations run free as they viewed the possibilty of taming remote river
basins with projects of engineering art, which were different for each
quirky site, thereby demanding complete, bottom-up analysis each
time. The CGT also strongly endorsed hydro, partially out of political
instinct, partially out of a mimicry of similar Soviet achievements, and
out of an implicit class analysis of the cost structure of the two technologies: hydro took capital from the owning class, while thermal took
income from the working class. Elementary cost-benefit analyses performed by the Modernization Commission for the Monnet Plan also
showed that if the nation was willing to invest the capital, hydro yielded
far greater benefits over the long term. Finally and of equal significance,
hydro dams had an important symbolic value—their immense, graceful
curves were totems of a new, high-technology, modernist France in
the making.

Hydro's unquestioned predominance was short-lived. As the political climate changed with the recognition of France's financial crises
and the onset of the Cold War, forces outside EDF pushed for the
adoption of thermal technology, even if it meant importing coal. There
was a strong element of revenge by the Corps des Mines against EDF
management. Lacoste appointed Gabriel Taïx to the EDF board as a
way to break the hegemony of the Corps des Ponts.[5] Taïx attacked the
hydro projects as baubles of "technicians' vanity" rather than coherent
efforts to develop cheap power resources.[6] For EDF Equipment Office
rationalizers such as Massé, hitherto a hydro proponent, the very specificity of each hydro site condemned it, for EDF could not benefit from
serial purchase prices on plant designs and components, as it could
with standardized thermal plants. Finally, economic logic and the exhaustion of sites ultimately doomed hydro and its proud supporters.
EDF, of course, developed the most promising sites first and, helped
by the Blue Note, found that each successive site was less economic
than the last. Faults in the Blue Note only accelerated the inevitable

[5] Picard et al., *Histoire(s)*, p. 71.
[6] Gabriel Taïx, *Le Plan Monnet*, pp. 86 and 150.

end of EDF's hydro era, with a calculable present-value loss of savings for each delayed project.

A small circle within the Research and Development Directorate of EDF (Direction des Études et Recherches, E&R), led by Pierre Ailleret, was initially well aware that hydro and thermal were not the only possible energy sources. Immediately after the nationalization, E&R inventoried the entire hexagon for possible wind-power sites and built a couple of experimental wind units during the Monnet Plan. The results were disappointing. Partially because of a penchant for large, central station generating units and partially out of concrete economic analysis, wind power was a technological cul-de-sac. Recognizing that hydro was ultimately doomed, however, E&R did pursue other alternative technologies as methods for energy-independent power production after hydro sites were exhausted. Aside from cogeneration, which was already widespread in France, the two alternatives envisioned by E&R were nuclear power, in its infancy until 1960, and tidal power.

A tide-driven plant at Rance in Brittany represented an entirely innovative technology, yet despite its appeal to hydraulic engineers and its publicity value for EDF, it never enjoyed strong support from within the firm. Ailleret himself saw the Rance project mainly as a pilot project for a grander scheme at the Iles Chausey, which was never built.[7] The brochures and internal memos of the CGT are surprisingly silent on the Rance project. The EDF Equipment Office was tepid on the project for the same reasons that it was reluctant to develop hydro. The Production and Transmission Office (until 1956, the Exploitation Directorate) and the load-management experts disliked the output curve of the projected plant, for its variation with the tides did not coincide with diurnal or seasonal variations in electrical demand. EDF managers consistently chose to delay starting construction at Rance throughout the 1950s, though the studies for the plant had long been completed. Finally, concurrent with the last gasp of nonnuclear technological audacity at EDF and after prodding by de Gaulle, EDF began the Rance project in the late 1950s.

De Gaulle cut the ribbon at the Rance project in 1966 after he was unable to inaugurate a new nuclear power plant. Though it included a dike several kilometers long and an impressive array of turbines, it was never a particularly spectacular plant from the perspective of production costs, as the Blue Note had predicted.[8] Nonetheless, it did

[7] Pierre Ailleret, "Les perspectives d'utilisation pratique de sources nouvelles d'énergie (énergie nucléaire exceptée)," *RFE* 85 (June 1957), 299.
[8] It is interesting to note, however, that the Equipment Office did not subject nuclear projects to Blue Note analysis on the logic that the intrinsic value of technological learning

foster the development of reversible turbines, the so-called bulb groups. Developed and manufactured by Neyrpic, the bulb groups were ideally suited, if a bit belated, for run-of-stream hydro, and with a few modifications, they became the basis for the turbine-pump combinations used in later pumped-storage hydro projects. Neyrpic enjoyed a healthy export business with this item. EDF benefited little from Rance, however, and it turned out to be another technological dead end.

Another alternative power source for EDF was natural gas. Until the discovery in 1953 of a major deposit at Lacq in the Southwest, France's only sources of methane were manufactured gas, a product of coal gasification technology, and high-furnace gas, which was a by-product of coke making. Manufactured gas was an uneconomical means for power production, and high-furnace gas, though economical as a joint-use product, was in very limited supply. The Lacq deposit, discovered by the nationalized oil exploration company (Societé Nationale de Pétroles Aquitaines, SNPA), was therefore quite an energy windfall. Once SNPA developed methods for cleaning the highly acidic gas, it faced a serious problem of transmission. Lacq is located in one of France's most remote and underpopulated regions, so almost any large-scale exploitation of the deposit demanded construction of expensive pipelines. The first obvious route would run from Lacq to Bordeaux and Nantes, but a lack of guaranteed buyers made the investment too risky. Gaz de France was interested, but could not guarantee sufficient demand. Gaspard, recognizing that it was cheaper to build power lines than gas lines and that EDF could easily convert its Nantes-Cheviré plant to burn gas, quickly sent Massé to negotiate with SNPA and received a low price for an allocation of one-third of the Lacq output. In a governmental meeting presided over by Roger Boutteville, Massé had managed to get the government to approve a fast-draw, low price policy for the Lacq fields.[9] Once EDF secured access to the gas supply, the Ministry of Industry insisted that EDF be prepared to cede its share of the gas as soon as it was needed by the private sector.[10] EDF soon consented to build and operate two 115-mw plants at Lacq-Artix for

could not be quantified, yet it did not allow the same latitude to the Rance plant. For an accessible summary of the Rance project, see Picard et al., Histoire(s), pp. 78–81.

[9] Louis Puiseux and Dominique Saumon, "Actors and Decisions in French Energy Policy," in Leon Lindberg, ed., The Energy Syndrome (1977), pp. 148–53. For an explication of the EDF-SNPA deal, see Editorial, "Le Gaz de Lacq et l'Électricité de France," RFE 83 (February 1957). For a full account of the Lacq exploitation plan, see André Decelle, "Production de l'électricité et démarrage de l'exploitation du gisement de Lacq," RFE 94 (February 1958).

[10] CAPV 132 (23 November 1956) and Picard et al., Histoire(s), pp. 230–31.

the exclusive use of Pechiney and converted its Nantes plants to gas. By 1960, slightly over 40 percent of EDF's thermal power was fueled by Lacq gas, only to decline rapidly after mid-1961, when Minister of Industry Jeanneney forced EDF to cede its portion of the gas.[11] EDF did, however, succeed in being paid not only for the retroceded gas, but also for the extra expenses of replacement fuel. In the end, Lacq was a promising direction for EDF, but once it gave the capacity assurances needed to place it into production at a low price, EDF was elbowed aside in favor of private firms. By the early 1960s, therefore, EDF's long-term energy future was in coal, oil, and nuclear energy.

France's oil consumption for power production was quite small in the early 1950s, accounting for an average of about 10 percent of all thermally based power, largely owing to concerns for energy independence and inadequate oil-transport infrastructures. With the French coal industry modernized as a result of the Monnet Plan, EDF opted to build most of its early thermal plants to burn coal. Nonetheless, in about 1951, the international oil companies began to target price their oil, selling it at a price just below that of imported American coal. Ever since the Achnacarry "As Is" agreements of 1928 had structured the global oil industry, the world's major oil companies (including Compagnie Française des Pétroles, 35 percent owned by the French government, the other portions largely controlled by remnants of the old Mercier group) had kept world oil prices stable, adjusting them to levels below competing forms of energy in respective domestic markets.[12] In response to low oil prices, EDF began to switch some of its older plants to oil and to build some of its new plants for oil. With the Suez Crisis of 1956, however, the price of oil skyrocketed and the question of secure supplies became paramount. In 1956 and 1957, EDF received its first taste of the dangers of a reliance on foreign oil, but did not draw the obvious conclusion. EDF did, however, begin to convert its thermal plants back to coal. To drive the point home even more strongly, report authored by Louis Armand for the European Economic Community (EEC) cautioned Europe against a dependence on foreign oil.[13] In 1958, oil prices gradually began a downslide that continued until 1970, falling 30 percent between 1960 and 1968 alone. Whether the oil giants at that time were target pricing their oil in order to undercut coal and nuclear power, as officials at EDF and CDF believed, or trying to keep prices

[11] Editorial, "Électricité de France et le Gaz de Lacq," *RFE* 130 (June 1961).
[12] John M. Blair, *The Control of Oil* (1976), pp. 54–71, and Anthony Sampson, *The Seven Sisters* (1975), chaps. 4–6.
[13] Louis Armand, "Un objectif pour Euratom," 9 May 1957, cited in Sampson, *Sisters*, p. 183.

at optimal levels (for them) amid a torrent of new crude supplies is unclear.[14] It is clear, however, that EDF and the French government fully believed that cheap oil was there to stay. In 1961, Minister of Industry Jeanneney therefore decided to phase out the French coal industry. A massive miners' strike in the spring of 1963 gave a slight reprieve to the coal industry, but not enough to save it from a slow regression or to save France from a dangerous addiction to foreign oil.

EDF managers fully supported Jeanneney's decision to slash coal production. EDF had a long rivalry with CDF and had been forced by the government to act as the guaranteed buyer of CDF coal. In addition, despite modernized facilities, French coal still cost more than either imported coal or oil, and after 1963, EDF had to buy large quantites of high-priced CDF coal just to soak up excess CDF production. Still facing higher oil prices than its neighbors and, after being told explicitly by an international oil official that oil was priced according to U.S. coal delivered at La Havre, EDF bought its own coal ship and saw its oil costs fall.[15] After 1958, EDF thus began to reconvert its plants to oil and to build almost all of its new plants to burn oil. By the late 1960s, EDF economists projected that oil was so cheap that the capital costs for highly efficient thermal plants (those with higher temperatures and pressures, and with reheated steam) were no longer justified.[16] EDF therefore consciously built less efficient plants, with thirty-year book lives, on the assumption of cheap oil. Low-priced oil was also a convenient foil for attacking the hydro and natural uranium technologies that the economist-managers rejected.[17]

In the mid 1960s, EDF's mathematical planning models assumed that

[14] Most experts on the subject reject any conspiracy theory, arguing that the influx of non–Seven Sister producers (particularly Occidental Petroleum) and a veritable uncontrollable flood of oil from Libya and Venezuela broke the pricing cartel of the majors; Sampson, *Seven Sisters*, chap. 7; Blair, *Control*, pp. 211–15; and Editorial, "Où va le prix de fuel lourd?" *RFE* 205 (November 1968), 60.

[15] Picard et al., *Histoire(s)*, p. 229.

[16] For plants of similar heat rates, plants able to burn both coal and oil cost only 4 percent more than conventional coal plants, and 15 percent more than oil-only plants; Roger Ginocchio, "L'utilisation des combustibles dans les centrales thermiques d'EDF," *RFE* 136 (February 1962), 286.

[17] EDF-EEG, "Intérêt économique des aménagements hydroélectriques: Révision de la 'Note Bleue,' " report to the EDF board's Equipment Committee (confidential), 24 October 1969. In response, hydro engineers wrote a counter report, "Révision intérimaire de la Note Bleue," in which they demonstrated the continuing lower production costs of hydro, even for plants not yet built. Hydro engineers from UNCM and the CFDT jointly fired off a report and letter to Maurice Luneau, the CFDT representative on the board, criticizing the fact that the economists had succumbed to mathematical rigor rather than responsible management, that they had severely undervalued the remaining hydro sites, and that they were entirely indifferent to the future of the hydro engineers themselves; letter from G. Rigal to Luneau, 22 October 1968, CFDT archives, Paris, Luneau papers. On management's resistance to natural uranium, see infra.

the drop in oil prices would continue into the 1990s, though Boiteux quietly admitted his own reservations.[18] Once mathematically validated, therefore, EDF began to reshape its system's geographic configuration in order to burn massive quantities of imported oil. Instead of a network of power looking inward toward domestic energy resources, the grid turned outward, opening up toward the multinational oil companies and OPEC members. The oil price shocks of 1970 and 1973–74 broke the euphoria generated by oil fumes, but by then EDF's total system had largely adapted to oil. EDF and France as a whole later paid for an indifference to the politics of supply. Perhaps Boiteux, like many French businessmen, believed that the American government would make the world safe for multinational capitalism. Little did he imagine that the American government saw a clear advantage for large U.S. firms were the world price of oil to skyrocket.[19]

There were many causes for the EDF management's decision to opt for near-total dependence on foreign oil. One must also look at cultural factors. American industrial styles were very popular among the French bourgeoisie in the 1960s, and EDF managers shared that enthusiasm. As the light-water nuclear reactor had an intrinsic value simply because it was American, so too was an oil-based economy worthy of emulation. The United States was the world's capitalist success story, and France's culture of high technology dovetailed well with an Americanization of French technique and French culture. The ideological satisfaction of an integration with multinational capitalism for EDF was also a contributing factor, proving that EDF, too, could be a part of the brave new oil-based world.

EDF Equipment-purchasing Policy: From Rival to Ally

EDF and its major suppliers both recognized the need to cooperate because of inevitable cohabitation, yet both jealously defended individual prerogatives. Rapid technological innovation and cost constraints demanded cooperation between the two. EDF followed a very

[18] "Allocation de M. Boiteux du 21 octobre 1968," EDF Archives, Centre de Documentation Murat-Messine, series E8: "Économie générale." As early as 1968, some experts began to fear concerted action between oil-producing countries and the majors: *RFE*, "Où va," p. 62. The same article also affirmed the conclusions of a governmental commission report that predicted oil at $10 to $12 a ton into the distant future.

[19] European analysts often cite the clear economic advantage for forces in the U.S. government and in U.S. industry to have aided the oil price shocks of 1970 and 1973–74; higher energy prices in Europe would raise production costs and make European goods less competitive in world markets relative to U.S. goods based on cheap energy; see, for example, Jean-Marie Chevalier, *Le nouvel enjeu pétrolier* (1974), chaps. 1 and 2, and Sampson, *Seven Sisters*, chaps. 12–14.

complex and changing strategy toward its suppliers between 1946 and 1970. Though the firm's attitude remained ambivalent throughout the period, it did shift from rivalry to cooperation as state policies and managerial perspectives became more rightist-technocratic after 1958.

EDF inherited in the nationalization a number of research and development consulting firms devoted to equipment, but EDF's top management decided to leave most research and development to the private sector. The structure of innovation thus paralleled that of military innovation in the United States. EDF was quite familiar with emerging technologies and technological potentials, yet it spawned innovation by ordering hardware with specific operational characteristics, not by its own systematic research and development. By dint of this indirect manner for initiating technological change, EDF's technical development depended on the producers' access to capital and to their anticipation of profitable production. EDF thus depended technologically on its suppliers, yet the suppliers faced a relatively monopsonist purchaser.

Electrical equipment production traditionally differed sharply from most other types of manufacturing. It was unusually capital-intensive and required extensive research and tooling costs. Extremely close machined tolerances on very large sized equipment and sophisticated tooling techniques applied to exotic alloys demanded a highly skilled labor force. The maximum feasible production capacity for each firm seldom exceeded three to five major components per year because of the large size of most generating plant subunits. Finally, electrical equipment manufacturers had to pursue innovation aggressively if they were to avoid obsolescence. Amortization of costly research and development expenses and standing capital therefore required regularized orders, stable markets and labor supplies, and production agreements or financial concentration.

A combination of war and economic depression had prevented any sizable orders for the fifteen years before 1946, leaving the electrical equipment sector with outdated tools and techniques. The bulk of the industry's products were based on foreign designs, for which the French firms paid license fees or acted as subsidiaries of the patent holders. The main exceptions to this pattern were Neyrpic and Merlin-Gerin, manufacturers of hydroelectric turbines and high-tension equipment (breakers, insulators, etc.), respectively.[20] Sales in export markets were often forestalled by the original patent holders, who easily underpriced French firms. French electrical equipment producers did not

---

[20] Germaine Veyret-Verner, "Deux usines pilotes," *Revue de Géographie Alpine* 60 (January-March 1952), 186 and 192–93.

consistently seek technological independence or technological leadership. Foreigners and EDF were reliable sources of innovation, and ententes and protective tariffs sheltered the manufacturers from competition. The electrical equipment entente, the Syndicat Général de la Construction Électrique (SGCE), headed by Henri Davezac, was among the strongest in France.[21] According to various sources, SGCE and its ally, the Syndicat des Constructeurs de Matériel d'Équipement Électrique, controlled 75 to 90 percent of the production in the heavy electrical equipment sector. SGCE could levy hefty penalties on firms that cut prices or exceeded their allocated market share.[22]

Two large and somewhat diffuse constellations and a small number of independent firms dominated the electrical equipment industry in 1950. A combination of cross-ownership, shared directorships, various technical relations (joint production schemes and joint patent licenses), and informal ties based on interpersonal networks among the financial and industrial élites marked the constellations. The largest was centered around Compagnie Générale d'Électricité (CGE) and the remnants of the old Messine electrical group. CGE was a modern, publicly held firm with a vast intercorporate network, linked interpersonally and financially to Pechiney, Ugine, Grands Travaux de Marseille (France's largest civil engineering firm), and to the Banque de l'Union Parisienne and the Banque de Paris et des Pays-Bas, two of France's largest investment banks. With many Polytechniciens on its board and in its front office, CGE represented the alliance of elite engineers with managerial capitalism. In 1939, 80 percent of CGE's activity was in electrical power distribution, but by 1946, that figure had dropped to 10 percent. CGE had dumped its utility stock between 1943 and 1945, selling it for considerable cash at an index of about 505 (1938 = 100).[23] The second major group, Jeumont-Schneider, with closely held and familial ownership, was tied to traditional steel-industry interests. Compagnie Electro-Méchanique (CEM), the French subsidiary of a major Swiss firm, was much smaller. Other firms in the sector either specialized in one type of equipment, or only tangentially manufactured electrical equipment.

The structure of the electrical equipment industry rendered entente control of prices and market shares difficult. While the two major constellations had strong incentives to maintain the entente, the foreign-based firms had fewer fixed costs to amortize because prices on the export market often excluded costs of tooling and research and devel-

[21] Ehrmann, *Organized Business*, p. 372, and Camille Albert, "Autour des projects antitrusts," *Le Monde*, 23 March 1953.
[22] Ibid.
[23] *Entreprise* 634 (4 November 1967), 42–47.

Table 2. Annual orders for hydro turbines, 1945-1961 (EDF and CNR combined)

Year	Megavolt-amperes ordered	Year	Megavolt-amperes ordered
1947	853	1955	1217
1948	9	1956	1160
1949	673	1957	536
1950	291	1958	8
1951	175	1959	89
1952	64	1960	550
1953	351	1961	830
1954	429		

Sources: Jean-Luc Wolfender, "Le coût des aménagements hydroélectriques," RFE 66 (July-August 1955), 411, and Gilbert Hurpy, "Les conséquences," p. 49. Hurpy's source is the EDF Equipment Office.

opment. Most of the exporters' fixed costs could be covered by sales in home markets. Because these firms maintained factories in France for their French sales, they were not subject to French import restrictions and duties. Overcapacity could also create incentives to cut prices. For example, once the electrical equipment sector was fully reconstructed and modernized toward the end of 1950, it had a total production capacity commensurate with the large Monnet Plan goals (Table 2). Overcapacity then brought a wave of price cutting.

Electrical equipment firms could mitigate risk by shifting some of their capacity to build nonenergy equipment. Few manufactured large electrical equipment exclusively and many also produced equipment for the rail, shipbuilding, and communications industries. These factors, along with decentralized purchasing of smaller equipment, somewhat countered the monopsonistic power of EDF. Nonetheless, for the corporate units specifically dedicated to large electrical equipment, EDF was by far the largest buyer, and the health of those units was closely tied to the pattern of EDF orders. Depending on the scope of the activities and the number of firms considered, between 44 and 75 percent of the sales of the electrical equipment sector were to EDF.[24] As early as 1952, the entente recognized its dependence on EDF and CDF; electrical equipment firms' "daily health and their future are tightly held between the hands of these two institutions, who can, according to their own whims, make them prosper or go bankrupt, and with

[24] Patrice Grevet ("EDF et les structures de l'industrie du gros matériel électromécanique," mémoire pour le diplôme d'études supérieures de sciences économiques, Université de Paris, 1966, p. 27) claims that the cartel controlled 44 percent of all production in its sector; SCME claimed that 75 percent of its sales were to the nationalized sector; Constructeurs de Matériel d'Équipement Électrique, Le matériel d'équipement électrique, pamphlet (Paris: SCME, 1958), p. 3.

them either aid the prosperity or unemployment of tens of thousands of manual, white-collar, and engineering workers."[25]

The irregular pace of EDF's orders plagued suppliers with very uneven capacity utilization. In 1958, Equipment Director Didier Olivier-Martin underlined the consequences of irregular orders:

> [Our policy] has resulted in a poor utilization of the personnel within the Equipment Directorate of EDF and of the facilities of both the civil engineering and electromechanical industries. On more than one occasion, we have gone to the factories of our suppliers and seen large and encumbering piles of parts in the latter stages of assembly, while at the front end of the production line, there are large quantities of idle machine tools. In like fashion, we have seen civil engineering firms, after having rushed to complete a project, find themselves without successive projects and forced to dissolve their laboriously constituted work forces and leave their equipment idle.
>
> Research and development personnel suffer more from the irregularities than do the personnel engaged in direct production. The lag time on research and development is in effect considerably shorter than that for actual production, and the absence of a series of successive orders in one year cannot be compensated by more orders in the following years. The research and development sections, which represent the future potential of these firms, are therefore submitted to a very demoralizing regime.
>
> The methods of work imposed by our irregular orders are incompatible with good productivity; they foul up our suppliers and sharply increase the costs of our investments.[26]

Delays in meeting orders somewhat compensated for this irregularity. EDF seems to have covered the costs of irregularity between 1946 and 1953, for the profits of electrical construction firms were quite high (Table 3).

The Equipment Directorate led EDF's efforts to frame a purchasing policy, and in general it hoped to find a way to help suppliers to cut costs, in the hope that they would pass the savings on to EDF. Early tactics focused on enhancing competition and enforcing price ceilings, but a later strategy involved standardizing designs, encouraging cooperation among suppliers, and pacing orders regularly. EDF managers never fully addressed two flaws in this approach, that there were few guarantees that cost savings would be passed through to EDF and that in any event, the suppliers would remain dependent on EDF. Later

[25] H. Fonty, "Les conditions d'activité des industries de gros matériel électrique," RFE 27 (January 1952), 117.

[26] Gilbert Hurpy, "Les conséquences de l'irrégularité des programmes d'équipement électrique de 1950 au IVᵉ Plan," thèse pour le doctorat ès sciences économiques, Université de Grenoble, June 1964, pp. 55–56.

Table 3. Net profits of France's top 37 electrical equipment firms, 1947–1953 (in millions of francs)

Year	Net profits (current francs)	Net profits (1947 francs)	Percent change (constant francs)
1947	1,104	1,104	—
1948	2,364	1,374	+ 24.5
1949	3,732	1,943	+ 29.3
1950	4,603	2,213	+ 13.9
1951	5,529	2,078	− 6.5
1952	6,798	2,445	+ 17.7
1953	7,390	2,789	+ 14.1

Sources: "CA," "Concentration, productivité et profits dans la construction électrique," Économie et Politique 8 (November-December 1954), 71–72 (based on SGCE's 1953 annual report); INSEE, Tableaux de l'économie française, 1970 (Paris: INSEE, 1970), 118; Pierre Massé, "L'électricité devant le nouveau plan," RFE 30 (April 1952), 222; and EDF-Direction Générale, "Évolution du financement des investissements," unclassified document, June 1981.

EDF managers came to assume that as private sector firms, the suppliers required profits to support their research and development, and that as the primary purchaser, EDF had to assure those profits.

Massé had long tried to standardize its equipment so that electrical equipment producers could reduce their research and tooling costs. As a first step, EDF standardized equipment definitions with a price list for specific items. The Equipment Directorate established base prices, then indexed them with a set of inflators specific to the structure of production costs for each major item. The price-series approach was too insensitive to inflation, however. Between 1947 and 1952, the indexed prices rose slightly faster than the overall rate of inflation, but price controls imposed in February 1954 forced prices far below the levels that a simple inflation index would have yielded.[27] EDF thus overpaid before 1953 and underpaid thereafter.

Genuine standardization raised deeper problems. If EDF introduced innovations with each successive unit (as it did until the mid-1960s), the manufacturers' cost savings were reduced, but EDF received more efficient equipment, with the caveat that repairs were more burdensome. On the contrary, if EDF demanded that all units in a series be identical, manufacturers' production costs fell, but EDF's operating

[27] Calculations based on EDF–Direction de l'Équipement, Service de la Construction du Matériel, "Indices des principaux gros matériels en juillet 1952," memo E/844, 15 September 1952, compared to INSEE indices. See also Hurpy, "Les conséquences," p. 38, and EDF–Conseil d'Administration, Commission de l'Équipement, "Procès verbaux des séances," confidential minutes of EDF Board of Directors' Committee on Equipment, mimeographed (hereafter CACE) 182 (21 April 1966), app.

efficiency stagnated.[28] The decision for or against absolute series regularity was never modeled, so EDF managers could not even pretend to choose rationally. In any case, the suppliers had little input.

Several of EDF's fundamental assumptions in its relationship with the electrical equipment sector were never questioned in the 1950s. EDF paid all the front-end costs for prototypes, so that research and development and tooling costs were fully rolled into the prices EDF paid for its equipment. Once EDF had admitted that it was to pay for the reconstruction of the electrical equipment sector directly after the war, it proceeded to pay for all modernization thereafter.[29] EDF expected to receive larger and larger rebates on subsequent orders because it had paid all front-end costs. EDF managers argued that if EDF were to play a "directing" role in shaping the electrical industry, it was incumbent upon EDF to pay for that privilege and ultimately to reap the benefits of the rationalization it induced. EDF's contracting practices often allowed it to take for itself most of the benefits from productivity gains in the electrical equipment sector.[30] However, since EDF paid front-end costs, electrical equipment firms could export at prices far below those they changed EDF and thus gain a position in the world market, where dumping practices were common.

EDF also tried to reduce the number of times it paid front-end costs because it made little sense to pay several times to reinvent the same wheel. Well into the 1950s, EDF avoided redundant front-end costs by buying foreign patents or prototypes and making them available to all the French manufacturers. It introduced in this way many of the subunits of the 125-mw thermal generating series (begun in 1951).[31] This approach remained insufficient for the Ministry of Industry. Beginning

[28] David Hounshell discusses in depth the contradictions of producing standardized products in *From the American System to Mass Production, 1800–1932* (Baltimore: Johns Hopkins University Press, 1984), pp. 263–80.

[29] Interview by author with Roger Gaspard, Paris, 3 June 1981; EDF even loaned tools and construction equipment to its suppliers, and in addition, prepaid some of its equipment orders in order to alleviate some of the cash-flow problems of its suppliers; see CAPV 41 (30 September 1949).

[30] A CEM official wrote in 1965, referring to the situation in the 1950s, that EDF had "a policy of forced and accelerated evolution; . . . this policy, which resulted in an appreciable reduction in costs per kwh . . . was evidently rational . . . but in the present state of administrative decisions, it was the manufacturers who paid the costs of it"; cited in Michel Herblay, *Les hommes*, p. 134. Author was an official in EDF's equipment office. See also SCME, *Équipement électrique*, p. 14.

[31] For the 125-mw thermal series prototypes, EDF bought the boiler from Combustion Engineering for Stein-Roubaix (CAPV 45 [27 January 1950] and CAPV 182 [21 April 1966]), the evacuation transformer from Charleroi (Belgian) for SW (CAPV 59 [23 February 1951]), the synchronous compensator from Westinghouse for Alsthom and SW (CAPV 72 [16 March 1951]) and helped the entry of Rateau into the production of thermal turbo-alternators by the purchase of another American turbo-alternator (Grevet, "Matériel électromécanique," p. 38).

in 1955, it encouraged joint production schemes and industrial concentration among electrical equipment firms on the assumption that
some were too small to achieve economies of scale. In this approach,
a lead firm would oversee development with its erstwhile competitors.
EDF well recognized the obvious dangers to price competition. Indeed,
when the Ministry of Industry's director of electricity criticized EDF's
dispersed ordering in 1955, Raymond Giguet, EDF's director of equipment, responded by implying that dispersed orders would keep prices
low.[32]

Soon thereafter, EDF managers began to argue the opposite position,
that the expenses of dispersed orders exceeded those of reduced competition. As it placed orders for its new 250-mw series of thermal plants
and for the new 380-kv grid in the late 1950s, the Equipment Directorate
explicitly tried to reduce the number of producers.[33] This policy met
with mixed reactions. Some firms insisted on the risk mitigation inherent in multiple product lines, and foreign patent owners restricted
interfirm cooperation. In addition, EDF as a whole remained deeply
ambivalent about concentration, but high unit costs for the 250-mw
series more broadly convinced EDF managers that concentration
among suppliers was essential. All EDF then needed was some mech-
anism to assure price competition.

EDF fully began to support consolidation among its suppliers when
France entered the Common Market (EEC). Competition within the
EEC offered EDF the opportunity to use foreign contracts (or the threat
of them) to compress the prices of increasingly oligopolized suppliers.
The state also hoped that foreign competition would reduce notoriously
high French prices and that competitive pressure would induce industrial fusions and joint production schemes so that French firms
could enjoy a large enough scale to compete in foreign markets.[34] Indeed, French firms were small in comparison to their foreign rivals: in
1956, Alsthom (France's largest electrical equipment firm) had total
sales of 600 million francs, compared to West Germany's Siemens at 2
billion francs, Westinghouse's 10 billion francs, and General Electric's
24 billion francs.[35] Electrical equipment firms responded to international competition with a decade-long series of mergers, which yielded
an industry dominated by two large combines, CGE and Jeumont-
Schneider, and one immigrant, CEM. Whether EDF intended it or not,
the promise of competition among French and foreign suppliers never

[32] CAPV 118 (22 July 1955).
[33] This position was also explicitly backed by the minister of industry; CAPV 161 (24
April 1959); see also Grevet, "Matériel électromécanique," p. 42.
[34] François Caron, Histoire économique de la France, XIXᵉ–XXᵉ siècles (1981), p. 250.
[35] Grevet, "Matériel électromécanique," p. 50.

materialized. EDF bought almost no foreign equipment in the 1960s. EDF ultimately faced not a cartel but a virtual monopoly.

Regularizing equipment orders also offered a way to reduce production costs for EDF's suppliers. This approach required close cooperation between EDF and the government client to regularize capital budgeting, and between EDF and the suppliers to exchange information. As early as 1953, in an EDF board meeting, Ambroise Roux, the Ministry of Industry representative and later the head of CGE, stated his ministry's view of the necessary EDF-supplier relationship: the suppliers are "the necessary extension of EDF."[36] In May 1955, the government created the Comité d'Équipement Électrique (CEE), composed of managers from the electrical equipment sector, EDF, and the state.[37] The CEE was set up to facilitate the contacts necessary to smooth relations among the actors and regularize orders, but internal cross-purposes rendered it useless. EDF wanted the CEE to pace orders and standardize equipment, but the Ministry of Industry and private sector officials wanted it to allocate markets and control prices. The Finance Ministry saw in it a way to cut the weight of EDF's equipment programs on the state budget. Larger electrical equipment firms in the entente were eager to cooperate with EDF, but on their own terms. Smaller firms were reluctant to work in the shadow of their larger rivals. The CEE was important, however, because it was the first attempt to foster cooperative relationships among EDF, the electrical equipment producers, and the state, and all parties had hoped that cooperative links would develop. Underlining this need after two years of failure in the CEE, Henri Davezac wrote: "These efforts must be extended much further. Public buyers and the private suppliers, despite the differences in their points of view—differences that are inherent their respective positions—are in fact in solidarity with each other."[38]

EDF managers in the 1950s increasingly came to view such cooperation as not only a simple exchange of information but also as a means of assuring profitability. Recognizing that innovation at EDF depended on the health of its suppliers, the economist-managers came to see that profitability as the sine qua non of EDF's technological vigor. Nonetheless, many members of the EDF community, unionists and middle-level engineers in particular, continued to resent EDF's suppliers. This sentiment always countered the increasingly cooperative attitude of

[36] CAPV 87 (24 April 1953).
[37] Jacques Bour, "La passation des commandes et des marchés à l'Électricité de France," *RFE* 112 (October 1959), 43, and "L'état-(bon) client," editorial, *RFE* 59 (December 1954), 81. See also Deglaire, *Recueil*, vol. 11, p. 425.
[38] Henri Davezac, "Les industries de la construction électrique en 1956–58," *RFE* 88 (July-August 1957), 646.

EDF top managers toward suppliers, making EDF's overall approach to its suppliers pervasively ambivalent.

The new political-economic context of the Fifth Republic strengthened the hand of those seeking more systematic cooperation. A decree of 1959 allowed EDF to have multiyear equipment programs within the context of the so-called law-programs, but capital budgeting remained tied to annual finance bills.[39] The EDF board had already officially adopted multiyear contracting in September 1958 by allocating equipment contracts according to the capacity utilization rates of its suppliers. This solved in a new way the problems posed by irregular orders. Henceforth, EDF's purchasing services no longer had to buy from the lowest bidder. At the same time, Massé negotiated an agreement with the electrical equipment entente, stipulating that EDF would guarantee regular orders at predictable prices and, in return, EDF would receive rebates on its purchases.[40] Under the new policy, EDF solicited bids, and once it received responses, it allocated contracts according to both price and production capacities. EDF assigned the largest order to the lowest bidder or least busy, climbing the bid ladder to divvy up the orders unless technical characteristics of specific firms' products gave better performance. No model was ever offered to facilitate choosing between price and the bidders' capacity utilization rates. For entente-priced materials such as transmission cable, allocation was simply on the basis of production capacities, and efforts to induce competition ceased.

The state itself after 1958 strongly pushed EDF to cooperate with its suppliers merely to increase their solvency. In 1960, the Finance Ministry instructed EDF to add 3 percent to all major equipment contracts in order to ensure that the producers could cover their research and development expenses. *Le Télégramme Économique* explained the method: "At a certain moment, . . . the nationalized firms that are clients of the electrical industry were asked [by the government] to be a bit less rigorous in contract negotiations. In the end, it [now] seems that the contracts will be negotiated and established according to the same methods of rigor, but that the final result would be hiked by 3 percent. The receipts resulting from this supplement would then be undoubtedly dedicated to the further development of the electrical industry."[41] While this measure can be seen as an intelligent way to compensate for EDF's monopsonist position, it offered no concrete

---

[39]At the time, Parliament was prorogued, and de Gaulle was empowered to legislate by decree. See Vilain, *La politique*, p. 182.

[40] CAPV 153 (26 September 1958).

[41] *Le Télégramme Économique*, cited in letter of Paul to Gaspard, 15 July 1960.

incentives to research and development. Suppliers were better able to amortize their front-end costs, but there were no direct rewards for the desired technical innovation—the bonus was forthcoming regardless of whether the products were standardized transmission cable or innovative new breakers. It did not wean the bulk of the sector from buying American patent licenses in place of developing its own technology.

Early Fifth Republic policies laid the groundwork for prosperity among EDF's suppliers. The change of regimes permitted EDF to regularize equipment orders, and a shift in thinking in EDF management and the Finance Ministry eased financial pressures on equipment manufacturers. The new measures did little to spur innovation, provide for technological independence, or cut costs. It is arguable that the earlier profit squeeze had spurred productivity gains. The two most innovative firms, Merlin-Gerin and Neyrpic, benefited less than the sleepy giants, CGE and Jeumont, who bought those firms in the early and mid-1960s. As long as the electrical equipment sector was private and EDF needed its output, it was essential that it remain able to innovate and increase productivity. In reshaping purchasing policies, EDF, the state, and the suppliers came to understand what Jean Monnet had said in 1950, that "the monies put at the disposal of the nationalized infrastructure of the economy are . . . only transferred through those firms by way of orders for equipment and civil engineering activities, and are finally distributed among the private equipment companies."[42]

The impact of shifts in purchasing policies can best be shown by examining the financial fate of EDF's suppliers. EDF's purchasing policies led first to excess profits for suppliers up to about 1953, then insufficient profits up to 1959. Despite irregular orders, EDF's early contracting practices allowed the rate of profit for a given volume of orders to more than double between 1947 and 1953.[43] EDF managed to benefit from the increasing productivity of electrical equipment firms, yet as *Revue Française d'Énergie* asserted, EDF was a very good client for its suppliers.[44] Profits remained high even after 1950, when the suppliers' entente began to erode in the face of price cutting and competition among its members, especially after reductions in the hydro program. In 1951, EDF established credible price targets and limited some of the higher equipment prices by implementing bidded contracting and soliciting foreign bids. Foreign bids were used only as

[42] Cited in Henri Coston, *Le retour des '200 familles'* (Paris: La Librairie Française, 1960), p. 43.

[43] Ibid.

[44] "L'état-(bon) client," *RFE* editorial, p. 81.

scarecrows to threaten suppliers, and foreign purchases were never more than 10 percent of all EDF orders.[45] EDF solicited foreign bids, then demanded that French manufacturers reduce their bids accordingly. This method successfully reduced equipment prices and established reference standards until midsummer 1953, when Minister of Industry Louvel prohibited foreign purchases. French electrical equipment manufacturers immediately raised prices behind the protective barrier.[46] Smaller equipment budgets after 1953 forced suppliers to cut prices competitively simply to amortize otherwise idle capacity. EDF took substantial advantage of a price freeze that the government initiated in February 1954 in an effort to quell inflation.

Under the price freeze of the mid-1950s, EDF forced its suppliers to cover virtually all production-cost increases. In addition, EDF used its position of relative security in terms of its own productive capacity and its ability to play on the hydro/thermal ratio to vary the timing and content of its orders and further compress its costs.[47] Through these measures, EDF achieved a 5 percent savings on the projected costs of its 1955 equipment program, managing to garner reductions of 40 percent on some contracts. The reductions were so sharp that Gaspard worried that some civil engineering firms were not sufficiently amortizing their own equipment.[48] On an installed capacity basis, EDF's Plan II (1954–57) equipment cost 35 percent less than that in Plan I in constant francs.[49] By 1957, the equipment firms publicly began to beg for mercy. Jeumont was probably justified when it claimed that the price freeze had cost it over a billion francs and that the selling prices were not high enough to cover new capital spending or research and development.[50] In 1957, a CEM official wrote: "This year, we must again denounce the grave insufficiency of our sale prices. This insufficiency, which began four years ago due to tight competition for limited orders has been artificially aggravated by the system of price controls. ... The price regulations have induced extracontractual costs, which have caused major losses on our sales of large electrical equipment."[51] The cries of the electrical equipment firms were probably a bit exaggerated, however, for no such firm went out of business, no major

[45] Giguet report, CAPV 87 (24 April 1953).
[46] For example, in a transformer deal in the fall of 1953, EDF found that Alsthom had hiked its prices, but when EDF tried to initiate a foreign order, Louvel blocked it; CAPV 94 (30 October 1953). Similar events occurred over the next two years, until the EDF purchasing section apparently gave up trying to initiate foreign orders.
[47] Grevet, "Matériel électromécanique," p. 40; see also CAPV 118 (22 July 1955).
[48] CAPV 118 (22 July 1955).
[49] Michel Vilain, La politique, p. 182.
[50] Herblay, Les hommes, p. 131. Author was an official in EDF's equipment office. See also SCME, Équipement électrique, p. 16.
[51] Cited in Herblay, Les hommes, p. 133.

product lines were dropped, and there were no desperate corporate takeovers or mergers in the sector.

The profits of EDF's suppliers shot up in 1958 and 1959 because of broad policy changes and the suspension of price controls. From a position of widespread operating losses in 1957, the electrical equipment sector enjoyed positive balances in 1958. Compared to year-earlier profits, in 1959, Alsthom saw an increase of 218 percent, Société Westinghouse (France) an increase of 89 percent, Jeumont an increase of 24 percent, and Forclum (a transmission-line installer) an increase of 12 percent.[52] Despite consistent increases between 1957 and 1960, their profits as a share of total sales were consistently only about one-quarter of that prevailing in the chemical and electronics industries.[53] Nonetheless, investments in new plant and equipment in electrical equipment manufacturing rose from 5 billion francs in 1956 to 15 billion francs in 1961, and EDF's suppliers were still not on solid financial ground.[54]

EDF became considerably softer on prices in the 1960s but still tried to keep equipment prices low in order to make the most of limited funds. The complete integration of EDF with its suppliers did not fully occur until the massive merger movement in the electromechanical sector in the 1960s and a massive nuclear push after 1975. The merger movement deprived EDF of the means of playing firms off against one another, and the nuclear decision of 1969 put EDF head-to-head with fully monopolized suppliers that purveyed technologies (imported from the United States) for which EDF could not estimate producers' costs. By 1970, equipment purchasing for EDF meant facing firms that routinely rigged bids and sold foreign technologies over which EDF had little control. The nuclear program after 1975 ended competitive bidding, but by that time, bidding was little more than a bureaucratic fiction, insisted on by EDF's own "anticapitalist" engineers.[55] Jules Horowitz of the Commissariat à l'Énergie Atomique (CEA) explained the reality of EDF contracting in the 1960s: "There was . . . a false competition and a false choice [among firms] for [equipment] systems. Indeed, 'someone' told me about the sacrosanct rule of competition!! A classmate of mine at Polytechnique, an important figure in the [equipment] industry, said to me, 'You laugh? Blood would run if the sup-

[52] From SGCE report, cited in letter from Paul to Gaspard, 15 July 1960, Éclairage archives, dossier: "Entreprises privées." It must be noted, however, that electrical equipment firms' profits had been unusually low in previous years.

[53] Grevet, "Matériel électromécanique," p. 46.

[54] H. Noel, "La construction du gros matériel électro-mécanique," RFE 134 (November-December 1961), 109.

[55] The term and argument are from Jean Cabanius, EDF Equipment Director, 1962–1967, cited in Picard et al., Histoire(s), p. 191.

pliers didn't take turns bidding on EDF contracts. When one firm's turn comes, the other holds back! . . . ' On the side of EDF, there was the illusion that real competition could actually exist when indeed there was competition only on paper to satisfy the rules."[56] Whatever EDF's intentions, by 1970, the contracting policies of its managers were either duplicitous, hopelessly naïve, or deeply ambivalent. From the start, EDF's technical success had hinged on the financial health of its suppliers, and this fact put the nationalized firm in a difficult dilemma. A public sector firm had to guarantee profits and mitigate risks for the private sector, but at the same it had to be attentive to its own expenses, its technological trajectory, and to possible improprieties. The systematic solution was structural, and it was implemented in the 1970s and 1980s—the nationalization of the suppliers.

The convergence of neutral technocratic conceptions and concerns for the health of EDF's suppliers can best be seen in a case in which economies of scale worked in reverse, with the increasing of thermal plant sizes. EDF began a 125-mw thermal generating plant series in 1951 and a 250-mw series in 1956. Engineers opted for a 250-mw series before an adequate performance record on the 125-mw series had been established. The 250-mw series was chosen on the technocratic assumption that larger scale and greater centralization imply greater efficiency, and the need for French equipment firms to have experience with a new, leading-edge technology in order to develop their export markets.[57] Close analysis shows that the 250 mw series yielded minimal cost savings.

Thermal efficiency in boilers had almost attained its highest possible level in the later units of the 125-mw series. The boilers in the 250-mw series therefore offered only a 7 percent increase in thermal efficiency— at the cost of a very sophisticated and expensive steel alloy in the boilers. In general, the price differences for the major components of thermal plants were only slightly cheaper for one 250-mw plant than for two 125-mw plants.[58] The EDF equipment section estimated that the cost savings were as follows: 20 percent on capital costs, 7 percent

[56] Ibid, p. 193.
[57] P. Guyot de Villeneuve, "Les centrales thermiques du palier technique de 250 MW," *RFE* 189 (April 1967), 241.
[58] Based on calculations from the contracted prices listed in the CAPV series, the savings on boilers was nil. This was admitted by the equipment office; CAPV 181 (24 March 1961); see also Jean Magoux, "Le nouveau palier technique de 600 megawatts des centrales thermiques," *RFE* 156 (January 1964), 157. By the same calculations, it can be noted that turbo alternators were about 13 percent cheaper and transformers were about 14 percent cheaper. Plant construction costs were lower owing to a smaller number of sites.

on fuel charges, and 40 percent on labor costs.[59] The direct cost advantages of the larger scale were annihilated by the poor operating record of the 250-mw series. The failure of a single plant of 250 mw removed twice the capacity from the total available power, implicitly raising the costs per failure. Repair time on the 250-mw series was about twice that on the 125-mw series.[60] These two factors were inherent in larger equipment and EDF should have considered them. Indeed, after several years of poor performance of the 250-mw series, Massé said, "The influence of larger dimension sometimes plays in a bad sense; it would be best to ask everyone not to sin by excessive optimism."[61] The 250-mw series also had a poorer overall operating record than its predecessor. Using conventional reliability theory, EDF managers assumed that the first three years of a new series would be affected by relatively high failure rates due to unforeseen design and production errors. This rule had held for the 125-mw series, but for the 250-mw series, "childhood illnesses" lasted fully eight years.[62] As a result, the rate of availability (the percent of time a plant or set of plants can be used) was 18.3 percent better for the 125-mw plants than for the 250-mw plants for the period from 1964 to 1969, when the 250-mw plants should have been beyond their youth stage.[63] The systematic failure of the 250-mw plants required that replacement power be generated by less efficient plants taken out of retirement for that purpose. For example, in the winter of 1966–67, 410 mw of retired capacity had to be brought out of mothballs to cover the failures of the 250-mw plants.[64] Such failures and the higher production costs associated with them negated the cost savings once promised by the upscaling.[65]

The axiom of "bigger is better" helped EDF open export markets for its suppliers and to allow suppliers to utilize the patent licenses they had recently bought from American patent holders.[66] Gaspard revealed

[59] De Villeneuve, "Les centrales thermiques," p. 249. According to calculations based on contracted prices, the 20 percent savings claimed by the equipment section was a vast exaggeration. Also, labor costs associated with operating the 250-mw plants were less than 10 percent of total operating costs.

[60] Ibid, p. 250.

[61] CACE 191 (26 April 1967).

[62] Calculated from EDF, Statistiques de production, p. 30.

[63] Calculated from EDF, Statistiques de production, p. 30.

[64] CAPV 243 (21 October 1966).

[65] The problems with the series were compounded by the systematic failures of the turbo alternators made by Jeumont, based on a Westinghouse patent but redesigned by Jeumont for the European market. Jeumont committed three separate design errors and paid for the repair of those errors when they were understood, but no attempt was made (or offered) to restitute to EDF the higher costs for replacement power; see CACE 192 (25 May 1967). The errors resulted from Jeumont's hasty efforts to get EDF contracts in order to open up export markets for its 250-mw turbo-alternator.

[66] Interview by author with Yves Morel, Embrun, 16 July 1981.

a business reason for upscaling to the 250-mw series when he recommended that all the parts in the 250-mw Albi plant be contracted
with Alsthom so that Alsthom could have a reference for the construction of an entire 250-mw plant, a major aid for exporting it.[67] EDF
managers repeated the upscaling error with a decision in 1961 to move
to a 600-mw series. The contradiction of upscaling indicates how there
was a convergence between the "scientific" propensities of the EDF
technocrats and the profitability of its suppliers. One need not presume
a conspiracy between EDF and its suppliers; as with rate making, the
way issues were framed evoked a limited set of results. In the end,
upscaling cost EDF and benefited its suppliers, and it revealed how a
"neutral" technocratic perspective (with its insistence on a law of scale
economies) indirectly placed the financial needs of suppliers above the
cost-effective operation of the power system.

The Nuclear Imbroglio

On 13 November 1969, Prime Minister Georges Pompidou announced to the assembled members of the press that his cabinet had
decided to adopt the American-designed, light-water model of nuclear
power plant and thus to abandon fifteen years of independent French
development of the natural uranium gas–cooled model. This decision
ended more than a decade's acrimony over the choice between light-
water reactors (LWRs) and the natural uranium (uranium naturel, gaz-
graphite, UNGG) technology (see Figures 2 and 3). As a decision-
making process, the battle over reactor designs underscored the rivalries within the French technological establishment—between engineers
and businessmen, public and private sectors, nationalists and multinationalists, Corps des Mines and Corps des Ponts, and among state
agencies. The economic and technical virtues of the two technologies
shifted with respect to each other throughout the period, as did decision makers' perceptions of the technologies and their context. A
study of France's decision to opt for LWRs can support and extend
David Noble's critique of the "Darwinian" notion of technical change,
that is, that successful technologies are "naturally selected" according
to economic and technical criteria, or that the technological environment, the nature itself, constructs the social environment rather than
being constructed by it.[68]

[67] CAPV 161 (24 April 1959).
[68] Noble, *Forces*, pp. 145–47. This is an implicit critique of the structural functionalist
approach used by Alfred D. Chandler in *The Visible Hand: The Managerial Revolution in
American Business* (Cambridge, Mass.: Harvard University Press, 1977) and by Thomas

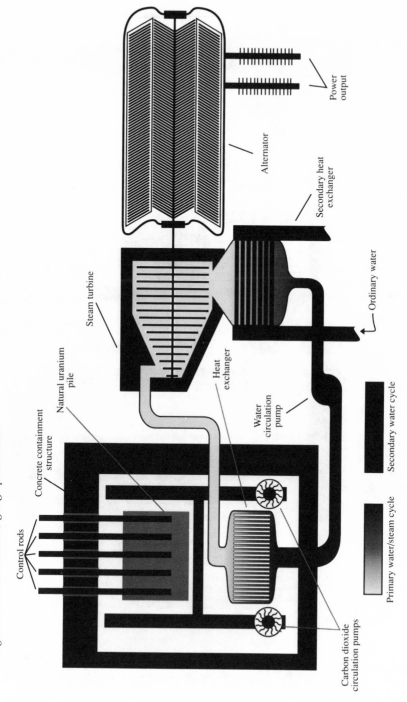

Figure 2. Natural uranium, gas-graphite reactor

Control rods

Concrete containment structure

Natural uranium pile

Steam turbine

Heat exchanger

Water circulation pump

Carbon dioxide circulation pumps

Alternator

Secondary heat exchanger

Ordinary water

Power output

Primary water/steam cycle

Secondary water cycle

Figure 3. Pressurized water reactor

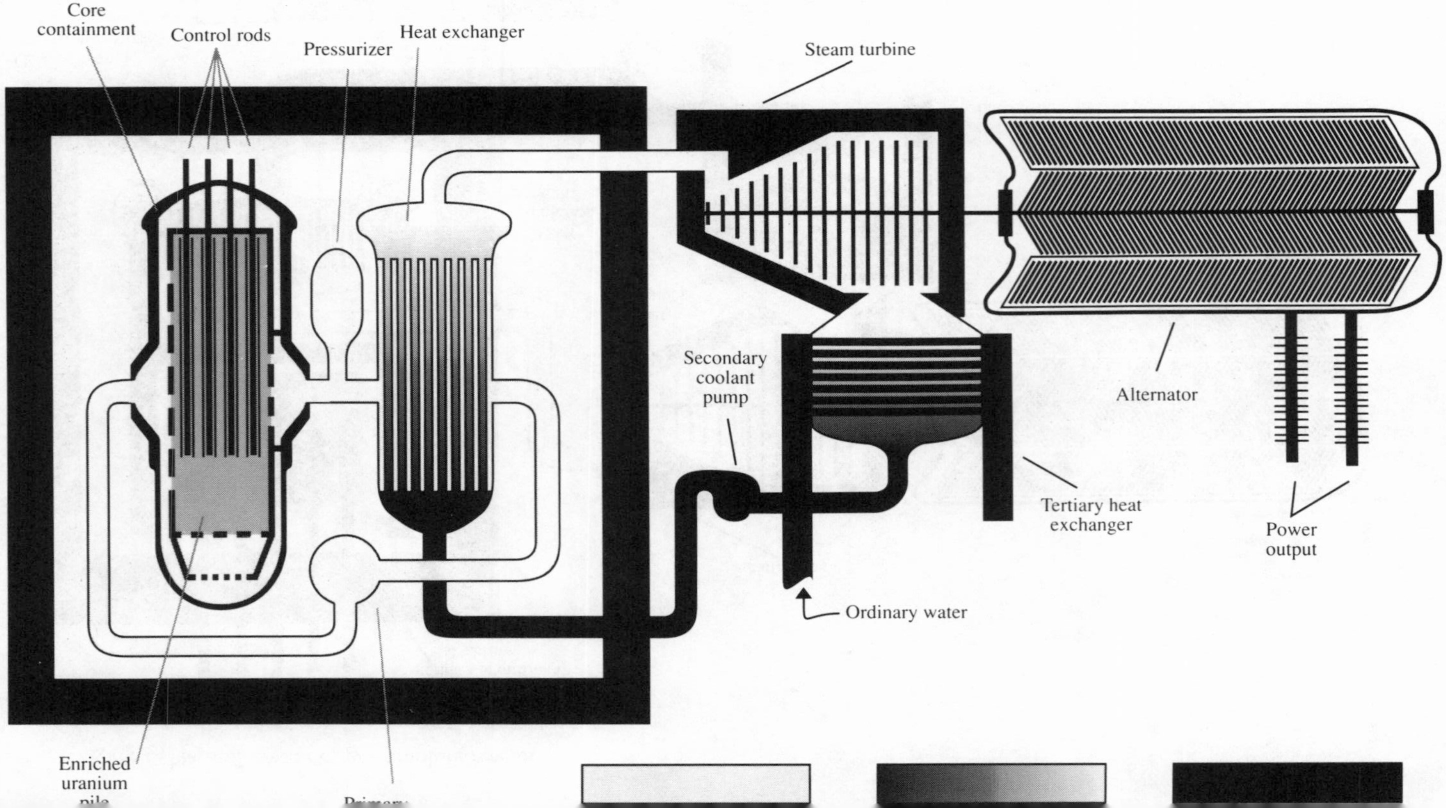

Core
containment

Control rods

Heat exchanger

Pressurizer

Enriched
uranium
pile

Steam turbine

Alternator

Tertiary heat
exchanger

Ordinary water

Secondary coolant
pump

Power
output

Primary

EDF entered the nuclear age in 1954, when Pierre Ailleret won approval from the Commissariat à l'Énergie Atomique (CEA) to use the waste heat from a nuclear pile to generate power. Though the result was far from being technically or economically viable—it was referred to as "Ailleret's toy"—the EDF community began to envision France's nuclear-powered future.[69] For trade unionists and hydro engineers, nuclear technology represented the perfect future: as the demand for their skills fell with the exhaustion of hydro sites, reemployment in nuclear construction offered a preservation of jobs and intrafirm status.[70] The UNGG pile developed by the CEA could be built almost entirely with domestic materials and technical resources, and it thus fit well into a strategy of national energy independence. Gaspard and Pierre Guillaumat, the director of the CEA, created an informal division of labor between the two agencies in 1954 with a surprising lack of bureaucratic rivalry. The CEA was to develop prototypes and EDF was to oversee the construction and operation of commercial nuclear power plants. Within prototypes themselves, the CEA oversaw the reactor section and EDF the generating portion. This left the heat exchanger in a contested zone, control over which was a ceaseless source of acrimony between EDF and CEA engineers.

We must look to the CEA's origins in order to understand its position on nuclear power. Weeks after the bombing of Hiroshima, de Gaulle's regime created the CEA as a cabinet-level agency to oversee France's journey into the nuclear age, even though in France the techniques for the military and peaceful uses of the atom remained only on the conceptual level. The first director of the CEA was a world-renowned Communist physicist with impeccable family ties, Frédéric Joliot-Curie, who brought together a highly sophisticated group of research phy-

---

P. Hughes in *Networks*. This direction for research on the question of technological choice was suggested by Langdon Winner, "Artifacts," pp. 121–36. For a superb set of articles on the social construction of technology, see Weibe E. Bijker, Thomas P. Hughes, and Trevor Pinch, eds. *The Social Construction of Technological Systems* (1987). The notion of a dialectical environment is fruitfully raised by Levin and Lewontin, *Biologist*, intro. and chap. 6.

[69] Picard et al., *Histoire(s)*, p. 187.

[70] For this reason, all but two of the six unions at EDF later strenuously opposed a shift to turnkey nuclear contracting in the late 1960s. The CFDT, which represented many of the hydro engineers, saw the death of hydro and the rise of turnkey contracting at that time as a threat to their métier; papers of Maurice Luneau (CFDT representative to the EDF board), CFDT-FGE offices, Paris. Similarly, the GNC said that the shift would "tend to limit the activities of the equipment section of EDF, then turn them toward stagnation and sclerosis and finally condemn them to disappear"; CAPV 238 (March 25 1966). A systematic reading of CAPV also reveals constant CFDT, GNC, and CGT resistance to any softening of EDF's usually parsimonious contracting methods. To the unions, a move toward LWRs implied a shift toward turnkey contracting; for this reason and a fear of abandoning the policy of energy independence, they resolutely opposed the adoption of LWR technology.

sicists atop the infant CEA. Following the lines of national independence (and after a brief flirtation with heavy water), they initiated development of what was to become UNGG technology. The CEA's choice of UNGG recognized France's limited supply of national resources. Under the McMahon Act of 1946, the United States held a nonexportable monopoly on enriched uranium, and France therefore had to use her own abundant supplies of natural uranium in metallic form. As a coolant and moderator, heavy water was in short supply in France, so the CEA opted for a gas coolant (regular water absorbed far too many neutrons) and a refined graphite moderator manufactured by Pechiney. Finally, the CEA was mandated to develop both weapons and power plants, and UNGG plants were generous producers of military-grade plutonium.

The onset of the Cold War in France spelled the ultimate end of Joliot's tenure at the CEA, and physicist-directors were replaced by research engineers, with Guillaumat at the top and Jules Horowitz as director of piles.[71] This change of métier implicitly pushed the CEA toward the territory of EDF engineers. The Guillaumat-Gaspard accords thus cut short the extension of the CEA toward EDF's domain, leaving CEA engineers the narrow realm between research scientists and electrical engineers. The resentment was considerable, symbolized by two corps of engineers performing the same work, jealously looking over one another's shoulders during nuclear plant construction. Finally, CEA engineers largely came from the Corps de Mines and professionally ranked above EDF engineers from the Corps des Ponts et Chaussées. Mines engineers felt upstaged by their inferiors and thus saw the 1954 accords as an affront to their professional pride and esprit de corps. Led by Horowitz, engineers of the CEA thus tended to contradict EDF's official positions out of sheer professional rivalry. According to EDF Director Boiteux, "Anytime EDF said 'black,' Horowitz and the CEA said 'white'; they contradicted everything we said."[72]

The Mines-Ponts rivalry has often been cited as the core of the battle over nuclear plant design.[73] Such lines cannot be drawn easily. One must instead draw them across agencies, between engineers and economist-managers and between nationalists and multinationalists. For

---

[71] The CEA remained anti-Communist for a number of years. EDF unionists suspected of Communist sympathies were sometimes forbidden to enter CEA research facilities, even though professional duties demanded that they do so; letter of Jacques Ribodoux to Marcel Paul, 12 March 1960, archives of the Confédération Générale du Travail—Fédération Nationale d'Énergie, Pantin, papers of René LeGuen, dossier: "Discrimination anti-syndicale."

[72] Picard et al., *Histoire(s)*, p. 196.

[73] Peter Pringle and James Spigelman, *The Nuclear Barons* (1981), p. 277; see also Philippe Simonnot, *Les nucléocrates* (1978), p. 27.

nationalist engineers, energy independence and the preservation of a powerful, proud, and vaguely anticapitalist profession remained at the top of the agenda. For the economist-managers, integration with multinational capitalism, conformity with procedures prevailing in the private sector, and the health of private firms worldwide took top priority. In the context of the battle over plant designs, Marcel Boiteux and Pierre Massé of EDF symbolized the multinationalists, as did Pierre Guillaumat, a longtime head of the CEA and later a chairman of EDF. Engineers in EDF's Equipment Directorate and in the CEA's Piles Directorate were nationalistic and often anticapitalist and tended to support UNGG technology. However, while EDF kept its internal battles from public view, the CEA was far less well ordered. While Guillaumat later cooperated with Boiteux to undermine UNGG, Horowitz of the CEA's reactor division determined the CEA's public image of support for UNGG. Politically supported by de Gaulle for purely patriotic reasons, the CEA was never held culpable for UNGG failures, and the CEA blamed UNGG plant failures on EDF's errors as architect-engineer. After UNGG plants broke down, de Gaulle attacked Massé "for not following the wise counsels of the CEA."[74] CEA Piles Directorate engineers thus appeared as the progenitors of a viable technology, which EDF managers failed to implement properly.

Gaspard remained tepid on nuclear power in the early 1950s, viewing it as a feasible future only on a thirty- to forty-year horizon.[75] Nonetheless, in 1955, the government created a study group called Péon (Comité sur la Production d'Énergie d'Origine Nucléaire), composed of EDF, CEA, and equipment-firm managers as well as state functionaries. Péon was charged with overseeing the trajectory of France's nuclear power development. Péon had no representatives from the engineering infrastructures of any of the agencies or firms. In cooperation with Péon, EDF made few extensive moves for a rapid development of nuclear power in the mid-1950s. After the creation of Euratom, a forum for European nuclear cooperation under the auspices of the nascent EEC, and following a tour of the United States in 1957 in which EEC and Péon representatives were subjected to a barrage of light-water marketing efforts, EDF embarked on a more intensive nuclear development program. Louis Armand, chief of the French group in the United States, argued that viable nuclear power was ten to fifteen, not thirty to forty, years distant. Armand also noted that the Suez Crisis underscored France's energy vulnerability.

EDF wanted to make nuclear power economically viable as soon as

[74] Massé, Aléas, p. 137.
[75] CAPV 109 (17 December 1954).

possible. It decided to increase its plant sizes considerably with each new unit after concluding that large plants could yield economies of scale.[76] Thus, the first EDF nuclear plant, EDF I, was started in 1956 at 70 mw, followed by EDF II in 1957 at 200 mw, and EDF III in 1959 at 480 mw. All were UNGG. CEA engineers argued against rapid up-scaling, preferring instead to perfect the technology before confronting the problems associated with larger dimensions. By 1961, top managers at EDF, attracted by the marketing efforts of Westinghouse and General Electric, began to argue for the abandonment of UNGG plants in favor of LWR plants. In 1960, EDF managers won approval for the construction of a Westinghouse LWR of 275 mw on France's northern border in a joint venture with a Belgian utility. EDF unions, engineers, and even the EDF board opposed the project. Increasingly, fundamental decisions on nuclear policy circumvented the board. Nonetheless, with the government's support, EDF broke ground on six UNGG plants up to 1966.

Engineers within the Equipment Directorate followed the logic of their distrust of the equipment manufacturers and solicited hundreds of separate bids for each plant.[77] EDF retained its role of architect-engineer, valorizing the engineers' skills and status, yet preventing the suppliers from gaining the experience necessary to export UNGG technology. EDF engineers' hammerlock on the architect-engineer role, along with contentious contracting methods, probably caused equipment manufacturers to view the abandonment of UNGG as the only way to gain even a modicum of control over, and exportability for, nuclear technology.

The technical attributes of UNGG and LWR designs moved toward closure between 1961 and 1964. A sufficient number of LWRs had been designed in the United States (though few were in operation) that design competition was possible. LWRs had several distinct advantages: (1) the radioactive zone was smaller, thus facilitating maintenance and repairs,[78] (2) because of a more powerful heat source, LWR

---

[76] EDF conceived its push for large plant sizes as part of a developmental strategy, in order to reach the economically necessary minimum scale as rapidly as possible. In this context, they chose an intensive rather than an extensive program, eschewing a large number of plants. EDF officials thus characterized their strategy: "To do enough of it to be ready in time [i.e., when UNGG plants became economically feasible], but not to do so much as to waste money"; anon., "Le programme nucléaire de l'EDF," *IDC* (February 1961), 2.

[77] In an interview with Philippe Simonnot, a former official of the Ministry of Finance underlined the manufacturers' opposition to EDF contracting practices, particularly to its maintenance of a blacklist of recalcitrant suppliers; Simonnot, *Nucléocrates*, p. 89.

[78] Note in Figures 2 and 3 that the radioactive zone in the UNGG plants includes the

plants were less complex, (3) with a fuel higher in heat content, the LWR was more compact, (4) LWR refueling was far easier, and (5) LWR fuel, though more radioactive, was far less flammable. UNGG had its own, less elegant technical advantages: (1) more accessible fuel supplies, (2) militarily useful by-products, (3) far less danger of catastrophic meltdowns, and (4) a reservoir of French technical experience. A comparison of the technical attributes of the two technologies was possible only on paper, because operating experiences were insufficient to judge concrete results. A combination of nontechnical, noneconomic factors still weighed to the advantage of UNGG, especially a certain technological nationalism and the prestige of French nuclear engineers. The technical and æsthetic advantages of the LWR, along with its American provenance, made it attractive to top EDF managers, given essentially even overall costs.[79]

Péon met frequently in 1964 to develop the nuclear power segment of the Fifth Plan for the years from 1966 to 1970. Within Péon, EDF managers argued for less aggressive UNGG development and more systematic efforts toward LWR development. EDF managers cited Britain's recent abandonment of UNGG technology as proof of its failings. EDF was outvoted within Péon, which in its report backed the UNGG path. Nonetheless, news of the rift leaked from the Péon meetings and the acrimonious and public war of plant types began. To the press, it was largely a battle between EDF and the CEA. De Gaulle continued to support UNGG technology, which he termed the "French model," out of patriotic fervor. EDF managers had little choice but to stall nuclear development. UNGG plant failures helped in these efforts. In 1959, the steel reactor casing on EDF I cracked, delaying completion of the plant for three years. EDF engineers had opted for a steel case against the advice of the CEA, so EDF took the blame for the failure. After a series of breakdowns on EDF I and II between 1963 and 1966 (due to failures in turbo-alternators, not reactors), UNGG's image declined further. The real break came in October 1966, when EDF III, online but a month and its official inauguration by de Gaulle scheduled to take place in a few days, sprang massive leaks in its heat exchanger. The manufacturer, Neyrpic, had installed a defective unit, but de Gaulle

---

entire volume within the containment structure; with the PWR, it is limited to the core containment and primary coolant circuit.

[79] After its own cost analyses comparing UNGG costs to those of oil-fired thermal plants (with oil at one centime per therm and a discount rate of 7 percent), EDF concluded in 1964 that UNGG technology was economically viable; EDF–Direction Générale, "Perspectives de développement des centrales nucléaires en France," mimeographed (1964), pp. 2–3, EDF archives, Centre de Documentation Murat-Messine, Paris, series E8: "Économie générale."

and the press held EDF culpable, and by dint of a poorly written contract, EDF paid the lion's share of the repair costs.[80] Badly burned by UNGG failures, EDF managers resolved to prevent any further development of UNGG technology and to push harder for LWRs.[81] The latter also offered EDF managers a public relations opportunity, because LWR failures could be blamed on the Americans, not on EDF. The impasse halted French nuclear power development in 1966. Ground was never again broken for any new UNGG plants. The battle over the question of French reactor design could not be resolved by interagency means, so by default the private sector and the government gained critical roles. Indeed the private sector and the state, allied with EDF management, largely determined the ultimate choice.

EDF's suppliers became restive following the LWR marketing blitz by General Electric and Westinghouse in the early 1960s, particularly after French suppliers bought LWR licences from the Americans. French firms began to see UNGG technology as a white elephant in a global market increasingly dominated by LWR technology. A heavily subsidized sale of a UNGG plant to Spain in the mid-1960s revived hope for UNGG exports, yet the French firms indifferently executed the contracts and the Spanish plant remained an orphan. Thus, equipment firm managers felt that the only option left was to adopt LWR technology, bought on a turnkey basis (i.e., contracted as a single unit, with the supplier as architect-engineer), in order to get EDF out of the architect-engineer business, utilize the American licenses, and develop markets for French nuclear industry exports. The wish among such firms to export French-made American technology was pure fantasy, however. They had been able to export high-tension and hydro technology on the basis of an undisputed French expertise, but their exports of American-based thermal technology had been minimal. Presumably, if foreigners wanted to buy LWRs, they would purchase them from the original developers, not from mere licensees.[82] Much later, when France did export LWRs, markets were opened by generous subsidies.

[80] On the allegations of EDF's culpability in the EDF III accident, see Puiseux and Saumon, "Actors and Decisions," p. 145. On the distribution of the costs of the EDF III accident, see CAPV 249 (10 March 1967) and CACE 190 (9 March 1967). For an astute study of the politics of failures, see Madeleine Akrich, "From Accusations to Choses," paper presented at the annual meetings of the Society for the History of Technology, Wilmington, Del., 21 October 1988.

[81] Ironically, EDF officials themselves admitted that the bulk of UNGG plant malfunctions were not in the reactors but in the peripheral equipment; "Les difficultés de réalisation des centrales nucléaires," IDC (December 1969–January 1970), 2. EDF President Massé held the equipment engineers culpable for the EDF III failure, thus justifying turnkey contracting in order to get EDF out of its architect-engineer role.

[82] Much later, France was able to improve LWR technology owing to its vast experience with LWRs after 1975. By 1988, over 70 percent of EDF's generating capacity was in

By the mid-1960s, with the technical and economic competition be-tween UNGGs and LWRs still at a draw, financial and political factors began to tip the balance. Recognizing that inexpensive fuel oil would postpone the day when nuclear power would become cost-competitive with conventional oil-fired plants, many French experts believed that the international oil companies intentionally kept fuel prices low.[83] This strategy coincidentally gave American reactor manufacturers time to prove that they could actually build large, functioning LWR plants. The critical gambit was, however, a LWR marketing blitz in the 1960s. Bupp and Derian as well as Pringle and Spigleman have well dem-onstrated that General Electric and Westinghouse used loss-leader pric-ing of LWR plants in order to defeat competition in the emerging world reactor market.[84] American firms tailored prices on LWRs of scales as yet unrealized to undercut the known prices of existing UNGG plants. The LWR reference prices used by Péon and the government in making cost comparisons between UNGG and LWR were thus entirely fictive. One must assume that the French licensees for LWR technology who participated in the Péon discussions knew this as well. Finally, because LWR technology implied a dependence on enriched uranium supplied by the American Atomic Energy Commission (AEC), American nuclear fuel prices became an essential part of the cost equations. Facing a relative excess of enrichment capacity at the time, the AEC obligingly offered below-cost prices for the fuel.[85] American oil and reactor firms thus shifted the comparative cost equations and effectively opened the French nuclear market.

The CEA's Horowitz and EDF's equipment director, Jean Cabanius,

---

LWRs, making France a viable LWR exporter, but only after American withdrawal from the field after 1978.

[83] This view prevailed among French policymakers; see Pierre Desprairies, "La con-currence de l'uranium et du pétrole," *RFE* 223 (July-August 1970), 467. See also Francis Perrin in *Le Monde*, 13 December 1969, and Marcel Boiteux, "Extraits de l'exposé de M. Boiteux devant la section de la Production Industrielle et de l'Énergie du Conseil Écon-omique et Social," mimeographed report, p. 11, EDF archives, Centre de Documentation Murat-Messine, Paris, dossier: série E8, "Économie Générale." Boiteux explicitly stated this to the EDF board; CAPV 277 (26 September 1969). See also "Où va le prix du fuel lourd?" editorial, *RFE* 205 (November 1968), 62. Using the neoclassic concept of cross-elasticities of demand, a similar point was made; "Baisse de prix de l'énergie première et développement électronucléaire," editorial, *RFE* 209 (March 1969), 264.

[84] Irvin C. Bupp and Jean-Claude Derian, *Light Water* (1978), pp. 48–49, and Pringle and Spigleman, *Barons*, pp. 264–71. The latter authors note that Philip Sporn, ex-chief of the American Electric Power Company, a respected doyen of American utilities, denounced the LWR price offers as "come-on bids" (p. 270). An EDF official, Pierre Bacher, termed the loss-leader strategy "an immense bluff," citing LWR contracts at $100 per kw installed, when actual costs for GE and Westinghouse were more like $500 per kw; communicated to author 12 June 1984 by Jean-François Picard.

[85] Boiteux recognized this fact in 1968 and noted that such underpricing would prob-ably not continue; CAPV 276 (22 June 1969).

met in early 1967 in one final attempt to solve the impasse on an interagency level. The impasse deepened as the two failed to reach a consensus. Also in 1967, Decelle retired as director-general of EDF and the entire top management was reorganized, in part because of de Gaulle's disdain for its pro-LWR position. Ironically, the new managerial group was equally in favor of the LWR (though more politically astute in promoting it), and the essence of the managerial change was the final victory of economists over anticapitalist engineers within the firm and the sealing of the political doom of the pro-UNGG unionists and engineers.

In the middle of 1967, the Franco-Belgian LWR at Chooz failed badly, yet the press quietly ignored the event, and the pro-LWR position was not eroded in any way.[86] A similar blithe indifference toward LWR flaws followed failures at two Italian plants at about the same time. In addition, in 1967, the CEA sucessfully put a small uranium enrichment plant into operation at Pierrelatte, thus implying that a French LWR choice would not mean dependency on American nuclear fuel and offering a non-UNGG source for fissionable weapons material. Nobody calculated the costs of manufacturing enriched uranium fuel, but there were suggestions that economies of scale demanded a large enrichment facility, predicated upon an EEC-wide demand and hence LWR domination of the EEC. Finally, at the end of 1967, de Gaulle met with the heads of EDF, the CEA, and relevant cabinet ministers and decided to reconfirm plans for a pair of 1000-mw UNGG units at Fessenheim but to allow EDF to proceed with plans to build a second Franco-Belgian LWR at Tihange.[87] The impasse therefore continued. Significantly, Massé had never consulted the EDF board concerning Tihange, resulting in a major blowup at the December board meeting. In addition, at that meeting Massé presented the bids EDF had received for the first Fessenheim unit. Acting against the wishes of the board, he grouped the bids into three subunits—reactor core, heat exchanger, and control and fueling systems. This was the first step toward a turnkey system of UNGG contracting, which the engineers and unions had strenuously opposed. Even with the cost savings promised by the new bid system, bids came back unrealistically high, and a number of

[86] Decelle report, CACE 203 (4 July 1967). The accident was far worse than that of EDF III, involving not only a core melt, but boiler contamination as well, requiring massive replacement of component parts.

[87] The commencement of construction on the Fessenheim I unit, slated for early 1968, was blocked by the Ministry of Finance for budgetary reasons. One must note, however, that the Ministry of Finance at this time was starting to oppose UNGG technology, primarily because the front-end costs of UNGG plants were higher than those of LWRs (with the high front-end costs ultimately compensated by lower fuel costs). This delay allowed EDF managers to slow UNGG construction even further.

board members viewed the high and probably rigged bids as a means to sabotage further UNGG development.[88]

Péon met in early 1968 to revise the nuclear plan for the balance of the Fifth Plan. By that time, the opposition of the manufacturers to UNGG technology was total. Within Péon, Ambroise Roux, chief executive officer of CGE, led the assault. The CEA's main spokesman in the meetings was Etienne Hirsch, an LWR supporter. As a result, Péon came to a solid pro-LWR consensus after cursory cost comparisons between the St.-Laurent (EDF IV) UNGG costs and projections of the already-troubled Oyster Creek LWR costs.[89] Péon then had to develop a strategy to kill UNGG without enraging de Gaulle. The scheme was complex: Péon verbally continued to support the UNGG project at Fessenheim, yet argued that LWR technology was cheaper and thus urged that France build a 600-mw LWR pilot project. However, to give the illusion that Péon was not killing the French design for the American one, Péon proffered the British gas-cooled high-temperature and the Canadian heavy-water, natural uranium reactors as viable alternatives. At the time, neither were as technically or economically advanced as UNGG, but the strategy was clear: to use the British and Canadian designs to undercut UNGG and give the illusion of a wide choice, then to use the opening to implant LWR dominance in France.[90]

The report, authored in April yet kept secret until December 1968, gave the press the impression of a balanced treatment of the issue.[91] Its expert cost comparisons went unquestioned and its facile support of the British and Canadian designs were believed. Because the report was advisory, the impasse continued until the conclusions were affirmed by the government. Delayed by the 1968 revolt, the resolution of the impasse did not occur until 1969. De Gaulle, UNGG's protector, retired in April, leaving the presidency to pro-LWR Georges Pompidou.

[88] CAPV 257 (22 December 1967). Boiteux openly stated that the high Fessenheim bids proved the economic nonviability of UNGG plants; CAPV 258 (26 January 1968). See also Frédérique de Gravelaine and Sylvie O'Dy, L'état-EDF, p. 217, from interviews with EDF officials.

[89] Regarding the cost analyses performed by the Péon group, Bupp and Derian wrote, "The Péon Committee's conclusion . . . was a seriously misleading estimate of the reasons for light water dominance. It disregarded self-interest, nationalistic concerns, and indicated the abiding willingness to accept self-serving promotional tracts as serious, independent analyses" (Light Water, p. 87). False cost information was thus consciously submitted to Péon. Massé later admitted that the cost difference of 14 percent was overshadowed by a 40 percent potential margin of error on the estimates; Aléas, p. 136.

[90] Ambroise Roux describes this charade in Picard et al., Histoire(s), p. 199. See also Simonnot, Nucléocrates, pp. 241–49.

[91] For the text of the report, see Commission Consultative pour la Production d'Électricité d'Origine Nucléaire, "Les perspectives de développement des centrales nucléaires en France: Rapport" (1968). Even RFE was fooled; see "Le rapport Péon," editorial, RFE 206 (December 1968), 112.

In October, shortly after its inauguration, a fueling mishap led to a partial meltdown at St.-Laurent I. The press again attacked the UNGG series, so in November Pompidou announced that Fessenheim was to be LWR, that no UNGG plants would be started in the foreseeable future, and that the government would help restructure the electrical equipment manufacturing sector in order to orient it toward series construction of turnkey LWRs.[92] Pompidou backed up his decision by referring to Péon's cost analyses, the results of which had already been belied by a worldwide drop in LWR orders due to rising costs.[93] Unionists and engineers within EDF and the CEA suffered a total defeat.

One can only guess whether UNGG technology would have ultimately succeeded in France. It is clear, however, that the operating histories and economics of UNGG technology were either equal to or better than LWR technology in the late 1960s, as EDF officials have since admitted. Indeed, when EDF III and St.-Laurent I (both UNGG plants) went on-line in 1966 and 1969, they were the largest nuclear plants in the world. After manufacturing defects were resolved, UNGG proved itself, even before 1969, to be a viable technology, though, like LWRs, not cost-effective in the face of cheap oil. The reasons for the death of UNGG technology rest not in the realm of technical or economic considerations, but in the domain of political and economic power.[94] In addition, one must note that EDF managers were enamored of the visions of the powerful, burgeoning American economy of the

[92] One of Pompidou's public rationales for the decision was to help electrical equipment manufacturers who had been hard hit by the pause in nuclear plant construction. The Péon report of November 1970 (cited in *Rapport de la Commission de l'Énergie du VIème Plan* [Paris: Commissariat du Plan, 1971], p. 198) said, in reference to the Pompidou decision, "Its central rationale was definitely to offer our electromechanical industry [a major opportunity] to extend [its] nuclear activities." The minister of research opposed the turnkey method because it forestalled the development of French expertise in LWR technology; CAPV 274 (25 April 1969).

[93] In the June 1969 board meeting, Boiteux himself admitted that LWR prices were rising at the rate of 20 percent per year, and that as of May 1969, UNGG and LWR technologies were absolutely cost competitive; CAPV 276 (27 June 1969). Nonetheless, when Boiteux spoke at the inauguration of the St.-Laurent I plant on 16 October 1969, he claimed that UNGG plants were technically, but not economically, viable; CAPV 278 (24 October 1969); see also AFP dispatch of 16 October 1969, "Vers l'abandon de la filière française." In Picard et al., *Histoire(s)*, pp. 200–201, an EDF official admits that EDF abandoned a technically mature UNGG design in favor of a less mature LWR design, and that this shift led to a major shortage of productive facilities in the late 1970s. Desprairies notes that the drop in LWR orders was due to the 68 percent cost overruns on the Indian Point LWR in New York ("La concurrence," p. 471); see also Bertrand Goldschmidt, "Les principales options techniques du programme français de production d'énergie nucléaire," RFE 215 (October-November 1969), 94.

[94] A former EDF cadre, Louis Puiseux, sees the abandonment of UNGG as part of a general process in energy policymaking by the French state, in which state sector technocrats abandoned their duty and allowed a fictive free market and a group of private sector managers to rule; Puiseux and Saumon, "Actors and Decisions," pp. 168–69.

1960s and imitated the economic and technological choices of the United States. In the final analysis, the political rejection of UNGG was the result of a successful campaign by private interests and by the victory at EDF of economists over engineers, which undercut the firm's original goal of national energy and technological independence. In opting for the LWR, particularly with the turnkey contracting method, EDF lost a large share of the control over the prices and technical characteristics of its own equipment. EDF became a large, protected, internal market for French nuclear equipment firms, though by maintaining its monopsonist power, EDF was able to prevent cost overruns in nuclear construction of the type that helped to kill that industry in the United States.[95]

A number of nontechnical and noneconomic factors were behind the decision to abandon UNGG technology. The Pompidou decision resolved three major axes of conflict. First, there was a long-standing battle for hegemony over French nuclear development between the CEA and EDF. Second, EDF's contracting and construction methods for UNGG plants prevented French nuclear equipment manufacturers from being able to export turnkey nuclear plants because they were not allowed the opportunity to develop sufficient experience as architect-engineers. Third, within EDF, the LWR decision symbolized the hegemony of economists over engineers at the top of the firm. The resolution of these contradictions was facilitated by the fact that French nuclear technocrats fell into two traps: the loss-leader pricing of LWR plants and enriched uranium in the 1960s and the pricing policies of multinational oil companies, both of which rendered the economic models inaccurate.

Labor and Technological Change

EDF workers often saw training and retraining as the solution to the dangers of obsolescent skills associated with changing technology. Since workers were essentially guaranteed lifetime job tenure at EDF, the company also had an interest in retraining. By this combination of factors, EDF workers seldom felt threatened by new technology and did not develop Luddite sentiments toward technical changes. Indeed, new technology, rather than constituting a dire catastrophe, often offered workers an opportunity to upgrade their skills and pay levels. Once the retraining system was fully understood by each worker, his

[95] Much of this success was due to standardizing plant designs, as the United States never did; Pierre Tanguy, "Safety and Nuclear Power Plant Standardization: The French Experience," *Public Utilities Fortnightly* 114 (31 October 1985), 22–23.

or her solidarity with the company and the front office deepened. EDF workers rarely faced technological unemployment because the overall strategy only shifted it, making it invisible and expressed only as a smaller number of hirings for each additional megawatt-hour of output.

Several factors explain the lack of Luddite sentiments beyond the fact of personal protections. From management's perspective, labor costs constituted less than one-quarter of total production costs, so the benefits to be gained by deskilling and cutting salaries were minimal in the face of inevitable worker resistance and cost reductions more easily attainable elsewhere. Workers were therefore faced with technologies to which they had to adapt—they faced a situation of utmost technological determinism. This does not mean, however, that management, especially after 1962, did not seek to limit salaries for symbolic and political reasons. More important, whatever Luddite instincts may have existed among individual workers (and there is little evidence to indicate them), there was no institutional framework for their expression. At the level of the EDF community, a technocratic ideology equating technological change with social progress remained essentially unquestioned. With respect to the CGT, a Marxist-Leninist view of technological change—perhaps a legacy of positivist influences on early Marxism—painted almost all technological change as unilinear and progressive, thereby rendering resistance to it atavistic.[96] For all four unions, the equation "technological change equals greater productivity equals rising incomes equals social progress" tied technological change to a better standard of living. The unions were not entirely Panglossian, however. They recognized that vigilance was necessary to prevent management from abusively introducing new technology as a way to achieve temporary gains over labor. The issue was not simply one of protechnology versus anti-technology, but one of control. Given that precondition, labor's consent to technological change effectively tied the shop floor to the home in a nascent consumerism, and EDF's consumer advertising became an effective medium for this message. More productive workers and machines would form the economic basis for a renaissance of the family, promising the ever-elusive "family wage" for male electrical workers.[97] Faced with managers legitimated by meritocratic selection, EDF workers remained largely quiescent as the na-

[96] This extends the argument made by Langdon Winner, *Autonomous Technology*, pp. 77–89.

[97] For a complete discussion of this issue, see Robert L. Frost, "La technocratie au pouvoir . . . avec le consentement des syndicats: La technologie, les syndicats et la direction à l'Électricité de France (1946–1968)," *Le Mouvement Social* 130 (January-April 1985), 81–96. For a discussion of the family wage, a level of remuneration for the male head of household sufficient to support a family, see Louise A. Tilly and Joan W. Scott, *Women, Work, and Family* (New York: Holt, Rinehart and Winston, 1978).

ture and character of their work was gradually transformed. The best way to elucidate this point is to examine two incidents of changes of technique and technology at EDF. Distribution services, where the bulk of the manual labor at EDF remained concentrated, were the center of contention over changing techniques.

The CGT successfully reduced the negative impacts of new technology and techniques as it responded to the reshaping of meter reading and billing procedures between 1948 and 1962. Many unskilled workers had been meter readers at the time of the nationalization, reading meters and collecting bills at the same time. This procedure had obvious drawbacks, not the least being the frequent absence of domestic users when the meter readers arrived. In addition, there were security and convenience problems with having the meter readers carry around receipts, money, and change. Though this method created jobs and gave EDF a personalized presence in every French home, it was labor-intensive and very inefficient. The CGT quickly understood that meter readers could well become victims of more rational methods.

As a first step in reorganizing meter reading, consumers were urged to pay their bills at post offices and banks or to pay by mail. In the second step, EDF cut the frequency of meter readings, even though that meant cash-flow problems for EDF, which had considerable uncollected revenues on the meters between readings. As early as 1948 the CGT demanded guarantees of job security and a normal promotion path for meter readers, and it led a campaign in defense of the meter readers throughout the 1950s.[98] When the state decreed in 1959 that the frequency of readings would be cut in half, the CGT pulled out all the stops and even managed to induce the Paris Municipal Council to vote against the change.[99] The other unions at EDF had criticized the CGT for leading what the CFTC called a "demogogic campaign" for the meter readers,[100] but the CGT succeeded in slowing the pace of the change. The CGT did exploit the meter readers' fears by claiming that the front office intended to replace them all by computers, to shift meter readings to consumers, and to use subcontractors, but it also managed to slow the transition so that there were few layoffs.[101] Most of the meter readers who did not leave by attrition were retrained as "commercial agents," going into the gaily colored and well-decorated neighborhood EDF offices and counseling domestic consumers on their electrical power and appliances. The CGT indeed ultimately won on

[98] Minutes of meeting between Éclairage leaders and Gaspard, 8 March 1948, Éclairage archives, dossier: "Releveurs-encaisseurs."

[99] Force-Information 54 (March 1959), 11.

[100] Gaz-Électricité 78 (May 1957).

[101] Force-Information 99 (January 1963), 57.

this issue, and the only costs to the firm were those of retraining and the difference between work force reductions by attrition and reductions by layoffs.

The introduction of a punch-card system for billing customers in 1953 evoked an amusing incident. The machines for reading and creating punch cards were not business computers in the modern sense, but merely elaborate mechanical sorting and tabulating devices. EDF did not want to lock itself into a transitional technology, so it leased rather than bought the machinery.[102] Needing semiskilled workers to operate the new machines, EDF proceeded to train people (mostly women), telling them that they had the rare privilege of becoming masters of a new technology. EDF then set up a number of keypunching centers and converted much of its domestic billing to the punch-card system. Within a decade, computer technology became available, making skills obsolete. The unions responded to the threat first by agitation, then by joint worker-manager sessions to determine the modalities of the introduction of the computers.

EDF had used computers since the mid-1950s in Direction des Études et Recherches (E&R) and EEG, but they were specialized devices designed to execute sophisticated programs on small numbers of variables rather than to process large data bases. Early computers were not intended to augment labor efficiency, but to perform hitherto impossible calculations. They represented no threat of unemployment and indeed required a new milieu of skilled workers. During 1960, the first rumors began to circulate among workers about the imminent introduction of administrative computers. Management initially kept quiet on the modalities of their introduction, but a systematic and coherent campaign on the part of the unions assured that the workers' positions were not only preserved but enhanced.

Éclairage pursued a complex strategy as it addressed the introduction of computers. In calling a Paris-region general assembly of EDF workers in June 1961 to deal with the computer threat, the CGT claimed that the front office intended to reduce the work force by 60 percent.[103] In a poster of February 1962, the CGT labeled computers as "monster brains" that would throw EDF workers out of jobs and degrade the quality of work life.[104] All the unions recognized that the new technology could be used either to upgrade skills and raise productivity, thereby justifying higher pay, or to degrade skills, erode pay, and

---

[102] CAPV 86 (27 March 1953).
[103] Éclairage leaflet for general assembly on computerization, Paris, 20 June 1961, Éclairage archives, dossier: "Ordinateurs."
[104] Force 105 (February 1962), poster format for display on union bulletin boards.

induce layoffs. The CGT wrote, "The CGT [electrical workers'] federation repeats that it is in favor of technical progress, but that it currently
struggles and will continue to struggle so that this technical progress
engenders social progress, higher skills, and greater well-being for the
workers."[105] Éclairage and the CFTC well understood the potential
dangers of computers. The CGT feared a more severe division of labor,
with low-skilled workers doing the robotlike work of data coding and
entry and extremely high-skilled workers doing the sophisticated tasks
involved in analysis of the output.[106] The CFTC worried about the
psychological fatigue and tension created by computerized work and
about the dangers of a work regime that would demand long work
days full of fast, repetitive work.[107] In 1967, the CGT defined its vision:
"The electronic era opens numerous and vast horizons for mankind.
The modern machine must serve society and not be used against it.
Electronic equipment at EDF and GDF as elsewhere serves to augment
surplus value. What is more natural for the work force [than] to demand
their due [when new technology is introduced]? . . . At present, the
machine has gone beyond the replacement of the human hand; it fulfills
certain functions of the brain. The social consequences are immense.
Our battle must be oriented so that the electron will be put to the
service of all, to the service of peace."[108]

Reflecting an ideological preoccupation that saw new technology as
unequivocally beneficial, EDF management never ceased to stress that
computers would improve work at EDF. Management claimed that
computer outputs constituted a more "noble" form of information,
thereby ennobling the workers dealing with them.[109] Conveniently ignoring the numbing work of data entry and verification, management
later elaborated on this position: "As to the climate of work due to the
introduction of computers, it must be noted that the machine will be
doing [the] fastidious and repetitive tasks; the workers who will be
reassigned as a result of it will find themselves with new tasks that
are of a higher level. This circumstance in and of itself should therefore

[105] *Force* 170 (January 1964).

[106] CGT responses ibid., p. 17; the CGT also noted that computers "often engender
more parcelized work, taking the management responsibilities [for day-to-day activities]
away from the workers, though at the same time, a higher level of knowledge is needed";
Force 196 (May 1967).

[107] Responses of the CFTC, in minutes of "Table ronde ordinateur," 19 March 1962,
p. 15, CFDT archives.

[108] Letter from the Syndicat du Personnel de la Production et du Transport d'Énergie
de la Région Parisienne to "Camarade Leroy," 9 January 1967, p. 5, Éclairage archives,
dossier: "Ordinateurs."

[109] Minutes of CSC-CMP meeting of 25 May 1961.

be favorable to the workers."[110] Management therefore denied that computers would aggravate the division of labor at EDF. At the same time, however, despite its claims that skill levels would rise as a result of computers, management tried unsuccessfully to use computerization as a method to chip away at a set of hard-won bonuses for hazardous and fatiguing punch-card work and to downgrade a number of job descriptions and pay levels. Though the workers who were reassigned as a result of computerization were guaranteed by the *statut* that the reassignments would not entail demotions, management did seek to demote the positions for new entrants.

Worker resistance to management's control of the computerization process began within the CMPs (works committees) and in the CSC-CMP (central council of works committees) in 1960, but the unions quickly understood that decentralized bodies could not deal directly with the central computerization plan, which management had recently developed. The unions demanded and won a series of "computer roundtables" between representatives of unions and managers. In the roundtables, which ran from 1960 through 1964, management presented its computerization plan and unionists advantageously modified it. Management implied that it wanted to use computers to erode the position of the workers, particularly those working on the precomputer punch-card machinery. According to management itself, computerization would mean the suppression of 4,495 jobs, mostly in the 151 punch-card shops around France.[111] Nonetheless, by the time the roundtable talks ended in 1964, the unions had won all of their original demands.[112] There were to be no layoffs, virtually no loss of the various punch-card bonuses, no loss of the normal promotion tracks, and all affected workers were to be retrained at the company's expense according to a program set up by the CSNP. The unions were also careful to make sure that everybody was well aware that "personnel management" done by computers (payrolling, pension and sick pay accounting, and productivity analyses) would not entail turning workers' lives into simple computerized data, "pushing the social context to the mar-

[110] Report of Koechlin (management representative) in minutes of "Table ronde ordinateur," 19 March 1962, p. 12, CFDT archives.

[111] Management representative report in minutes of "Table ronde ordinateur," 6 January 1964, p. 7. For information on the conversion from punch-card machines to computers, see Rémi Sadoux, "À l'EDF les 'computers' transforment les habitudes de gestion," *Entreprise*, 12 January 1967, p. 1.

[112] "Agents des ateliers mécanographiques dont le poste sera supprimé," EDF-Inspection Générale document of 7 January 1964; Blom report in minutes of "Table ronde ordinateur," 6 January 1964, p. 9; CGT leaflet of 25 March 1964; untitled EDF-Inspection Générale document of 16 January 1964. The CSNP also won the right to intervene in the drawing up of job descriptions for computer workers; Claude Flandre's (GNC) notes from undated "Table ronde ordinateur" [1962?], Éclairage archives, dossier: "Ordinateurs."

gins."[113] The unions also elicited a commitment from management that no computer work would be subcontracted. Finally, when a number of computer and punch-card activities were transferred to a suburb of Paris, Issy-les-Moulineaux, in 1964, the unions won a better work regimen for the transferred workers, along with generous housing and transportation allowances.[114]

The victory of the workers on the computerization issue was not total. Management responded only verbally to the workers' fear of becoming simple data in computerized personnel management models; it took no concrete steps to avoid that degradation. All of the unions sought pay increases as a result of the enhanced productivity due to the introduction of computers, but speaking for management, Pierre Valle sidestepped the issue, claiming that only the government could decide such issues, even though EDF retained power to to assign various bonuses.[115] Indeed, in the 1964 to 1974 computerization plan, 280 former punch-card workers lost their "active service" bonuses and 300 lost their punch-card bonuses.[116] Perhaps the greatest shortcoming of the settlement went unrecognized by all sides: though there were no layoffs as a result of computers, the normal increase in the number of jobs at EDF over time was reduced, thereby diverting the social costs of computerization from the present work force to the future work force and from within EDF to the society as a whole. This tendency was most pronounced with computer technology, yet it was true as well for all productivity measures.

Nonetheless, the unions successfully turned aside management's attempts to undercut the workers' situation through the introduction of computers. Moreover, though it took a number of years to be recognized by the workers, computer technology provided a powerful alternative to striking as a means of resistance and protest, as we shall see, shutting down power entailed enormous costs in terms of public support for the workers, but blocking the computerized billing process could cut off the revenue flow to EDF without affecting consumers.[117] Computers controlled by the workers raised the vision of a new, high-technology form of workers' action. In that context, workers were able to struggle on the most politically legitimate terrain within the EDF community, control over work based on specialized skills and expertise.

[113] EDF-Direction Générale document (untitled) of 4 January 1964, CFDT archives.
[114] "Décision," EDF/GDF Directions Générales, 21 April 1964, CFDT archives, "Table ronde ordinateur."
[115] Responses of the FO in minutes of "Table ronde ordinateur," 19 March 1962, pp. 13–14.
[116] "Incidence de l'automatisation sur les effectifs et les fonctions du personnel," appendix to minutes of "Table ronde ordinateur," 2 July 1963, table 2.
[117] De Gravelaine and O'Dy, L'état-EDF, p. 83.

CHAPTER 6

The Forces of Production: Work and Work Life at EDF, 1954–1970

A strong and institutionalized presence of labor in the daily life of EDF represented the sweetest fruit of the nationalization for electrical workers. Codeterminist bodies in which the unions had a strong voice treated questions of workplace discipline, promotions, assignment of responsibility for accidents at work, and (to a far lesser extent) job assignments. Though decrees of the Cold War era limited the unions' power, their sheer presence and engagement remained a bulwark against any return to a paternalist or favoritist managerial style. Because workers had voice only through the unions, each worker had a strong incentive to join. Many probably joined the CGT, by far the largest and most influential union, simply because it was most able to deliver for its members. The CGT's power of numbers prevented any major erosion of its influence, and its institutional power tended to depoliticize it. It was relegated to the role of a paperwork processor and conciously chose to be the major defender of pay levels at EDF. The CGT became primarily a service union, and by the mid-1950s, bureaucratic expertise, not "militance in the gut," made a good union leader.[1]

The educational system at EDF remained inadequate through the 1950s, but the unions and the EDF front office joined efforts to expand it considerably between 1958 and 1962. This reflected a quiet quid pro quo struck between unions and management: because the front office could offer few solutions to the pervasive salary crisis, it compensated by offering ways to enhance skills and thus gain individual wage in-

[1] René Le Guen, cited in Picard et al., *Histoire(s)*, p. 168.

creases. Weak as it was, this compromise helped maintain unity between workers and the front office.

The political problems inside and outside EDF in the 1950s never fully annihilated the reforms won through the nationalization. The unions' loss of control over the benefit system was the only major casualty. The superiority of the EDF workers' situation over that of virtually all other French workers and the hegemony of the culture of high technology weakened the impulsions to reform EDF internally. Pay remained the major problem for EDF workers, a problem that could not be resolved in-house. That fact reinforced the CGT's penchant for targeting its demands at the state itself and largely to ignore political relations within the firm. As a result, the CGT expended minimal efforts to resist the evolution of EDF management away from the early productivist alliance. The CFTC attempted reforms, but its position was weak and its ideas were not fully developed, remaining in gestation and only breaking loose with the crisis of 1968.

Union Strength and Politics

Unions were strong but deeply divided at EDF. The CGT very slowly lost members to other unions, but the deterioration was too slow to be explained by simple attrition. Most new workers continued to join the CGT's two main electrical federations, Éclairage and the GNC. Virtually all EDF personnel (save a dozen top executives) belonged to one of the unions. Figure 4 indicates the relative strength of the unions at EDF. Relative union power varied by region. Force Ouvrière was strong in Amiens, Béziers, Roanne, Lille, Bayonne, and Laval—all areas with significant Socialist party electoral strength. The CFTC was better distributed regionally, for it had a presence almost everywhere, though more strongly in the East and the lower Loire valley. It enjoyed considerable power only in Nancy, Metz, and Sélestat, with majorities in both blue- and white-collar categories only in the latter two, as well as strong support among clericals in the Parisian central offices.[2] The CGT had majorities or pluralities virtually everywhere except among white-collar workers in the research and development section (Paris), and in Besançon and Cherbourg. UNCM (white-collar workers only) had pluralities only in the research and development section (Paris) and in Cherbourg; nowhere did it enjoy majority support among white-collar workers.[3]

[2] *Gaz-Électricité* 32 (February 1951).
[3] "Résultats des élections des commissions secondaires du 27 avril 1960," appendix

Figure 4. Relative strength of unions at EDF, 1947–1969

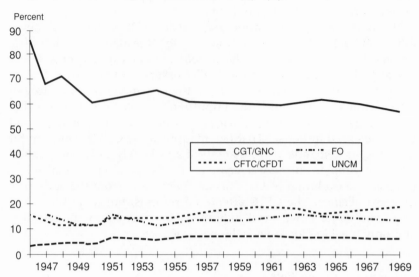

Sources: Results of CCOS/CCAS, CMP, and CSNP elections, listed in *Gaz-Électricité* 42 (June 1955), *Gaz-Électricité* 77 (April 1957), *Force-Militant* 38 (16 September 1965), and J.-F. Picard et al., *Histoire(s) de l'EDF* (1985), p. 166.

The unions did not become decadent and detached from their members. In the first place, union rivalries forced each union to maintain close contacts with its members and to compete in delivering services. Secondly, without a system of dues check-off, stewards had to collect union dues on a monthly basis, thus assuring regular contacts. Though there were pressures for workers to join certain unions (the promise of better career advancement in central services for UNCM members and the strong daily presence of CGT militants among blue-collar workers), they do not seem to have been unusually strong. Presumably, however, peer pressure compelled new entrants to join the largest union in their work centers.

After 1950, the Communist party and the national CGT doctrinally denied that nationalizations had benefited workers. They reverted to the Communists' analysis of nationalizations from the the mid-1930s, that nationalization only offered a method for capitalism to run better. René Guiart wrote in a Communist theoretical journal in 1954 that "contrary to the myth that is widely accepted at present, the state is an efficient and competent capitalist; the workers in the state industries

to CSNP minutes, meeting of 7 March 1961, GNC archives, dossier: "Commissions secondaires."

and services are as systematically exploited as the workers in the private monopoly sector." He also said that the nationalized sector aided the private sector through guaranteed orders and cheap tariffs. In addition, as the nationalized sector was concentrated in the economic infrastructure, it formed the precondition for monopoly profits in heavy industry.[4] Nonetheless, Éclairage and the GNC never broke from their implicit alliance with the front office of EDF. The CGT's demands necessarily had to be aimed at the state because regardless of any analysis of the political-economic status of nationalized enterprises, the state controlled EDF salaries. The state could safely meet the demands of the CGT by promising a share of the fruits of progress without undermining the structure of power. Serge Mallet argued that the CGT believed that cooperation with management could bring material rewards and that the CGT's demands could be integrated into the system—if it ignored the questions of workplace control and industrial management.[5] The plan's promise to share the gains of increased productivity could coopt a CGT that had centered its strategy on increasing the standard of living.

The CGT and PCF implicitly shifted toward Éclairage's less draconian position in 1955 as PCF chief Maurice Thorez promulgated his "pauperization" theory. He argued that the working class suffered not only a relative impoverishment, with the rich getting richer relative to the poor, but an absolute impoverishment, with the real living standards of the workers actually falling. This formulation, which the party forced upon its members, finally pushed Pierre Le Brun, the CGT's most competent electrical engineer-manager, out of the PCF/CGT orbit. Le Brun conceded the fact of relative impoverishment, but he argued that the rise in popular living standards in the 1950s belied any claim of absolute impoverishment.[6] The pauperization theory ironically opened up a possibility for cooperation with the existing political system. In the first place, cooperation might slow the pauperization process. This explains Éclairage's preoccupation with returning to the "democratic management" model of the late 1940s by simultaneously cooperating with management and by attacking the "technocrats installed in the Finance Ministry by the monopolies" as the hatchet men on EDF pay levels.[7] With salaries thus at the top of the agenda, consumerism became a political program and, for Marcel Paul, the washing machine

---

[4] René Guiart, "L'oligarchie financière et l'état," *Économie et politique* 5–6 (1954), 192.
[5] Cited in Pierre Brachet, *L'état*, p. 98.
[6] Jacques Fauvet, *Histoire du Parti communiste français* (1977), pp. 453–54. Thorez's position is clearly expounded in Maurice Thorez, *La paupérisation des travailleurs français* (1961), passim.
[7] *Force-Information* 110 (January 1965), 14.

became an instrument of class struggle.[8] This strategy impelled the CGT to focus its demands on pay and to seek better vacation centers, summer camps, and the like—precursors of the "socialist consumer society of the future."[9]

The CFTC saw the nationalization as an unmitigated victory for the workers, but one that had to be reinforced and extended by the active participation of the workers in the daily activities of the firm. For the CFTC, the working class's apprenticeship to become the future ruling class would be in the nationalized sector.[10] It feared that the nationalized sector could become a progressive ghetto and attempted to broaden its purview of union activities to include the character of local communities and the relation of wages to prices in the economy. The CFTC tried to open up the EDF community to the outside by seeking a closer cooperation with local communities through decentralization measures and through expenditures of EDF's workers' social funds on projects that benefited both non-EDF and EDF workers. On the issue of salaries, the CFTC recognized the problem of the wage-price spiral and once even offered to limit wage demands if the government guaranteed price stability.[11] For similar reasons, the CFTC opposed state support for EDF because subsidies would only reproduce the notorious inequities of the French tax system. The CFTC saw the nationalized sector as a starting point for the participation of workers in an economically democratic future. The key vehicle for this was the plethora of codeterminist bodies at EDF, especially the works (or mixed production) committees (CMPs). The CFTC's Catholic affiliation became increasingly anomalous as it became more radical and codeterminationist. For that reason, the CFTC Gas and Electric Federation played a major part in breaking from the church in 1964, thereby becoming the Confédération Française Démocratique du Travail (CFDT).[12]

Neither UNCM nor FO offered a systematic strategy beyond a parochial defense of their constituencies' interests and a deep anti-Communism. Both unions occasionally signed agreements when the other two unions demanded better settlements. After trying to conduct joint actions, the CFTC wrote of FO, "Continuing contacts cannot be maintained with a federation that has only the negative 'anti' attitude and rarely does anything constructive."[13] The CFTC did not even con-

[8] Paul's report to the 25th CGT Congress, June 1955, cited in Picard et al., Histoire(s), p. 375.
[9] Frédérique de Gravelaine and Sylvie O'Dy, L'état-EDF, p. 110.
[10] Gaz-Électricité 44 (December 1952).
[11] Gaz-Électricité 11 and 12 (January-February 1948).
[12] For a complete history of the radicalization of the CFTC and its evolution to the CFDT (leaving a small rump of CFTC loyalists), see Paul Vignaux, CFTC à la CFDT.
[13] Gaz-Électricité 43 (October-November 1952).

sider the UNCM to be a union. "No relationship is possible with UNCM: [it is] an organization with the character of a professional club in which the representatives regularly vote for the positions of the bosses."[14]

The unions were forced to develop clear conceptions of the position of cadres (middle and upper managers) and their relationship to blue-collar workers and to the working class as a whole because a hierarchy of technical power operated the firm. UNCM was the easiest union to understand in this respect because it viewed cadres as a class apart and acted to buttress the "rights" of cadres against blue-collar workers. Its position also sought to place a barrier against the growth of CGT power and that of its blue-collar constituency. The UNCM rarely conducted work actions on issues other than salary levels. FO similarly rejected class politics. It largely limited its activity to pay issues, much like its allies in the American AFL-CIO. FO urged its members to defer to authority, raise productivity, and await the benefits of greater production—to struggle to increase the size of the economic pie rather than to squabble over its division. Work actions were occasionally necessary, however, to preserve workers' rightful share of the pie.

The CGT considered cadres a part of the working class, but wished the two parts separate and unequal. It defended the strength of the managerial hierarchy, posing it essentially as a natural and necessary phenomenon in complex social and technical organizations. The CGT strongly supported the salary hierarchy and maintained a strict division of labor between the issues germane to the GNC and those treated by Éclairage. The GNC focused on larger managerial issues—tariffs, state and private sector relations, and equipment programs—while Éclairage concentrated on traditional labor issues. GNC loyalists benefited from the strategy of stratification, for though they were often closed out of top management, they enjoyed promotions at a rate equal to or better than those of members of other unions. As EDF managers, GNC members sometimes worked against their union interests. The CGT sensed no betrayal because it distinguished between "union" and "professional" activities. In the years when the GNC and Éclairage were absent from the EDF board, the GNC rarely received information that routinely went across the desks of its members, even though its members permeated the EDF hierarchy. The GNC's belief in professional standards and secrets prevented it from threatening EDF managers or from constituting an alternative hierarchy.

The CFTC tried hard to understand and shape the cadre mentality. It was consciously structured to have cadres and blue-collar workers

[14] Ibid.

mix within the same federation. The mixed structure was initially intended to reinforce hierarchies and build respect for superiors, but through the 1950s, the CFTC began to use it to blunt the elitism of managers.[15] The logic behind the link was thus fully reversed. Initially, it was done so that the cadres could reinforce cooperation with the blue-collar workers and edify them, then it was done to keep class issues always present in the minds of the cadres. For the later CFTC, autonomous cadre unionism would only create a castelike structure of power within the firm.

The CFTC tried to address the problems faced by workers confronting managers at several junctures in the 1950s by focusing on paternalist mentalities and sociotechnical chasms. The CFTC also recognized that high levels of technical knowledge conferred considerable social power to cadres, and that they sensed contested (rather than shared) power between themselves and workers. As a union strong among foremen, the CFTC also recognized foremen's and cadres' fears of usurpation when faced with the rising skill levels of the workers and their uncomfortable tasks in implementing sometimes unpopular policies. The CFTC did not attack the hierarchy directly before 1964. Indeed, in 1952, the CFTC wrote, "It is crucial that blue-collar and clerical workers understand that the hierarchy is indispensable and that [it] must offer appreciable [financial] advantages for those who enjoy power within it." Popular access to the routes into the managerial structure for workers would compensate for the managers' high social status.[16] The CFTC was thus the strongest supporter of codetermination and in-house education and training programs, first to legitimate the hierarchy, then to find ways to overcome it.

Remuneration

The central issues for all unions were pay, benefits, and job classifications. EDF unions struck over few other issues before 1968. This preoccupation with bread-and-butter issues reflected the pervasive low salaries at EDF throughout the period. Centering agitation around wage issues also reinforced the solidarity between EDF managers and unions because such issues could only be resolved only at the level of the government. Until the late 1950s, workers and managers often allied against the government on the pay issue. The low salaries that prevailed throughout the 1950s and 1960s were a major issue, but in order

[15] Based on author's interviews with militants of the CFTC/CFDT, CFDT-FGE offices, Paris, March-April 1981.
[16] Gaz-Électricité 21 (July-August 1949) and 40 (March 1952).

to address the full range of remuneration we will first discuss nonwage compensation.

Managers and workers at EDF found in productivity bonuses an opportunity to circumvent governmental pay freezes. Decisions for their allocation were left to EDF itself. Productivity bonuses also reinforced EDF's image as one of France's most productive enterprises in terms of output or value added per worker. In the Gaspard years, management assumed that workers were the source of higher output and that they should enjoy pay increases roughly equivalent to EDF's productivity increases. Popularized by a number of "productivity missions" to the United States by French managers as a part of the Marshall Plan, the productivity bonuses at EDF appealed to a broad community of modernist policymakers in the early 1950s. EDF replaced irregular bonuses in 1951 with a permanent and regular productivity bonus. The Financial Committee of the board wanted to make *all* pay productivity-based and tied to individual productivity, but union opposition blocked it.[17] The 1951 system split bonuses between individuals and work groups, with 40 percent of it allocated according to managers' opinions of individual worker productivity. The unions resented pitting workers against each other and fought hard against the new system. In some areas, they pooled individualized bonuses and divided them equally among all workers within a given unit.[18] The split system continued for several years, but in 1955 bonuses were evenly allocated and became little more than a 4 to 5 percent supplement to regular pay, regardless of unit or individual productivity. Productivity bonuses were allocated only to currently active workers and thus excluded retirees from many pay increases. Widows and workers on various types of paid leave (illness, maternity, etc.) were also excluded from them. The CFTC, FO, and UNCM consented to this exclusion in the 1951 pay agreement and it remained until 1968. Though much of the high productivity was the logical result of the very capital-intensive nature of electrical power services, only later did the *rentabilité* school of EDF managers make that distinction.

Promotions also allowed pay hikes without raising the politically important base pay figure. Many of these promotions necessarily reflected rising skill levels. The *statut* set seniority advancements, and they were awarded to an average of 17 percent of all EDF workers per year in the mid-1950s. The CSNP and secondary commissions (local versions of the CSNP) controlled job upgrades, and about 9 percent of all EDF workers received them each year in the mid-1950s. As the pay

---

[17] CAPV 68 (23 November 1951).
[18] *Gaz-Électricité* 38 (December 1951).

problems deepened, the rate of classification promotions increased.[19] CSNP decisions upgraded entire job titles at once, so salary levels only obliquely corresponded to actual job activities. By 1959, this practice had virtually empied the bottom six slots in the twenty-tier wage scale. The lack of a direct tie between functional job titles and pay levels worked to the advantage of both management, which could then exercise favoritism, and unions, which could raise pay levels by ultimately seeking promotions for all workers in a given category. By 1955, the lack of links between job titles and pay levels had badly tangled the salary structure. Unions and managers agreed that coherence had to be reëstablished, and negotiations accordingly began in the CMPs, secondary commissions, and the CSNP to make that link. The CGT's reticence and the complexity of of the task prevented resolution until 1960.

The constant job upgrading and the lack of a coherent tie between pay and job function systematically eroded the salary hierarchy. The gap between highest and lowest levels steadily closed, primarily because the lowest paid had to be kept above the poverty line. Because reranking demanded that functional pay categories be redefined, the process took several years. In the interim, conceptually tangled job announcements confused hiring and promotion procedures.[20] The reranking was passed in 1960. In a move surprisingly uncontested by the CGT, unit managers' and cadres' classifications were set apart from the other workers', creating a three-tiered pay hierarchy (in place of a unified ranking) with limited passage from tier to tier. An internal caste system began to rise from the wreckage of once-clever strategies to increase salaries.

EDF workers enjoyed a benefit package second to almost none. Their benefits included free or discount-priced gas and electricity, baby bonuses, paid leave for a variety of personal reasons (including births and deaths within workers' families), and half-time pay for the wives of local distribution center managers.[21] Perhaps the most stunning benefit was the "thirteenth month" of pay each year, which had its origins in the formalization of the prenationalization Christmas bonuses. The

[19] *Gaz-Électricité* 73 (December 1956) and Secrétariat d'État aux Affaires Économiques, Direction de la Coordination et des Entreprises Nationales, *Rapport sur l'évolution de la situation économique et financière des entreprises nationales du secteur industriel et commercial au cours des exercices 1955 et 1956* (1957), p. 12.

[20] "Voeux émis des commissions secondaires, Rennes, séance n° 150 du 27 novembre 1962," Éclairage archives, dossier: "Commissions secondaires," and *Gaz-Électricité* 67 (December 1955).

[21] At times the requests for the extension of benefits reached absurd proportions, such as when Paul sought two days' paid leave for stillbirths, one under the rubric of birth leave, one as death leave; letter of Paul to Gaspard, 21 April 1960, GNC archives, dossier: "Revendications générales." Paul's request was denied.

government, EDF managers, and the unions battled in the 1950s over the inclusion of such benefits into the calculation of salary packages, with the government seeking total inclusion, Gaspard favoring a partial inclusion, and the unions favoring total exclusion. The acrimony of negotiations within EDF on these issues led the CFTC to characterize the talks as "dialogues of the deaf," and Gaspard saw his greatest union opposition in 1955, when he attempted to count promotions as pay hikes.[22] The government and Gaspard tried to include the workers' own reduced-price utilities into the 1955–56 agreement, and the CGT responded with a rare attack against the company itself by calling for EDF workers not to pay their utility bills, infuriating Gaspard to the point that he cut off negotiations.[23] Benefits and promotions were not systematically calculated into salary agreements until 1963. In return for not counting benefits in salary packages, pay was not adjusted for overtime work, and the usual work week ran between forty-five and forty-eight hours until the mid-1960s. Only after the economist-managers gained control of the firm were benefits calculated into salary settlements. Then a ninety-minute cut in the workweek was termed a pay hike.

Educational and training activities at EDF (called PROFOR, an acronym for "professional formation") were large relative to other firms, and they continued to expand throughout the 1950s and 1960s. PROFOR activities covered both continuing education for enhancing and updating skills and special training for entering EDF from the outside. Not only was the educational network needed to train workers for the standardized and specific technology, it was also necessary because low wage levels precluded EDF from hiring all of the skilled workers it needed. At the same time, only one of three applicants for EDF schools was accepted for training and (implicitly) later hiring.[24] Between 1958 and 1961, training activities expanded considerably as EDF recognized that a new generation of technology required even higher skill levels.

Updating the skills of current workers was as important as having highly skilled workers enter EDF. PROFOR conducted retraining sessions, correspondence courses (in which close to 10 percent of the EDF work force were engaged at any given time), and "workers' information" sessions. The latter provided training for foremen and cadres when new technologies or techniques were introduced. The foremen

---

[22] *Gaz-Électricité* 67 (December 1955).
[23] *Gaz-Électricité* 68 (January 1956).
[24] "La formation et le perfectionnement du personnel de l'Électricité de France et du Gaz de France," *IDC*, article 18 (July 1959), 3.

and cadres then trained the workers under them when they returned to their home centers. For new equipment that necessitated more in-depth training efforts, entire teams of workers were sent to training centers and instructed in operations and maintenance activities. This was the case with the initiation of the 250-mw thermal series and the introduction of work on charged transmission lines.

While the unions strongly supported all of the PROFOR programs and backed the CSNP's efforts to increase PROFOR's activities, the jewel of the PROFOR program was the "workers' promotion" program. In PO (as the "promotion ouvrière" program was called), blue-collar workers could take courses in economics, engineering, and manage-ment and ultimately become managers themselves. Between 1946 and 1958, about eight hundred workers (2 percent of the cadres in 1958) became cadres via the three-year PO program. About 10 percent of the cadres in 1970 had been through PO. A lack of financial support for PO trainees and a requirement that entrants have a *baccalauréat* hind-ered the success of the program. The CFTC and FO pressed EDF to provide a concrete system of grants, scholarships, and loans for PO entrants, but without success.[25] They *did* win a system to prepare for the *baccalauréat*. The PO system explicitly reinforced internal social cohesion, and its expansion in the 1960s reflected the need to revive a sense of community, particularly on a meritocratic basis, and to give blue-collar workers a sense that there were avenues for upward mo-bility within the firm.[26] While PO did help a number of blue-collar workers to cross the class line, it did little to break the gender division of labor—between 1947 and 1975, only six women received technical training in the PO program.[27]

EDF training schools, like their private predecessors, undoubtedly helped to socialize workers into the firm's internal culture. PROFOR brochures stressed that a major facet of the training at EDF schools was "humane, . . . based essentially on self-discipline, concentrat[ing] on the development of the notion of public service . . . and increas[ing] the sense of initiative and responsibility," and PO classes explicitly sought to inculcate students in "cadre culture."[28] Such training also reinforced deference to a technically expert hierarchy. The CGT suc-ceeded in its efforts to organize the teachers at the EDF schools around 1960. With CGT members as teachers, the hierarchy and internal ide-ology of EDF were not to be threatened by EDF's own educators.

[25] CAPV 139 (24 May 1957).

[26] Marta Ormos, *La montée: La promotion ouvrière dans une grande entreprise publique, EDF-GDF* (1982), pp. 35, 68, 198–99.

[27] Ibid, p. 159.

[28] "La formation et perfectionnement," p. 2, and Ormos, *La montée*, pp. 100–101.

The pay at EDF remained abysmal. From 1953 to 1962 real salaries at EDF remained essentially unchanged, while those of Paris-region metalworkers (to which the pay of EDF workers was often compared) rose over 50 percent (see Appendix fig. A9). From 1962 to 1968, real EDF salaries declined slightly.[29] Despite proof that the press overstated nationalized sector pay, EDF workers struggled throughout the 1950s to surpass their 1953 real pay levels—which were well below those of 1938.[30] A 1954 strike wave led pundits to assume that the nationalized sector in general and EDF in particular were at the leading edge of social agitation and pay hikes. Though EDF salaries were lower than those for comparable work elsewhere, the government and private sector looked at percentage increases rather than actual pay levels. Gaspard himself said, "In the final analysis, EDF and GDF can no longer discuss the most minimal increase in salaries without all of [the workers in] the other sectors demanding similar increases."[31] In order to increase salaries, Gaspard utilized the little power left him in the domain of salaries to increase various bonuses. The unions consistently sought to increase base pay. An increase in the base required governmental approval, and the government only considered pay hikes in the midst of a social crisis, then often reneged once the pressure abated. Despite the government's explicit refusal to bargain with the unions, Gaspard often negotiated (pursuant to Article 9 of the *statut*), even though it was a safe bet that the government would ignore the results.

Continual increases in benefit and pension charges undermined public confidence in EDF's labor costs.[32] Many private sector employers asserted that France's unusually high employer-paid social charges made French goods uncompetitive in world markets. This position contained a grain of truth, yet it was self-serving and ignored the reluctance of France's private sector to innovate. Social charges in the nationalized sector were somewhat higher than those in the private sector. At EDF, these expenses added 49.4 percent to basic salaries in 1954, rising to 52 percent in 1955 and 53.2 percent in 1956.[33] The high scale of these charges reflected the use of productivity bonuses as an alternative to direct wage increases and, most important, high pension

[29] Comparison made on Paris-region EDF salaries, presented in: EDF-Direction du Personnel, *Statistiques du personnel: Année 1970* (1970), pp. 68–69. Price indices and Paris-region metalworkers' salaries are from INSEE, *Tableaux de l'économie française, 1970* (Paris: INSEE, 1970), p. 114. All calculations are based on constant 1950 francs. More generally, Pierre Bauchet, *Propriété publique et planification* (1962), pp. 211–13, indicated that nationalized sector salaries fell steadily after 1955.

[30] CAPV 136 (22 February 1957) and 108 (26 November 1954).

[31] CAPV 108 (26 November 1954).

[32] This is a recurring criticism of EDF, most recently in François de Closets's bestselling *Toujours plus!* (1982), chaps. 8–10.

[33] Secrétariat d'État aux Affaires Économiques, *Rapport*, p. 21.

costs arising from a growing rate of retirements in the mid-1950s—the legacy of utility expansion in the 1920s. EDF assumed pension costs for all of the workers it inherited from the private power companies and often received less than a decade of labor from such workers, but paid all of the pension costs. EDF had only partially inherited the private companies' pension funds (many of which were depleted by the former owners between 1944 and 1946) and the inflation of the late 1940s eroded the rest. Finally, EDF funded its pensions on a pay-as-you-go basis. This problem was even graver at GDF, and since Parliament usually saw only combined EDF-GDF figures on pensions, EDF pensions appeared to be more costly than they actually were.

The procedures for setting salary increases at EDF generated considerable acrimony from the start. Article 9 of the labor *statut* had called for negotiations between EDF management and unions, with arbitration by the minister of industry, but it was followed only until the fall of 1947. From then until 1953, precipitous governmental decisions usually set salaries. The government took formal control over salaries in May 1953, but at the same time, it did not disavow Article 9. The EDF unions and the minister of industry signed the agreement of January 1960, but again, it developed no systematic negotiation procedure.

Following a massive miners' strike early in 1963, Prime Minister Pompidou set up a committee of experts to develop procedures on which the government could negotiate salaries or, lacking the unions' assent, impose pay settlements in the nationalized sector. Pierre Massé, then the plan commissioner, presided over the committee of three. The Massé committee published its report in April 1963, and the unions hotly contested a number of items. The report introduced the notion of the "total salary bill," which included everything from straight pay to productivity bonuses, discounted utilities, day-care subsidies, the "thirteenth month," and payments into the workers' benefit (CCOS) fund. The Massé commission drew comparisons between the public and private sectors, and in calculating private sector labor costs, it averaged in the remuneration of workers in firms employing ten or more workers, thus integrating the low-pay small business sector into the indices. Nonetheless, counting all of the benefits received by EDF workers and averaging in some of the lowest paid private sector workers in that index, the Massé commission conceded that EDF pay had eroded between 3.1 percent and 3.6 percent between late 1958 and January 1963.[34]

The conceptions behind the Massé commission report were as ques-

[34] Pierre Massé et al., "Document: Rapport sur la situation des salaires du secteur nationalisé," *RFE* 143 (March 1963), 287–94.

tionable as Massé's Blue Note or Boiteux's Green Tariff: all three represented "scientific" methods for applying private sector business concepts to EDF. The unions deeply resented the Massé committee report, yet they felt powerless in the face of decisive Gaullism. The Massé report recommended a permanent committee of experts to oversee pay levels in the nationalized sector and to assuage resentment by pegging pay increases to the Plan Commission's forecasts for overall GNP growth. As later events were to show, the promises of scheduled pay increases were, as before, routinely ignored by the government.

The committee of experts called for by the Massé commission was set up by Pompidou in the fall of 1963, as a part of the government's austere anti-inflation Stabilization Plan. The context was not propitious for EDF workers: the admitted goal of the Stabilization Plan was to reduce overall consumer demand and price levels, and thus to free capital for productive investment. This implicitly demanded retrogressive salary packages. The Toutée Commission, as the second committee of experts was called, was also to take pay decisions away from negotiations between the ministries and the unions. Instead, experts working under the government's instructions would set the confines of any possible settlement, ostensibly guided by nationwide price and productivity forecasts, then negotiations could proceed only to allocate a preordained total salary bill. Unions could not question the "objective" economic indicators formulated by the Toutée Commission. This solution to salary determination only created an illusory technocratic smokescreen between the unions and the government, which continued to hold all of the reins. Massé and modernist state managers saw the procedure as a way to bring unions in as subordinate partners in the salary determination process, in contrast to private sector employers, many of whom preferred to eschew negotiations entirely. The unions saw it all as an elaborate ruse to defuse resistance to the policy of salary restraint under the mantle of economic management. The Toutée procedure also reduced hierarchical salary coefficients, thereby further closing the gap between the highest and lowest paid at EDF. As a result of the Toutée procedures, between 1960 and 1968, the ratio between the highest and lowest paid workers' salaries fell considerably, and between mid-1963 and the end of 1964, real earnings for EDF workers fell 12 percent.[35]

The subtext of the new salary negotiation procedures was that EDF workers went from being respected actors in the daily life of EDF to

[35] On the politics of labor negotiations in the Fifth Republic, see Bernard Moss, "La réforme de la législation de travail sous la Vᵉ République: Un triomphe du modernisme?" *Le Mouvement Social* 148 (July-September 1989), 63–91, esp. pp. 65 and 69. On workers' salaries, see René Gaudy, *Les porteurs*, 67.

being simply another cost of production—and an irritable one at that. Such policies and procedures had long been in gestation among the moderates in the Finance Ministry and among economist-managers at EDF. Integration into the modernizing capitalist economy of France in the 1960s required a systematic dehumanization of management's conceptions of EDF workers to a level comparable to that in private industry, and the Massé and Toutée commissions did precisely that. Workers were too divided and dispirited to resist it until the events of May 1968, when they rid EDF of the Toutée procedure, easily as a feather in the wind.

Changes in Work Methods and Workers' Response

Work techniques and productive technology at EDF changed rapidly in the transitional period. Automated production techniques and control over production and transmission by long-distance communication links began to replace older methods. Many in the mid and late 1950s saw the increasing automation of work as a way to liberate workers from mundane manual tasks, and they began to envision a push-button world of the future. The major push for expanding training programs reflected a recognition that the EDF workers of the future would indeed be highly trained button pushers, that mental labor would replace manual labor. Unlike André Gorz and a small circle of intellectuals, who began to critique automated work in the early 1960s, few recognized how boring and mind-deadening the work of monitoring dials, gauges, and computer printouts would be in the high-tech world of the future.[36] The EDF community believed that higher technology would enrich the workers in the checkbook and on the shop floor.

The unions had long consented to push productivity as a means to defend EDF from antinationalization attacks. They correctly assumed that if EDF could prove itself to be a highly productive enterprise in terms of value added per worker, the attacks would weaken. That strategy left its legacy in a veritable cult of productivity at EDF. The CGT had been virtually Stakhanovite in its productivity push, but that impetus ultimately backfired. Productivism defended the firm in the short term, but over time, the introduction of new technology and new work methods meant the relative (and ultimately, the absolute) decline of the CGT's membership base among unskilled workers. In the end, the unions couched productivism in a vague language that validated technocratic management and an apolitical culture of technology.

[36] André Gorz, _Strategy for Labor_ (1967), chaps. 1 and 2.

Blinded by the glare of chromium and silicon artifacts, the unions later consented to managers who used the old productivist language for far different political ends.

The nationalization law set an unrealistic boundary for EDF's activities. The law limited EDF's purview to the connections on the input end of low-voltage meters, but the old utilities had often overseen internal wiring, meter installation, appliance sales and maintenance, and verification that internal wiring was safe and conformed to industry norms. Because few private firms existed in 1946 to take over these activities, EDF naturally assumed them on a temporary basis, guided in the largest sense by a perception that EDF had to win the confidence of the mass of consumers. In addition, most of the concession contracts between EDF and local communities specified that EDF had to oversee several consumer-safety regulations and assure that users' interior wiring did not inhibit the operation of EDF's facilities. Three factors in the late 1950s and early 1960s modified this situation. First, many of the workers engaged in such activites began to retire and their work was turned over to private firms. Second, in order to implement a new low-voltage rate schedule, EDF's purview was extended to include the circuit breaker below the low-voltage meters. Finally, EDF's continual budgetary problems and a nationwide shortage of skilled workers made hiring new workers at EDF particularly difficult. To this last element must be added the perception of a number of EDF local distribution center managers that personal career advancement and departure from some of France's more remote regions would be hindered were they to seek authorization to hire more workers.[37] Subcontracting work to private firms offered an easy solution, particularly for distribution services, but also for a number of high-skill, in-house activities.

The shortage of personnel put both workers and managers in an awkward position. Workers were far from happy with the overtime work needed to deliver more services with a short work force, though the unions rarely protested mandatory overtime.[38] In addition, workers often spurned unpleasant cleaning and maintenance activities, hoping to avoid them—if possible by promotion.[39] Subcontracting could be

[37] Gaz-Électricité 73 (December 1956).

[38] In only one instance did the workers themselves mention this problem, and when they did, they made it clear that they preferred overtime to subcontracting; transcript of the meeting of the CMP for the Paris Region Production-Transmission Group, 23 May 1958.

[39] The CGT saw the danger of subcontracting in precisely the opposite fashion: in which the more interesting work would be subcontracted and EDF workers would be left to do only the worst tasks; note from Pauwels to Tougeron, 16 November 1963, Éclairage archives, dossier: "Entreprises privées." See also Paris-Électricité (Paris region GNC journal) 24 (29 August 1960).

used to reduce overtime and to allow EDF workers to perform tasks more exciting than cleaning. Economist-managers saw subcontracting as a way to limit "labor costs" in the long run. Subcontracting, though more costly in the short term, was cheaper over time because subcontractees received few benefits or employment guarantees and were not vested in pensions. Subcontracting also enhanced EDF worker-productivity figures because it was concentrated in the most labor-intensive activities.

EDF unions, with the exception of UNCM, were unified in opposition to subcontracting for a number of reasons. At first glance, they saw subcontracting as an erosion of the nationalization. The CGT quickly noted that one of the major subcontractors in the Paris region, a firm called Versilles, was operated by an "ex-CPDE fascist," precisely the type of person the CGT had tried to keep out of EDF in 1946.[40] Similarly, the unions felt that subcontracting threatened EDF workers by creating a parallel and underprivileged labor force next to them.[41] Union leaders also argued that subcontracting, particularly in the way it was set up by a number of local managers, demoralized EDF workers.[42] The CGT specifically saw the threat of layoffs in subcontracting, though subcontractors really replaced only workers who had left by attrition. All unions shared the perception that subcontracting, particularly when it covered the installation and maintenance of domestic meters and the verification of wiring, endangered good customer relations. Domestic consumers would henceforth only see EDF workers at their doors to collect bills and read meters. In this light, the unions feared that subcontracted labor was insufficiently imbued with the public service spirit and would thus alienate the EDF clientele.[43]

The ways that managers utilized subcontracting and the often contradictory responses and practices of top EDF managers compounded

[40] Note from Ripoteau to Paul, undated (1960?), Éclairage archives, dossier: "Entreprises privées."

[41] In a memo to Éclairage locals from the national office, 19 May 1960, the CGT wrote, "The goal of the front office is to use the private firms in order to create a secondary, nontitled work force, which they would be free to use against EDF and GDF workers whenever they feel like it"; Éclairage archives, dossier: "Entreprises privées." The same position was the consensus of the workers' representatives in the Lyon-Rhône distribution CMP; transcript of CMP meeting for the Lyon-Rhône distribution center, 26 January 1960.

[42] Transcript of CMP meeting for the Auxerre distribution center, 28 November 1958; letter from Paul to Gaspard, 26 November 1958, Éclairage archives, dossier: "Entreprises privées." See also note from [unnamed] Éclairage steward in the Gap distribution center, "Situation des entreprises privées," 18 June 1960, Éclairage archives, dossier: "Entreprises privées."

[43] Letter from FO Gas and Electric Federation President Werbrouck to Gaspard, 25 May 1950, Éclairage archives, dossier: "Entreprises privées," and transcript of sub-CMP meeting at Carpentras, 30 June 1960.

many of the unions' fears. Stewards and managers bickered endlessly over what work could legally be subcontracted in the vast gray areas on EDF's frontier. The EDF labor *statut* prescribed that all work on the system, with the exception of "large maintenance" and "first installation" activities, had to be performed by titled EDF workers. Both terms were terribly vague: how "large" was "large" to be, given the situation that an insufficient work force meant slighting daily maintenance and thus ultimately requiring "large" maintenance?[44] For "first installation," the *statut* obviously meant that EDF workers would not build power plants, but were they allowed to in install modernized domestic electrical meters? This vagueness could be played to the hilt by any manager, who, given wide powers to subcontract, could assign EDF workers to dull and/or dirty maintenance work and allow subcontractors to do more exciting tension-change and meter-updating work.[45] In particular, EDF managers opted to raise the capacity of the low-voltage network from 120V to 220V, so EDF workers potentially faced considerable work in rewiring all low-voltage installations. While management claimed that voltage changes were "first installation," the unions saw them as maintenance work; both positions were certainly arguable and management's upper hand gave major opportunities for subcontractors.[46] Though the bulk of subcontracting was concentrated in the distribution services, maintenance of large generating equipment was often subcontracted to the relevant equipment manufacturers; day-to-day operations on the transmission network were subcontracted as well, as were hydro-siting studies. Occasionally, even routine typing, bookkeeping, and card punching were subcontracted.[47] The scope of

[44] The Bayonne distribution-center workers noted this problem directly; transcript of CMP meeting for the Bayonne Mixed Distribution Center, 27 May 1960.

[45] Transcript of CMP meeting of the "Paris-Électricité" distribution center, 13 July 1960.

[46] CAPV 164 (24 July 1959); letter of distribution services director Pagès to CSC-CMP President Blanchard, 30 January 1961, Éclairage archives, dossier: "Entreprises privées." The voltage change, decided after EDF learned the method on a technical mission to the United States in 1954, was seen by EDF managers as a quick-fix method for raising distribution system capacity for a minimum cost. Once the tension change was decided, the low-voltage grid had considerable slack capacity, thereby necessitating the "blue meter" campaign to yield better system utilization and to lower kwh operating costs. The tension change was also an opportunity to install the new meters for the Universal Tariff, again necessitating more workers. Ironically, this set of decisions demanded more workers on the distribution network at precisely the moment when the shortage of workers at EDF was most broadly recognized. The interphase method used for the tension-change operation was far more dangerous for the consumers because appliances were not fully "off" when the switches indicated it. According to the CGT (*Force-Information* 109 [December 1964], 13), seventeen domestic consumers died from electrocution in 1963 alone as a result of the interphase wiring method.

[47] Transcript of meeting of the CSC-CMP, 16 December 1965, and transcript of meeting of the CMP for the Seine Regional Production/Transmission Group, 9 February 1963;

Table 4. Value of subcontracted and in-house maintenance work in 1963 (in millions of francs)

Activity	Subcontracted work	In-house work
Distribution	353	136
Transmission	79	33
Hydro production	62	21
Thermal production	97	30

Source: "Official EDF internal document," reproduced in unsigned CGT memo, 1963, Éclairage archives, dossier: "Entreprises privées."

subcontracted work could include virtually any EDF activity except the supervision of EDF workers. When confronted by the workers, the managers usually claimed that the practice was only temporary or "exceptional" and that it would end when sufficient workers arrived from EDF's schools.

EDF workers waited forever for additional workers to arrive. Subcontracting expanded considerably after 1959 in both the number of workers and the activities performed. Using its broad definition of subcontracted activity (based on a narrow definition of "large maintenance" and "first installation"), the CGT claimed in 1965 that the parallel work force employed about 10,000 workers, more than 10 percent of the current size of the EDF work force.[48] In 1963, an internal EDF memo cited considerable subcontracting of maintenance work, as shown in Table 4. While the volume of subcontracting rose considerably between 1959 and the mid-1960s, the number of EDF workers in the five lowest job classifications—those where most maintenance workers were concentrated—fell. Their numbers rose from 76,053 in 1955 to 77,177 in 1959, but dropped to 72,984 in 1964.[49] Combined with the subcontracting of labor-intensive work, this enhanced the illusion that EDF had fewer and fewer manual workers. The totality of EDF activity probably became *more* labor-intensive owing to the growth of the total quantity of equipment that had to be maintained, repaired, and upgraded, particularly in the distribution network. The number of production workers per kwh fell and the number of white-collar workers

---

untitled CGT document, 31 May 1965, Éclairage archives, dossier: "Entreprises privées"; transcript of CMP meeting for the Third Alpine Hydro Equipment Group, 25 February 1958, *Paris-Électricité* 24 (29 August 1960); and transcript of CMP meeting for the Third Thermal Group, 28 April 1960.

[48] *Force-Militant* 38 (16 September 1965), 4.

[49] *Force-Militant* 38 (16 September 1965), 2; end-of-year figures, and these figures include GDF workers, but subcontracting practices were the same in both firms. These figures must be viewed with a bit of scepticism in light of the redefinition of job categories in 1960.

rose, but the number of subcontracted maintenance workers sky-rocketed.[50]

The replacement of low-skilled EDF workers by subcontractees posed problems for the CGT, for though it was well represented in all of the job categories, its strongest support was in the lowest five categories. If for no other reason than self-defense, the CGT led the fight against subcontracting. Roger Pauwels of the Éclairage national office wrote to the Lille local, after noting that subcontracting had damaged morale: "The union cannot help but to draw an incontestable benefit from publicizing [management's practice of subcontracting]. The massive use of private subcontractors in effect is continually more irritating to the workers, and the workers are waiting for us to take a firm position on the issue."[51] Union efforts against subcontracting focused on the CMPs. In its resistance, starting in 1958, the CGT again saw a useful role for the CMPs. The CMPs provided a particularly appropriate forum opposing subcontracting because most subcontracting was imple-mented by local managers—precisely the same people who faced the workers within the CMPs. Discussions often revealed, however, that much of the irregularity came not from the physical character of the subcontracted work but from the poor scheduling of work on the part of the managers themselves.[52] The Nancy CMP solved this problem by creating a foremen's or crew chiefs' work group to set up better sched-uling and provide for routine preventative maintenance. A similar plan was drawn up for maintenance in thermal production plants.

The Nancy solution was illusory, however. While it eroded much of the impetus for subcontracting, it was a far more bureaucratic method of organizing work. More important, the workers felt that it lowered the intellectual level of their work: "The worker is henceforth only a

[50] It is unfortunate that precise figues for this are unavailable—EDF managers were careful not to give any coherent sense of the total scale of subcontracted work, particularly maintenance activities. The question of the overall levels of skill and the mix of skills is very complex, and it raises a number of important issues concerning the nature of high-technology industry. It is obvious that over time the EDF work force on the average became more skilled, yet it remains unclear how much those higher skills made for higher per-worker productivity. The productivity of the workers in expanding activities is unmeasurable in terms of the overall productivity of the firm, for it is impossible to distinguish between new activities and the elaboration of older ones. One can also note that higher technology often means greater complexity and thus lower reliability, thereby requiring a larger number of maintenance workers.

[51] Memo from Pauwels to Dervaux, November 1958, Éclairage archives, dossier: "En-treprises privées."

[52] Transcript of CMP meeting for the Lille distribution center, 22 February 1960. See also transcript of CMP meeting for the Third Alpine Hydro Equipment Group, 7 May 1958; transcript of CMP meeting for the Regional Transmission Equipment Group, 27 May 1959; transcript of CMP meeting for the First Region Thermal Equipment Group, 1 July 1959, and transcript of CMP meeting for the Douai Mixed Distribution Center, 14 October 1960.

robot instead of a thinking person, instructed to do his work without knowledge [of it] and without interest."[53] The workers in Nancy agreed with this critique. The Lille manager promised to involve execution workers themselves in the scheduling process to allay such fears, so the Lille workers accepted the new method, hoping that it would help end subcontracting. Both resolutions remained exceptional. When other CMPs raised the issue, management most often temporized, saying that the practice would soon pass, vaguely promising to end it. Both of these responses were essentially subterfuges, for subcontracting continued unabated.

EDF workers conducted only two notable work actions to resist subcontracting. After a local manager in Nice had repeatedly refused to discuss subcontracting with the CMPs—even after ordered to do so by Gaspard—the workers began daily strike actions in May 1960. These took the form of "turning strikes" in which one or two members per work group would go out for a short period, thereby stopping all work every morning over a two-week period. After a half-day of negotiations, management consented to discuss all proposals to subcontract with the CMP.[54] A month later, the Paris-region workers went out for forty hours to end subcontracting with the Versilles firm. Ninety percent of the workers participated, though the FO and CFTC leadership opposed the action. The goal was not only to stop the use of the Versilles firm, but to initiate joint discussions with management in order to define "first installation." Because of a combination of disunity and the higher stakes involved, the strike failed.[55]

Top EDF managers generally responded to these pressures by claiming to oppose subcontracting and by encouraging the CMPs to discuss the issue. This tended to make subcontracting appear to be a matter of bad managers rather than company policy, but at the same time, recalcitrant managers were not reprimanded. Each time a wave of resistance to subcontracting swelled, Gaspard ordered another inquest, the results of which were ignored. Whatever Gaspard's intentions, these strategies effectively defused the opposition.

Resistance to subcontracting generally failed. As economist-managers replaced social productionists atop EDF, a determination to ignore union resistance eclipsed Gaspard's more subtle approach. Once Gaspard retired in 1963, the front office ceased its efforts to allay work-

---

[53] Statement of CGT steward, transcript of CMP meeting for the Lille distribution center, 22 February 1960.

[54] Memo from Éclairage national office to Éclairage locals, 19 May 1960, Éclairage archives, dossier: "Entreprises privées."

[55] Memo from Ripoteau to Paul, 18 June 1960, Éclairage archives, dossier: "Entreprises privées."

ers' fears and began to subcontract far more systematically. The unions could not stop subbing in the face of Gaspard's vacillation, and they were less able to resist once it became policy. The reluctance of union leaders to encourage strike actions and their readiness to accept promises made by local and central office managers undercut effective opposition. Subcontractors ultimately became permanent fixtures next to EDF. In this fashion, many labor and CGT-intensive jobs disappeared from EDF, thus facilitating the construction of EDF's new face, that of an apolitical corps of elite and highly trained technocrats and technical workers. The unions' failure to stop subcontracting reflected their broader inability to deal effectively with issues that concerned the composition and character of work.

"Cogestion Manquée"

The CGT profoundly changed its position regarding comanagement with the onset of the Cold War. It continued to support the codeterminist labor councils, but as arenas for exercising the CGT's power. In a continuing defense of its turf, the CGT implied that the operation of comanagement bodies hinged on its continued power within them. For example, when the elections for representatives on the local secondary commissions (codeterminist personnel boards) in 1960 indicated a slight erosion of support for the CGT and implied a reallocation of seat assignments, the CGT attempted to change the method of seat allocation. Failing that, the CGT tried to keep the secondary commissions from convening. The secondaries did not meet for several months and many of the promotions set for the end of 1960 could not proceed. In a circular to its locals, Éclairage wrote, "While they are illegally constituted, the new secondary commissions will not function; the personnel must be gathered together any time that the secondary commissions try to meet in order to show the highest combativeness against them." In order to deal with end-of-year promotions, the circular suggested that CGT representatives meet with management behind closed doors. Because the CFTC was a beneficiary of the reallocation, the CGT baited it for its leftism.[56] Gaspard and the other unions ultimately backed down and allowed the CGT to have its way.

The CGT was even less interested in the consultative comanagement

[56] Circular from GNC Federal Bureau to local stewards, 27 December 1960, and circular from Éclairage Federal Bureau to local stewards, No. 39, 24 November 1960; GNC archives, Pantin, papers of René Le Guen, dossier: "Commissions Secondaires"; Éclairage leaflet: "Pas de fonctionnement des commissions secondaires illégalement constituées," 20 January 1961.

bodies, especially the CMPs. Set up by a CGT aflush with Liberation enthusiasm in 1946 to facilitate the battle of production, the CMPs were politically buried by the CGT in 1949. Pasquier stated the CGT position in 1952: "In the present political [-economic] regime, we do not want to facilitate the functioning of the CMPs; in another [political-economic] regime, they would be extremely precious to us."[57] For the CGT, co-management would only fool the workers into believing that workers' opinions could be respected in a capitalist system. Though moribund in the early 1950s, the CMPs continued to exist formally. The CGT tried to subordinate CMP functions to those of the secondary commissions and CSNP, where the CGT still held considerable power. This was particularly true with the various health and safety bodies, which multiplied as a result of tangled prerogatives and powers. The health and safety committees, the local committees for workplace medicine, and the medical-social committees were all created to perform similar functions. A multiplication of such committees diluted the force of each and all.

The reluctance of many managers (who presided in CMP meetings) either to conduct the meetings seriously or to heed their resolutions undermined the credibility of the CMPs. A CMP activist complained of infrequent CMP sessions with vacuous agendas and reluctant chairs in a report to the CFTC central office: "These presidents, rather than attempting to facilitate debates, try to relegate the meetings to a state of total lethargy."[58] Similarly, according to a CFTC delegate, whenever any suggestions were made that demanded expenditures, management usually denied that funds were available: "Money is the master, money is the king: the demands pass from office to office, bureau to bureau; all responsibility is annihilated in the hierarchy, everybody covers his ass and nothing gets resolved."[59] In addition, many distribution center managers considered their service areas as personal fiefs and ignored the CMPs, the personnel bodies, and even their superiors in Paris.[60] The decentralized structure of the CMPs diffused their power, and their national council, the Superior Consultative Council of CMPs (CSC-CMP), was little more than an "in" basket for the Paris filing system. The CMPs' localized scope also minimized the breadth of their activities. CMPs could criticize petty bosses and local practices, but top

---

[57] Cited by Decaillon in *Gaz-Électricité* 40 (March 1952). Citing American ECA documents, Warren Baum blames the Communists for the failure of the *comités d'entreprise* (codetermination bodies) in other firms by the CGT's "packing" practices, *The French Economy and the State* (1958), pp. 182–83.
[58] *Gaz-Électricité* 41 (May 1951).
[59] Ibid.
[60] *Gaz-Électricité* 55 (October 1954).

managers who shaped the overall direction of the firm remained safely insulated.

The CFTC frequently tried to revitalize comanagement. Though the CMPs were initially empowered only to discuss ways to economize labor time and materials, the CFTC wanted them to be forums to discuss management practices in general. The front office was initially reluctant to permit that expansion of the CMPs' activities. For example, once Central Services had devised methods for comparative productivity analysis at the level of distribution centers, Yves Morel asked that the studies be passed on to the CMPs for discussion. Gaspard hedged, arguing that workers should not try to manage the firm. When Morel assured him that the CMPs would use the studies for "informational" purposes only, he consented.[61] The CFTC did not, however, pose the CMPs as an alternative to technocratic management. Speaking of the tasks of a CMP member, the CFTC argued: "In a nationalized firm, he must not draw out the opposition between the firm and the workers because the process of tying the workers to the daily activities of the firm must lead them to search out the common welfare of all. It is toward this common welfare that our efforts must be focused."[62] Nor did the CFTC wish to see the CMPs as a shadow management within EDF. It argued that the task of management rested with the board of directors, where unions (but not the CGT at the time) had direct input.[63]

The CFTC's analysis of the CMPs had several radical elements though it was initially rather corporatist. Comanagement was to "humanize" work relations through collective participation and responsibility, "to give the hierarchy, from top to bottom, the sense of participation and responsibility for the daily workings of the firm."[64] More profoundly, the CMPs were to be the laboratory for developing the modes of democratic management for a future society, going beyond the problems of everyday life: "For workers to demand a normal life is insufficient. To believe that the well-paid will deal with the question of work life is an error. It is of the utmost necessity to escape the rule of both men and machines. . . . We want to escape the conditions both of the wage-earning class and the technocracy. . . . In order to perform its apprenticeship as the future ruling class, the working class needs to assume its responsibilities in the mixed committees."[65] The CFTC did not hold naïve hopes for the CMPs. Mulling over the question of whether ef-

---

[61] CAPV 106 (24 September 1954).
[62] CFTC-Fédération Gaz-Électricité, "Pour une action efficace au sein des comités mixtes à la production," *Gazelec* (special issue, April 1957), 8.
[63] Ibid., p. 6.
[64] *Gaz-Électricité* 44 (December 1952).
[65] *Gazelec*, "Pour une action efficace," p. 9.

fective *cogestion* could occur under capitalism, it answered by admitting that it was indeed a very difficult task, but that "it's a stage which presents a certain interest: it can be an excellent means for workers' education." The CFTC saw the peril of socialism in one firm and called for working outside EDF as well, extending comanagement practices beyond the nationalized sector. The CFTC also feared that the workers' representatives could be cut off from the rank and file, enabling the comanagement bodies to act as corporatist organisms *against* the rank and file. In addition, if the comanagement process were to be cut off from the community as a whole, it could result in a hermetically sealed fortress and systematically ignore the needs of the consumers and the nation as a whole.[66]

Gaspard was initially quite careful to limit the threat that the CMPs posed to the hierarchy: "Since the final responsibility for management rests with the board and the General Directors of EDF and GDF, the CMP and sub-CMP presidents [local unit managers] must entirely preserve their hierarchical prerogatives and those of their superiors; they must not participate in the votes that the worker representatives may seek by setting choices among a number of options. They shall act in the meetings only within the confines of their delegated power."[67] In April 1950, however, Gaspard instructed local managers to take the CMPs far more seriously and to use them as alternatives to resolving conflicts via the hierarchical structures.[68] Armed with the new memo, the CFTC campaigned to resuscitate the CMPs. In 1952, it began a series of workshops and conferences to train CFTC militants for effective action in the CMPs. The CFTC developed a work program for its activities in the CMPs that went far beyond the confines of "economies" in its 1955 congress. The program called for CMPs to address questions of the organization of work, subcontracting practices, rate making, local equipment-purchasing practices, the use of overtime work, hiring and pay problems, and the like.[69] Despite the CFTC's enthusiasm, and probably because of the indifference of the CGT and the local managers, the CMPs remained dormant.

Under pressure from the CFTC and the CGT (which was beginning its struggle against subcontracting), in late 1955 Gaspard initiated an inquest to discover why the CMPs were not operating. He was careful to reiterate that the tasks of the CMPs did not include local contracting per se, but only oversight of the "conditions" (not modalities) of sub-

[66] *Gaz-Électricité* 44 (December 1952).
[67] Cited ibid., p. 21.
[68] Cited in *Gazelec*, "Pour une action," p. 21.
[69] Ibid., pp. 23–24 and 33–34.

contracting.[70] The inquest had been completed and discussed within the CSNP by late 1957, and as a result Gaspard wrote a memo that expanded the CMPs' power. A brief new solidarity spilled over into the new CMP memo, where Gaspard said: "The CMPs and sub-CMPs [can] deal with all of the questions that arise in the respective units and subunits, within the confines of Article 33 of the *statut*. The CMPs [shall] have the latitude to deal with any question, whether or not it has previously been raised in the sub-CMP, and they can instruct the sub-CMPs to study and discuss certain questions."[71] Until that time, the CMPs (and indeed, the CSC-CMP) could only address issues that arose from the lower organisms. The new approach gave the comanagement bodies hierarchical powers of their own. In addition, a CSNP decision in 1955 had given the CMPs the power to oversee subcontracting and purchasing procedures on the local level. The CFTC had high hopes for the use of these new powers: "Too many private firms view EDF as a fatted calf which can be used to hike profits. With representatives of the personnel in permanent contact with these realities, the workers can discern all of the anomalies practiced during contracting, and they can use these powers to roll the pretensions of the private firms back to their proper proportions."[72]

The CMPs gleefully used their new powers in the campaign against subcontracting, only to fail. They remained merely consultative, and enforcement power remained with the usual hierarchy. The CMPs and Parisian management could well admonish local bosses, but basic power remained in the hands of management. The failure to end subcontracting demoralized the CMPs, which remained dormant until the self-management thrust of the events of 1968 reawakened interest in them.

The comanagement bodies that had binding decision powers fared much better because day-to-day personnel matters depended on them. Seat allocation battles damaged the internal esprit of the CSNP and secondary commissions, but their power remained. With these bodies the CGT really delivered services for its members, assuring easier promotions and helping to hire the sons of its members. This was a particularly valuable service in a firm where nearly half of all personnel had a close family member employed by EDF.[73] It is arguable that the CGT's strength at EDF was based on its power in the codeterminist personnel organisms, thus creating a strong incentive for EDF workers

[70] Cited ibid., p. 34.
[71] Cited ibid., p. 7.
[72] *Gaz-Électricité* 76 (March 1957).
[73] Ormos, *La montée*, p. 55.

to join the CGT regardless of whether they agreed with its politics. This explains both the pervasiveness of the CGT's power and its inability to mobilize large numbers of EDF workers for work actions unless it was allied with one or more of the other unions. In any event, the CGT's power within the personnel bodies assured the symbiotic survival of both.

The decree of 4 May 1950 had seriously undermined the power of the CSNP to override the managerial hierarchy at EDF. Similarly, a 1959 decree created interregional secondary commissions as intermediaries between the locally based secondaries and the CSNP.[74] Regional managers were to preside over the interregional secondaries. The unions united to resist the measure, for they feared it would become a bureaucratic screen for managerial power.[75] The workers' influence remained strong in the secondary commissions because they operated on a local level, where daily social peace demanded that problems be rapidly resolved. The strong presence of the unions within the firm assured them a decisive role in the CSNP. The interregional secondaries would be cut off from the power of the workers at the base and from the unions at the top. The interregional managers would be able to override the local secondaries and thus stop appeals to the CSNP. Gaspard limited the implementation of the decree after union pleas, but he insisted that the interregional managers sit in local secondaries and have voting powers on matters concerning their level of the hierarchy.[76] Evidently, a number of local managers deferred to the interregional managers, resulting in a de facto implementation of the original decree. In response, the CGT, CFTC, and UNCM organized boycotts of the secondaries in which the interregional managers sat. The unions also conducted several local work stoppages around the issue and managed to limit the interregional managers' power within the secondary commissions, yet the issue was not fully resolved until 1968.

The union-operated benefit system (CCOS) remained an ugly scar at EDF throughout the 1950s. A decree of 1955 restituted workers' control to the CCOS (with a name change to Caisse Centrale d'Action Sociale, CCAS), but union rivalry prevented the full return of the CCAS to the unions until 1963. The personality of Marcel Paul remained a major barrier for the re-creation of the CCAS, which, though more decentralized in its new form, still required a president. Éclairage in-

[74] Letter of Gaspard to Decaillon (CFTC), CFDT archives, papers of Yves Morel.
[75] Note by "RLG" (René Le Guen), 4 April 1962, and letter of Paul to Gaspard, 6 October 1961, both in GNC archives, dossier: "Commissions secondaires."
[76] Letter of Gaspard to Paul, 13 September 1961, GNC archives, dossier: "Commissions secondaires," and letter of Gaspard to Decaillon.

sisted that Paul be the president, as he had been until 1951. The government appointed a new CCAS in 1960, yet refused to allow Paul to preside.[77] The CFTC, UNCM, and FO long tried to block renewed CGT control of the CCAS. Nonetheless, when the unions regained control of the CCAS, the CGT regained its old position of power, albeit without Marcel Paul presiding. The CGT kept the well-endowed CCAS tightly closed, making its services available only to EDF workers and their families.

When Striking Is Too Powerful: Methods of Workers' Action

At 6 A.M. on 16 October 1957, the EDF community shut down almost all of France's electrical power system. The issue was pay levels, and all four unions at EDF, along with the uppermost managers of the firm, supported the strike. As a show of internal solidarity against the government's salary policies, the strike succeeded stunningly, but an ugly human tragedy turned public opinion against the firm. The strike marked several significant turning points. First, it was the last decisive act by the long-standing alliance between the unions and the management at EDF. Second, the workers turned their technical knowledge and skills to meeting their own needs. Finally, the public backlash against the strike underscored how carefully public sector workers had to use labor's traditional weapon.

The erosion of the salary levels at EDF reached a crisis point by the fall of 1957. Inflation had severely eroded purchasing power, yet the government steadfastly refused to take any measures to approve any pay raises, despite a resolution in Parliament instructing it to do so.[78] A study commissioned by Parliament's Industrial Production Committee in February 1957 found the following wage gaps: entry-level skilled workers at the Seine Préfecture made 63.6 percent more than comparable EDF workers; highly skilled oil industry workers made 56 percent more, and skilled workers in the private metals industry made 34 percent more; finally, on average, even state tobacco-industry workers made from 30 to 38 percent more than EDF workers.[79] The government ignored the crisis and based its anti-inflation strategy on limiting public sector wage demands. Business leaders strongly sup-

---

[77] *Force-Information* 107 (October 1963), 15.
[78] Cited in a letter from National Assembly deputy André Le Troquer (SFIO) to Werbrouck (FO), no date, Éclairage archives, dossier: "Grève du 16 octobre 1957"; and *Force* 80 (November 1957).
[79] *Rapport N° 4110 de la Commission de la Production Industrielle de l'Assemblée Nationale,* separate reprint from *JO* of 13 February 1957, pp. 3–5.

ported the government's tactics. In a business roundtable, an unnamed industrialist said: "It is crucial not to budge an inch at EDF and GDF. It would be better to have a fifteen-day electricity strike and bring Marcel Paul and his CGT people to their knees than to allow a chain reaction of wage hikes to start. Today you have the public sector, tomorrow you will have the private sector."[80] Finally, in the fall of 1957, the cabinet allowed Minister of Energy Ramonet to negotiate with Gaspard over EDF salaries. Gaspard and Ramonet reached a tentative agreement in the first week of October, but Minister of Finance Gaillard had the cabinet reject the package, and for reasons unrelated to EDF salaries, the Cabinet collapsed soon after. The resentment at EDF was universal. Patience had been strained to the breaking point, and workers and managers alike agreed that all other options had been tried and had failed, so a strike had to be called.[81]

In the few days before 16 October, EDF cadres and workers inventoried the electrical power needs of literally every hospital, health facility, and factory, warning consumers of the coming shutdown, urging them to confirm that their emergency power units worked, and offering to supply emergency power if they had no backup supplies. The unions officially notified Gaspard of their intention to strike (though he was already well aware of it through informal channels) on the afternoon of the fifteenth. Gaspard then began to make sure that emergency power would be available, only to find that such tasks had already been done.[82] In Témoignage Chrétien, Philippe Myot later wrote, "All necessary warnings had been given by the unions [and] all possible precautions had been taken by the strikers."[83] At 6 A.M. on the sixteenth, therefore, the power in France went off, under the total and united control of the EDF workers and managers. The exceptions were few: here and there a hospital without an emergency power generator received power, as did a number of aluminum producers, whose equipment would have been severely damaged without constant power supplies. At 4:45 in the afternoon, a gradual phase-in to full power began, and by 5:00, the entire system was back to full power. The strike was a total technical success. The EDF workers and managers showed to the world that they had the technical expertise to cut off (significantly) almost all power, while assuring emergency power to consumers who could not do without it. Before the completion of the

[80] L'Information Industrielle et Commerciale, 13 December 1957.

[81] Leaflet authored by CGT, CFTC, FO, and UNCM, 14 October 1957, Éclairage archives, dossier: "Grève du 16 octobre 1957."

[82] CAPV 143 (25 October 1957).

[83] Philippe Myot, "Responsabilités et droit de grève," Témoignage Chrétien 695 (1 November 1957).

transport grid, such an action would have been impossible. The strike indicated the dual nature of high-technology productive facilities, that while the grid could serve the needs of consumers in a highly reliable fashion, it also placed a powerful tool in the hands of the workers who were willing to use it—though its use was predicated on total unity within EDF. In addition, the technical sophistication necessary to operate the system prevented the government from using strikebreakers, as it had before.

But a baby died in an incubator in Argentan. The moderate and rightist press immediately pulled out all of the stops: "Wednesday's Cutoff of Current Has Killed a Baby" headlined *L'Aurore* (18 October). *Paris-presse l'Intransigéant* (19 October), *Figaro*, and *France-Soir* (both of 22 October) all used the imagery of the dead baby to deride EDF workers, unions, managers, and the nationalized sector generally. The provincial press took a similar tack. EDF was broadly characterized as a bastion of greedy Communist baby killers. The attacks were off the mark, however. All hospitals in France eligible to receive patients on the national social security accounts were required by the Ministry of Public Health to have emergency power units. Many of the hospitals that bothered to observe the regulation did so by purchasing generators left behind by the American army in 1945. Many hospitals simply ignored the regulation and therefore fraudulently received payments from the social security account. Presumably, administrators at the Argentan hospital had misinformed EDF workers in the days before the strike by claiming that it had an operable emergency power unit, as required by law. This fact probably explains why the medical community leveled the most vicious attacks against the strikers—providers had a strong incentive to befog the issue by charging EDF workers with greed and irresponsibility.[84] Public opinion nonetheless remained negative.

The rightist press concentrated on the baby-killer theme and a number of provincial and financial papers red-baited the EDF community. *Les Échos* (17 October) described the strike as insurrectional. *La Provençale* of Marseille (22 October), Socialist leader Gaston Defferre's paper, backed FO's activity in the strike but red-baited the other workers, claiming that FO should have struck alone. A very ugly attack came from *La Dépêche du Midi*: "The truth is simple, cruel. M. Marcel Paul and his Communist co-conspirators are the secret and fearsome masters of energy in France. The director general of EDF [Gaspard] conspires with them, some say by [political] inclination, others say by oppor-

---

[84] The two most relevant ministers conceded that the EDF workers were not culpable for the death of the baby: Minister of Industry Ribeyre in *JO, dp*, 14 December 1957, p. 5366, and the minister of public health in *JO, dp*, 5 December 1957, p. 5186.

tunism. It is always [the Communists] who influence the nominations to the EDF front office and who dominate its administrative life. The government and the general directors always retreat before the Communists." The author closed by calling for a government of public safety to prevent a Communist dictatorship in the public services.[85] The worst red spectre was conjured by Socialist Senator Georges Lamousse (Haûte-Vienne), who claimed that the strike was not really over pay at EDF, but a dress rehearsal by the Communists for the power cutoffs that they would execute as the Red Army approached from the East.[86]

The death of a baby and the red-scare stories rendered the strike a failure. Though the strike did force the government to allow a salary increase, public backlash permanently damaged the internal solidarity of EDF. In the board meeting after the strike, Chairman Flouret criticized the action, which the board had implicitly supported because the strike "went so tragically beyond the goals intended for it."[87] FO and UNCM both scrambled to explain to their members outside EDF why they had struck, and UNCM even threatened to sue several newspapers for the attacks.[88] Paul sent an urgent memo out to the other EDF union leaders on the twenty-fifth, calling for a joint defense against the press attacks. The most telling consequence of the strike, however, was that henceforth Gaspard and other top EDF managers systematically distanced themselves from the union leaders, and the internal social alliance eroded accordingly.

The 1957 strike showed that in a public service industry, the classic labor strategy of total shutdowns was perhaps too powerful a weapon. No antistrike legislation was passed right after the strike, though there was significant public support for it. Nonetheless, EDF workers eschewed total cutoff strikes after 1957. Instead, they invented more imaginative methods of agitation. These included well-targeted, lightning local strikes—sudden so that management would not be able to inform factory managers of imminent power cuts. All four of the EDF unions in the Paris region supported this strategy because, with the proper precautions, it did the least damage to small and domestic consumers.[89] Another strategy, though used only occasionally because of adverse effects on consumers, was the "regional turning strike," in which power would be cut region by region in succession. More effective strategies involved no cuts at all; they included paperwork and

[85] André Lafond, "Sainte Pagaille," Le Dépêche du Midi (Toulouse), 21 October 1957.
[86] Georges Lamousse, "La grève de l'EDF était une répétition du dispositif communiste," Le Populaire du Centre, 24 October 1957.
[87] CAPV 143 (25 October 1957).
[88] Le Figaro, 24 October 1957.
[89] "Rapport de Raymond Ripoteau au XXIIᵉ congrès," Force-Information 102 (April 1963), 37.

administrative strikes, meter-reader strikes, and brownouts during normal working hours. Many of these strategies were obviously quite
popular with consumers. Finally, only after the imagination explosion
of May 1968 did EDF workers discover the most ingenious methods:
computer strikes and refusals to turn off expensive peak-power plants
during off-peak hours. Many of the new tactics bordered on illegal-
ity. The French Constitution protected only the right to simple work
stoppages. More innovative approaches, which, legally speaking,
amounted to industrial sabotage, had no legal protection. Management
later placed power dispatching, which offered immense potential for
consciously misoperating the system, under the control of politically
reliable workers. Parliament passed systematic legislation limiting the
right to strike in the public sector after the 1963 miners' strike. New
legislation outlawed all turning strikes, required a five-day warning
before any work action, and (in order to prevent rolling strikes, in
which each worker in a work group would go out one hour in succession) deducted a full day's pay for each hour of illegal stoppages.
This law remained in force until 1968, after which it became a dead
letter.

High technology and the sophisticated skills necessary to operate it
entirely changed the traditional notions of striking. Strikes risked al-
ienating the public and creating a widespread backlash. Electrical
power production is, after all, a public service. In addition, the political
complexity of workers' protest grew when they began to understand
how to use the high-technology system to their own advantage, thereby
creating a distance between unionists and managers. Sophisticated use
of technology therefore became the byword for both workers and managers. Gradually, managers and workers applied different meanings
to the status high technology conferred them. Managers already understood how the culture of high technology could be manipulated for
political and social ends. Workers were only beginning to rediscover
the links between skills and power.

All in the EDF Family

Management extended its efforts to reinforce the culture of high
technology in the 1960s. It attempted to displace internal discontent
by presenting new technology as a solution to social problems, and by
giving workers the sense that they were on the leading edge of progress. Myths of high technology made it ideologically autonomous from
its social context. The struggle for workers in the 1960s needed to
demystify technology and reinvent it as the tool for social progress that

the framers of the nationalization had intended. Before that could happen, however, labor had to learn how to pose this issue; until it did, management could manipulate labor's tacit consent. Corporate paternalism and gender chauvinism offered effective vehicles to win that consent.

EDF workers suffered along with other French citizens from France's postwar housing shortage. In addition, EDF personnel, particularly young managers, were subjected to frequent transfers. EDF built its own apartment complexes and houses as a response to both problems. EDF also began a home-loan program in 1951, but it covered only the purchase of new homes and did nothing for renters. The EDF board later approved loans for older homes and occasionally offered loans and grants to help workers gather sufficient funds for down payments. Finally, when EDF was unable to give any financial assistance, it did offer "stability of employment" statements for its workers so that they could have better access to mortgage money. Home ownership, the sign of middle-class success, remained impossible for young, gypsy EDF managers. Finance ministry representatives on the EDF board protested the expenses of providing above-average housing, but Gaspard responded that high-stress, high-technology workers deserved it.[90]

The physical characteristics of EDF housing symbolized the closed and hierarchical nature of the EDF community. During a board discussion on a proposed EDF housing project, Morel noted that EDF often separated its community from possible neighbors, thereby forestalling a sense of community outside the firm.[91] This problem was exacerbated by EDF's penchant for placing worker housing very close to EDF workplaces or on the upper floors of new distribution-center buildings. EDF workers could rarely escape their workmates, and undoubtedly, they often felt a bit suffocated. Even when EDF workers vacationed at CCOS/CCAS facilities, they usually only saw colleagues and their families. EDF housing also underlined the hierarchy: in one EDF-only community, there were fifty-four duplexes, thirty-six four-room flats, and ten six-room houses—different housing for each major pay category.

Women's status at EDF was not enviable. Technical jobs went overwhelmingly to men. Men and technology seemed to go together like boys and toys. Balkanization (sexual segregation) of jobs was a virtually ironclad rule, and most EDF women were clerical workers. Women rarely held managerial positions. For a period in the early 1960s, one

[90] CAPV 154 (24 October 1958).
[91] CAPV 155 (24 November 1958).

of the highest-ranked women at EDF was a consultant in the section promoting electricity use, giving her inherently valuable woman's advice on which domestic appliances should or should not be recommended. Few women were admitted into EDF technical training or retraining schools, and when specific jobs became more technical, women were often elbowed aside. For example, women had long overseen customer accounts in EDF consumer centers, but when computer terminals replaced ledgers, men replaced women.[92] Women thus rarely enjoyed the upscaling of skills and salaries associated with new technology at EDF. The percentage of women workers at EDF rose steadily as the firm became more bureaucratic. In the five years between 1959 and 1964, the percentage of women as a part of all workers at EDF rose from 12 to 14 percent. Almost half (47.2 percent) of the personnel in the Parisian central administration in 1964 were women; in the paperwork-intensive divisions of equipment and research and development, women were about 21 percent (20.7 and 22.1 percent, respectively) of the work force, but only 13.8 percent of the workers in distribution services, where the work was far more manual-intensive, were women.[93]

The CFTC addressed the balkanization question in the early 1950s, but it did not abandon many traditional assumptions about womens' capacities for various types of work. The CFTC strongly supported EDF's principle of equal pay for equal work, but it protested that the rule was often ignored. Pay levels among accounts clerks in provincial centers often depended on the sex of the worker. The CFTC also saw that there were few promotion tracks out of women's jobs. Not only were stenotypists' jobs underrated, they were locked into one job classification and could not advance because the necessary stenographic skills for advancement into higher levels of clerical work were rarely utilized. The CFTC also recognized that keypunching, primarily a woman's activity, was routine, dull, and repetitive. It therefore suggested that jobs be rotated every six months and that no keypuncher be forced to work more than fifteen years at that job.[94]

The CFTC's traditionalist views of women's social roles countered its progressive view of women's labor in the early 1950s. Though it understood that women worked for more than pin money and that working women had to carry on household tasks, it said nothing about the relations of women and men in the home. The CFTC blamed bal-

[92] Ormos, *La montée*, p. 164.
[93] Calculated from figures presented in *Force-Militant* 38 (16 September 1965), 4. Inexplicably, over one-third of the workers who designed the configuration of the high-tension grid were women.
[94] *Gaz-Électricité* 36 (September-October 1951).

kanization as much on women as on the employer, for women were considered to have "inferiority complexes," which kept them out of men's work. According to the CFTC, job segregation was due in part to "women's preference for work in which the concrete results [were] immediately observable" and to "the intellectual capacities of women, which [were] generally less logical and less powerful [than those of men], and better for analytic than for synthetic thinking. . . . [Women] have more perseverance, but less brilliance."[95] Despite its sexist assumptions, the CFTC successfully organized the majority of the women clericals in the central administration. Its success most likely came from its strong defense of better pay levels and job classifications for women.

The CGT saw women in a more progressive and egalitarian light. It did not try to delve into the depths of women's consciousness. Instead, it simply observed the discrimination women faced and offered solutions. It sought to counteract the balkanization problem by calling for equal access to all jobs and for women to be trained for traditionally male jobs by better access to PROFOR's PO program. The CGT's program for women in the 1950s could scarcely have been more progressive for its day: the CGT demanded day-care services or allowances, job-security guarantees, full access to all social benefits, better pensions, upgrading of women's job classifications, and the like. Along with the bulk of French society, the CGT did not, however, break from traditional principles concerning women's domestic role. Women were still expected to pursue the class struggle with their washing machines. The CGT sought more flexible work hours for women so that women's family duties could be better met through more generous baby bonuses and maternity leaves.There was no mention of child-rearing leave for men. In the CGT's nineteen-point program for women's job rights in 1954, eight issues concerned women's role as primary child raisers.[96] The CGT's positions on women did not change substantially through the 1950s. The set of demands arising out of a 1962 CGT-EDF women's conference differed little from those of 1954, the only major difference being a call to break from the sexist assumption that women's work was only for pin money.[97]

EDF remained a citadel of male power with women filling roles as support staff for men who were primary decision makers. Both the CGT and the CFTC helped lead the way in French society in developing programs to deal with the direct on-the-job discrimination women faced. However, neither union attempted to break the association be-

[95] Germaine Benoît, "Le rôle des femmes à l'EDF et GDF," Gaz-Électricité 53 (March 1954).

[96] Force-Information 4 (July 1954), 36.

[97] Force-Information 150 (February 1962), 23.

tween men as conceptualizers of technology and women as users of it. As a result, EDF made little progress toward breaking the gender division of paid and domestic labor. The distinction between men as conceivers and women as utilizers or nurturers was carried into the EDF advertising campaigns, reflecting the old consensus that women's place was at home. Men designed appliances for women to use in the hope that women could be the queens of households made richer by high technology and their husbands' productive efforts.

The CGT strongly supported an emerging domestic consumerism, seeing it as a forerunner to a more egalitarian, socialist, consumer society. It backed the sales and promotion campaigns because they offered avenues for continued employment and promotions for the strongly CGT meter readers, and because they conformed to the CGT's dream of a link between technical and social (meaning consumerist) progress. Most of the CGT's criticisms centered on complaints that EDF never installed enough electrical equipment.

The CGT and CFTC were quite conscious that management constantly tried to promulgate a new style of industrial paternalism based on the technical expertise of the cadres.[98] The CFTC even recognized the pure opportunism of a number of the careerist cadres when it noted that many of them had used the CGT as a ladder to rise within the EDF hierarchy, but then acted like all other kinds of bosses.[99] Much later, GNC chief René Le Guen noted that in the years after 1958, a strong "house mentality" and a "corporatism" had emerged among the cadres.[100] As the largest union, the CGT was the obvious candidate to lead resistance against the new ideological framework, but a combination of bureaucratization, a belief in the gospels of growth, technical expertise, and consumerism dulled the necessary sensitivity.

Resistance to the new in-house ideology was halfhearted because that ideology was at best only half understood. The explosion of May 1968 marked a critical turning point in understanding technocorporatism. At that time, the CFDT began to criticize the simple equation between more electrical use and a better quality of life, implicitly placing the entire productivist ethos on the line. That criticism was based on a new discomfort with the ideals of the consumer society on which the electricity-promotion campaigns had been built. More important, the

---

[98] Claude Flandre noted directly that EDF house magazines were used by top management to make middle cadres, engineers, and technicians tools for the top managers; Flandre report to Éclairage's Twenty-Third National Congress, cited in *Force-Information* 102 (April 1963), 44. In a resolution from its Thirteenth National Congress, the CFTC Fédération Gaz-Électricité called for resistance to what it considered a growing wave of paternalism among *cadres*; cited in *Gaz-Électricité* 55 (October 1954).

[99] *Gaz-Électricité* 73 (December 1956).

[100] Le Guen, *Voyage*, p. 164.

events of 1968 forced workers to reexamine the CMPs, which had been virtually dormant since the end of the antisubcontracting campaign in 1963. The technocorporatist ideology of the firm and the paternalism of the managers was directly criticized in the CMPs after 1968. Finally, the events of 1968 yielded the pay increases that EDF workers had long been seeking.

Visions of Liberated Work and Technology: 1968

The revolt of May 1968 in France was not spontaneous, contrary to a number of popularly held assumptions. The forces for an explosion had been building for a number of years, and the situation at EDF in the mid 1960s was indicative of the gathering storm. Several major factors fed into the tensions that burst forth in May. EDF had absorbed many repatriated Algerian gas and electrical workers in 1962, thereby creating both downward pressure on salaries and a slowing of normal promotion tracks. The Toutée procedures had compressed salary levels and disempowered EDF workers. Finally, the secularization of the CFTC in November 1964 via the creation of the Confédération Française Démocratique du Travail (CFDT) facilitated cooperation with the CGT, as did the CGT's new national strategy to form broad fronts with other progressive unions. When the student movement effervesced in the spring of 1968, however, the CFDT and Éclairage viewed the student movement differently, with the CFDT fully supporting the students' demands and Éclairage following the line of the CGT national office, totally opposing the students. Éclairage was so forcefully against the student movement that in the first week of May, Éclairage members at GDF-Paris demonstrated *against* the students. Out of a rather obvious fear of being politically left behind, the CGT only started to support the student movement when it began to broaden into a workers' movement in mid-May. The CGT realized that if it remained opposed to the May movement, it would be powerless to influence and redirect it.

From the outset, the CGT and CFDT were at loggerheads on how to deal with the revolt. The CGT wanted to revive the spirit of 1946 within the firm, replete with its cryptomilitarist conceptions of workplace hierarchies. It gave only lip service to the very popular conceptions of workers' control, workers' democracy, and *cogestion*. In reference to the May movement, René Le Guen wrote: "In our two [gas and electric] industries the major problem is to return the nationalization to its original applications. The ideas of 'cogestion' and 'workers' control' can only dilute the objectives of the struggle.[101] In essence,

[101] Ibid., p. 257.

while the discourse of 1968 idealistically tried to do away with bosses, the CGT's spirit of 1946 merely attempted to implant socially and politically conscious managers. Éclairage leaflets constantly stressed the need for "realism," eschewing discussions of what it derisively termed "the construction of the world."[102] Éclairage was very clear, however, about the need to loosen the grip of the monopoly capitalist private firms over EDF.

The CFDT's evolution made it open to learning from the student and young workers' movement. In the mid-1960s, the CFDT had closely examined the Yugoslavian experiments in workers' democracy, and it tried to develop new conceptions of workplace relations. They took special note of the analyses of André Gorz and Serge Mallet, the "new working class" theory. That theory had special relevance for EDF, for a central axiom in the Mallet analysis was that as skill levels of workers rose, as they did at EDF, workers would demand a greater voice in determining the character of work and work relations.[103] At EDF, however, precisely the opposite had happened: as average skill levels rose, managerial control became stronger. In particular, the CFDT noted how the CMPs and other workers' participationist structures had atrophied over the years. Routinization and bureaucratization had systematically weakened the CSNP. In addition, the CFDT began to recognize that the famed PROFOR apparatus merely augmented the skills and qualifications of those who already had them. The CFDT was also trying to move away from being essentially the foremen's union, which it had been in the 1950s, toward becoming a union of mid-level technicians.

The CFDT and CGT thus took far different approaches toward the May movement, though both formally supported it. The CGT allied with FO and UNCM against the "ultraleftist" thrust of the movement while the CFDT openly supported it.[104] While the other unions sought to retain or even buttress the hierarchies at EDF, the CFDT attacked them. Éclairage tried to forestall discussion of character-of-work issues by concentrating on winning a large pay increase. Of course, the CFDT did not oppose pay increases, but it preferred not to negotiatiate on pay questions alone. The CFDT was willing to continue striking over nonpay issues and would have done so had the other unions not ceased striking after a large salary increase was won.

A strike at EDF began and extended during the week of 20 May, but

---

[102] GNC leaflet, 21 May 1968, Éclairage archives, dossier: "Grève de mai 1968."
[103] Gorz, *Strategy*, and Serge Mallet, The *New Working Class* (1967).
[104] Resolution of the CFDT confederal council, meeting of 18 May 1968, cited in *Syndicalisme*, supplement to no. 1188 (20 May 1968); see also CFDT-Fédération Gaz-Électricité leaflet, week of 20 May 1968, CFDT archives.

it was far from typical. The workers decided that rather than shutting down the power, they would occupy their workplaces and continue working, assuring management that the plug would be pulled at the slightest provocation. Even the power dispatchers joined the action. In addition, as a show of strength, EDF workers dropped the frequency of the power from 50 to 49 hertz—a greater drop would have damaged EDF and consumers' equipment. By 22 May, the "strike" was total. Negotiations began on twenty-fifth and the Toutée system was ignored from the start. Boiteux tried but failed to negotiate with each union separately. The unions for the most part won what they had sought for years in procedural matters: talks between the unions and the front office, pursuant to Article 9 of the *statut* with arbitration by the minister of industry. The strike demands were presented to the union negotiators in Paris as classic *cahiers des doléances* from local EDF workers' general assemblies held during the first week of the strike. They often diverged from the simple quantitative salary demands sought by the leaderships of the CGT, FO, and UNCM. The workers strongly supported raising the lowest salaries more than the higher ones, reviving codeterminist councils, improving PROFOR programs, instituting measures against the dictatorial pretensions of some managers and the paternalism of others, enforcing a forty-hour workweek, indexing pay on inflation, taking a fifth week of vacations, and ending subcontracting. Interestingly, the workers in the various research and development arms reflected many of the sentiments cited by Mallet, seeking a larger voice for workers in determining modes of management, changes in PROFOR in order to provide ongoing education and technological adaptation, and a better system of paid leave and retirement for women workers. research and development workers explicitly supported the students and they reiterated the students' demands for democratizing education.[105] Only the CFDT was willing to push the nonpay issues particularly hard in the negotiations, and pressure from the local general workers' assemblies forced the other unions to consider such issues, albeit without enthusiasm.

Negotiators reached a tentative agreement on 31 May after considerable discord among the unions. The centerpiece of the agreement was an average 11 percent pay hike, weighted favorably toward the lower pay categories. It was set in such a way, however, that comparability with other firms was virtually impossible, thus meeting one of Boiteux's key goals—not to set the basis for wage hikes across the economy.[106] The major qualitative victory for the workers was the end

[105] From assorted reports from local workers' general assemblies held during the week of 20 May 1968, Éclairage archives, dossier: "Grève de mai 1968."
[106] Boiteux report on May 1968 strike wave to EDF board, CAPV 263 (14 June 1968).

of management's tie-breaking vote in the CSNP, a managerial prerogative that had begun in 1950 and gave to CSNP procedures only the illusion of being codeterminist. This made the CSNP far more democratic. Most of the other concrete gains were unimpressive: one hour less of work per week, an extra two days of paid vacation per year, pay for the strike days, a slight cut in the retirement age, the integration of one-third of the productivity bonuses into the base for calculating pensions, and paid time off for perfoming union functions. For the more important qualitative issues, the CGT, FO, and UNCM were willing to go back to work after eliciting only promises. Significantly, these included a promise by management (again) to set up committees to examine the issues of subcontracting, PROFOR activities, and methods for reviving the CMPs. Clearly, all unions except the CFDT tried to end the strike as soon as the quantitative demands were met.

For the first time ever, the tentative agreement reached in Paris was submitted to local workers' assemblies for approval. To the CGT, this meant that work would resume immediately upon reaching the tentative agreement, before the local votes, thus stacking the deck for acceptance, even though the strike officially continued until the locals accepted the contract on 4 June.[107] An examination of the votes shows that where the votes were done by raised hands, acceptance of the contract was strong, but when done by secret ballot, the results were very mixed, indicating severe pressure from the CGT to vote to go back to work. Virtually all of the research and development sections voted to stay out.[108] An internal Éclairage memo stated that "the level of worker discontent remains very high and many of them are willing to stay out until all of their demands are met."[109] Among the millions of strikers in May, the EDF and GDF workers were the first to go back to work, and their decision helped to break the momentum of the still-expanding strike movement.

Life was never the same at EDF after May 1968. The CFDT emerged from the movement as the union furthest to the left, pushing aside the CGT and making the CGT seem aged, conservative, and outworn. The CGT's demands for a return to the spirit of 1946 were insufficient and outdated. In 1946, the French state and economy reflected the old structure of local provincial power and family owner-managers; in 1968,

[107] Interview by author with Ernest Anzalone, CFDT negotiator during May 1968 strike, Paris, 9 July 1981.
[108] Summaries of back-to-work voting results, 4 P.M., 4 June 1968, Éclairage archives, dossier: "Grève de mai 1968."
[109] Ibid, appended note. Ernest Anzalone observed that the CGT virtually strong-armed the workers back to work; interview with author, Paris, 9 July 1981.

the workers faced a refined, centralized, and modernized capitalist state. In 1946, the EDF community viewed the capitalist economy as a rival; in 1968, EDF had a symbiotic relationship with it. In 1946, technically trained managers supervised largely unskilled or semi-skilled workers; in 1968, economist-managers oversaw technically trained workers. Technological and economic change had transformed the very function of management. The issues at EDF had fundamentally changed because France itself had been transformed. A reexamination of the modes of workplace democracy moved to the top of the agenda as many workers began to reexamine the new set of work relations that technological, economic, and political change had wrought. Renewed militance and imagination vied with the culture of high technology in the workers' collective mentality, and at the end of the 1960s, the agenda remained open.

Epilogue

The transitional period at EDF, 1954–62, took a toll on internal solidarity. The firm made great technical gains, but the social advantages of working at EDF stagnated and, relative to other firms, declined. The alliance between the unionists and the social technocratic managers eroded, and it was slowly—indeed, for the CGT, imperceptibly—replaced by quiescent labor and economistic managers, held together by a strong mythology of high technology. The unions preserved their right to have a voice in determining the character of the daily life of the firm, but those who enjoyed that voice found increasingly that the most important issues were decided before they were presented in the participationist forums. Indeed, governance at EDF began to replicate the operation of the Plan, which preserved the niceties of participation yet relegated most decisions to groups of experts[1] (particularly under the tenure of Pierre Massé).

Economist managers have commanded EDF with little internal opposition from 1962 to the present, with a brief hiatus in 1968 and 1969. As the Gaullist state routinized the rule of experts, outsiders—whether labor, small business, or retail consumers—were systematically disempowered. Nonetheless, the French economy, with EDF at the leading edge, delivered vast quantities of material goods to French citizens in the 1960s and only the intrepid could resist. The movement of May-June 1968 opened an entirely new potential trajectory for the French society and polity, but the risks of inventing a new postcapitalist and postmodern social order gave pause to many. EDF workers glanced

[1] Peter A. Hall, *Governing the Economy: The Politics of State Intervention in Britain and France* (1986), p. 158.

into the yawning abyss of an uncertain future in May 1968 and retreated. France followed. An alternative future could not be invented overnight, and progressive unionists and intellectuals began to search for a more careful path. The events of 1968 opened an entire set of issues concerning the quality of work and the quality of life, and the habits of the EDF community were sufficiently shaken to allow many to imagine that the firm could again become the leading edge of a newly defined social progress.

The reverberations of 1968 echoed through EDF for several years. A reinvigorated socialist movement promised an electoral route to a participatory economic democracy. Within EDF, comangement bodies enjoyed a brief renaissance, and on the periphery, consumer groups began to demand a voice through their new organizations. The potentials for reform were considerable, yet they depended on momentum, a willingness of threatened institutions to reform, and a continuation of the prosperity that allowed the luxury of posing postscarcity political issues. EDF management and the CGT had little interest in pursuing reforms that would have eroded their own power. Force Ouvrière briefly toyed with extreme leftism but abandoned it rapidly. The CFDT tried to keep the spirit of 1968 alive, but lacked the power to deliver very much. Inflation probably constituted the major factor that destroyed the potentials of 1968. Businesses responded to wage increases in 1968 just as they had in 1936—with a systematic set of price increases. Currency fluctuations following the American double devaluation and float exacerbated inflation. The wage gains of May were already eroding by September, and the unions were kept busy simply preserving the material gains of May. By 1972, the momentum was effectively broken.

In the 1970s and 1980s, EDF managers gained the charmed position of France's most respected technocrats. Their victory in the battle over reactor designs and their key role in breaking the momentum of the May 1968 strike movement made EDF a perfect candidate for an experiment in recasting the relations between the nationalized sector and the state. The Nora Commission of 1967 had specifically examined the long-dormant issue of controls over the nationalized sector and the broader issue of greater autonomy for managers. It concluded that when the accumulated set of controls worked, they inhibited managerial initiative, and that when they did not, they wasted managerial time and talent.[2] The report recommended that the government pursue a contract strategy with the nationalized firms, setting the broad lines

[2] Groupe de Travail du Comité Interministériel des Entreprises Publiques, *Rapport sur les Entreprises Publiques* (1967).

of each firm's performance and allowing it to reach specified targets following its own methods.

EDF management signed a Program Contract with the state in December 1970, which ironically set performance specifications for EDF according to indicies that EDF itself had developed. Economists within EEG had developed mathematical and econometric models for measuring factor productivity in the 1960s—the "total factor productivity" models—and the contract specified that total factor productivity would rise at an annual rate of 4.85 percent. EDF designed the model, and the government had EDF run it to measure the firm's performance. Similarly, the contract required a *rentabilité* of invested capital of 8 percent in 1971 and 8.3 percent in 1972. Again, EDF developed and ran the measure of its own performance. EDF was restricted to rate increases of no more than 1.85 percent per year. Any revenues gained by EDF through productivity increases beyond the targets could be retained by the firm. This would be useful for EDF because the state was determined to reduce state subsidies for EDF's capital budget, forcing it to finance new equipment by bond issues and retained earnings. A Progress Contract was supposed to link the Program Contract to a labor agreement that guaranteed cost-of-living and productivity-based salary increases. The CGT resisted but finally signed in late 1971.

The success of the contract strategy of the early 1970s hinged on several factors. First, the state had to assume the political neutrality of EDF managers, and Boiteux's rhetoric about the "objective" character of economic models convinced state officials. Secondly, labor had to agree to a formalization of corporatist arrangements with management, and after a largely symbolic resistance, the unions accepted their partnership role. Finally, EDF's cost structure had to remain steady, which, of course, it did not do after the oil price explosion of October 1973. Until that time, according to its own measures, EDF met and exceeded contract goals. Changes in oil prices and a massive nuclear program rendered many of the presumptions in the contract approach absurd.

Oil prices at French ports of entry rose almost fourfold in the winter of 1973–74. At first blush, the price shock embarrassed EDF, pointing up the blithe indifference with which EDF managers had treated oil supply issues. The EDF board discussed the 1970 oil price hike by OPEC, yet seems not to have taken it seriously, for the firm continued to build its new series of 600-mw, oil-fired plants.[3] Suddenly, production costs rose, and EDF had neither the coal supplies nor the coal-burning capability to allow it a substitute heat source. Nonetheless,

---

[3] CAPV 288 (25 October 1970).

EDF managers turned embarrassment to advantage. High oil prices allowed EDF to begin to define its new and now best-known image—that of the world's most aggressive nuclear utility.

The Péon Commission report of 1968 and the Pompidou decision of 1969 were both framed on the assumption that nuclear power was still not quite economically or technologically mature. For that reason, the nuclear program of the Fifth Plan still spoke in terms of prototypes and the need to investigate alternative nuclear designs—it admitted that artifactual closure had not yet occurred with nuclear power.[4] The Sixth Plan (for 1970 to 1975) had cautiously set EDF nuclear construction at 8,000 mw—about 1,600 mw per year. Nonetheless, by March 1974, nuclear technology was suddenly assumed to be mature, and EDF managers and the state framed an aggressive new program for 5,400 mw of light-water reactors to go into construction in 1974 alone, with an additional 6,300 mw slated for 1975. In February 1975, EDF was scheduled to start construction on 12,000 mw in 1976 and 1977, with an additional 5,000 mw slated for 1978. Also in 1975, EDF opted to standardize plants on the Westinghouse-designed pressurized water reactor against General Electric's boiling water reactor.

The decision for a single nuclear design with a single supplier marked a significant shift in EDF purchasing policy. Bidding procedures became impossible, and EDF had to move toward a system of account surveillance to assure cost controls. More significantly, in order to avoid improprieties, CEA (the agency that had lost in the design battle of the 1960s) bought 30 percent of Framatome, the French manufacturer of LWRs, and EDF agreed to a gradual purchase of Westinghouse's PWR patent. Framatome was largely linked to Jeumont-Schneider, so Alsthom-CGE and CEM, Jeumont-Schneider's rivals, lost. To compensate, EDF guaranteed that it would purchase its turbo-alternators from Alsthom-CGE and CEM. CGE was nationalized in 1982. By restructuring the electrical power industry and its suppliers around nuclear technology, EDF and the state created the managerial modus operandi toward which they and the suppliers had been moving for years, with decisions made by closed circles of experts outside the scope of the EDF board and parliamentary politics.

EDF began to invent a specific nuclear logic as it opted to pursue the aggressive nuclear program. At a time when many felt that energy demand should be reduced, power produced under the new program would exceed even EDF's habitually optimistic supply projections. EDF

[4] For a discussion of artifactual closure, see Trevor J. Pinch and Weibe E. Bijker, "The Social Construction of Facts and Artefacts, or How the Sociology of Science and the Sociology of Technology Might Benefit Each Other," in Bijker et al., eds., *Social Construction*, pp. 17–49.

managers insisted not only that electrical demand would continue to double every ten years, but that electricity would replace other forms of energy in heating, cooking, and the like.[5] This satisfied EDF's long pretension to become France's energy broker and led EDF into an unpopular campaign to promote and subsidize electrical space heating. EDF never convinced the public that the logic of nuclear energy—that it operated best as a supply for base load—meant that switching to less efficient electrical heat would conserve resources.

Nuclear logic extended further. For EDF managers and the state, the choice of an enriched uranium design seemed to imply that France needed to deal with all phases of the nuclear fuel cycle. However, most fuel facilities were highly capital intensive and attained economies of scale only when they were far larger than necessary to meet France's needs. Each facility was designed on the assumption that most of the industrial world would also opt for similar nuclear power programs and that France could easily sell its excess fuel-treatment capacity. This meant that France signed long-term contracts for fuel supply and waste treatment with other powers. CEA thus built a uranium-enrichment facility at Tricastin, which required four 900-mw power plants simply to supply it with power. Similarly, in collaboration with German and Italian utilities, EDF built a 1,300-mw fast breeder reactor at Creys-Malville in order to assure supplies of fissionable fuels.[6] Finally, the CEA built a plant to reprocess highly radioactive spent fuels in Brittany, signing long-term contracts to receive spent fuel, from which it would recover fissionable materials. Once the rest of the world began to abandon nuclear power in the late 1970s, France was left with considerable slack capacity in its fuels plants. Similarly, as French citizens proved reluctant to substitute electricity for other energy forms, EDF's production capacity became too large in the mid-1980s, when over 60 percent of its power was nuclear-based.

Antinuclear protests remained smaller in France than elsewhere, despite EDF's aggressive program. EDF approached the public with promotional zeal, and its rhetoric of progress generally, and of nuclear power in particular, succeeded. Public confidence in EDF remained high and EDF promulgated a public image of highly skilled experts overseeing virtually failure-proof technologies. By standardizing plant designs early, EDF was also able to keep construction costs low, thereby minimizing rate increases. France's small antinuclear movement did, however, help to recreate an internal sense of besiegement at EDF, not

[5] Albert Robin (General Director of EDF), "Croissance énergétique zéro: Quand et à quel niveau?" internal EDF paper, April 1976.

[6] Breeder reactors take uranium^{238}, add a neutron, and yield plutonium. Because of its high operating temperature, the Creys-Malville plant is sodium-cooled.

unlike that of the Cold War era. The CGT again closed ranks with EDF management to defend the besieged citadel, and the CFDT, which alone opposed the nuclear program, faced accusations of treason to the enterprise. Internal unity against the antinuclear movement also served to close off discussion of many of the lingering issues of 1968. Labor again deferred to heroic managers.

Nuclear technology was equally important for its symbolic impact. A vast network of nuclear plants reiterated many of the cultural pre-dilections of the EDF community—that bigger is better, that high technology is always more capital-intensive, that "progress" is best led by centralized authority, and that newer and better technologies are inherently more complicated, demanding control by experts. The script for the future promulgated by EDF effectively closed off debate about the future. Creys-Malville, with its thirty-story containment building, its white-coated technicians, and its solar-heated visitors' center outside the security perimeter, became the totem of the new EDF, just as the Monnet Plan dams once had been. Those not intimidated by the self-verifying and self-referential rhetoric of nuclear technology need only visit Creys-Malville to be cowed by the new images of power.

François Mitterrand and the Socialists were elected in 1981 on a platform to decelerate EDF's nuclear program. In May 1981, Mitterrand suspended the program in order to reevaluate it. In the end, only the hotly contested plant at Plogoff was scrubbed and the rest of the program remained intact. EDF had finally succeeded in making its expertise and programs unassailable by political authorities of any persuasion. The Left conceded power to EDF's technocracy and in so doing closed off an entire range of public discourse about France's future. In the late 1980s, when EDF faced vast nuclear overcapacity (the consequence of its refusal to recognize that the French populace only reluctantly changes its consumption habits), the Socialist government finally decided to scrub several of EDF's nuclear construction projects.

The Mitterrand regime also proceeded to nationalize many of the private firms with which EDF had had close links, including Pechiney (by then, Pechiney-Ugine-Kuhlmann, PUK), Compagnie Générale de l'Électricité, and Framatome. Corporate policies changed little. Jacques Chirac and the Right denationalized several firms in the mid-1980s, but corporate policies again remained unchanged. The pirouettes around the issue of nationalization in the 1980s underlined an important fact, that regardless of who owned France's industries, the personnel and policies would remain the same. The only difference became one of how the capital of a firm would be composed—entirely by debt if nationalized, and a mix of debt and equity if private. In either case, the same people would hold the paper. An entire trajectory of political discourse withered under a set of broadly held assumptions about linear progress and the legitimacy of expertise. EDF symbolized that end of ideology.

Appendix

Figure A1. Values of utility stocks, 1925–1938

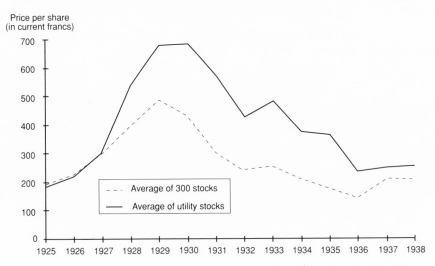

Source: Jean-Marcel Jeanneney and Claude-Albert Colliard, *Économie et droit de l'élec-tricité* (1950), Table 42.

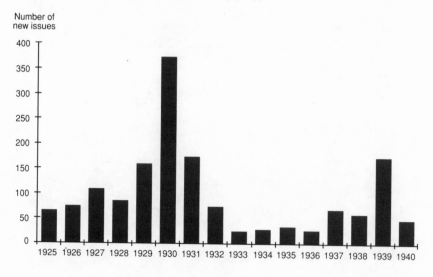

Figure A2–a. New utility securities issues, 1925–1940

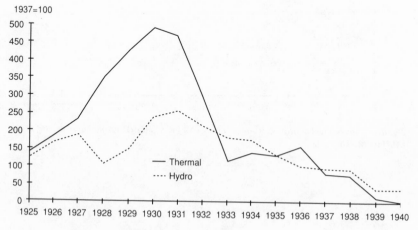

Figure A2–b. Indexes of utility capital spending, 1925–1940

Source: Jean-Marcel Jeanneney and Claude-Albert Colliard, *Économie et droit de l'électricité* (1950), Table 20.

Figure A3. Utility stock price indexes, 1938–1945

Price indexes
(1938=100)

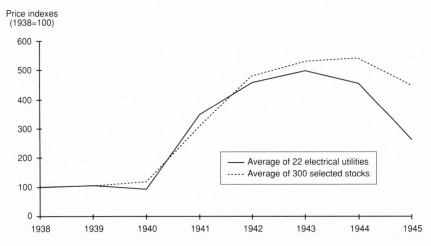

Source: Edmond Roux, *Nationalisation sans spoliation* (1945), 26.

Figure A4. Composition of the EDF Board, 1946–1970

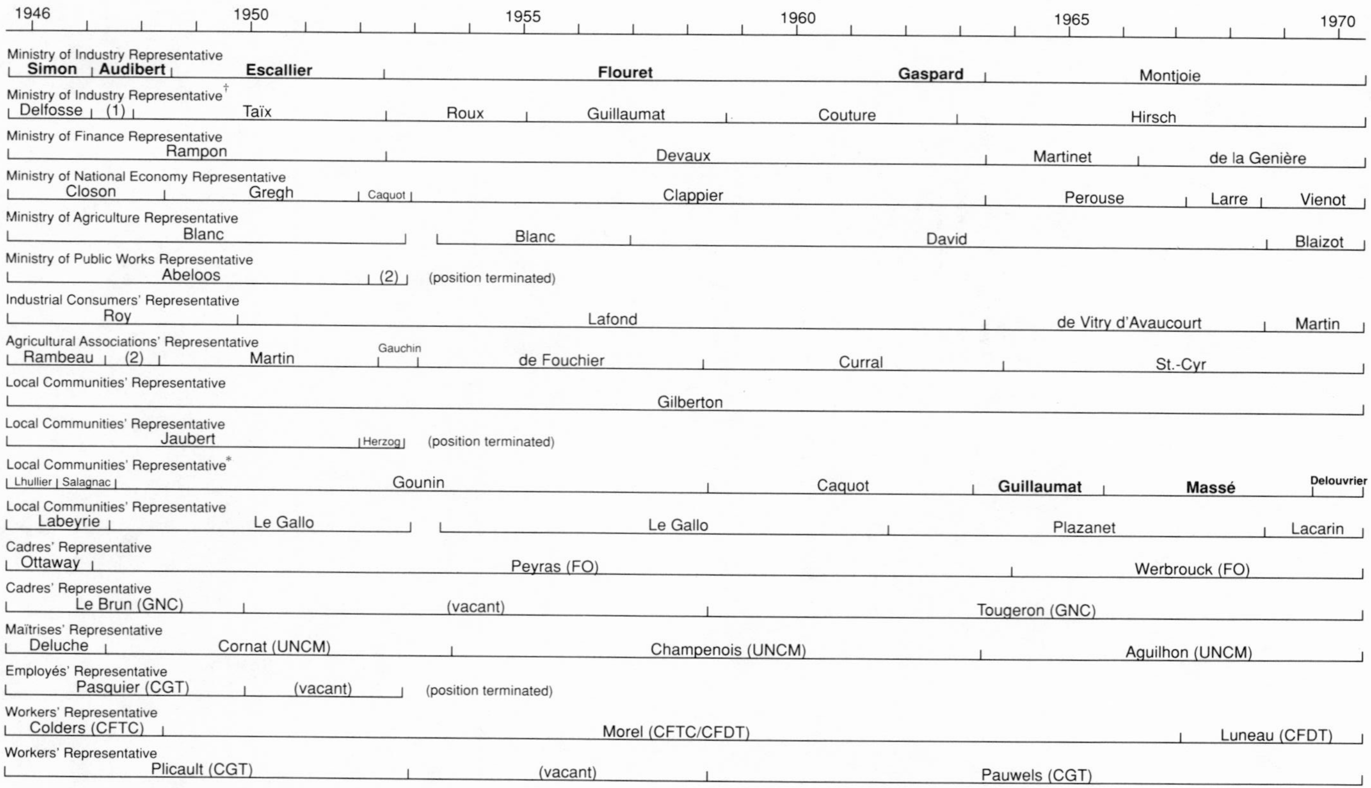

	1946	1950	1955	1960	1965	1970

Ministry of Industry Representative
Simon | **Audibert** | **Escallier** | **Flouret** | **Gaspard** | **Montjoie**

Ministry of Industry Representative†
Delfosse | (1) | Taïx | Hirsch

Ministry of Finance Representative
Rampon | Devaux | Guillaumat | Couture | Martinet | de la Genière

Ministry of National Economy Representative
Closon | Gregh | Caquot | Clappier | Perouse | Larre | Vienot

Ministry of Agriculture Representative
Blanc | Blanc | David | Blaizot

Ministry of Public Works Representative
Abeloos | (2) | (position terminated)

Industrial Consumers' Representative
Roy | Lafond | Martin

Agricultural Associations' Representative
Rambeau | (2) | Martin | Gauchin | de Fouchier | Curral | St-Cyr

Local Communities' Representative
Gilberton

Local Communities' Representative
Jaubert | Herzog | (position terminated)

Local Communities' Representative*
L'huillier | Salagnac | Gounin | Caquot | **Guillaumat** | **Massé** | **Delouvrier**

Local Communities' Representative
Labeyrie | Le Gallo | Le Gallo | Plazanet | Lacarin

Cadres' Representative
Ottaway | Peyras (FO) | Werbrouck (FO)

Cadres' Representative
Le Brun (GNC) | (vacant) | Tougeron (GNC)

Maîtrises' Representative
Deluche | Cornat (UNCM) | Champenois (UNCM) | Aquilhon (UNCM)

Employés' Representative
Pasquier (CGT) | (vacant) | (position terminated)

Workers' Representative
Colders (CFTC) | Morel (CFTC/CFDT) | Luneau (CFDT)

Workers' Representative
Plicault (CGT) | (vacant) | Pauwels (CGT)

†Seat reassigned to CEA in 1958
Chairmen of the board are in **boldface**

Figure A5. State controls over EDF, 1960

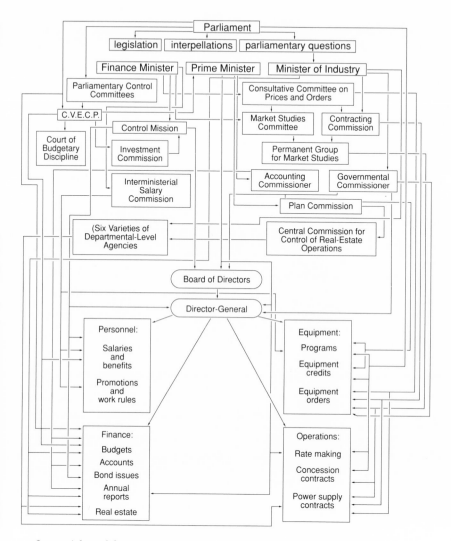

Source: Adapted from Georges Lescuyer, "Les interventions de l'état dans la gestion de l'électricité de France," *Revue Française de l'Énergie* 110 (July-August 1959), 36.

Figure A6. Sources and volume of EDF capital budgets, 1948–1970

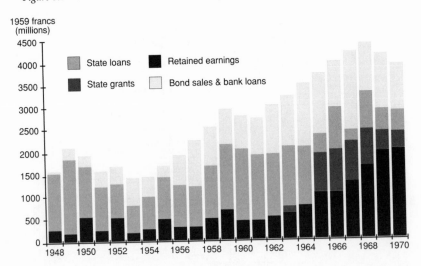

Sources: For 1948–51, Pierre Massé, "L'électricité devant le nouveau plan," *Revue Française de l'Énergie* 30 (April 1952), 222; for 1952–70, EDF-Direction Financière, "Évolution du financement des investissements," loose document (1981); indexing derived from INSEE, *Tableaux de l'économie française, 1970* (Paris: INSEE, 1970), p. 138.

Figure A7–a. Composition of EDF capital spending, 1950–1961

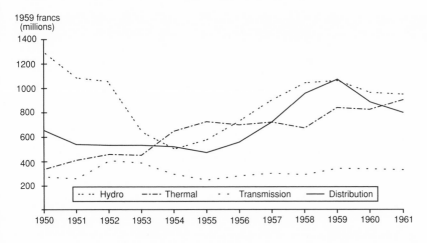

Figure A7–b. Composition of EDF capital spending, 1950–1961 (categories aggregated)

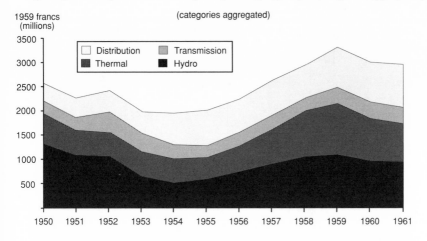

Source: Gilbert Hurpy, "Les conséquences de l'irrégularité des programmes d'équipement électrique de 1950 au IVe Plan," doctoral dissertation, Université de Grenoble, 1964, p. 133.

Figure A8. Composition of EDF Management, 1946–1970

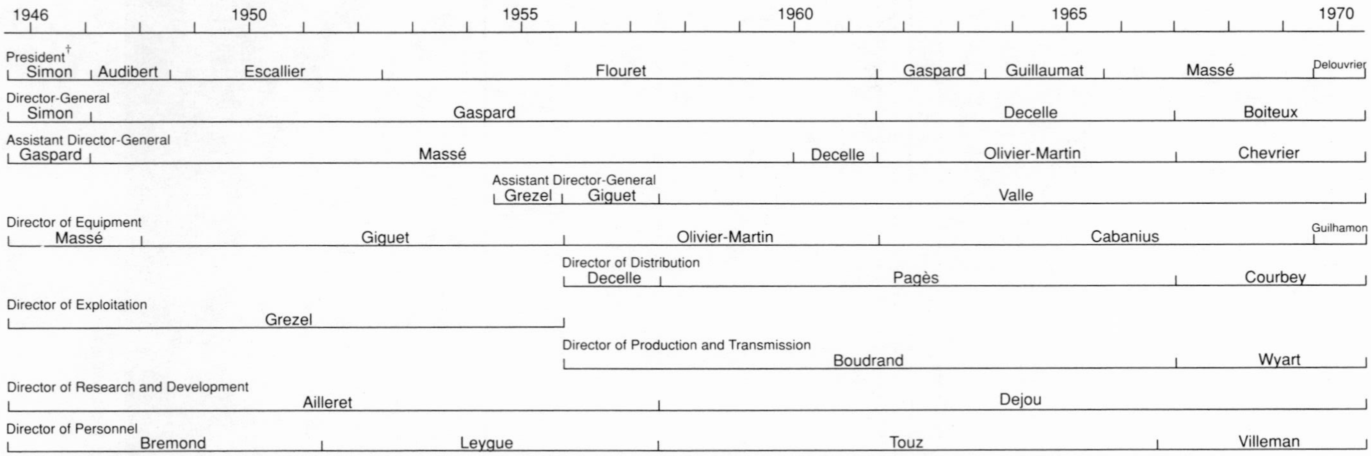

1946 | 1950 | 1955 | 1960 | 1965 | 1970

President[†]
Simon | Audibert | Escallier | Flouret | Gaspard | Guillaumat | Massé | Delouvrier

Director-General
Simon | Gaspard | Decelle | Boiteux

Assistant Director-General
Gaspard | Massé | Decelle | Olivier-Martin | Chevrier

Assistant Director-General
Grezel | Giguet | Valle

Director of Equipment
Massé | Giguet | Olivier-Martin | Cabanius | Guilhamon

Director of Distribution
Decelle | Pagès | Courbey

Director of Exploitation
Grezel

Director of Production and Transmission
Boudrand | Wyart

Director of Research and Development
Ailleret | Dejou

Director of Personnel
Bremond | Levgue | Touz | Villeman

†President and director-general posts separated in 1947

Figure A9–a. Comparisons of EDF base salary to consumer price index and metal-workers' salaries, 1946–1969

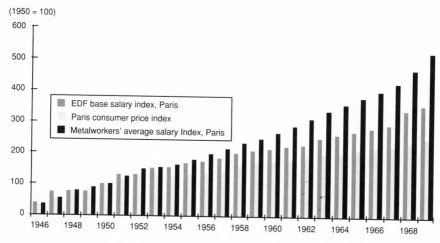

(1950 = 100)

Figure A9–b. Comparison of EDF and metalworkers' living standards in Paris, 1946–1969

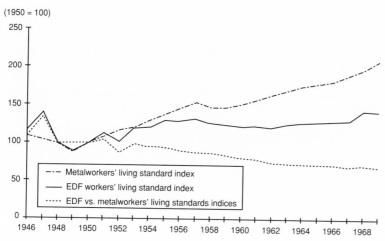

(1950 = 100)

Note: EDF base represents take-home pay of lowest-level EDF workers in Paris, on which all other EDF salaries are based; Paris consumer price index and metalworkers' salaries are INSEE indices. Living standard indices represent respective salary indices + Paris consumer price index; comparative index is EDF salary index + metalworkers' salary index.

Sources: EDF-GDF Direction du Personnel, *Statistiques du personnel, 1970* (Paris: EDF-GDF, 1970), pp. 68–69, and INSEE, *Tableaux de l'économie française, 1970* (Paris: INSEE, 1970), p. 118.

Selected Bibliography

Archives

Archives of Électricité de France (EDF—Centre de Documentation Murat-Messine, Paris VIIIe)

REH Alpes I and GRPH-Savoie dossiers on Tignes, CMP dossiers (inquest on subcontracting, 1960), série E.8.

Confédération Française Démocratique du Travail (formerly, Confédération Française des Travailleurs Chrétiens), Fédération Gaz-Électricité.

Personal papers of Ferdinand Hennebicq and Yves Morel.

Research dossiers.

Confédération Générale du Travail, Fédération Nationale de l'Énergie (formerly, Fédération Nationale de l'Éclairage et des Forces Motrices; hereafter CGT-FNE; Pantin), and CGT, Groupement National des Cadres (CGT-GNC; Pantin); unprocessed archives.

Personal papers of Marcel Paul, René Le Guen, Émile Pasquier, and Claude Flandre.

Various research dossiers.

Électricité de France, Conseil d'Administration, "Procès verbaux des séances," Nos. 1–280 (1946–70), and appended documents and reports; closed record series.

Électricité de France, Conseil d'Administration, Commission de l'Équipement, "Mémentos des réunions," Nos. 1–170 (1946–69), and appended documents and reports; closed record series.

Institut d'Études Politiques, Paris: Press clippings dossiers.

Ministry of Industry Archives, Archives Nationales, Paris: Série F14, Dossiers F/4956–F/10117ter.

264

Interviews

Anzalone, Ernest. EDF offices, Paris. 20 November 1980, 12 December 1980, 16 January 1981, 19 February 1981, 19 March 1981, 9 July 1981, and (on Paris-Lyon SNCF line) 16 April 1981.
Boyer, Jean-Marie. EDF offices, Paris. 4 November 1980.
Gaspard, Roger. Private office, Paris. 3 June 1981.
Morel, Yves. Private residence, Embrun. 16 July 1981.
Pauwels, Roger. CGT-FNE offices, Pantin. 18 February 1981.
Puiseux, Louis. École des Hautes Études en Sciences Sociales, Paris. 18 February 1981.
Thomas, Jean. CGT-GNC offices, Pantin. 21 April 1981.

Unpublished Sources

Beltran, Alain, and Jean-François Picard. "La nationalisation du gaz et de l'électricité." Paper presented at conference Nationalisations et Formes Nouvelles de Participation des Ouvriers à la Libération (1944–1951), Paris, May 1984.
Boiteux Marcel, and Paul Stasi. "Sur la détermination des prix de revient et de développement dans un système interconnecté de production-distribution." Report VI, UNIPEDE conference, Rome, September 1952.
Bouthillier, Guy. "La nationalisation du gaz et de l'électricité en France." Doctoral thesis, Université de Paris, 1968.
Confédération Générale du Travail. "XXVIe Congrès national, Paris, 28–30 avril, 1946: Compte-rendu sténographique." Typescript.
Électricité de France et Gaz de France. "Rapport sur l'activité d'EDF et de GDF depuis la nationalisation." Mimeographed report, 31 March 1948.
Francony, M. "La tarification au coût marginal en théorie et en pratique: L'expérience de l'Électricité de France." Paper presented at the CIREC Conference on Electrical Ratemaking, Liège, 29–30 May 1979.
Frost, Robert L. "France's 'False Start' in Nuclear Power: The Failure of Independent French Nuclear Technology, 1954–1969." Paper presented at the annual meeting of the Society for the History of Technology, Cambridge, Mass., November 1984.
Gabet, M., and M. Francony, M. eds. "Aspects économiques et tarifaires de la modulation des charges à l'Électricité de France." Paper presented at the Conference on the Covering of Load Curves in Future Electrical Production Systems by the European Economic Community's Committee on Electrical Energy, Rome, October 1977.
Grevet, Patrice. "EDF et les structures de l'industrie du gros matériel électromécanique." Mémoire pour le diplôme d'études supérieures de sciences économiques, Université de Paris, 1966.
Holter, Darryl O. "Miners against the State." Ph.D. diss., University of Wisconsin–Madison, 1978.
Hurpy, Gilbert. "Les conséquences de l'irrégularité des programmes d'équipe-

ment électrique de 1950 au IVᵉ Plan." Thèse pour le doctorat ès sciences économiques, Université de Grenoble, 1964.

Lorgeou, Jean. "Tariff Framing for Low Voltage Supplies in France: Theoretical and Practical Aspects of Developing the Universal Tariff." Paper presented at the UNIPEDE Conference on Electricity Tariffs, Madrid, April 1975.

——. "La tarification de l'électricité." Internal EDF working document, No. AC/T 700, May 1978. Mimeographed.

Puiseux, Louis. Seminar on French Energy Policy. École des Hautes Études en Sciences Sociales, Paris, spring 1981.

Rouchon, J. "Une expérience de mise en place d'une réforme tarifaire en basse tension: Les problèmes posées par l'introduction en France du tarif universel." Paper presented at the UNIPEDE Conference on Electricity Tariffs, Madrid, April 1975.

Section Française de l'Internationale Ouvrière (SFIO). "Congrès National Extraordinaire, Paris, 9–12 novembre 1944, compte-rendu sténographique." Microfilm No. 270/36 ext., Bibliothèque de Documentation Internationale Contemporaine, Nanterre.

Stasi, Paul. "L'utilisation rationnelle de l'énergie électrique: L'apport de la tarification." Paper presented at the UNIPEDE Conference on Electricity Tariffs, Warsaw, May 1962.

Staudenmaier, John M., S.J. "Perils of Progress Talk: Some Historical Considerations." Paper presented at the Technology and Epistemology Symposium, San Jose, Calif., February 1985.

Government Documents

France. Assemblée Nationale Constituante. *Journal officiel, débats parlementaires.* 21–26 March 1946.

——. Commission Consultative pour la Production d'Électricité d'Origine Nucléaire. "Les perspectives de développement des centrales nucléaires en France: Rapport." Paris: Ministère de l'Industrie, April 1968.

——. Commission de la Modernisation de l'Électricité. *Rapport.* Paris: Imprimerie Nationale, 1946.

——. Commission de Vérification des Comptes des Entreprises Publiques. "Rapports d'ensemble." *Journal officiel, annexe administrative.* Paris: Imprimerie Nationale, 1949–1970.

——. Groupe de Travail du Comité Interministériel des Entreprises Publiques ("Commission Nora"). *Rapport sur les entreprises publiques.* Paris: Imprimerie Nationale, 1967.

——. Institut National de la Statistique et des Études Economiques (INSEE). *Tableaux de l'économie française, 1970.* Paris: INSEE, 1970.

——. Journal officiel, "Textes d'intérêt général: Électricité, Concession d'alimentation générale en énergie électrique." Extract from *Journal officiel*, N°. 58–2115 (December 1958), Arrêté du 27 novembre 1958.

——. Ministère des Finances. "La réglementation actuelle des prix." *Statistiques et Études Financières* 74 (February 1955), 113–22.

——. Secrétariat d'État aux Affaires Économiques, Direction de la Coordination Économique et des Entreprises Nationales. "Rapport sur l'évolution de la situation économique et financière des entreprises nationales du secteur industriel et commerciel au cours des exercices 1955 et 1956." Paris: Imprimerie Nationale, 1957.

United States. Chief Engineer, U.S. Forces, European Theater. *Report on Electric Power in France*. Washington, D.C.: U.S. Army, 1946.

Books, Articles, and Pamphlets

Adam, Gérard. *La CFTC, 1940–1958: Histoire politique et idéologie*. Paris: Armand Colin, 1964.

Aharoni, Yair. *Evolution and Management of State-owned Enterprises*. Melrose, Mass.: Ballinger, 1986.

A.I.I.I. [pseud]. "L'Électricité de France en 1955." *Les Documents Politiques, Diplomatiques et Financiers* (August 1956), 27–37.

Ailleret, Pierre. *25 ans de vie technique et économique d'EDF*. Paris: EDF, 1972.

Amoyal, Jacques. "Les origines socialistes et syndicalistes de la planification en France." *Le Mouvement Social* 87 (April-June 1974), 145–63.

Andrieu, Claire, Lucette LeVan, and Antoine Prost, eds. *Les nationalisations de la Libération: De l'utopie au compromis*. Paris: Presses de la Fondation Nationale des Sciences Politiques, 1987.

Antoine, Aristide. *Les relations d'Électricité de France avec l'étranger*. Paris: Société des Ingénieurs Civils de France, n.d. [1956?]. Pamphlet.

Armand, Louis. "Entreprises nationalisées et entreprises privées." *Bulletin ACADI* 53 (December 1951), 415–37.

Armengaud, André, ed. *Vingt ans de capitalisme d'état*. Paris: SPID, 1951.

Association pour l'histoire de l'électricité en France, ed. *L'électricité dans l'histoire: Actes du colloque de l'association pour l'histoire de l'électricité en France, Paris, 11–13 octobre 1983*. Paris: Presses Universitaires de France, 1985.

Audibert, Etienne. *Conférence de presse de M. E. Audibert du 16 février 1948*. Paris: EDF, 1948. Pamphlet.

——. "Le fonctionnement financier de l'EDF." *Documentation Française* 848 (11 March 1948), 3–7.

Auriol, Vincent. *Mon septennat*. Paris: Fayard, 1974.

Baby, Jean. "La formation des trusts." *Économie et Politique* 5/6 (1954), 53–64.

Bardin, J.-P. "De l'association 'capital-travail' à la 'cogestion'." *Revue Politique des Idées et des Institutions* 67:13 (July 1958), 374–79.

Bauchard, Philippe. *Les technocrates au pouvoir*. Paris: Arthaud, 1966.

——. "Une nouvelle planification," *Revue Économique* 101 (1966), 231–47.

Bauchet, Pierre. *L'expérience française de planification*. Paris: Éditions du Seuil, 1966.

——. *Propriété publique et planification*. Paris: Cujas, 1962.

Baum, Warren C. *The French Economy and the State*. Princeton, N.J.: Princeton University Press, 1958.

Baumol, William J. *Public and Private Enterprise in a Mixed Economy.* New York: Macmillan, 1980.

Berthomieu, Claude. *La Gestion des entreprises nationalisées.* Paris: Presses Universitaires de France, 1971.

Bessière, Francis. "La méthode des modèles élargis: Application à un modèle de choix des investissements." In *Proceedings of the Fourth International Conference on Operational Research.* New York: Wiley, 1966.

Bijker, Weibe E., Thomas P. Hughes, and Trevor Pinch, eds. *The Social Construction of Technological Systems.* Cambridge, Mass.: MIT Press, 1987.

Billoux, François. "1944–1947: Des Communistes au gouvernement." *Cahiers d'Histoire de l'Institut Maurice Thorez* 34 (n. s. 6, January-April 1974), 136–62.

Blair, John M. *The Control of Oil.* New York: Random House, 1976.

Bloch, Marc. *Strange Defeat.* New York: Norton, 1968.

Bloch-Laine, François, and Jean Bouvier. *La France restaurée, 1944–1954 : Dialogue sur les choix d'une modernisation.* Paris : Fayard, 1986.

Blum, Léon. *À l'échelle humaine.* Paris: Gallimard, 1945 and 1971.

Boiteux, Marcel. "Sur la détermination des prix de revient et de développement dans un système interconnecté de production-distribution." *Revue Générale de l'Électricité* 68 (August 1949), 43–62.

——. "Sur la gestion des monopoles publics astreints à l'équilibre budgétaire." *Econometrica* 24 (1956), 22–40.

Boiteux, Marcel, and Louis Puiseux. "Neutralité tarifaire et entreprises publiques." *Bulletin de l'Institut International d'Administration Publique* 12 (1969), 109–21.

Boutteville, Roger. "La modernisation de l'électricité." *Documentation Française* 562 (3 March 1947), 14–19.

Bouvier, Jean. "Financement public et re-démarrage industriel en France, 1944–1950: Une prise de relais ambigüe pour l'investissement." In *Le rôle des capitaux publics dans le financement de l'industrie en Europe occidentale aux XIXe et XXe siècles,* pp. 89–110. Bruxelles: Établissements Émile Bruylant, 1981.

Brachet, Philippe. *L'état-entrepreneur.* Paris: Editions Syros, 1976.

——. *Les nationalisations: Quand la droite se sert de la gauche.* Paris, Éditions du Cerf, 1978.

Braudel, Fernand, and Ernest Labrousse, eds. *Histoire économique et sociale de la France, tome IV: L'ère industrielle et la société d'aujourd'hui;* 4–1: *Panoramas de l'ère industrielle;* 4–2: 1950 à nos jours. Paris: Presses Universitaires de France, 1979 and 1982.

Braun, Madeleine, et al. "Le Front National." *Cahiers d'Histoire de l'Institut Maurice Thorez* 8 (n.s. 39, November-December 1974), 87–95.

Brown, Donald J., and Geoffrey Heal. "Equity, Efficiency, and Increasing Returns." *Review of Economic Studies* 46 (October 1979).

Buchanan, J. M. "Peak Loads and Efficient Pricing: Comment." *Quarterly Journal of Economics* 80 (1966).

Bupp, Irvin C., and Jean-Claude Derian. *Light Water.* New York: Basic Books, 1978.

Burawoy, Michael. *Manufacturing Consent.* Chicago: University of Chicago Press, 1979.

Cardot, Fabienne, ed. *L'électricité dans l'histoire. Problèmes et méthodes.* Paris: Presses Universitaires de France, 1985.

——. *L'électricité et ses consommateurs.* Paris: Association pour l'Histoire de l'Électricité en France, 1987.

——. *La France des électriciens.* Paris: Presses Universitaires de France, 1985.

Caron, François. *Histoire économique de la France, XIXᵉ et XXᵉ siècles.* Paris: Armand Colin, 1981.

Carré, Jean-Jacques, Paul Dubois, and Edmond Malinvaud. *La croissance française: Un essai d'analyse économique causale de l'après-guerre.* Paris: Éditions du Seuil, 1972.

Castagne, Bernard. *L'équilibre financier des entreprises publiques.* Paris: Armand Colin, 1971.

Catholique de la Résistance, Un. "Pour la France de demain." *Les Cahiers Politiques* (clandestine) 2 (June 1942).

Chenot, Bernard. "Direction et contrôle des entreprises nationalisées." *Le Fonctionnement des Entreprises Nationalisées en France: IIIᵉ Colloque des Facultés de Droit, Grenoble, 9–11 Juin 1955.* Grenoble: Université de Grenoble, 1955, nonpaginated.

——. *Organisation économique de l'État.* Paris: Dalloz, 1965.

——. "Les paradoxes de l'entreprise publique." *Revue Française de Sciences Politiques* 4 (October-December 1955), 725–35.

Chevalier, Jean-Marie. *Le nouvel enjeu pétrolier.* Paris: Calmann-Lévy, 1974.

Choffel, Jean. *Seule, une femme: Alice Saunier-Sëité.* Paris: Flammarion, 1979.

Cicchetti, Charles J., ed. *The Marginal Cost Pricing of Electricity.* Cambridge, Mass.: Ballinger, 1977.

Cicchetti, Charles J., and Wesley K. Foell, eds. *Energy Systems Forecasting, Planning and Pricing: Proceedings of a French-American Conference, University of Wisconsin–Madison, 23 September–3 October 1974.* Madison: University of Wisconsin, 1975.

Claude, Henri. "Les nationalisations ont-elles réduit la puissance du capital?" *Économie et Politique* 7 (October 1954), 60–67.

Clemens, Eli W. "Marginal Cost Pricing: A Comparison of French and American Power Rates." *Land Economics* 40 (November 1964), 40–54.

Cohen, Stephen S. *Modern Capitalist Planning: The French Model,* 2d ed. Berkeley: University of California Press, 1977.

Combet, Roger. "L'administration et les affaires nationalisées." *Revue des Arts et Manufactures* 59 (November 1956), 41–53.

Comité Général d'Études (CGE). "Pour une nouvelle révolution française." *Les Cahiers Politiques* 5 (January 1945), 5–12

——. "Sur les réformes à apporter au régime politique de la France." *Les Cahiers Politiques* 3 (August 1943), 1–17.

Comité pour l'Équipement Électrique Français. *Cinq jours au pays du kilowatt.* Paris: CPEEF, 1949. Pamphlet.

Confédération Française Démocratique du Travail. *Les dégats du progrès.* Paris: Editions du Seuil, 1977.

Confédération Française Démocratique du Travail–Fédération Gaz-Électricité.

L'utilisation des entreprises privées à EDF-GDF. Paris: CFDT-FNE, 1981. Pamphlet.

Confédération Française Démocratique du Travail–Syndicat de l'Énergie Atomique. *L'électronucléaire en France.* Paris: Éditions du Seuil. 1975

Confédération Française des Travailleurs Chrétiens. *Programme révendicatif de la CFTC du XXIᵉ Congrès de la CFTC.* Paris: CFTC, 1945. Pamphlet.

——. *Rapport sur les nationalisations.* Paris: CFTC, 1945. Pamphlet.

——. *XXIᵉ Congrès, 15–18 septembre 1945.* Paris: CFTC, 1945.

——. *XXIIᵉ Congrès, 8–10 juin 1946.* Paris: CFTC, 1946.

Confédération Française des Travailleurs Chrétiens–Fédération des Syndicats Chrétiens des Services Publiques et Concédés. "A propos des nationalisations." *La Voix des Services Concédés* 6 (February 1946), 1–4.

Confédération Française des Travailleurs Chrétiens–Fédération Gaz-Électricité. *Pour une action efficace au sein des comités mixtes à la production.* Paris: CFTC-FGE, 1957. Pamphlet; reprint from *Gazélec*, special issue of April 1957.

Confédération Générale du Travail. *Programme d'action gouvernementale.* Paris: CGT, 1945. Pamphlet.

——. "Rapport sur les comités d'entreprise." *La Voix du Peuple,* January 1946, 93.

——. *Les responsables de la scission démasqués.* Paris: CGT, 1948.

Confédération Générale du Travail–Fédération de l'Éclairage. *Gaillard-Pflimlin et le gouvernement actuel conduisent le pays à la récession.* Paris: CGT, 1958. Pamphlet.

——. *Pétition pour une politique française de moyens énergétiques dont l'urgence est criante.* Paris: CGT, 1959. Pamphlet.

——. *Les tarifs-cadeaux.* Paris: CGT, 1954. Pamphlet.

Conseil National de la Résistance (CNR). *La charte démocratique* (clandestine): May 1943. Pamphlet.

Constructeurs de Matériel d'Equipement Électrique. *Le matériel d'équipement électrique.* Paris: SCME, 1958. Pamphlet.

Courtin, René. *Rapport sur la politique économique d'après-guerre.* Algiers: n.p., 1944.

Crozier, Michel. "La participation des travailleurs à la gestion des entreprises." *Preuves* 93 (November 1958), 50–58.

de Brunhoff, Suzanne. *Capitalisme financier public.* Paris: SEDES, 1958.

de Carmoy, Guy. *Le dossier européen de l'énergie.* Paris: Éditions d'Organisation, 1971.

de Closets, François. *Toujours plus!* Paris: Grasset, 1982.

Deglaire, Simone, ed. *Recueil des lois, décrets, arrêtés, circulaires et cahiers des charges intéressant la production, le transport et la distribution de l'énergie électrique,* vols. 9–15. Paris: Direction du Gaz et de l'Électricité du Ministère de l'Industrie, 1947–1965.

Deglaire, Simon, and Edmond Bordier, *Électricité, service public.* Tome 1, *La nationalisation.* Paris: Berger-Levrault, 1963.

de Gravelaine Frédérique, and Sylvie O'Dy. *L'état -EDF.* Paris: Alain Moreau, 1978.

Dejonghe, Etienne. "Les houillères à l'épreuve." *Revue du Nord* 57:227 (October–December 1975), 643–66.

Delion, André. "Le contrôle des entreprises publiques." *Droit Social* 22:1 (January 1959), 1–9, and 22:5 (May 1959), 265–74.

———. *L'état et les entreprises publiques.* Paris: Sirey, 1959.

Delouvrier, Paul, and Robert Nathan. *Politique économique de la France.* Paris: Cours de droit, 1958.

Direction des études et des recherches d'Électricité de France. "Il faut penser dix ans d'avance." *Industries et Techniques* (March 1963), 83–94.

Documentation Française, La. "Électricité de France: Entreprise nationale, industrielle et commerciale." *Notes et Études Documentaires* 4575–4576 (10 June 1980), passim.

———. *L'électricité en France.* Serial N° 178. Paris: La Documentation Française, June 1962.

Dreyfus, Pierre. *Une nationalisation réussie: Renault.* Paris: Fayard, 1981.

Drèze, Jacques. "Some Postwar Contributions of French Economists to Theory and Public Policy." *American Economic Review* 54 (June 1954), 1–64.

Dubois, Joseph, and Géraud Jouve. *La bataille de l'électricité.* Paris: SEI, n.d. [1946?].

Durand, Pierre. *Marcel Paul: Vie d'un 'pitau'.* Paris: Temps Actuels, 1983.

Earle, E. M., ed. *Modern France: Problems of the Third and Fourth Republics.* Princeton: Princeton University Press, 1951.

Ehrmann, Henry. *French Labor from Popular Front to Liberation.* Ithaca: Cornell University Press, 1947.

———. *Organized Business in France.* Princeton: Princeton University Press, 1957.

Électricité de France. *Dix ans de progrès.* Paris: EDF, 1956.

———. *EDF '72.* Paris: EDF, 1972.

———. *Statistiques de production et de consommation, 1969.* Paris: EDF, 1970.

———. *Valeurs d'exploitation électricité, 1965–1974.* Paris: EDF, 1976.

Électricité de France, ed. *Le Service et les hommes.* Paris: EDF, 1971

Électricité de France–Direction de la Distribution. *Bien connaître le tarif vert.* Paris: EDF, 1976.

———. *Statistiques électricité.* Paris: EDF, 1972–1974.

Électricité de France—Direction des Études et Recherches. "La direction des études et recherches d'Électricité de France: Il faut penser 20 ans d'avance." *Industries et Techniques* (March 1963), 87–94.

Électricité de France–Études Économiques Générales. *Le calcul économique et le système électrique.* Paris: Eyrolles, 1979.

Électricité de France—Inspection Générale pour la Coopération hors Métropole. *Manuel de l'expert d'Électricité de France en mission de coopération technique.* Paris: EDF, 1967.

Électricité de France—SEPAC. *La tarification de l'électricité.* Paris: EDF, 1978. Technical pamphlet.

Électricité de France et Gaz de France–Direction du Personnel. *Statistiques du personnel: Année 1970.* Paris: EDF, 1970.

Elgey, Georgette. *La république des contradictions, 1951–1954.* Paris: Fayard, 1968.

——. *La république des illusions, 1945–1951.* Paris: Fayard, 1965.

Empis, Philippe. "Les aspects financiers d'Électricité de France." *Nouvelle Revue de l'Économie Contemporaine* (March 1950), 6–12.

Fajon, Étienne. "Les Communistes et les nationalisations." *Cahiers du Communisme* 4 (February 1945), 13–15.

Faure, Edgar. "Quelques aspects du problème des nationalisations." *Revue Politique et Parlementaire* (December 1945), 11–19.

Fauvet, Jacques. *Histoire du parti communiste français.* Paris: Fayard, 1977.

——. *La Quatrième République.* Paris: Fayard, 1961.

Fédération Nationale des Collectivités Concédantes et Régies. *Bulletin d'Information* 100, numéro spécial (February 1973).

"Formation du personnel à l'Électricité de France et à Gaz du France, La." *Moniteur des Travaux Publics et du Bâtiment* 44 (1 November 1969), 17–30.

Fridenson, Patrick. *Histoire des usines Renault.* Tome 1, *Naissance d'une grande entreprise, 1898–1939.* Paris: Editions du Seuil, 1972.

——. "L'idéologie des grands constructeurs dans l'entre-deux-guerres." *Le Mouvement Social* 81 (September–December 1972), 45–68.

——. "Intervention à propos de la communication de M. Bouvier." In CNRS, ed., *Libération de la France, colloque,* pp. 863–66. Paris: CNRS, 1976.

Fridenson, Patrick, and André Straus, eds. *Le capitalisme français XIXe-XXe siècle. Blocages et dynamismes d'une croissance.* Paris: Fayard, 1987.

Frost, Robert L. "De quelques effets d'une gestion scientifique." *Revue Française de Gestion* 70 (Sept.–Oct. 1988), 108–20.

——. "Economists as Nationalised Sector Managers: Reforms of the Electrical Rate Structure in France, 1946–1969." *Cambridge Journal of Economics* 14 (Fall 1985), 285–300.

——. "The Flood of 'Progress': Technocrats and Peasants at Tignes (Savoie), 1946–1952." *French Historical Studies* 14:1 (Spring 1985), 117–40.

——. "Skill and Technological Innovation in French Electrical Power: A Reassessment of the Deskilling Thesis." *Technology and Culture* (October 1988), pp. 865–87.

——. "La technocratie au pouvoir . . . avec le consentement des syndicats: La technologie, les syndicats et la direction à l'Électricité de France (1946–1968)." *Le Mouvement Social* 130 (January–March, 1985), 81–96.

Gabet, Marcel. "L'entreprise publique en France au XXe siècle." In *Le rôle des capitaux publics dans le financement de l'industrie en Europe occidentale aux XIXe et XXe siècles,* colloquium, pp. 112–27. Bruxelles: Établissements Émile Bruylant, 1981.

Gaspard, Roger. "Dix ans de politique financière à l'Électricité de France." *Arts et Manufactures* 34 (December 1956), 31–34.

Gaudy, René. *Et la lumière fut nationalisée.* Paris: Éditions Sociales, 1978.

——. *Les porteurs d'énergie.* Paris: Temps Actuels, 1982.

Gauron, André. *Histoire économique et sociale de la Ve république,* 2 vols. Paris: La Découverte, 1983.

Gazier, Albert. "Les entreprises publiques seront-elles étatisées?" *Revue Banque et Bourse* 99 (July-August 1953), 291–95.

Gendarme, René. *L'expérience française de la nationalisation industrielle.* Paris: Librarie de Medicis, 1950.

Gilly, Jean-Pierre, and François Morin. "Les groupes industriels en France." *Notes et Études Documentaires* 4605–4606 (10 February 1981), passim.

Ginocchio, Roger. *Aménagements hydroélectriques.* Paris: Eyrolles, 1959.

——. *Législation de l'électricité.* Paris, Eyrolles, 1977.

Giscard d'Estaing, Edmond. *Les nationalisations.* Paris: Comité d'Action Économique et Douanière, 1945. Pamphlet.

Goetz-Girey, Robert. *La pensée syndicale française: Militants et théoriciens.* Paris: Armand Colin, 1948.

Goldschmidt, Bertrand. *Les rivalités atomiques, 1939–1966.* Paris: Fayard, 1967.

Gorz, André. *Adieu au prolétariat.* Paris: Éditions du Seuil, 1979.

——. *Strategy for Labor.* Boston: Beacon, 1967.

Graham, B. D. *The French Socialists and Tripartisme.* Toronto: Toronto University Press, 1965.

Granick, David. *The European Executive.* New York: Knopf, 1958.

Granou, André. *La bourgeoisie financière au pouvoir.* Paris: Maspero, 1977.

Grelon, André, ed. *Les ingénieurs de la crise.* Paris: Éditions de l'EHESS, 1986.

"groupe d'abonnés, Un." *Note sur la nationalisation de l'électricité.* Paris: n.a., 1946. Pamphlet.

Groux, Guy, and Mark Kesselman, eds. *1968–1982: Le mouvement ouvrier français.* Paris: Éditions Ouvrières, 1984.

Guiart, René. "L'oligarchie financière et l'état." *Économie et Politique* 5–6 (1954), 181–204.

Hall, Peter A. *Governing the Economy: The Politics of State Intervention in Britain and France.* New York: Oxford University Press, 1986.

Halphen, Étienne, and Georges Morlat. "Sur la valeur industrielle d'une chute d'eau." *Annuaire Hydrologique de la France* (1945), 65–97.

Heilbroner, Robert. "Do Machines Make History?" *Technology and Culture* 8 (1967).

Herblay, Michel. *Les hommes du fleuve et de l'atome.* Paris: Pensée Universelle, 1977.

Hincker, F. "L'énergie en Europe et en France." *Économie et Politique* 64 (November 1959), 44–62, and 65 (December 1959), 10–15.

Holter, Darryl O. "Mineworkers and Nationalization in France: Insights into Concepts of State Theory." *Politics and Society* 11:1 (Spring 1982), 3–21.

Houille Blanche, La, ed. *Tignes.* Paris: Eyrolles, 1959.

Hughes, Thomas P. *Networks of Power: Electrification in Western Society.* Baltimore: Johns Hopkins University Press, 1983.

Hutter, R. "Qu'est-ce le coût marginal?" *Revue Générale des Chemins de Fer* (February 1950), 53–63.

Hyperion [pseud.]. *Servir l'homme.* Paris: n.a., 1946. Pamphlet.

"Interview avec Marcel Paul." *Énergies* 799 (26 March 1971), 17–23.

Jaubert, François. *L'Électricité de France et l'histoire du droit de l'électricité.* Paris: n.a., 1973. Pamphlet.

Jeanneney, Jean-Marcel. *Forces et faiblesses de l'économie française, 1945–1959.* Paris: Armand Colin, 1959.

Jeanneney, Jean-Marcel, and Claude-Albert Colliard. *Économie et droit de l'électricité*. Paris: Domat-Montchrétien, 1950.

Jouhaux, Léon. "Les nationalisations en France." *Annales de l'Économie Collective* 433 (July-October 1949), 185–91.

Julliard, Jacques. *La IVe République*. Paris: Calmann-Lévy, 1968.

Kolboom, Ingo. "Patronat et cadres: La contribution patronale à la formation du groupe des cadres (1936–1938)." *Le Mouvement Social* 121 (October–December 1981), 71–95.

——. *La revanche des patrons: Le patronat français face au Front populaire*. Paris: Flammarion, 1986.

Kolko, Joyce, and Gabriel Kolko. *The Limits of Power*. New York: Knopf, 1972.

Kuisel, Richard F. "Auguste Detoeuf, Conscience of French Industry: 1926–1947." *International Review of Social History* 20 (1975), 149–74.

——. *Capitalism and the State in Modern France*. New York: Cambridge University Press, 1981.

——. *Ernest Mercier, French Technocrat*. Berkeley and Los Angeles: University of California Press, 1967.

——. "The Legend of the Vichy Synarchy." *French Historical Studies* 6 (Spring 1970), 365–98.

——. "Technocrats and Public Economic Policy: From the Third to the Fourth Republic." *Journal of European Economic History* 2 (1973), 53–99.

Lacoste, Robert. "Liberté et production." *France-Documents* 9 (July 1947).

Lacroix, Annie. "CGT et action ouvrière de la Libération à mai 1945." *Revue d'Histoire de la Deuxième Guerre Mondiale* 116 (October 1979).

——. "La nationalisation de l'électricité et du gaz." *Cahiers d'Histoire de l'Institut Maurice Thorez* 6 (n.s. 34, January 1974).

Lacroix-Riz, Annie. *La CGT de la Libération à la scission (1944–1947)*. Paris: Éditions Sociales, 1983.

——. "Majorité et minorité de la CGT de la Libération au XXVIe Congrès confédéral, août 1944–avril 1946." *Revue Historique* 540 (October-December 1981).

Lange, Peter. *Union Democracy and Liberal Corporatism: Exit, Voice and Wage Regulation in Postwar Europe*. Ithaca: Cornell Studies in International Affairs, Western Societies Papers No. 16, 1985.

Laniel, Joseph. *La nationalisation de l'électricité: Un cri d'alarme*. Paris: Parti Républicain de la Liberté, 1946. Pamphlet.

Lanthier, Pierre. "Les dirigeants des grandes entreprises électriques en France, 1911–1973." In Maurice Lévy-Leboyer, ed., *Le patronat de la seconde industrialisation*, Cahiers du Mouvement social, no. 4, pp. 106–10. Paris: Éditions Ouvrières, 1979.

——. "The Relationship between State and Private Electric Industry, France, 1880–1920." In Jürgen Kocka and Norbert Horn, eds., *Law and the Formation of the Big Enterprises in the Nineteenth and Early Twentieth Centuries*, pp. 590–601. Göttingen: Vadenhoeck & Ruprecht, 1979.

Latour, Bruno. *Science in Action*. Cambridge, Mass.: Harvard University Press, 1987.

Launay, Michel. *La CFTC: Origines et développement (1919–1940)*. Paris: Publications de la Sorbonne, 1987.

Lauriol, Paul. "Tarification de l'énergie électrique." *L'Éclairage Électrique* 33 (1902), 325–37.

Lavigne, Pierre. "Aspects juridiques de la dotation en capital des entreprises nationales." *Revue des Sciences Financières* 51:2 (April-June 1959), 189–203.

Le Brun, Pierre. "La nationalisation nécessaire de la production et de la distribution de l'électricité." *Revue Syndicale Économique et Sociale* 3 (September 1937).

Lecerf, Jean. *La percée de l'économie française*. Paris: Arthaud, 1963.

Lefaucheux, Pierre. "Passage au socialisme, Pt. 2." *Les Cahiers Politiques* 9 (April 1945).

Lefranc, Georges. *Les expériences syndicales en France, 1939–1950*. Paris: Aubier, 1950.

———. *Le mouvement socialiste sous la Troisième République (1875–1940)*. Paris: Payot, 1963.

———. *La nationalisation des industries clefs*. Paris: CGT, 1936. Pamphlet.

Le Guen, René. *Voyage avec des cadres*. Paris: Éditions Sociales, 1978.

Lepage, Henri. *EDF et la tarification au coût marginal*. Paris: Documentation Française, 1988.

Lescuyer, Georges. *Le contrôle de l'état sur les entreprises nationalisées*. Paris: Librarie Générale du Droit et de Jurisprudence, 1962.

Levin Richard, and Richard Lewontin. *The Dialectical Biologist*. Cambridge, Mass.: Harvard University Press, 1985.

Lévy-Leboyer, Maurice, ed. *Le patronat de la seconde industrialisation*. Paris: Éditions Ouvrières, 1979.

———. "Le patronat français a-t-il été malthusien?" *Le Mouvement Social* (1974), 3–49.

Lipsey, R. G. and K. Lancaster, "The General Theory of Second Best." *Review of Economic Studies* 24 (December 1956), 11–52.

Loiseau, Pierre. *L'indemnisation des entreprises nationalisées*. Paris: Éditions de la Cigogne d'Alsace, 1950.

MacKenzie, David. "Marx and the Machine." *Technology and Culture* 25 (1984), 473–502.

Maier, Charles S. "Between Taylorism and Technocracy: European Ideologies and the Vision of Industrial Productivity in the 1920s." *Journal of Contemporary History* 5 (1970), 27–61.

———. "The Politics of Productivity: Foundations of American International Economic Policy After World War II." *International Organization* 31:4 (Autumn 1977), 607–18.

Maillet-Chassagne, Monique. *L'influence de la nationalisation sur la gestion des entreprises publiques*. Paris: Société d'Édition d'Enseignement Supérieur, 1956.

Malégarie, Charles. *L'électricité à Paris*. Paris: Baranger, 1946.

Maleville, Georges. *Conseiller d'état, témoignage*. Paris: Librairies Techniques, 1979.

Mallet, Serge. *The New Working Class*. London: Spokesman Books, 1964.

Maréchal, G. "L'autofinancement." *Économie et Politique* 62 (September 1959), 24–33.

Marty, André. *L'affaire Marty*. Paris: Éditions des Deux-Rives, 1955.

Massé, Pierre. *Aléas et progrès: Entre Candide et Cassandre*. Paris: Economica, 41984.

——. *Le plan ou l'anti-hasard*. Paris: Gallimard, 1963.

Mater, André. "Réflexions d'un juriste sur une nationalisation." *Revue Juridique de l'Électricité et du Gaz* 15 (November-December 1948).

Meynaud, Jean. "Études et documents sur l'entreprise publique." *Revue Économique* 4 (July 1959), 610–15.

Mioche, Philippe. *Le Plan Monnet. Genèse et élaboration*. Paris: Publications de la Sorbonne, 1987.

Moch, Jules. *Guerre aux trusts*. Paris: Éditions de la Liberté, 1945. Pamphlet.

——. *Le parti socialiste au peuple de la France*. Paris: Éditions de la Liberté, 1945.

——. [pseud. JM]. "Réflexions sur les socialisations." *Les Cahiers Politiques* (clandestine) 8 (March 1945).

——. *Socialisme, crise, nationalisations*. Paris: Librairie du Parti, 1932. Pamphlet.

——. *Socialisme et rationalisation*. Paris: Librairie du Parti, 1924. Pamphlet.

Monnet, Jean. *Memoirs*. New York: Doubleday, 1978.

Monnier, Lionel. *Capitaux publics et stratégie de l'état*. Paris: Presses Universitaires de France, 1977.

——. "La complémentarité des capitaux publics et privés." In *Le rôle des capitaux publics dans le financement de l'industrie en Europe occidentale aux XIXe et XXe siècles*, pp. 177–205. (Bruxelles: Établissements Émile Bruylant, 1981.

——. "La tarification de l'électricité depuis la crise du pétrole." *Revue de l'Énergie* (June 1978), 297–311.

——. *La tarification de l'électricité en France*. Paris: Economica, 1983.

Morlat, Georges, and Francis Bessière. *Vingt-cinq ans d'économie électrique*. Paris: Dunod, 1971.

Moss, Bernard. "La réforme de la législation de travail sous la Ve République: Un triomphe du modernisme?" *Le Mouvement social* 148 (July-September 1989), 63–91.

Naville, Pierre, ed. *L'état-entrepreneur: Le cas de la régie Renault*. Paris: Éditions Anthropos, 1971.

Nelson, James R., ed. *Marginal Cost Pricing in Practice*. Englewood Cliffs, N.J.: Prentice-Hall, 1964.

Nissel, Hans. *The Electrical Rate Question: Europe Revisited*. Washington, D.C.: Electricity Consumers' Resource Council, 1976.

——. "Incremental Cost Pricing and U.S. Utility Rates." *Public Utilities Fortnightly* 84:19 (14 August 1969).

——. "Price Signals or Load Management?" *Public Utilities Fortnightly* 97:1 (1 January 1976).

Noble, David F. *America by Design*. New York: Knopf, 1977.

——. *Forces of Production: A Social History of Industrial Automation*. New York: Knopf, 1984.

Nordengren, Sven. *Economic and Social Targets in Postwar France*. Lund, Sweden: Belingska Boktryckriet, 1972.

Oizon, René. *L'évolution récente de la production énergétique française*. Paris: Larousse, 1983.

Ormos, Marta. *La montée: La promotion ouvrière dans une grande entreprise publique, EDF-GDF*. Toulouse: Éditions Erès, 1982.

Panich, Leo. "Trade Unions and the Capitalist State: Corporatism and its Contradictions." *New Left Review* 125 (January–February 1981), 21–44.

Parti Communist Français. *Rapports au dixième congrès national du parti communiste français*. Paris: PCF, 1945.

——. *Rapports du comité central pour le dixième congrès national*. Paris: PCF, 1945.

Paul, Marcel. "Les nationalisations et la lutte pour l'indépendance nationale." *Cahiers du Communisme* 35 (October 1959).

——. *Le statut national*. Pantin: CGT-FNE, n.d. Pamphlet.

Paval, Valéry. "Une vieille illusion réformiste: Les nationalisations, moyen de lutte anticapitaliste." *Critiques de l'Économie Politique* 2 (n.s., January-March 1978)

Paxton, Robert O. *Vichy France: Old Guard and New Order, 1940–1944*. New York: Norton, 1972.

Pellenc, Marcel. *Les méfaits des nationalisations*. Paris: SPID, 1951 Pamphlet.

Picard, Jean-François, Alain Beltran, and Martine Bungener. *Histoire(s) de l'EDF*. Paris: Dunod, 1985.

Pineau, Christian. "Sur la gestion des entreprises nationales." *Revue Banque et Bourse* 14 (June 1950), 251–54.

Pringle, Peter, and James Spigelman. *The Nuclear Barons*. New York: Holt, Rinehart and Winston, 1981.

Puiseux, Louis, and Dominique Saumon. "Actors and Decisions in French Energy Policy." In Leon Lindberg, ed., *The Energy Syndrome*, pp. 119–72. Lexington, Mass.: D.C. Heath, 1977.

Radosh, Ronald. *American Labor and U.S. Foreign Policy*. New York: Random House, 1969.

Ramadier, Paul. "Les entreprises nationalisées devant les problèmes de l'expansion économique." *Annales de l'Économie Collective* 514–521 (combined, April-November 1955), 199–222.

Rice-Maximin, Edward. "The United States and the French Left, 1945–1949: The View from the State Department." *Journal of Contemporary History* 19 (October 1984), 729–47.

Robrieux, Philippe. *Histoire intérieure du parti communiste*, vol. 2. Paris: Fayard, 1981.

Rôle des capitaux publics dans le financement de l'industrie en Europe occidentale aux XIXe et XXe siècles, colloquium. Bruxelles: Établissements Émile Bruylant, 1981.

Rosenberg, Nathan. *Perspectives on Technology*. New York: Cambridge University Press, 1976.

Rousso, H., ed. *De Monnet à Massé: Enjeux politiques et objectifs économiques dans le cadre des quatre premiers plans (1946–1965)*. Paris: Éditions du CNRS, 1986.

Roux, Edmond. *Énergie électrique et civilisation*. Paris: Flammarion, 1945.

——. *L'industrie électrique au service exclusif de la nation*. Paris: SPPDEE, 1946. Pamphlet.

——. *Nationalisation sans spoliation*. Paris: SPPDEE, 1945. Pamphlet.

Ruggles, Margaret. "Recent Developments in the Theory of Marginal Cost Pricing." *Review of Economic Studies* 17 (1949–1950), 107–26.

Sabel, Charles F. *Work and Politics: The Division of Labor in Industry*. New York: Cambridge University Press, 1982.

Saint-Geours, Jean. "L'état et les entreprises publiques." *Droit Social* 16:9 (November 1953), 509–13.

Sampson, Anthony. *The Seven Sisters*. New York: Viking, 1975.

Sauvy, Alfred. *Les chances de l'économie française*. Paris: Presses Universitaires de France, 1946.

Section Française de l'Internationale Ouvrière (SFIO). *Résolutions du Congrès National Extraordinaire, Montrouge, 29–31 mars 1946*. Paris: Librairie du Parti, 1946.

——. *XXXVIIᵉ Congrès national, Paris, 11–15 août, 1945*. Paris: Éditions du Parti, 1945.

Sheahan, John. *Promotion and Control of Industry in Postwar France*. Cambridge, Mass.: Harvard University Press, 1963.

Simonnot, Philippe. *Les nucléocrates*. Grenoble: Presses Universitaires de Grenoble, 1978.

Singer, Daniel. *Prelude to Revolution*. New York: Hill and Wang, 1970.

Société Française d'Études et de Réalisations d'Équipements Électriques. *SOFRELEC*. Paris, SOFRELEC, 1965. Publicity pamphlet.

Sorlin, Pierre. *La société française*. Tome 2, *1945–1970*. Paris: Arthaud, 1971.

Staudenmaier, John M. *Technology's Storytellers, Reweaving the Human Fabric*. Cambridge, Mass.: MIT Press, 1985.

Steiner, Peter O. "Peak Loads and Efficient Pricing." *Quarterly Journal of Economics* 71:3 (November 1957), 585–610.

Sturmthal, Adolph. "Nationalization and Workers' Control in Britain and France." *Journal of Political Economy* 61 (1953), 121–34.

Syndicat des Constructeurs de Matériel d'Équipement Électrique (SCME). *Le matériel d'équipement électrique*. Paris: SCME, 1958. Pamphlet.

Syndicat Professionnel des Producteurs et des Distributeurs de l'Énergie Électrique (SPPDEE). *Réflexions sur l'équipement électrique en France*. Paris: SPPDEE, 1946. Pamphlet.

Taïx, Gabriel. *L'énergie et son utilisation*. Paris: Groupe Parisien de l'Association des Ingénieurs Anciens Elèves de l'Institut Electrotechnique de Toulouse,1949. Pamphlet.

——. *Le Plan Monnet est-il une réussite?* Paris: R. Pichon, 1953.

Tanguy, Pierre. "Safety and Nuclear Power Plant Standardization: The French Experience." *Public Utilities Fortnightly* 114 (31 October 1985), 21–24.

Tarrow, Sidney. "The Crisis of the Late 1960s in Italy and France and the Transition to Mature Capitalism." In *The Political Economy of Southern Europe*, edited by Giovanni Arrighi. Beverly Hills: Sage Publications, 1985.

Tenaille, R. "La politique économique de demain." *Défense de la France* (clandestine) 40 (2–5 October 1943), nonpaginated.

Thépot, André, ed. *L'ingénieur dans la société française*. Paris: Éditions Ouvrières, 1985.

Thorez, Maurice. *La paupérisation des travailleurs français*. Paris: Éditions Sociales, 1961.

Tillon, Charles. *On chantait rouge*. Paris: Laffont, 1977.

Tilly, Louise, and Joan Scott. *Women, Work and Family*. New York: Holt, Rinehart, and Winston, 1978.

Tinguy, R. "Les entreprises nationales et le parlement." *Revue Politique des Idées et des Institutions* (30 October 1955), 482–89.

Touraine, Alain. *La prophétie antinucléaire*. Paris: Éditions du Seuil, 1980.

Toutée, Jean. "Mission sur l'amélioration des procédures de discussion des salaires dans le secteur public: Rapport." *Droit Social* 27:5 (May 1964), 278–86.

Tussau, Guy. "Les industries électriques et électromécaniques." *Notes et Études Documentaires* 4563–4564 (27 March 1980), passim.

Union d'Électricité. *Assemblée générale, compte rendu de la séance du 18 mai 1945*. Paris: Union de l'Électricité, 1945. Pamphlet.

Union des Cadres Industriels de la France. "Programme d'action de la Résistance." *L'Industrie Française* (clandestine, April-May 1944).

Union des Ingénieurs et Techniciens Français. *La politique d'équipement électrique*. Paris: UITF, 1952. Pamphlet.

Union pour l'Étude du Marché de l'Électricité (UNIMAREL). *L'alimentation en électricité des établissements industriels*. Paris: UNIMAREL, 1958. Pamphlet.

Uri, Pierre. "La querelle des nationalisations." *Les Temps Modernes* 45 (July 1949).

Vanoli, André. "Le capital financier." *Économie et Politique* 5–6 (1954), 165–70.

———. "Les monopoles." *Économie et Politique* 5–6 (1954), 13–52.

Veblen, Thorstein. *Engineers and the Price System*. New York: Holt, 1919.

Veyret-Verner, Germaine. "Deux usines pilotes." *Revue de Géographie Alpine* 40:1 (January-March 1952), 183–96.

———. "Trois faits marquants dans l'équipement hydro-électrique du sud-est de la France." *Revue de Géographie Alpine* 40:3 (July-September 1952), 509–14.

Vignaux, Paul. *De la CFTC à la CFDT, syndicalisme et socialisme: Reconstruction (1946–1972)*. Paris: Éditions Ouvrières, 1980.

Vilain, Jean. *La politique de l'énergie en France*. Paris: Cujas, 1969.

Villey, Daniel. "Contre l'idéologie des réformes de structure." *Les Cahiers Politiques* 11 (June 1945).

"Vingt ans de capitalisme d'état." *France-Documents* 52 (1951), passim.

Wall, Irwin. *French Communism in the Era of Stalin*. Westport, Conn.: Greenwood Press, 1983.

Weart, Spencer R. *Scientists in Power*. Cambridge, Mass.: Harvard University Press, 1979.

Werth, Alexander. *France, 1940–1955*. New York: Macmillan, 1956.

Wieviorka, Michel, and Sylvaine Trinh. *Le modèle EDF*. Paris: Éditions de la Découverte, 1989.

Winner, Langdon. *Autonomous Technology: Technics-Out-of-Control as a Theme in Political Thought*. Cambridge, Mass.: MIT Press, 1977.

———. "Do Artifacts Have Politics?" *Daedalus* 109:1 (Winter 1980), 121–36.

Index

ACADI. *See* Association des Cadres Dirigeants de l'Industrie
AFL. *See* American Federation of Labor
Alphaville, 156
Alsthom, 17, 178, 183, 186, 250
American Federation of Labor (AFL), 89–90, 211
  activity in France, 89
Armand, Louis, 106, 118, 169, 191
Armengaud law, 100–101
Association des Cadres Dirigeants de l'Industrie (ACADI), 117–18, 123
autoproduction, 100

Blue Note, 114, 166–67, 219
  development of, 137–41
Blum, Léon, 51
Blum-Byrnes Accords, 90
Boiteux, Marcel, 116, 130–31, 136, 143–48, 150–53, 171, 191, 244, 249
  rise to prominence, 130
Boutteville, Roger, 30, 35, 78, 168
Brown, Irving, 89

cadres, 81, 82, 97, 113, 154, 211, 241
  politics and union analyses of, 211, 212, 214, 216, 241
  recruitment and salary problems, 154–55
capital expenditure budgets, 85, 105, 117, 120–23, 131, 179–82, 249
capital financing, 9, 11, 18, 37–39, 57, 66–70, 75, 85–86, 100, 115, 131, 149, 249
Cartel des Gauches, 13
cartels and oligopolies, 22, 118, 172, 179

CCOS. *See* Conseil Central des Oeuvres Sociales
CEA. *See* Commissariat à l'Énergie Atomique
CFDT. *See* Confédération Française Démocratique du Travail
CFTC. *See* Confédération Française des Travailleurs Chrétiens
CGE. *See* Compagnie Générale d'Électricité
CGT. *See* Confédération Générale du Travail
Christian Democrats. *See* Mouvement Républicain Populaire
clerical workers, 212, 238
CMP. *See* comanagement; Comités Mixtes à la Production
CNR. *See* Conseil National de la Résistance
coal, 11, 131
  supply issues, 19, 29, 35, 36, 121, 122, 140, 151, 165, 170, 249
codetermination, between labor and management, 71–73, 210–12
COEE. *See* Comité d'Organisation de l'Énergie Électrique
cogeneration, 58, 67–68, 145, 167
  denationalization of, 100, 101
Cold War, 75, 82–83, 92, 97, 109, 112, 114, 120, 166, 190, 206, 227, 252
comanagement (*cogestion*), 48, 72–73, 82–83, 95, 113, 227–31. *See also* codetermination; Comités Mixtes à la Production
Comité d'Organisation de l'Énergie Électrique (COEE), 29, 30, 35

281

Comités Mixtes à la Production (works
    committees), 72, 83, 204, 210, 214,
    242–43
    success and politics of, 225–31
    see also codetermination;
        comanagement
Comité sur la Production d'Énergie
    d'Origine Nucléaire (Péon), 191–98,
    250
Commissariat à l'Énergie Atomique
    (CEA), 186, 189–92, 197–99, 203
Communist Party and Communist poli-
    cies, 25, 31–35, 73, 113, 189, 208,
    235–36
    approach to nationalizations, 40–63
    facing Cold War from within EDF, 87–
        110
    role in founding EDF, 77–80
Compagnie Générale d'Électricité (CGE),
    16, 67, 111, 128, 173, 179, 181, 197,
    250
Compagnie Nationale du Rhône, 15, 69,
    85
Compagnie Parisienne de la Distribution
    Électrique (CPDE), 16, 18, 222
computers and computerization, 201,
    202, 203, 204, 205
concessions for distribution services, 12–
    17, 26, 30, 79, 102, 105, 221
Confédération Française Démocratique
    du Travail (CFDT), 241–45, 248, 252
    creation of, 210, 242
Confédération Française des Travailleurs
    Chrétiens (CFTC), 25, 28, 31–32, 65,
    71, 73, 78, 88, 92, 94, 99–100, 105,
    107, 112–13, 125, 135, 201, 203, 207
    ideology, 210–16 passim
    position on nationalizations, 54–56
    role in setting up EDF, 80–81, 83
    union activities, 226–42 passim
Confédération Générale du Travail
    (CGT), 25–28, 31, 33, 35, 40, 46–53,
    63–65, 72–74, 77, 80–82, 105, 111–12,
    128, 135–39, 158, 160, 166–67, 240–
    41, 252
    approaches to new technology, 200–
    203, 214–34
    facing revolt of May 1968, 242–49
    position on nationalizations, 87–99
    strength with respect to other unions,
    206–11
    see also Éclairage, Fédération de l'
Conseil Central des Oeuvres Sociales
    (CCOS), 71, 76, 95–96, 217, 232, 238
    police action against, 96
    see also comanagement; Comités
        Mixtes à la Production

Conseil National de la Résistance
    (CNR), 40
consumerism and consumerist ideology,
    156–58, 200, 209, 241
CPDE. See Compagnie Parisienne de la
    Distribution Électrique
Crédit Lyonnais, 16
Creys-Malville breeder reactor, 252
criteria for technological choice, theories
    of, 164
Croix de Feu, 23

Davezac, Henri, 60, 117, 173, 179
de Gaulle, Charles, 33, 43, 52, 58–59,
    118, 144, 191, 197
    role in nuclear choices, 193, 196
Democratic Charter, 40
Direction des Études et Recherche,
    167
discount rate used in evaluating proj-
    ects, 138–41, 148
division of labor, 48, 203, 204, 211
domestic electrical tariff model, 150
domestic electric imagery, use of, 160
domestic sales campaigns, 159–60
Durand power utility group, 16, 27, 30,
    77–79

Éclairage, Fédération de l' (CGT), 70, 73,
    144, 148, 227, 232
    facing Cold War from within EDF, 88–
    97
    formation of, 25–27
    positions on comanagement, 202–7
    reaction to May 1968 revolt, 242–45
    in Resistance and Liberation, 30–35
    role in nationalization process, 43–49
    role in setting up EDF, 77–83
    strength and politics, 207–11
    see also Confédération Générale du
        Travail
École Polytechnique and alumni, 6, 16,
    22, 23, 30, 78, 106, 130, 154, 173
École Supérieure d'Électricité, 16
economies of scale, 5, 64, 135, 178, 184,
    192, 196, 251
Empain, Baron, 17, 30, 67
employee benefits, 24, 71, 73, 77, 103,
    210–17, 232, 240
equal pay for equal work, principle of,
    239
equipment purchasing practices, 172–84
étatisation (state control), 12, 79, 125
    defined, 57
    fear of, in nationalization, 61–65

family wage, 200

Fédération Nationale des Communes Concédants et Régies (FNCCR), 44, 78–81, 105, 135
FNCCR. *See* Fédération Nationale des Communes Concédants et Régies
FO. *See* Force Ouvrière
Force Ouvrière (FO), 106–7, 111–12, 233–36
  facing May 1968 revolt, 243–45
  founding of and Cold War, 90–97
  strength and politics, 210–16
foreign consulting, 156–58

Gaspard, Roger, 31–32, 53, 81, 85, 101, 106, 111–12, 154, 168
  managerial style and practices, 126–37
  policies toward conservative regimes, 91–93
  policies toward nuclear power, 189–91
  relations with unions, 213–17, 226–27, 230–36
gender division of labor, 216
General Electric, 178
GNC. *See* Groupement National des Cadres
Green Tariff, 165, 219
  defined, 125
  development of, 143–53
grid, need for and configuration of, 10–13, 29, 35, 171, 178, 235
Groupement d'Électricité, 15
Groupement National des Cadres (GNC), 49, 78, 150, 155, 207, 209, 211, 241
  facing Cold War and conservative regimes, 82–97
  formation, 27–28
Guillaumat, Pierre, 130, 131
  role in nuclear plant choices, 189–91

hiring of employees, and criteria, 70–71, 200, 214–15, 221
Horowitz, Jules, 183
hydroelectric power, 29, 36, 37, 98, 101, 110, 114, 116, 121, 129, 131, 141, 156, 189
  early development, 10–20
  programs at EDF, 165–72

indemnification of former owners, 45, 53, 56, 58, 61
  charges and payments, 86, 98, 99
  debate in nationalization, 61, 65–67

Jeumont-Schneider, 67, 129, 173, 178–82, 250
Joliot-Curie, Frédéric, 189

Konkouré hydroelectric project, 157

Labor Charter, 31, 32, 35
labor *statut*, 26, 27, 82, 92, 204, 213, 217, 223, 244
  establishment of, 48, 70–74
  political attacks upon, 106
Lacoste, Robert, 35, 51, 52, 68, 79, 85, 88, 91, 92, 166
Lacq natural gas deposit, 168–69
Laniel, Joseph, 59, 60, 115
Le Brun, Pierre, 44, 49, 56, 81, 88, 93, 209
Liberation coalition, 43
Louvel, Jean-Marie, 45, 54–55, 64–68, 83, 94–95, 101, 104–6, 113, 118, 143, 182
luxury market for electricity, 12

"malthusian" investment policies, 21, 118, 141
marginalist economics, use of in management, 4, 143–53
Marshall Plan, 70, 86, 213
Massé, Pierre, 31–32, 78, 101, 102, 113, 116, 120, 151–54, 176, 180, 185, 191, 196, 247
  approach to equipment issues, 166–68
  approach to salary issues, 217–20
  management style, 129–41
May 1968 revolt, 242–46
Mendès-France, Pierre, 57, 118
Mercier, Ernest, 16–17, 30–31, 60, 130, 134
  politics of, 19–23
Moch, Jules, 14, 21, 52, 67–68, 88, 91
models, use in management, 3–6, 113–16, 147, 153, 165, 199, 205, 249
  notion of shadow profits in, 133–38
  private sector as normative reference in, 163
Monnet Plan, 35, 83–84, 101–2, 105, 110, 116, 120–22, 137, 174
  hydroelectric plan under, 165–69
Morel, Yves, 71, 92, 113, 125–26, 135, 157, 229
Moulinex, 160
Mouvement Républicain Populaire (MRP) (Christian Democratic Party), 62–66, 73
  position on nationalizations, 44–58
MRP. *See* Mouvement Républicain Populaire
municipal socialist movement, 13

neo-liberalism, 6, 23, 42, 79, 87, 90, 105, 115

neo-liberalism (*cont.*)
  adaptation to rightist technocorporatism, 118
  approach to nationalizations, 51–65
  defined, 57
Nora Commission, 248
nuclear plant choices, 186–99

oil-burning thermal power, 121–22, 131, 153, 195, 199, 249–50
  conversion of power plants to, 169
  shift toward, away from coal and hydro, 163–71
Organization Committees, 29–31
overtime work, 215, 221, 222, 230
  mandatory, 93

paternalism by employers, 20, 22, 24, 28, 32, 54, 71, 72, 134, 156, 158, 206, 212, 238, 241, 242, 244
Paul, Marcel, 112, 209
  as minister of industry, 43–48
  in 1957 strike, 232–36
  role in building EDF, 76–87 passim
  role in nationalization, 56–74 passim
  state actions against, 88–96 passim
Pechiney, 17, 78, 100, 110, 130, 145, 152, 153, 157, 169, 173, 190, 252
Péon. *See* Comité sur la production d'énergie d'origine nucléaire
Pleven, René, 45, 57
PO. *See* Promotion Ouvrière training program
Popular Front, 15, 18–20, 26, 28, 47
productivity bonuses, 112, 213, 217, 245
PROFOR (in-house employee training), 215–16, 240, 243–45
Promotion Ouvrière training program (PO), 216, 240
purges
  anticollaborationist, 32–35, 49–51, 59
  anti-Communist, 87, 90, 91, 94, 95, 97, 106, 109

Ramadier, Paul, 85, 89, 103, 132, 146
  role in nationalization process, 45–68 passim
Rance tidal power plant, 167
rationing of electricity, 30, 36, 49, 85, 131
Redressement Français, 21–24, 30
régies, municipal and cooperative utilities, 64, 68, 80, 81
reliability of power equipment, 140, 185
Renault auto works, 42
rentabilité and use of financial rates of return, 102, 113, 116, 132–39, 213

retraining of employees, 199, 202, 215, 239
Roux, Ambroise, 111, 127, 128, 179, 197

sabotage during Liberation, 31, 32, 36
salary categories and hierarchy, 214
salary levels, 71, 73, 82–85, 93, 124, 126, 154, 155, 233–34, 239, 244
  freeze, 1945–47, 49
  modes of determination, 27, 71, 75, 82, 88, 93–94, 105, 107, 112, 119, 125, 209, 210–20, 233, 249
  before nationalization, 24–30
  patterning of private sector, 73, 103, 134, 234, 244
  politics of, among unions, 199–210 passim
schools for training employees, 25–26, 76, 206, 215–16, 224, 239
self-management by workers, 33, 50, 55
Simon, Pierre, 72, 77–88 passim
skill, role in electrical work, 24, 26, 206, 212–15, 239
  technology and effect upon, 25, 26, 28, 84, 199–204 passim, 237, 243
"socialist accumulation," 41, 46
Speer, Albert, 30
Stabilization Plan (1963), 219
standardization of equipment, 58, 166, 175–81 passim
  effect on worker training, 215
  nomenclature, 176
  of nuclear designs, 250
  of thermal plants, 138
state regulation and control over utilities, 12. *See also étatisation*
strike actions, 49, 78, 88, 91, 93, 94, 96, 107, 110, 217, 226–27, 233–48 passim
  alternatives to, 205, 236, 237
subcontracting of labor, 27, 96, 112, 122, 201, 205, 221, 230, 231, 244, 245
  movement against, 221–27, 242
Suez Crisis, 122, 169, 191
suppliers' capacity utilization rates, 180

tariffs for power sales, 12–18, 37, 70, 72, 82, 85, 101, 104, 108, 121, 122–26, 130, 135, 157, 209, 211
  ratemaking principles, 14–15, 80, 142
  see also Green Tariff: development of
technocorporatism, 20–25, 28–29, 42, 53, 58, 106, 114, 118, 134, 241, 242
technological Darwinism, 163–64
thermally based power generation, 12, 20, 25, 36, 100–102, 120–21, 194
  choice for, within primary heat source strategies, 166–70

decision for, contrasted to hydroelectric alternative, 19, 101, 110, 137–39, 165
in equipment planning models, 140–41
research and development strategies with, 177–84 passim
Toutée pay procedures, 131, 219, 220, 242, 244
training for employees, 26, 199, 212–216, 220, 239. See also schools for training employees

UNCM. See Union Nationale des Cadres, Techniciens et Agents de Maîtrise
Union d'Électricité, 16
unionization in electrical power, 26, 28
Union Nationale des Cadres, Techniciens et Agents de Maîtrise (UNCM), 27, 32, 35, 49, 73, 79, 107, 222, 232–33, 236
activity in Cold War, 88–97 passim, 111–12
analysis of cadres by, 210–13
foundation of, 27
role in May 1968 revolt, 243–45
support for, 207–8
union strength and membership, 207–12
Universal Tariff model for domestic uses, 150
utility holding companies, 25

wind-power, 167
women, position of, within EDF, 202, 216, 238–41, 244
works committees. See comanagement; Comités Mixtes à la Production

X-Crise, 23–24, 30, 117

Library of Congress Cataloging-in-Publication Data

Frost, Robert L., 1952-
    Alternating currents : nationalized power in France, 1946-1970 / Robert L. Frost.
      p.   cm.
    Includes bibliographical references and index.
    ISBN 0-8014-2351-1 (cloth : alk. paper)
    1. Électricité de France. 2. Electric utilities—France. 3. Electric utilities—
Government ownership. 4. Electric utilities—Technological innovations. 5. High
technology industries. 6. High technology industries—Employees. 7. Government
business enterprises. 8. Government business enterprises—Employees. I. Title.
HD9685.F84E52   1991
333.79'32'0944—dc20   90-55727